PRODIGAL HUMAN

Also by Michael Adzema

From the Return to Grace Series

Culture War, Class War: Occupy Generations and the Rise and Fall of "Obvious Truths." Volume 1. (2013)

Apocalypse Emergency: Love's Wake-Up Call. Volume 3. (2013)

Apocalypse NO: Apocalypse or Earth Rebirth and the Emerging Perinatal Unconscious. Volume 4. (2013)

Wounded Deer and Centaurs: The Necessary Hero and the Prenatal Matrix of Human Events. Volume 5. (2016)

Planetmates: The Great Reveal. Volume 6. (2014)

Funny God: The Tao of Funny God and the Mind's True Liberation. Volume 7. (2015)

Experience Is Divinity: Matter As Metaphor. Volume 8. (2013)

Falls from Grace: The Devolution and Revolution of Consciousness. Volume 9. (2014)

The Necessary Revolution. Volume 2. (forthcoming)

Back to the Garden: The Psychology and Spirituality of Humanicide and the Necessary Future. Volume 11. (forthcoming)

Primal Return: Renaissance and Grace. Volume 12. (forthcoming)

From The Path of Ecstasy Series

The Secret Life of Stones: Matter, Divinity, and the Path of Ecstasy. Volume 1. (2016)

Womb with a View. Volume 2. (forthcoming)

Cells with a View. Volume 3. (forthcoming)

PRODIGAL HUMAN

THE DESCENTS OF MAN

Return to Grace, Volume 10

MICHAEL ADZEMA

Gonzo Sage Media: Eugene, Oregon: sillymickel@gmail.com
ISBN-13: 978-1530838134

For the Millennial Generation, shouldered with making the turnabout that we have needed since the dawn of civilization, and admirably struggling to do it.

CONTENTS

PREFACE

Falls from Grace, Prodigal Human, Back to the Garden, Primal Return ... Overview

"We are prodigal or fallen ... therefore we do not have to be. This book shows the dark side of civilization and by contrast reveals the bright side of human potential, within Nature, which we left behind and could embrace again.... The prodigal human will be welcomed back into the fold of Nature, if and when we have finally had enough and decide to make the journey home."

The book that precedes this one in the Return to Grace Series, *Falls from Grace: The Devolution and Revolution of Consciousness* (2014), has not presented an optimistic portrait of the human condition. We learn that coming into the world we go through four major traumas, each of which further constrict the expanded consciousness of Divinity, which is our innate nature. They are conception, birth, the primal scene at the age of four or five, and the identity stage in adolescence or young adulthood. The end result — the world around — is a person with huge amounts of repressed pain, who is separated from self, Self, Divinity, and Nature, which that person acts out in all kinds of counterproductive, self-defeating, self-destructive, destructive, aggressive, and harmful ways. This has resulted in the atrocities of history — which is one of human's unique distinctions from Nature. Most pressing for our place in the timeline, it has led to the imminent humanicide (suicide of the human race) and ecocide (the death of all life on this planet) which we humans are bringing about.

The question might arise, Is this scenario true for all people? Has it always been true? Is it this way in all cultures? What are the roots of this dismal human predicament?

Finally, and not the least of these, Is there anything we can do about it? What is the alternative? What would something better look like in our current situation?...

What can we do?

Prodigal Human

This book, *Prodigal Human: The Descents of Man* (Volume 10), and the ones to follow in the Return to Grace Series, especially, *Back to the Garden: The Psychology and Spirituality of Humanicide and the Necessary Future* (Volume 11) and *Primal Return: Renaissance and Grace* (Volume 12), will address these questions and those like them.

We begin by looking more closely, here in *Prodigal Human*, at the "evolutionary" and historical aspects of this situation. I address the first four of those questions above, which pertain to the origin and pervasiveness of this human condition: Specifically, what are its roots? Is it true for all cultures? All people? And has it always been true?

The book following this, *Back to the Garden*, begins to address the other questions: Specifically, is there anything we can do about it? What is the alternative? What would something better look like in our current situation? What can we do?

The book following that, titled *Primal Return*, addresses all four of those questions but focuses in particular on, What is the alternative? And, what would something better look like in our current situation? That book, indeed, will provide a vision, a workable one beginning from the place that we now are, of what an alternative, life-affirming societal and global construct would look like as contrasted with our current life-negating, humanicidal and ecocidal one.

But first we have to look at from where we have come in order to have an inkling of where we ought to go. We have to clearly understand the problem — and my part in that will be to reveal the deepest roots of it — before we can hope to see any possible paths forward for addressing or going beyond it. The deeper we go in understanding our dilemma, the more transcendent our visions, the more effective our solutions. Seeing clearly the deepest, the primal, the prehistoric roots of our current predicament is what this book is about.

The Descents

If the previous book, *Falls from Grace*, could be said to describe the ontogenetic or "developmental" arc of the devolution of consciousness that has led to our estranged state, this book, *Prodigal Human*, can be called the phylogenetic arc of that perspective — the falls from grace, not occurring in one's individual history, that is, over the course of one's lifetime, but unfolding over the course of history and prehistory for our species, human.

Hence, *The Descents of Man* is used for the subtitle. However much that reminds of Darwin's classic work of the same name, indeed, this current work actually does pertain to man's evolution as being a "descent" — the popular connotation of the term — or as I call it a *devolution*.[1] What this book describes is human's descent from Nature into civilization; also it details human's estrangement from the Divine over that same period. For in my conceptualization of the Divine as being All That Is, and Nature also being All That Is, Nature and the Divine are identical. (See also, my Return to Grace, Volume 8: *Experience Is Divinity*.) And in these ways, what I will be describing is most assuredly a *descent of man* from our most authentic and noble place among our honorable fellow planetmates. (See, also, my Return to Grace, Volume 6: *Planetmates: The Great Reveal.*)

Of course, for the purposes of this book, you do not need to agree with *my* "theology." If you simply can entertain the notion that the fact that being, as we are, on the edge of environmental apoca-lypse and having built the means of nuclear destruction of all life on this planet many times over points to something massively wrong with humans and their conceptualizations of themselves and their role in Nature, then we are on the same page. For that is the essence of this book: Which is that something is wrong with humans that would cause us to be able to annihilate, not just ourselves, but along with us all life on this planet we inhabit.[2] If that is not considered suicidal or homicidal, it must be acknowledged to be at least *stupid*. And it is definitely ecocidal.

Or maybe you do not yet see this. Much could be said on our current trajectory, concerning the results of climate change, world-wide pollution, and the like, but the purpose of this book has not to do with addressing that. That was the purpose of *Apocalypse Emergency* (2013) and *Apocalypse NO* (2013). More will be said in *Back to the Garden,* as well. Let me here advance just one aspect of our problem, one alone which ends our species, brings down life on this planet … one, only, of several other extinction level events that have already occurred. This has to do with the increasing nuclear radioactivity of the Earth.

If you have a problem with the notion that it is all life that is at risk, as most people do and do not want to know otherwise, remember that virtually no life can live in an environment of radiation. There are only a few microscopic animals — called Tardigrades, or "water bears," who have been found to be able to exist around the radioactivity at the mouths of volcanoes — who can survive nuclear radiation. Second, Fukushima alone — being so dire, so catastrophic that neither nations nor news reports are brave enough to face the issue — is an extinction-level event, continuing to radiate the planet even now.

This is in addition to the 444 nuclear power plants still operating in the world. Note also that at this time there are sixty-three more under construction and they operate in thirty countries. Now, all of these plants emanate at least some radiation, and all are in danger of even greater leaks and meltdowns. All have no way of disposing of their nuclear waste, which amounts to 2,000 to 2,300 metric tons per year, with each individual plant contributing approximately twenty metric tons a year. Of this waste, one of its fission products, Tc-99, has a half-life of 220,000 years and another one, I-29, has a half-life of 15.7 million years. That's right, I said *million*.

Let us take the more commonly explored component of that waste, plutonium. It has a half-life of 25,000 years or more, and needs to be guarded that entire time. Plutonium, in fact, is still deadly for 250,000 years or more. To further make your day, plutonium is so deadly that less than two kilograms of it distributed to everyone in the world would kill everyone. One *millionth* of a gram of plutonium, inhaled, guarantees lung cancer. Ralph Nader has called it "the most toxic substance known to mankind." However since then, 1995, the Japanese have claimed to have created an even more toxic substance. Put that in your #thanksalot folder, won't you.

According to the Nuclear Information and Resource Service, I quote,

> *Each 1000 megawatt nuclear power reactor annually produces about 500 pounds of plutonium, and about 30 metric tons of high-level waste in the form of irradiated fuel. After several years, when removed from the reactor core, the fuel is about one million times more radioactive than when it was loaded. This irradiated fuel is currently stored at the reactor sites.*

So, each of the 444 reactors produces five hundred pounds of it *a year* and only about two pounds of plutonium is enough to end humanity. Some 222,000 pounds of plutonium *per year* is created in the nuclear waste of reactors and a mere two of those pounds is enough to kill us all off. If you are still giddy with optimism after that, keep in mind that there have been many nuclear waste leaks over the years, into the environment, never reclaimed, bound to make it into the ecosystem in due course. One alone, which happened at the Hanford Nuclear Reservation in Washington State, a half century ago, involved a leakage of over 400,000 gallons. It went on for a long time before it was even discovered to have happened.

But there have been many other leaks at Hanford, Helen Caldicott (2009) writes, "The DOE calculates that 450 billion gallons … of radioactive waste has been 'released' into the ground, some of which is approaching or has entered the Columbia River."[3] Not bad enough, there has been a tendency for those in the know to cover these matters up and to delete documents related to it. In one instance alone, the General Accounting Office undertook an investigation, in 1991, of the "mysterious disappearance" of key documents that calculated the leaks from the radioactive waste tanks.

Since then, in 2016, there has been another major leak at Hanford of 3,000 to 3,500 gallons. It was discovered and reported on just this past April, 2016. It was described as a "catastrophic" event.

Hanford is the site where folks were making the plutonium for nuclear bombs. Oh, you want more? Wow, you're a tough one....

Okay, well, Hanford has been called an American Fukushima and Physicians for Social Responsibility call it "the most contaminated nuclear site in the world."

Now, how much did they tell you about these developments on the nightly news amid their incisive reports on new innovations in education or the like. Oh, I must tell you that my local news reported several times last night, with actual interviews, several-minute reports on a young man's apartment having been ransacked and his friend's ashes having been spilled. Yes, we have time on our airwaves for all the "pressing" and important developments of our day. *sarcasm*

So, there must be something awry in humanity to have brought about the end of life on Earth, which includes our own — for us to be committing humanicide. We are the prodigal daughters and sons of Nature and the Divine, no doubt about it. And this book reveals exactly what constitutes that twistedness — that "original sin," if you will.

However, think about the fact that it is only because we are on the doorstep of apocalypse that we, not only can envision a re-evaluation of human evolution and our role in Nature, but we are *forced to*. A revisioning of human's presumed role as "crown of creation" and "pinnacle of evolution" is not just warranted but *required*. If you are with me on that, do not worry, you need not accept my metaphysic. However, if you do see any higher powers that might exist in Reality as being inclusive of both Nature and Isness Itself, then so much the better.

of "Man"

Furthermore, though feminists, including myself, might wish, at first, to take issue with my use, in the subtitle, of the term, *man*, as referring to the entirety of all humans, I have purposely retained the term from Darwin's usage as a title in his famous work to point to the fact that this *descent,* this *devolution,* had a lot to do with the rise of patriarchy. It was predominantly a descent of *men*, of males … a descent from our natural and fitting nobility within the magnificent tapestry of an integrated and harmonious Nature. Though the devolution of humans involved men *and* women, of course, the most extreme example of it is represented by the patriarchal ethic — which is our distinct neurosis, married with civilization — and it is exhibited most strongly by men.[4]

I wished, in the subtitle, to point to that, as well as to give a tip of the hat to women who, perhaps because of their deep connection to Nature and the biological in that they give birth and actually emanate new life that way, are indeed less "fallen" from grace in Nature. Indeed, feminism and the feminist ethic have a lot to tell us about the ways we *should* be looking at ourselves and our relationships to each other and Nature if we are to avoid the apocalyptic omega point these *descents of man* are marching us toward.

Therefore, this book will address the questions of origins and then will lay out the distinctly human cultural qualities that grew from them.

The Arc of Fall and Return

The most thorough response and effort at solutions will be brought out in Volume 11 of this Return to Grace Series. For *Primal Return: Renaissance and* Grace, will carry the highlights of solution unveiled in *Prodigal Human* and *Back to the Garden* forward and pattern them into a panorama of an overstanding[5] of what an alternative might look like. Furthermore it will lay out — as important if not more so — the way to it.

Finally, *Primal Renaissance,* the book following *Primal Return*, will bring everything now known about our condition, from the previous twelve books, together into a look at the highest potentials of humans on Earth, reunited with Nature, now, and the Divine. Volume 13 in the Return to Grace Series — *Primal Renaissance* — will expand the overstanding of our natural home, reconnected with

Nature and as revealed in Volume 12, *Primal Return*. This will be an unveiling of a humanity, returned again and reunited with Nature, while having retained the products, awarenesses, and advances acquired through our long long arc of descent and return. It will be the clearest vision of a utopian future that is possible for humanity.

I want to mention that there is a plan for a final volume, a Volume 14 of the Return to Grace Series, which would be titled, *Return to Grace: The Crisis and Opportunity of End Times* and would be a consolidation of the highlights from the previous thirteen volumes into a coherent statement and vision.

Altogether the first four of these works being described — Volumes 9 through 12, which are *Falls from Grace, Prodigal Human, Back to the Garden,* and *Primal Return* — trace an arc of fall and return, of fall from grace and return to grace. This is the grand human adventure. We descend from grace; we find ourselves estranged from Nature, or prodigal; and we therefore need to *return* to grace.

We fall from our identity with Divinity and our union with Nature for many reasons. These reasons are explored in my books, *Experience Is Divinity* (2013) and *Funny God* (2014). For whatever reason, though, we set about a process of forgetting who we really are, in essence. And this all happens in the course of every lifetime, beginning with conception and continuing with the second fall of birth, the third fall of the primal scene, and the fourth fall of ego identity and consolidation at the adolescent and young adult time of life. This overall fall — this line of descent in our individual lives — I describe in *Falls from Grace*.

However, there are reasons why we, humans, of all species of planetmates undergo this fall, while other planetmates do not. Oh, yes, there are metaphysical reasons. And I tease some of those out in *Funny God* and *Experience Is Divinity*, regardless that the greatest overstanding of the reasons for our distinction in that regard will be forever hidden from us while in the Form State, that is, the embodied state.

Yet, we *can* know how, in evolution, we came to have this distinction ... or to be afflicted with this abomination. This process is accessible by science. This route of retreat from inclusion and harmony with Nature, along with a detailed exposition of the actual resulting state of falleness, as it is built up over time, is what is laid out in this work. The devolution involved in our, so-called, "evolution" over time to become human is explained as to how it began, how it proceeded — in a step-by-step process of descent occurring over the course of millions of years — and how it built up, then coalesced into what we call *human* ... and into what we call, specifically and mistakenly, our *human nature*. Thus, the falls from grace of Volume 9 is explained and explored in this volume, Volume 10, resulting in an *overstanding* of the human state or human predicament, our existential situation, as well as an *understanding* of how we are the prodigal human needing *redemption*, to use an old-fashioned word, or into needing a *return to grace*, which is my term.

Completing the arc, then, will be the purpose of the next two books in the series, *Back to the Garden* and *Primal Return*. For they will begin with our existential state of fallenness or prodigality or estrangement; and they will tell us what amounts to getting back our rightful place among the noble of Nature, what we can do to get it back, and what getting it back looks like. These books will describe the process of return as well as the state of being returned. They will provide the greatest overstanding of the arc as well as a vision of a possible humanity in a relatively near future. They will show humans finally returned to, included in, and reintegrated with Nature. This is not a return that loses all we have learned in the course of our arc of fallenness; rather, it is one that remembers and indeed redeems or blesses that ad-venture of the lonely human. It is a vision within which what we are and what we have learned are cross-fertilized to create a renaissance or flowering of the human condition and the human presence on Earth in our immediate future.

Return to Eden

As mentioned, *Primal Renaissance* will continue that vision in laying out an end point of a truly evolved humanity in some possible future beyond the immediate one. It will unveil our potential omega state, our end state, our utopian possibility on Earth in reunion with Nature and with the vastest awareness of ourselves, our physical world, the Universe, and our place in it all — the Cosmos and the Divine.

So, we prodigal humans need to get ourselves back to the Garden, we need a primal return, which is a return to grace. Doing so will create a renaissance of human awareness and the human condition in the arc of history. *Primal Return: Renaissance and Grace* and *Primal Renaissance* will unveil the profile of a lodestar for human evolution, actual evolution this time, characterized by a flowering of the human condition and a return to our identity with God and Nature ... our grace.

In *Prodigal Human,* this book, we will look at how we came to be estranged and see that state is actually one that is less than what we are potentially: We are prodigal or fallen ... therefore we do not have to be. This book will show the dark side of civilization and in so doing, by contrast, reveal the bright side of human potential, within Nature, which we left behind and so could embrace again ... and thereby be redeemed as a species and liberated as individual humans. The prodigal human will be welcomed back into the fold of Nature, if and when we have finally had enough and decide to make the journey home.

One might look at the five books this way:

- *Falls from Grace* — how the devolution happens to each of us in our individual lives;

- *Prodigal Human* — how this devolution and separation from Nature came about over the course of human "evolution" and history;

- *Back to the Garden* — what it is, now in context, and what it means we need to do;

- *Primal Return* — solutions, how to get it back;

- *Primal Renaissance* — vision and prophecy, the utopia possible for humanity.

The Descents of Man

Doing an overview of this book before you, now, these descents, in relative order of their appearance in time or, if they occurred concurrently, their priority as being causative were as so,

- First Descent — Bipedalism

- Second Descent — Birth Trauma

- Third Descent — Prematurity

- Fourth Descent — Fetal Malnutrition

- Fifth Descent — Ego

- Sixth Descent — Basic Mistrust

- Seventh Descent — Hunting

- Eighth Descent — Murder

- Ninth Descent — Horticulture, Farming

- Tenth Descent — Husbandry, Domestication of Planetmates

- Eleventh Descent — Sedentary Living

- Twelfth Descent — Accumulation

- Thirteenth Descent — Hierarchy ... control of others, inequality, domination and submission, class war

- Fourteenth Descent — Misogyny ... oppression of women, domination and submission brought into the family

- Fifteenth Descent — Child Use and Abuse ... domination and control of offspring, mistreatment and exploitation of children, family "armies" and work groups

- Sixteenth Descent — Work ... the commercializing — the buying and selling — of time and the experience of living

- Seventeenth Descent — Religion ... instead of spirituality; the beginnings of impersonal and ritualized practice in relation to Divinity and authority, sycophantic worship instead of connection with Divinity, phantom and transcendent gods

- Eighteenth Descent — Culture ... the maze and the Matrix substituting for felt experience and authenticity

- Nineteenth Descent — Soul Murder ... control of thoughts and self, avoidance-denial of pain, ultimate loss of empathy and conscience (the sociopaths of today and of history) and, thus, the ability to engage in war, hate crimes, burning of Jews and witches, genocides, ecocide, and to murder from afar and upon command.

All Aboard the Devolutionary Tour

A lot to take in, huh? Well, let us go through this again in a much more leisurely way and this time with our eyes open and exploring. Let us take a scenic tour along the route of "man's" descent from Nature to the apocalyptic crisis besetting us today.

First stop, bipedalism.

1

The First Descent — Bipedalism:

Our Separation from Nature Began When We Stood Up

"We remain ... one of the few species whose bodies have adaptations suited to water as well as land."

"...bipedalism is rare in Nature. As bipedal humans, we were beginning a whole new adventure for life on planet Earth."

Humanity's First Home Was the Trees

A long long time ago ... we're talking millions of years, double digits millions ... our ancestors lived in trees in a region of the Earth now called Africa. Our primate forbears were arboreal, scurrying along tree limbs and with a small amount of ability to brachiate, that is, to swing below the limbs and branches, like some primates do today. We slept in branches, and we took nourishment from the trees. We were primarily fruitarian, augmenting our diet with insects, caterpillars, and the like. We did not hunt or eat meat. Foraging was the way to go and was eminently sufficient during normal times. Life was good; but as happens, it did not last forever.

A change came upon the Earth. It was a global warming during the Miocene Era. The Miocene Era lasted from 23 to 5.3 million years ago and included periods of both warming and cooling of the Earth's climate, though overall it was warmer than the preceding Oligocene Era and the following Pliocene. Before sharp drops in temperature at around fourteen million years ago and again at eight million years ago, the Earth had experienced a particularly torrid time. This warming began at around twenty-one million years ago and receded only about fourteen mya. Life was no longer so good. The days were hot and discomforting. Rising temperatures meant tree lines receded, leaving open space in Africa for savannah and desert. Vegetation was harder to come by. Very many, most actually, of our would-be progenitors died off. That would have been the end, and we would not be around today, except for....

Water.

Our Second Residence Was Waterfront Property

Luckily for us, some of our ancestors did live near oceans, streams, marshes, rivers, and lakes. And what a relief it was to have water to cool off with on those hot scorching days.

Furthermore, this was the best possible place to forage. Vegetation still grew prodigiously near water sources. Sure, we had to share those waterholes with other planetmates, which included lions and other carnivores; and that was occasionally fatal.

But the water was also the best place — and oftentimes, along the seashores, the only place — to escape from predators. So in addition to our former way of seeking refuge in the trees, around water we could make our way out into it as well to escape. Most carnivores looking at us as lunch were averse to water. Their loss, our gain.

Even better, there were other ... different and more varied ... food sources that came with water. Shorelines, marshlands, and lakesides provided both welcome relief from the increased temperatures as well as served up succulent new foods such as fish, crab, kelp, snails, and items comparable to what we know of as oyster, lobster, and mussels, today. This was in addition to the lush vegetation that grew near water.

Whereas most of our species at that time died off, those who had waterfront property thrived.

Which, strangely enough, is exactly the opposite of what will happen in the near future with climate change and the sea and ocean levels rising today. There's a cruel karmic justice for ya.

But back then, it was an advantage to be by the sea. We were still planetmates and Earth Citizens, of course, and we belonged in Nature. We retained our planetmate nobility and took our honored spot in the ecosystem of Gaia. We were still in Eden, so to speak.

Then a fateful development ensued.

Our First Split with Nature Began When We Stood Up

You see, in the water there is a huge advantage in foraging to be able to raise oneself up on one's hind legs. One could go out further in the water, much further. Naturally, those that did increased their success in acquiring food. They survived; they reproduced. They won out in the process of natural selection.

There was an even greater advantage attached to water in terms of safety from predators. Again, wading out as far as possible brought the greatest security.

For both reasons, over time our primate ancestors found it increasingly advantageous to stand up. And not just to stand up, but to stay up! And for long periods of time. Considering the reasons — food acquisition and safety from predators, which both involve survival and with one of them being extra motivating to endure long periods of uprightness so as to avoid a ghastly and brutal end — there was huge incentive to stay out in the water for extensive lengths of time, standing. And to avoid being eaten as well as to get the best things for eating, oftentimes it was the most benefit to be standing as far out in the water as could be, with only one's head above the surface.

At first we were practicing our new skill of keeping our "chins up" (old chum) only in water. Eventually, for other reasons we found it helpful to be bipedal on land as well. These included keeping one's hands and arms available for carrying an infant, for with our loss of hair ... oh, did I fail to mention that? ... yes, we lost our hair like all other mammals who go out to sea ... and I assure you, we were not the first. Anyway with our loss of hair, infants could no longer hold onto fur, as our primate relatives do. Furthermore, with humans being born more helpless than our cousins and staying that way for a longer period of time after birth, our very young ones were not developed enough to cling anyway. We'll get into that in the next few chapters, with prematurity of birth and secondary altriciality.

The Naked and Aquatic Ape

Now, over the course of millions of years, because of our semi-marine lifestyle, our bodies changed in myriad ways. We lost our hair, as I said: It was helpful, when in water and especially when swimming, to not be encumbered with fur. Yet the hair on our heads remained and grew longer. For in water, a toddler could grasp its mother's hair, while she was foraging, so as to stay in proximity with her and avoid the dangers of being separated and possibly even drowning.

Our fingers became more sensitive and more useful, for that was a great help in finding and acquiring food items beneath the water.

Our eyesight was already pretty good. Having been tree-dwellers, it was hugely important to be able to distinguish shapes and patterns and for our vision to have keen three-dimensionality and binocular perspective to be able to judge limbs and distances well to keep from falling and possibly dying. Well, in the water, super-duper vision was nice to have, too; but we developed it even more. For looking through the water to find food was aided considerably by better eyesight.

But what was not that important anymore was the sense of smell. Whereas our primate sisters and many mammalian cousins have a keen ability to make out odors and scents, we began losing ours. In the water, there were nowhere near the complex odors and scents as on verdant land with its intricate, multi-aspected vegetation, infinitely complex dirt and ground cover, and varied beings … all emitting different, intense, and "highly informative" smells.

There, in the forest, it was a huge advantage to have super smell. Not so much in the water, surrounded by bland smelling ocean or sea water, with little complexity or variation to it. Even worse, the chemical substances eliciting smell, so abundant in the woods, would be washed away, while in water. Or they would drift off on the breeze and not linger as long, like they did when there was vegetation and trees all around.

Additionally, while foraging in water, it was an advantage to communicate with others of our own. Smell was a good way for land-dwellers to convey emotion and messages. The scents of the forest and other planetmates, particularly our own kind, were rich and revealing. The water, much less so.

So for informational purposes, we developed two of our abilities exceedingly — the ability to make meaningful sounds to communicate and a refined capability to convey emotion, thought, and intent through facial expression. The first would lead to language, over a very long time. The second grew out of the fact that in water, at times, it was only or primarily our heads that were visible.

It was quite an advantage in acquiring food to be able to communicate with our own, so being able to send and receive signals by way of facial expressions was a huge boon. We could not use our body language as much in water. Being often up to our heads in it, sometimes we could not wave our arms to signal alarm. It was difficult to indicate displeasure or irritation with one's body posture alone. Signals for happiness, pleasure, and direction were similarly muted. As mentioned, using smell for communication, as many in our extended family did to achieve the same ends, was no longer possible.

Hence, we became ever more adept at portraying messages through our faces, culminating in tiny but finely tuned movements in facial muscles and the ever more refined changes in facial expression that would make possible. On the other side of that, we became skilled readers of each other's facial expressions. To this day, we might not be very good at reading body language, but if you look at actors and the way they can convey so much information with a slight change of lip, eyebrow, head movement, or such — sometimes movements of muscles in the face practically imperceptible, yet we get the message — you will see how profoundly good we got at understanding each other's feelings, emotions, and even thoughts that way. We can tell a lot by "the look on his (her) face."

These are only a few of the many ways our bodies changed, and in these kinds of changes we were not all that unusual in Nature. Other species had been land-dwelling and had actually made a complete change of residence to the sea. Among these are the seals, dolphins, whales, walruses, and dugong, also known as sea cows. They had all once lived on land. The whale was once a land dwelling quadruped, like any other of the furry animals we see around us today. And the manatee evolved from a creature that had similarities to both an elephant and a rabbit. Imagine that.

The changes in their bodies were huge … as were the changes in their sizes, by the way. Limbs that were important on land became rather useless in the water, and flippers and fins and the like were better things to bring to water. In water, removing the limitations of gravity as it did, meant that size, shape, and weight were not constrained. Sea mammals became big and blubbery. Which is something that we only now, with our corporate control of food pushing nutritionless starchy, sugary, and salty foods to the near elimination of all else, are pulling off with *our* increased weight and heft.

World-Straddlers … Return to the Interior

However, we never made that complete transition to water like they did. We remain to this day one of the few species whose bodies have adaptations suited to water as well as land. Our cohorts in that regard are pigs and elephants, interestingly enough. Nevertheless, with a status midway between primates and dolphins, this was the first of many instances where humans found themselves on the borders of erstwhile hard and fast categories. Not only would it not be the last, but it is one of the things that ended up defining us. We were world-straddlers, like it not, for good or ill. And oftentimes it was for the worst.

Part of the reason we never became fully aquatic was also due to climate changes. Days were getting cooler again, and those of us who lived along the seas would begin making our way increasingly toward the interior of the continent and begin spending more of our time on land.

Perhaps it was that those who were inland thrived more, but it is also possible that those ancestors of ours with oceanfront property worked their way up the rivers back to Africa central. Or both of those factors contributed. For one thing, now that the Earth was cooling again, it was not as crucial to be in water. It was not as comfortable either. How our desire to go swimming changes on cool and cloudy days, eh?

There might also have been more disincentives to forage in waters in the interior than there were down by the sea. If it had been the case that our direct ancestors first evolved along the ocean, then when it got cooler, they might actually have wanted to follow the rivers and streams inland for more comfortable, warmer weather. However, along the ocean, there would be relatively few dangers in the water. Sharks were rather uncommon and only occasionally fatal. Other dangers, such as sting rays, could be survived. Whereas, inland there would be more dangers to survival in the water. There were crocodiles and alligators and their like; there were poisonous water snakes in more abundance than by the sea. These, along with the fact that the land surrounding began giving up more in the way of groceries were incentives to stay on the land more and to seek food there more often.

Indeed, while our ancestors came from the interior of Africa and were marsh, swamp, stream, and lake likers, we eventually had less and less need to go into the water; and we found more and more reasons to be on land. Our bipedalism at least made that an interesting change from those we saw around us who were loping about on four legs.

For certainly, bipedalism is rare in Nature. As bipedal humans, we were beginning a whole new adventure for life on planet Earth.

2

The Second Descent — Birth Trauma:

Birth Trauma Makes Us Humans … and Mistrustful of Everything

Bipedalism Caused Painful Births, Which Caused Bigger Brains, Which Caused "Intelligence," Which Caused Culture

Birth Pain Causes a Feverish Human Mind, Struggling Against Nature and the Divine, Which We Call "Intelligence"

The more civilized the people, the more the pain of labor appears to become intensified — Grantly Dick-Read, M.D., Childbirth Without Fear.

Giving birth is like taking your lower lip and forcing it over your head. — Unknown

To the woman He said, "I will greatly multiply your pain in childbirth, In pain you will bring forth children; Yet your desire will be for your husband, And he will rule over you." — Genesis 3:16

So you have it, the most significant change in our bodies that resulted from foraging in water was bipedalism. It altered the fate of humanity. Over the course of over ten million years, we became gradually more bipedal, till eventually we stood upright as we do today. We know we were walking around upright at least 3.6 million years ago, and no doubt that mechanism of mobility was in place long before that. However, this change in posture required a momentous and fateful change in our pelves to pull it off.

These changes in our pelvic structure are characteristic of *Homo sapiens* today and existed in all members of the Genus Homo. Indeed, they were present in the Australopithecines, our earliest known hominid ancestors. The most crucial change occurred in the overall orientation and configuration or the pelvic bones. Not only the angle of the pelvis, but specific bones needed to change, which included major adaptations in the ilia and the sacrum.

We gradually developed narrower hips, which were more conducive to uprightness. The pelvis of *Homo Erectus* was relatively very narrow. It included long femoral necks, which is the arm of the thigh bone attaching it to the pelvis. This aided us in running and striding, but it also had the drawback of making for a very small birth canal for women.

So, our bone structure in general changed, to accommodate bipedalism, but the crucial change had to do with the pelvis and in particular the pelvic ring. Whereas our cousins the apes have a pelvic opening that either in front-to-back or side-to-side orientations is greater than the size of the head of the ape to be born, we do not. In gibbons, gorillas, and chimpanzees, for example, the pelvis has a size making it that the infant, by twisting its head, can relatively easily make it out of the birth canal. But humans' pelvic rings are smaller than our neonates' heads … along *either* dimension. Sounds impossible, does it not?

Well, we are able to accomplish birth with two adaptations that our primate relatives did not have to make. The one is the release of special hormones by the mother that relax the mother's pelvic area, stretching and lubricating it at the time of birth. (ouch!) This, even before we in modern times and in Western societies began to give episiotomies, where the vagina is surgically cut to make it larger and more accommodating to the passage of a big-brained neonate.

The other is that the skull bones of the human-to-be adapted to be softer than in chimps and other relatives at that stage of birth. The skull being easier to be pressed a little smaller and molded, we get our big heads out of our womb-without-a-view. (double ouch!)

We can see the effects of that squeezing in human babies after birth whose craniums often show shapes indicating compression. These deformations of the head later subside, become normal, so our skulls are not so obviously molded. However, the heads of some people, look closely, still reflect that imprint of having been pressed inside a vice. Sometimes the skull will have a flatter plane on one side of it; sometimes the top back area of the skull is elongated a little, similar to our depictions of aliens with bigger brains than us, or like we are sprinting directly into a strong wind and our heads are becoming streamlined, to cut the friction. Other sorts of shapes indicating pressure can be noticed, too.

In any case, the for-the-first-time-questionable benefit of upright-ness led to narrower pelves, a different angle of the plane of the pelvis, and a smaller pelvic/vaginal opening, which narrowed the birth canal and gave us no end of problems getting out into the light at birth. In females this created more painful births. However, it caused even more trauma for the neonate.

You suddenly have a headache, you say? I am not surprised.

How about the mother's pain? Well, as I said their muscles had to relax. But beyond that, just ask any mother. Or keep in mind the quote at the beginning of the chapter: "Giving birth is like taking your lower lip and forcing it over your head." I'm not a woman, so have not given birth, not in this lifetime anyway. However, that analogy sat me up straight and made me glad I wasn't. It gave me great respect and put me in awe of mothers who do, too!

Skull Size, Pelvic Size, and Birth Pain

In this regard, it is interesting to note biological anthropologist Jim Moore's (1987) comments in a talk given at the University of Califor-nia, San Diego, concerning pelvic size, birth, and secondary altricial-ity. Jim Moore pointed out that the paleontological evidence from the bone records of our protohuman and hominid line show several fascinating developments occurring simultaneously and over the course of millions of years.

We are going back as long as six to seven million years here. One is an increase in skull size. Another is a decrease in the size of pelvic bones, which occurs alongside and is a consequence of our gradual evolution to bipedalism from being, like our primate relatives, quadrupeds.[1]

Most folks know about the increase of skull size that occurred over the course of our evolution. Humans enjoy touting their big brains almost as much as men enjoy crowing about some of their dimensions. However, what is only rarely considered is what effect this increase has on the process of birth. Nor has this been laid alongside the related factor of reduced pelvic size. But doing so leads to some fascinating conclusions.

To begin, it is reasonable to suppose that this increased skull, and brain, size in hominids contributed greatly to birth pain, for both mother and infant. This is so for the obvious reason that the size of the head is the determining factor in the size of the vaginal opening required for delivery. That is, because skull bone is mostly unyielding when pressured from outside, its diameter must be less than or equal to the maximum diameter of the vaginal opening through which it must pass at birth. If the skull is too big for the opening, the child simply cannot get out. And the factor that most determines the maximum diameter of the vaginal opening is the configuration of the bones, especially pelvic bones, that are involved.

Keep in mind that this kind of birth pain would not have occurred when the skull was smaller. A smaller head would pass, in general, with considerably more ease for infant and mother. In support of this we note that this is exactly the case for all our primate relatives, all of whom have proportionately smaller skulls. Note they also have larger, wider pelvises, proportionally, than us, and thus wider vaginal openings at birth time. Correspondingly, they do show observably much less difficulty and pain in birth, for both mother and newborn. So, along with this trend to increasing skull size in humans and reduced pelvic size we can surmise a corresponding trend to increasing birth pain, birth difficulties, and, consequently, increasing birth trauma for hominid newborns.

The Vicious Cycle of Skull Size and Birth Pain

Brain Size and Primal Pain: Brain Size Related to Degree of Unconscious Pain Needing to Be Repressed

About this factor of birth trauma, keep in mind that it is demonstrated neurophysiologically (Janov, 1971; Janov & Holden, 1975) that much of the increased brain size in humans is tied up with processing unconscious pain. That is to say, that we require the expanded capabilities inherent in neocortical expansion and larger brains to keep traumatic experiences repressed. A bigger brain is needed to keep our primal pain from overwhelming us.

Bipedalism → Narrower Pelvic Opening →
Birth Pain → Increased Brain Size →
Increased Skull Size → Birth Pain →
More Increase in Brain Size → around and around

What I am saying is that increased brain size and painful birth become, then, phylogenetically linked in a vicious cycle — one producing the other. Said another way, over the course of millions of years skull size and birth pain increased each other: Greater pain in birth requires, later on, greater repression of pain in order to survive, which leads to the development of greater neocortical capacities for processing and keeping that pain repressed. This leads to actual physical neocortical expansion, which results in greater skull size.

Then, that bigger head causes greater pain in childbirth for both mother and infant. This increased birth pain causes greater birth trauma in neonates. Finally, this birth trauma leads to greater repression of pain, then, to expanded brain size, then, increased birth pain, birth trauma, a need for more repression … round and round and round again. This goes on imperceptibly over an extremely long time in the course of our evolution.

Keep in mind, however, that this is a chicken-and-the-egg correlation. There is no way of knowing what came first. Whether changes in skull size and expanded neocortical capacity, or greater repression of feelings and pain (possible as a consequence of increased social behavior, requiring increased repression/control of individual behaviors), or increased birth trauma (either on its own, for some unknown reason, or more likely because of skeletal changes occurring through increasing bipedal locomotion and upright posture) came first is irrelevant. These are mutually arising causative factors. It is enough that we notice their interrelationship.

At any rate, all this trauma in infants pushed the development of neural cells to deal with — primarily to repress — such birth trauma. We needed to do this in order for us to not be overwhelmed with its erstwhile psychological aftermath — think of that as a kind of PTSD (post-traumatic stress disorder) from birth. Such a festering unease, in us as children or adults, would have disrupted our ability to survive, if we had not found all kinds of conscious and unconscious ways around it. With additional skillful cognitive tricks — however corrupting of our handle on our reality — we were able to hop around our underlying unhappiness. Still, unacknowledged, our birth trauma presses on us throughout our lives and alters our attitudes, thoughts, and behavior. Much of this book is about what that means for us.

At the beginning, however, this increase in neural cells — the result of the need to repress birth trauma — furthered brain growth even more, of course. Even greater increases in skull size ensued.

And, of course, increasing brain and skull size created even more pain and trauma for both mother and child at birth. Something had to give.

For millions of years these factors played out. At 1.9 million years ago, the time of *Homo Erectus,* we had the big brains we've come to boast about. Whereas we were well along the road to bipedalism long before that, at 3.6 million years ago.

Pelvic Size

In this light it is interesting to point out that Moore (1987) presented evidence of the significantly larger pelvic size in our ancestral line of hominids which would have either (1) allowed for a gestation period of up to twelve months or (2) allowed for an exceptionally easy birth — the increased brain size being much more readily passed through a larger opening. Either of these propositions, or a combination, is provocative in light of the above.

In other words, we can speculate that either (1) increased pelvic size in females was naturally selected for as brain size became larger, so as to minimize the deleterious effects of painful birth ... as in creating neurosis in the adult, hence reduced reproductive fitness ... or (2) gestation period was prolonged, with increasing brain size, to minimize the deleterious effects of imperfectly met biological needs which are a consequence of that extra time of helplessness after birth and during the brain's maturation, which is called *secondary altriciality*, by the way.[2] More about that very soon now.

In this second instance, the disadvantages of secondary altriciality are lack of precociousness in the infant, requiring an increase in maternal care after birth and reducing the economic potential of the female during that period. But it logically follows that there is a limit to which gestation can be allowed to go on without itself becoming an economic disadvantage to the female — certainly the proposed gestation period of two years — twenty-one months to be exact — for full precociousness at the level we see in nonhuman primates would be a substantial economic hardship on the female. Thus it would be selected against, in evolutionary terms.

Furthermore, increasing bipedalism was always at work against the larger pelvis. A narrower pelvis aided ambulation. Better abilities for running and darting about most definitely were survival advantages. In particular, a mother having her arms free so as be able to carry her infant, while dashing away from a danger, would assist in natural selection toward bipedalism. A mother being able to run with an infant, as opposed to having the infant in the womb at that time, would no doubt also have contributed to survival. Thus there were pushes on natural selection in the direction of increasing bipedalism and decreasing durations of pregnancy.

In any case, the demands of survival worked against such a long gestation of even twelve months. *Homonin* females would have fared poorly by being inhibited this long from foraging and other activities important for survival. They would have died off.

As mentioned, we see in the fossil records some evidence that our pelvic bones became wider for a while, which would have made birth somewhat easier. But what this probably meant, in actuality, is that the baby, needing twenty-one months in the womb, ideally, (we'll get to that next chapter) was coming out at some point after nine months. It has been said, the bone records show a gestation of twelve months at one point. This would have been assistive to birthing ape-sized heads and with minimal birth trauma. What is more likely is that our skulls were the larger size and some of that extra gestation needed for the bigger brain's maturation was still happening in the womb, and there was roughly the same amount of pain involved in birth as there is today.

Birth Pain Makes Us Humans

Birth Pain Caused the Feverish Minds of Humans, Which We Call Intelligence

To continue, remember that what is universally acknowledged to distinguish humans from other species is our intelligence and the elaboration of culture that comes from that. However, with the understanding of skull size, birth, and repression described above, we see these much-touted distinctions and claims to superiority to be merely the byproduct of our neocortical attempts to deal with unconscious pain, specifically, that of birth trauma.

"We Are a Fever, We Ain't Born Typical"

Birth pain caused the feverish minds of humans, which we call our intelligence. "We are a fever. We ain't born typical," is the way The Kills have sung it. And those spinning excess wheels of mental fibrillation, driven by human birth trauma, are the gears in the machine of our manic material culture.

These factors vied against each other for a long time, with wider pelves and narrower ones competing for ascendance. No doubt, gestations and the amount of birth pain varied as well. Regardless, the skull size had only one direction, up, for it to go. For whatever the compromise of that time in prehistory in terms of the width of pelves, there was more and more pain to be repressed in order for the organism to not be overwhelmed during the course of its life. And this required continued, ever increasing, growth in neural cells, thus brain size, thus skull size. This increased to the point we are today where in order to fully gestate the brain we ended up with, we would have had to have a twenty-one-month gestation, which we never got. There had to be another way.

Human Nature

How we solved that problem of getting a big head out of a small opening, at this point in our evolution, was to be born earlier than would be ideal. The ever bigger skulls of neonates led to a tendency for newborns to be born more and more prematurely, for with skulls at smaller sizes these prematures would be able to make it out of the womb. Barely. The larger heads still meant greater pain for mothers as well as the newborns themselves than planetmates in Nature needed to endure.

Therefore, we may speculate that a combination of these factors resulted in a compensatory system wherein the fact of increasing brain size is eventually resolved, to date, by a comparatively reduced gestation period accompanied by increased need for child care after birth; increased need for economic dependency overall (both during and after gestation) by the female; increased need for male parental investment in providing for both female and child; and increased birth pain correlating with increased cultural development to offset or mitigate the effects of birth pain.

The net effect is a species with prolonged child care; increased tendency toward single-family units; increased brain size; greater cultural elaboration; increased birth pain for the neonate; increased "intelligence"; and increased neurotic and psychotic behavior (thus idiosyncratic and variable behavior) which requires further cultural accommodation, hence cultural elaboration — all evolving simultaneously, interrelating and mutually reinforcing each other. All in all, with these considerations, we have the basic factors which outline our distinctive human nature — that is, which constitute, for good or ill, our fundamental distinctions from other species.[3]

Next, "External Gestation" and the Origins of Culture

Nevertheless, the critical change in all that is our most unusual premature births. And this is what we look at next ... the earlier births required of human babies. And coincident to that, I address *secondary altriciality*, which has to do with the extra time needed for growth outside the womb and in the company of family and society. Gestations were cut short. "External gestation" — which is what some scholars have called this period of brain maturation occurring outside the womb and in the company of society — was prolonged

Next stop, though, the earlier births of humans — our prematurity.

3

The Third Descent — Prematurity:

Secondary Altriciality, "External Gestation," and the Origins of Culture

Why We Can't Get No Satisfaction and What It Has to Do
With Being Born Helpless. Parents Are Imperfect ...
Biology Is Relatively Perfect

Human Nature, Culture, Pelvic Size, and Plato's Cave:
Needs Which We as Newborns Ache to Fulfill Are
Satisfied by Other Species Perfectly

For millions of years, the factors of mothers needing wide pelves to accommodate birthing healthy twenty-one month gestated newborns, vied for natural selection against the economic pressures for females to have shorter gestations to return to full foraging and to be able, with smaller pelves, to move and while carrying something, like a baby, run more quickly.

Prematurity Was the Compromise

Gradually over that time, the compromise we have today was arrived at. Pregnancies would be shorter — nine months — allowing for the economic and survival advantages of that. As for the long period of maturation required for the brain, that would be taken care of by the infant being born more and more premature in order to get the head out at all, regardless that it was still traumatic. Thus, roughly half the brain's development would occur in the womb under the direction of a process of Nature determined and perfected over the course of millions of years. The other half would happen after birth, under the care and direction of considerably less perfect humans.

We are born premature. Relative to virtually all the rest of Nature, whose development of its brain occurs under the aegis of Nature, that is, before birth, we are *half-borns*. We are only half ready for life at the time of birth.

Prematurity was the compromise, the imperfect solution. It meant that, in order to make up for the loss of all that time of maturation in the womb which other species are afforded, we would have a longer time of abject helplessness after birth. This postnatal time of one year, comparable to the time our nearest relatives in Nature spend in the womb, would require careful, focused, and thoroughly all-encompassing care by the mothers or other caregivers. It would be accordingly exhausting and time intensive. This meant that needs of the infant could never be perfectly satisfied.

Human mothers now needed also more expertise in child-caring than those in Nature. The knowledge and skill required could never be ideal. Indeed, there would be a gap in what the baby needed and what mothers could provide. Compared to Nature, human infants were needy, difficult, time-consuming, and frustrating in their being so helpless and so long to mature. This would have consequences for child abuse later on, but in the beginning it simply meant human mothers had a much greater and more difficult workload than their sisters in Nature.

Thus, premature birth and narrower pelves — concomitant with bipedalism — won out. Survival advantages won out over healthy, happy newborns and relatively easy, painless births with long gestations and the near perfect nurturing for an additional twelve months by a Divinely-designed biological process in the womb.

We began the process of becoming human, meaning being separate from all other Earth Citizens, at the time that narrow pelves, nine-month (premature) gestations, birth pain and trauma for mothers and newborns, and dependency on caregivers for the first few years of life became the norm.

So it was that standing up ... while not strictly a fall from grace, in and of itself ... set the whole process of human's descent from Nature in motion.

Secondary Altriciality and the Origins of Culture

The other part of prematurity is the helplessness after birth and the extra dependency of the baby on maternal care for survival and growth. The additional time of helplessness that humans have is termed *secondary altriciality*.

With prematurity came secondary altriciality. And with secondary altriciality came culture.

Let me explain.

Sociability

The intensive care required of newborns created an exceptionally important time of one-on-one engagement of the infant with its caregivers, usually its mother. Right at the start, we are forced into socializing, however we can. We need to communicate in any way possible to get our needs met. And we are helpless to any ministrations that our caregivers might put upon us.

We become more social than our relatives in Nature. By that I mean the increased dependence required of human infants resulted in much greater maternal care and interaction between mother and infant. Thus the need to communicate and nurture led to cooing, led to *motherese* — which is the baby talk and cooing that mothers adopt naturally and for humans universally, as the way to talk to its baby.

Language

This motherese and cooing during evolution led eventually to language. Certainly the roots of language are in the need for communication around survival while foraging in water. However, with secondary altriciality and the long extra time of mothering, that language ability was facilitated and enhanced. Along the same lines, the intense interaction between mother and child led to extra facility in what we had already been developing in facial expressions for the purpose of communicating. Like language, it is in the mother-infant interaction that particular skill is refined.

The uniqueness of this mother-infant time is easy to see when you compare us with other species. For example, think for a moment of the way we normally see a chimp or gorilla baby with its mother. Certainly they interact. Definitely they will occasionally play. However, to a much greater degree, what you observe is a detached attitude of the mother with little to no eye-to-eye contact. That makes sense, when you think of it. For the babies being more mature when chimps and gorillas are born, they are past that time of excessive dependency required of humans. That means that chimps and gorillas can much more take care of themselves, even to the point that they do not need to be held but can cling to the mother's fur. It follows that extra motherly attention is not necessary.

Now, think about humans' mother-infant interaction. Compare the two. When we observe human mothering, let us say the mother is breast or bottle feeding her child, you might see the mother and baby looking deeply and for prolonged periods into each other's faces. The same kind of intense interaction is characteristic of play times between the two. Each is fully attentive to the nuances of facial expressions and sound emitted by the other. This is a lengthy intensive education for human infants in the finer points of facial expression. The mother might be making sounds, cooing, using words and talking, perhaps singing or humming in order to soothe and pacify.

Lay that alongside what we normally see in the mother-infant interaction of our primate relatives. Let us take, for example, chimps and gorillas. In Nature, chimps and gorillas do very little of that. A mother might be observed nursing, but her face is often looking off into the distance. When not nursing, the child might be clinging to the mother's fur, oftentimes not even in direct view of the mother's eyes. At any rate, the mother, being clung to, appears unaffected and seemingly absent-minded, or watching and monitoring its environment and the behavior of others in the social group in its vicinity.

Do not think this means planetmate mothers are detached and unfeeling toward their infants. Quite the contrary! They will show such a dedication to the care of their youngest as to put many human mothers (not all) to shame. Mother and child will stay together for life, in some species. Planetmate mothers have been known to die of grief if their infant dies. Just that the crucial and delicate time of infant vulnerability for humans has been gone beyond for our primate relatives, during their time in the womb. They are "past all that." This delicate time, this "external gestation" for humans requires incredibly more focus on the part of human mothers. The bonding that results from all that effort and mothering has some salutary benefits. The fact that it cannot be done perfectly? As it is done for primates during their corresponding development which occurs in the womb? Well, not so much.

In addition, the tasks of mothering, for that devil-may-care chimp mother includes nothing like what is required of human mothers in terms of pacifying the infant. Being more mature and less helpless, chimp and gorilla babies do not need to, nor have they evolved to be able to, scream and wail for attention and to express their needs like human newborns do. That is another thing that is distinctly different between us and our relatives in Nature: Human babies require more pacifying, thus more attention in that regard.

Granted, human babies are in more pain because their needs are greater, being more helpless; and those needs cannot be perfectly satisfied, so they cry about that.

And for certain, our infants are required to do more communicating about their needs to try to get them met; for we are more helpless and needy after birth, less able to fend for ourselves. For example, we cannot even turn over or crawl, let alone grasp — as our chimp and gorilla relatives can — until considerably later after birth. We need to shake our arms and wail and can do little more. Holding out our hand or reaching, or indicating the object of our desire by pointing, is not even possible till later. Meanwhile, our nearest relative infants are already able to reach out and grab.

Thirdly, with the additional load of birth trauma, and trauma from fetal malnutrition, which we will get to next, you can imagine how much more unhappy we are than our cousins.

We come into the world weeping and wailing, screaming and turning red and flailing about. Our cousins do not. Hence during that extra time of dependence and even for a while afterward, there are additional emotional needs that human mothers have to take care of that their sister mothers do not have to do. Babies are often in pain; mothers must coo, pacify, hum, rock, and make nice. You can see where this is a considerable prod for even more mother-infant interaction and communication — both verbally, audibly, in the direction of increasing facility in language, and visually, by means of facial cues and body language.

Culture

The point is that this intensive mother-infant interaction is the foundation for the extra sociability required of humans and for culture, with all its components of language, need for communication, and structure in our social groups.

So, because of secondary altriciality ... that extra time of dependency as infants ... which is caused by prematurity, which is necessitated by the size of our skulls and brains, which size is the result of the overwhelming birth trauma of humans with its consequent need to be repressed in order for humans to function, which was caused because we began standing up and so altered the arrangement of our pelvic bones, we developed both language as well as the need for human interaction, the sociability, which is the basis for culture as well as human empathy.

Regarding empathy, humans have been fitted to survive in groups where there is extensive communication of needs and desires. While other mammals care about the pain of their offspring and seek to mollify them and are capable of grieving, we are the only species who developed the ability to empathize to such an extent that we are the only ones to have psychotherapists. Oh, and shamans and priests

… oh, and sympathetic lovers. But then, being as fucked up and neurotic as we are, simmering in pain atop a hill of trauma, we are the only species who needed to.

At any rate, that extra socialization, with its language and refined communication by way of sound, facial expression, and body posture, lays the foundation for human culture. Indeed, culture steps in to make up for the lack of instinct in humans. More about that, as well, later on.

Monogamy

Secondary altriciality had other consequences which shaped human behavior and human culture. For mothers required assistance, during vulnerable times in pregnancy as well as the busy and all-consuming mothering times after the child's birth, with food acquisition, safety, and surviving. This need for outside support contributed to monogamy as the desired way to go for male-female reproductive pairing … at least for women.

We see the differences in male and female tendencies in that regard even today. First of all, however, throughout our history this extra assistance needed by mothers has pushed for single male-female units — monogamy — with exceptions to the contrary pushing through only occasionally and to various degrees in only some cultures, but if so, especially among the well-to-do in those societies. For in some societies, men with excess resources have the luxury of time for such dalliances, the resources to facilitate them, along with, importantly, the power to keep from being pressured by others in the group to do otherwise and to be like the rest in the group, for example, through moralizing. They are above such restrictions as falls upon the rest of their group, and in such a situation, we see the tendencies of men to manifest as they would.

The point is we have polygamy and polyandry as human potentials, but polygamy — that is, one man with two or more women — vastly trumps polyandry in terms of its occurrence. Furthermore, and just ask any woman, it is the man who is more likely to cheat. That is more than just a complaint or criticism from women, it is actually the case, statistically, and in virtually all cultures. Whether it is considered "cheating," however, is culturally variable.

Thus, there are measurable differences between women and men in their desires for protection versus for risk-taking; for nesting as compared to wandering; for family-home life as against adventure and a shackle-less existence; and finally, for analytical detached pursuits of a solitary nature versus social, people-oriented, playful, and family pursuits. That hardly means the potential for both tendencies does not exist equally in both. Yet, statistics indicate that secondary altriciality with its demands for mothering had an effect on male and female behavior, needs, and desires. Women have stronger desires for, and more actual need for, security. Whereas men are more likely to feel relatively more unattached to relationship, to family, and even to nurturing and providing ... despite what men say.

Social Structure

As a consequence of secondary altriciality, humans have a distinct social structure in the family and the group. Indeed, the natural social configuration has women at the center, dispensing care and nourishment, and men on the peripheries, doing whatever they can find to do when they are absolutely not needed for reproduction, defense, or nonessentials and luxuries like meat and "entertainment" — that is to say, ritual, religion, and performance.

Division of Labor

Thus secondary altriciality can be seen to be responsible, as well, for the division of labor we notice in all societies between men and women, with it being extremely pronounced in some cultures and in others not as much, though it exists. The increased dependence of the infant on its mother after birth contributed to a division of labor with women needing protection during their times of increased vulnerability and incapacitation and time being taken up in the care of the very young. It contributed to gender roles, therefore.

Family Units

Beyond that, these tendencies, rooted in that dependency of infants, pushed for the creation of family units. Remember, families are not a big deal to our primate relatives. In chimps they do not exist at all.

Primates are rarely monogamous, for starters. Among our fur-bearing cousins, only the gibbons mate for life. Chimps are promiscuous and the fathers are not involved at all in the care of the young. Being non-monogamous as well as promiscuous, for one thing, paternity is not known. Some other mammals, such as wolves, pair off for life; and the males are protective and caring of the young, as the mothers are, but the paternity is known. They essentially have family units. Not so for our more closely related mammal planetmates.

However, all these factors of sociability, monogamy, division of labor, and many other changes that came with infant helplessness made it so natural selection would favor those of us who mated for life, were monogamous, and had male assistance for the mother at and around the times of its roles of mothering. Thus, families.

So, culture is born in the helplessness of the human infant.

Why We Can't Get No Satisfaction

Let us now add another factor to this development of supposed intelligence and culture. As I have been saying, *altricial* means humans are born helpless. We would die if not cared for. Secondary altriciality of humans, and only humans, means our brains and consequent functioning are even less advanced than other species at birth. We are, in essence, born premature relative to other species. We are born *even more* helpless. And the later development of our brains comes in a social, not biological, surround.

The period after birth requires that the newborn get its needs met indirectly, that is, through someone else. In the womb, one's needs are handled automatically by Nature and biology. One does not have to cry in order to get nutrients. However, the human newborn, in order to get its needs met in that time of dependency *must* communicate. At the same time, it also helps to be non-fussy, to smile a lot, and to be adorable. So these social requirements — conflicting as some of them are (that is a whole other story; we'll get to it) are put upon our infants. Humans thus learn sycophancy and conformity right at the beginning, even prior to any enculturation in society which might push those tendencies even further.

The infant has complex needs, which are as complex and demanding as those that are taken care of by other species in the womb, and must rely on human adults, with all their flaws, shortcomings, and imperfections to somehow be able to attend to and satisfy them. Rarely can humans do it well, and never can they do it as well as Nature does for primates in the womb.

By comparison, all other mammals, when born, are more able to provide for themselves, are further along in their development toward independence when born, are more capable of bringing about or at least initiating the satisfaction of their needs . . . hence they are less dependent, and vulnerable, than are human infants.

Secondary altriciality in human infants means that there is a greater need for care, for "mothering" — because of the newborn's greater helplessness, greater dependence, greater vulnerability — than that of all other mammals postnatally. However even the best mothering cannot be as perfect in satisfying the infant's biological needs as was the situation for it in the womb. Hence, there is going to be a gap between need and fulfillment inherent in this prematurity, an inherent frustration of need to at least some extent, and, it follows, inherently an increase of at least some amount in the degree of pain suffered by the newborn and infant in the nonsatisfaction or incomplete satisfaction of its biological needs.

Yet secondary altriciality is important in another respect. Since this phase represents a dependent phase that corresponds to phases that occur to other species in utero, it leaves *Homo sapiens* vulnerable to neurosis and mental illness — its roots in the pain of unmet biological need — to an extent unprecedented, in any other species. This also contributed to increased brain size, increased secondary altriciality, and so forth in the way discussed above for birth. Thus, we have another vicious cycle, again with "fevered" brains and culture the byproduct.

4

The Fourth Descent — Fetal Malnutrition:

Standing Up Had Us Starving and Suffocating in the Womb

"We feel ourselves to be a victim to our surroundings and begin doing the opposite of what all other species and even our earliest ancestors did during their times in late gestation: We split off from our rootedness in the mother and we cast that unyielding surround of the womb and placenta — and the mother, by proxy — into 'the enemy,' needing to be fought. We create a duality between us and Nature, us and other people ... and in terms of how this comes out later in rampant misogyny, between us and women, if we are male."

While many of our descents occurred over time, in a historical progression, one following the other, others happened concurrently, or else we have no way of knowing which development came earlier than another. When they developed together or around the same time, for the most part, in ordering these descents of man, I put the development of greatest import, with the greater impact on the ones that follow, before the ones that are a consequence of the one before or they are of lower importance in their effect on our "descents."

Prenatal Suffocation and Starvation ... Fetal Malnutrition

Fetal malnutrition is one such development that happened concurrently with birth trauma and prematurity, with its resulting secondary altriciality.

Andre Briend (1979) brought this to our attention relatively recently as our evolutionary science goes.[1] What it basically means is that during the last month of gestation the growth of the prenate, as measured by its weight, slows down, levels off. The way this looks on a chart is that the curve of growth, undeterred and relatively perfect in its progression for the first eight months, begins to flatten out. The fetus is no longer growing optimally, as it had been.

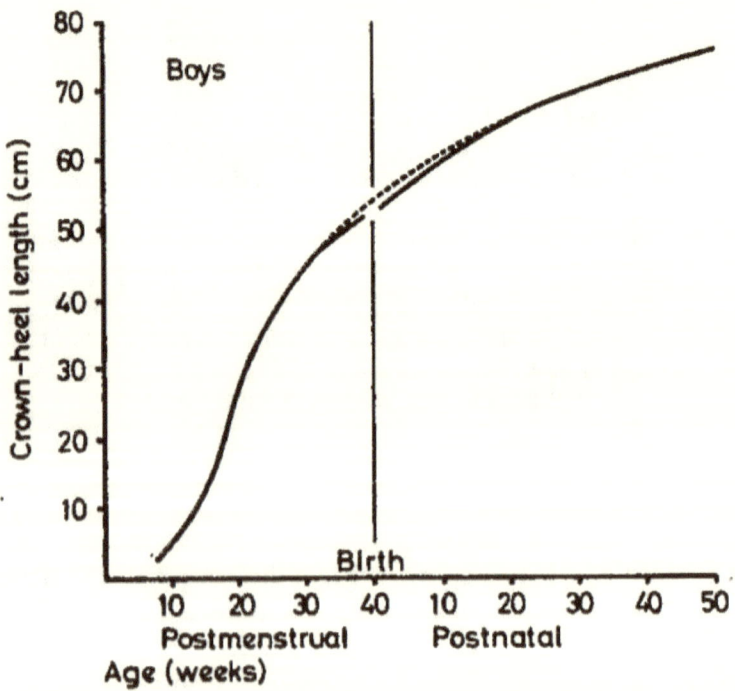

Why? Well, what happens is a direct result of bipedalism. Whereas primate young, whose parents go about on four legs, hang loosely underneath the mother's torso in her normal posture of standing on four legs, the weight of human prenates sits smack atop several arteries and veins important for the fetuses health.

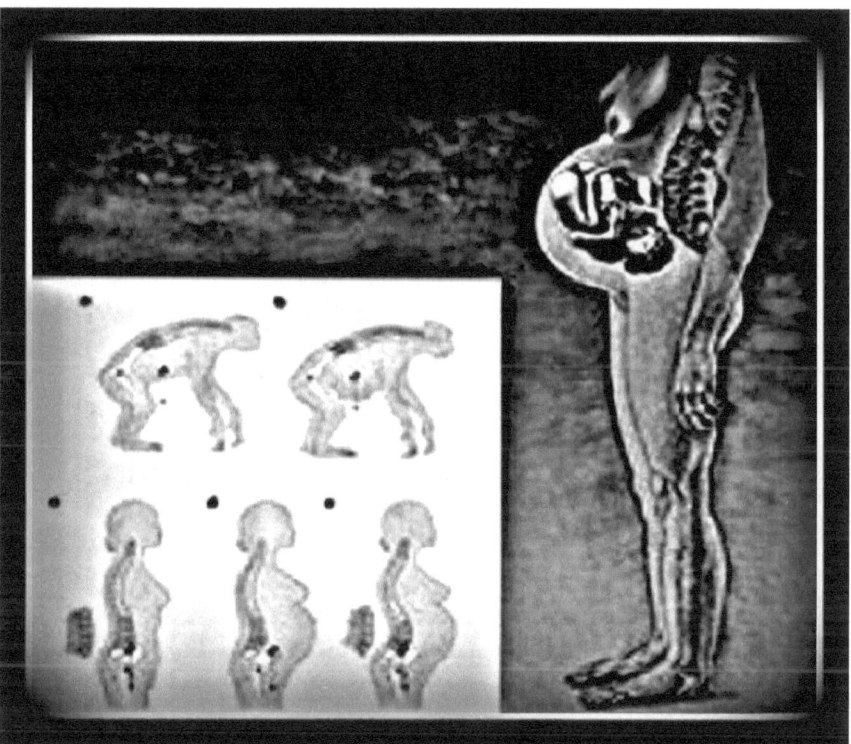

As Briend explains it, becoming bipedal did more than make birth more difficult for humans, which scientists commonly acknowledge, it caused the lower lumbar of the vertebrae and the sacrum to be thrust forward. This unique human skeletal modification reduced the space in the female body for the uterus and resulted in a significant interference with maternal hemodynamics, that is to say, blood flow. Specifically, when the mother is lying down or standing this reduction in blood flow is pronounced. It is only alleviated somewhat when the mother is lying down and in a lateral position, which is to say when she is lying down on her side. Now, this is rarely the case.

This deleterious effect on the prenate of its mother standing up is particularly at work in societies and classes where demands on the mother to be productive and laboring right up to the time of delivery are in place. While much bed rest, and in a lateral position, would help, this is not only hardly allowed — let alone is it even common knowledge that this would be advantageous — it is impractical; it is virtually impossible.

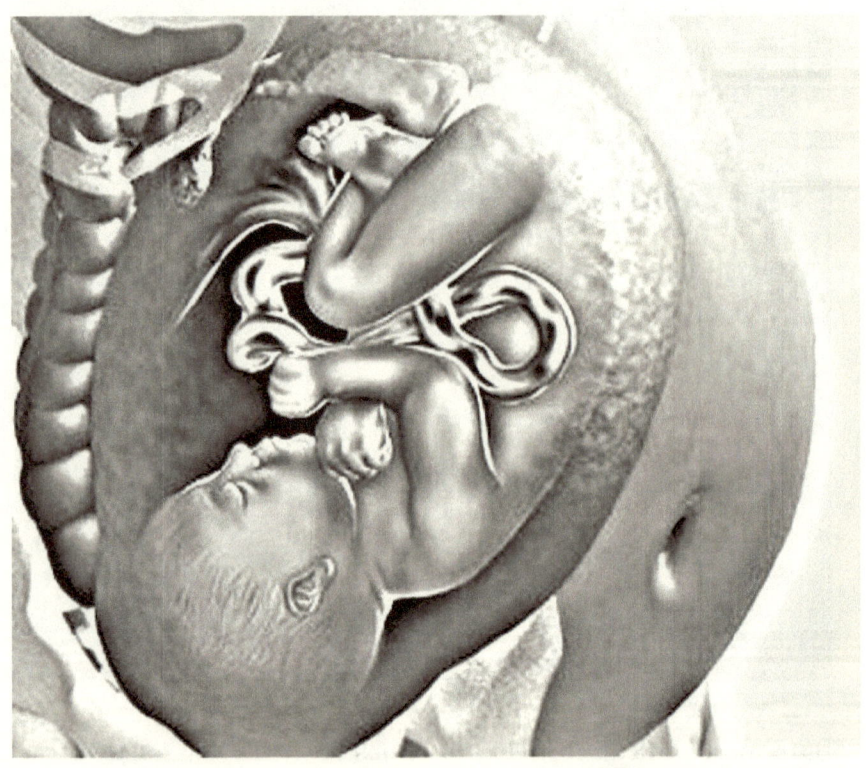

In the supine position, lying on one's back, face up, the arteries that go down along the lumbar spine, which are the vena cava and the aorta, are compressed. As Briend explains, compression of the aorta causes a drop in arterial blood pressure distal to the lumbar lordosis. This directly impacts the nutrition of the prenate, in that it reduces blood flow involving the uterus. Additionally, pressure on the inferior vena cava causes a reduction in blood volume and a decrease of cardiac output. This is highly significant for the fetus in that both of these, blood volume and cardiac output, prior to this in the prenate's gestation, had been substantially increased to facilitate the prenate's extraordinary development.

Those are the effects on blood flow when the mother is lying down on her back; yet standing upright, there is a similar impairment of blood flow to the placenta. Briend points out that in a mother's being up and about, the effects of gravity, that is to say, of the weight of the fetus on the mother's internal system, has a negative effect on the hydrostatic pressure in the veins. Both of these factors of reduced arterial and decreased blood flow in the veins are especially impactful for the growth of the prenate during the last few weeks of gestation.

The conclusion is that uprightness of posture had adverse effects on the neonate and its mother at birth, in creating the most difficult births of humans among all planetmates; but also in the last month of gestation, in creating such a reduction in the flow of oxygen and nutrients to the fetus as to cause it to radically abate its ability to continue growing.

Veins which remove the waste products of food conversion are pressed upon as well. With blood vessels compressed, blood flow to the fetus is reduced, while the mother is standing, especially, but in other positions as well, except the lateral position. This involves lying on one's side, hence it is not a position frequently adopted.

So in most situations the prenate is not getting enough nutrition to grow at its previous pace. However, remember that the fetus does not breathe air like it will later. It gets *all* its oxygen through the arteries coming to it from the placenta. Therefore it will be starved for oxygen along with all other nutrients. Conceivably, with oxygen being the primary nutrient required for life, this *prenatal suffocation* has at least as much, if not considerably more, influence on the growth of the prenate.

Concomitant with this reduction of resources, the blood flow necessary to remove the byproducts of food conversion is itself impaired. With a backing up of toxins, this way, there is a buildup of noxious substances in the fetal surround. The fetus feels itself not just hungry and "gasping," but poisoned and irritated as well.

We experience feelings of being force-fed impurities, with our impurities being inadequately removed. This leads to a complex of feelings that are kind of a prenatal disgust. I call this *prenatal revulsion.*

In addition, with the fresh sensitivity of newly acquired and unimpaired senses, we feel this toxicity around us, not just being fed us. With this we experience a situation something like a bath in slightly acidic water. And that feels like a kind of burning on our delicate skin surfaces. It is an irritation not alleviated till after birth. This is what I have termed, *prenatal irritation* or *prenatal burning.*

As I said, the fetus is starving and suffocating in there in the last four weeks of its gestation, which is *prenatal suffocation* or *prenatal gasping.* Furthermore, it experiences prenatal irritation or burning, from the toxins in its surround. And along with the rest it feels something like a sickening or poisoning — what I have termed *prenatal disgust* or *prenatal revulsion* — caused by the backup of toxins affecting how it feels about what is coming into it, not just in its surround.

How We Know How Fetuses Feel

Most of us can only imagine the unbelievable trauma involved in this. Indeed, we might not have even recognized the traumatic nature of this development of fetal malnutrition if it were not for the fact that over the course of the last sixty years, since the experimentation that began with LSD in the Fifties, there have been people who have re-experienced parts of this time.

Subsequently, other modalities arose allowing non-drug access to and reliving of this time in utero for some people. I am one of them.

The paramount researcher in the LSD-assisted as well as non-drug exploration of these early times is Stanislav Grof.[2] Grof's particular portrayal of this pain, based on his extensive research, subsumes such trauma of the last four weeks under a category of *perinatal* events that can occur earlier in the womb, having to do with toxins ingested by the fetus because of what the mother takes in during that time. His theory holds that if the intake of air, food, and drugs by the mother is ideal, that is, relatively non-toxic, this kind of prenatal pain of poisoning and "sickness" does not occur. My position on this is that he has misattributed this prenatal pain and that, instead, it occurs virtually to all of us in those last four weeks and has characteristics of suffocation, poisoning, and skin irritation or "burning."

I am not alone in asserting this. In fact, my earliest ideas about this, outside of the experiences of it in primal re-experience I had two decades previous to reading about it, came to me via Lloyd deMause (1982, 2002) in his important works. He sums up these experiences with the term, the *suffering fetus*, and he proposes as the reason for our trauma that we are connected to our mothers through a *poisonous placenta*.

A sidenote: Some prenatal and perinatal psychologists question the existence of this pain. Thomas Verny, a primal therapist and the author of *The Secret Life of the Unborn Child* (1981), is reported to have said he never heard of such trauma around fetal malnutrition being described as occurring in the course of the primal therapy that he, and other primal therapists, facilitated in people. However, I contend that the reason they have not is that they are confusing the pain of this time with two other times perinatally — earlier in the womb, as I have stated … and at the time of birth. In addition, I can tell you I re-experienced it. Furthermore, the re-experience of it comes only after many years of primal re-experience of easier to integrate traumas, and few people stay with this kind of inner journeying and healing that long, as I have.

This pain shows up quite a bit in Grof's work where he, and I assume the client, mistakenly relate it to earlier in the womb. This no doubt is often the case and sadly has increased in modern times: We are sickened and traumatized earlier in the womb when our mother consumes or breathes in toxins — be they from smoking, from drinking alcohol, from ingestion of drugs and pharmaceuticals, from inhalation of polluted and toxic air, or from consumption of toxic, additive-ridden food.

However, I submit that it happens to us all, virtually, except for very early premies being born prior to that eventful last month. And it is not merely the result of what the mother ingests, but it is a consequence of what the mother is breathing and eating not getting to the fetus sufficiently, because of a constricted blood flow, and along with that, on the egress side of fetal dining, the prenate's byproducts of food conversion not being removed as efficiently. The prenate's waste matter must be removed by that blood flow as well. So there is a discernible, to the fetus, buildup of toxic waste products when the veins are restricted. The "garbage" backs up in the system, leaving us, as prenates, stewing in it.

The other pain that is misattributed in Grof's schema is the one at birth where he describes the filthy, even *scatological* (associated with feces), aspect of birth. He says that we are born into the mother's feces, which are released at the time of birth. While it is no doubt true that happens if the mother does not receive the standard pre-birth enema needed, the mother *does* have this taken care of in any of our modern times. Hence, how clients could be experiencing wallowing in shit and other filth is hard to understand, unless one does, as Grof is wont to do, attribute it to the transpersonal facet of the perinatal matrix or constellation of events.

This is saying that he would attribute the existence of such filth around the time of birth, when it did not happen in that individual's actual life, to the fact that it presumably has happened for the vast majority of humans for the greatest extent of our time as a species. Additionally, he might bring in archetypal elements — such as those involving filthy, disgusting hells and murderous, blood-thirsty mother and evil goddess figures — to explain it. This application of arche-typal understandings is saying that Grof might, for example, relate it to the archetype of Mother Kali, from Indian literature, or to any of the other fiercesome mother archetypes, as well as to ideas about hell which involve it being dirty, revolting, and involving burning or fire.

Sure enough, though, applied to this prenatal time of fetal malnutrition — which involves a seemingly "blood-sucking" placenta, which is associated with a feminine figure, a "goddess," who is one's mother and which threatens death, along with this existence of ours prenatally going on for what seems an eternity in a "hell" of backed up toxins — there is no doubt these archetypal elements are mixed in. Though not with the time after birth, but prior to it.

Therefore, I believe Grof overlooks the effects of fetal malnutrition; I have never heard or read of him mentioning this event. So he misses the obvious fact that such wallowing in toxicity by the prenate in the last four weeks of gestation has all the characteristics of what he describes as scatological and happening at the actual time of birth. Wallowing in feces is metaphorically identical to simmering in the waste products of one's food conversion in the womb. How can these two times be confused? Believe me it is not hard to do.

36

As I have written again and again, how what happens to us prenatally is interpreted is all important and that interpretation is influenced by our knowledge of what is supposed to happen. Swami Guru Muktananda (1974), in his autobiography, said he "hopped like a frog" in his spiritual "practice." However, he might have related it instead to a time as a fetus, kicking in the womb, or at birth, pushing with his legs to get out ... that is to say, in re-experiencing it, like he wished he could but was not able to do at that time ... or even cellularly, where in re-experiencing our time as a sperm one will kick frantically in a way like the sperm does to propel itself via its long tail. That is, Muktananda might have interpreted his experience that way, instead of describing it as being frog-like, if he had known such possibilities of re-experiencing early events exist.

Can re-experiencers make such a misattribution? Absolutely, yes. In the course of a session, experiences come one upon the other, often. And fractals of a feeling are mixed with times both before and after the time one thinks one is re-experiencing. It is the feeling that is the central quality and determines what will be experienced. The feeling is the core and draws to it various events, which happened at different times, which contain that same core feeling or trauma. These are feeling *complexes;* Janov used the term *compound feelings* to describe this tendency to feel earlier and later fractals of the same feeling as occurring either simultaneously, with one feeling overlying and often mixed with another, or happening in close temporal proximity to each other. Thus, often the exact time of the experience one is reliving must be deduced. There were no wristwatches in the womb. Nor did we have graphs on the womb walls of prenatal and postnatal development nor charts of the events that usually occur then.

Yet, there is the fact that fetal malnutrition is externally observable and measurable, not simply deduced from sessions of re-experiencers. It does exist and is calculated in terms of the weight of the fetus over that period of time and has been measured related to the heel-to-crown size of the fetus. There would seem to have had to have been a huge emotional corollary to an event of such an incredibly profound impact on a prenate's development that it would actually slow down, practically halting, its growth. Imagine how much one would have to starve oneself or suffocate oneself when one is growing as a child or an adolescent to bring that about. Sure, it happens, as can be seen in the growth of children in impoverished areas of the world. Still, it requires quite a bit of very painful and torturous starvation for reduced nutrition to slow down one's growth. Add the factor that there is oxygen deprivation at the same time, and even non-re-experiencers will have to conclude it to have been an extraordinarily hellish time.

The Prenatal Matrix of Human Events and The Roots of All Evil

At any rate, I have laid out the details of this trauma in my book, *Wounded Deer and Centaurs,* especially in Part Two: "The Prenatal Matrix of Human Events." And I have shown how it has led to the atrocities of all times.

For during that time we are crowded; we are compressed in the womb, too. This leaves us ever afterward thinking we need more room (more womb) personally. We fight over property and boundary lines. And as nations, we engage in wars of "expansion." Further, we experienced a suffocation that makes us feel ever after that we can never get enough of what we need, which leads to greed for oneself and oppression of others who we fear might take what we want. That time of suffering also involved a kind of sickening or poisoning, because of the buildup of toxic waste products not being removed enough, which has many of the elements of paranoia. And this we carry with us into life. Historically we have acted this out in blatant ways on minorities, for example, the Jews at the time of the Third Reich; on witches in Medieval times; and upon homosexuals, in "civilized" cultures, right up to today. We also experienced a prenatal irritation or burning which makes us push people away and persecute minorities, which makes us unable to accept love and to be uncomfortable and even enraged by closeness, and which results in all kinds of angry and hateful acts as adults.

For the complete explanation, see my work (2016b). For our purposes, it is important to point out that the growth of the neonate, for about five weeks after birth, speeds up so that its rate of acceleration exceeds that during the uninhibited growth in the womb prior to fetal malnutrition. Thus, it catches up to what it would have weighed had it not had an arrested development, caused by nutritional insufficiency, just prior to that. After this acceleration which is required in order to catch up, development continues along the same arc of growth established in the first eight months of gestation.

Indeed, based on what we can see from the outside, there is no problem here. What the fetus does not get in the womb and does not experience as growth then is made up for after birth by utilizing whatever nutrients it gets to make up for that and by accelerating its growth. However, this is once again removing the human from the equation; this is looking at us as though we are unfeeling machines, not fully feeling subjective beings. For, as I have said, this is an horrendous time as felt for a prenate, having vast psychological and emotional consequences for each of us individually as well as historically as a species.

How it affects us? Well, it is another trauma, a significant one, that needs more repression, thus a bigger brain in order to keep it from affecting our ability to function.

Yet the effect most immediately, at that time in the womb, the last four weeks, is that it confronts the fetus with its biggest trauma to date. It might really be the only major trauma up to that point. For previous to that in the womb and even earlier, at the cellular level, for the most part our lives are literally ... awesome. We are content, often blissful, and glorying in many things, such as our supreme ability to pull off this explosive multiplication of cells to create all our components. We built this body on verve and vigor. There is no doubt in my mind that feeling back to this time prior to the Big Pain is the foundation for incredible self-confidence. And much more.

So it is, then, that when the womb gets too crowded, we doubt. When we suffer a simmering suffocation, we go into a despair about the powers in the world surrounding us that have up to that time facilitated us wonderfully. When we experience prenatal poisoning or sickening, we experience overwhelming fear, anxiety and consequent paranoia. We suspect the worst. This is the ultimate in "negative thinking." We mistrust the powers and forces we initially had identified with, and subsequently, felt at least a solid connection with ... like Adam and Eve did with God in Eden.

When we have the prenatal irritation, we are enraged about having anything around us and we want to throw off all bonds. If nothing else it is like having multiple itches that must be endured for they cannot be scratched. Regarding the compression and trapped feelings, when we in later life come across a trace of that early crowdedness in our psyches, we want to explode. Hollywood movies, and similar entertainment media including and especially video games, exploit these feelings for considerable profit in providing us innumerable and repetitive scenes involving fiery explosions. We want to "jump out of our skin" is one way it comes to us. We want to be suicide bombers, if we could.

This crowdedness is one of the roots of our development of bombs, in particular, nuclear ones. For it creates in us an unconscious draw toward events of being blown up. We experience a vicarious thrill when we observe the bombing — the shock and awe (notably phrased) — of a battle like was seen at the beginning of the Second Iraqi War. A part of us that we will not acknowledge knows that that thrill is actually our hidden delight of blowing up and exploding out of the womb at that hellacious unending time of crowdedness and suffocation.

Thus the idea of nuclear annihilation at any time — the possibility that one will be, figuratively, "blown up" — has an unacknowledged psychic resonance with us. It feels somewhat comforting, even desired, this idea of exploding violently, much the way we might feel about ripping the scab off a wound or scratching an itch that we cannot reach. It has an unconscious draw ... or appeal. We want to "just get it over with."

And that enchantment with it keeps us from being appropriately disturbed by such an unbelievable catastrophe and allows us to live with it; though if we were sane, it would not. Indeed, there is an element of counterphobia in our reaction to nuclear annihilation, with roots in that time of crowdedness and suffocation at fetal malnutrition, a kind of machismo, if you will, that pushes us to feel and act like, "Come on! Bring it on! Do your worst!"

Blank Slate and Forgetting

The upshot of all this is that humans, unlike all other species, experience a forgetting, caused by trauma, at our very roots and even before birth. We forget our connection to the Universe, to Nature, and to the Divine. We forget our past lives, even. We are beginning to become that blank slate we will say afterwards that we were at our birth.

However, at the time it is not experienced as a blank slate or nothingness, as we experience ourselves as riddled through with fear and negativity. We feel ourselves to be a victim of our surroundings and begin doing the opposite of what all other species and even our earliest ancestors did during their times in late gestation: We split off from our rootedness in the mother and we cast that unyielding surround of the womb and placenta — and the mother, by proxy — into "the enemy," needing to be fought. We create a duality between us and Nature, us and other people ... and in terms of how this comes out later in rampant misogyny, between us and women, if we are male.

Culture Versus Instinct

That supposed "blank slate" we are born with — wrought of a process of forgetting utilized to fend off the overwhelming trauma of the time — has another important ramification. You might say that most species are born and are either immediately or soon enough able to fend for themselves. How they are able to do that is attributed to what we refer to as *instinct*.

We arrive at this determination of a factor of instinct, not empirically, but conveniently. By that I mean that *instinct* is not a thing-in-itself that we have discovered in Nature. No. We see that other planetmates are able to do all kinds of things without being taught, and since we do not have that same thing we cannot understand it. Not able to understand it we give it a name — *instinct*. Problem solved.

But what is it? Well, we say it is genetic. It is behavior laid down in the genes. And we have this further rather magical idea that somehow the pattern of molecules in a part of our bodies, inside ourselves, creates behavior. Things create actions; items in the physical world impel beings to do particular things in particular ways, simply by the fact of their existence. This is like saying that my rock garden ... I'll even give you, the *pattern* of my rock garden ... conceivably makes me, want to or not, get up at 7am, make coffee, put particular and specific clothes on, and travel in a particular car, to a particular place, to engage all day in particular and precise actions, at a particular job. Why, how fantastic!

Or, you might say, it is like our DNA are like gears in a magnificent watch which, energy applied, results in all kinds of specific actions. However, this is looking at planetmates as things and objects — which is a byproduct of the objectification of Nature, wrought of our Newtonian-Cartesian dualism — which posits that the world is a machine with no consciousness. Disregarding for a minute the fact that that objectification of Nature is a mistake we make in our devolution from Nature through the process I am describing in this book, at least consider that reasoning has it that you do not exist either. Oh, your body exists, in this formulation, but you are not an experiencing being ... are you now? Hell, even mechanically you are reading these words with no consciousness or awareness in the mix!

Or else this reasoning posits that you exist, but that you are different and superior to all the rest of Nature, to all other planetmates, which is a kind of egotism, specifically *anthropocentrism*, that is not consistent with true understanding. Such egoistic, anthropocentric, thinking only finds what it posits in the first place.[3]

Beyond that, what necessarily follows is that the machine is so wonderful it is able to perform exactly appropriately in applying its mechanical actions to an infinite number of situations and nuances of events. It apparently knows, ahead of time — that is, it is built perfectly into its configuration of molecules of DNA — when that bird is going to come across that twig, of that size, at that position in space (and time), and angle in relation to it, so that it will reach down its beak and grasp that twig and pick it up and move it to the side and over to a stack of other twigs, perfectly arranged previously in the shape of a nest, all performed perfectly, albeit somehow magically. And the bird will fit that twig into where it will most optimally bring about a further addition to that nest.

That's quite the watch!

It assumes, also, that all the learning that we observe planetmates doing concurrent with the manifestation of said instinctive acts are not actual "learning" but are part of that clockwork-like predetermination of any and all events — no matter how tiny or insignificant — which is caused by the infinitesimal configuration of its inner "gears" of DNA. And, remember, no consciousness involved! Hell, that's not necessary, right?

Not fantastical enough, this behavior is not just of a crude sort, for example, a bird's ability to create a nest. No, somehow instinct is said to account for the fact that birds are able to, not only fly in formation, but make specific synchronous movements in full flight among all of them, and to do it always and an infinite numbers of times, all without any blemishes in their choreography, or mistake, or collision among them. Supposedly, these genes of millions of years development know when and how each individual bird in flight, throughout that span of eons, is supposed to move in any particular millisecond that each individual bird is in flight.

So these genes of instinct evolved over millions of years somehow knew in advance, millions of years before now, what a particular flock of birds was going to do at a particular millisecond of time (and *all* birds in all flocks in every millisecond of time over the course of millions of years). Yet instinct is supposed to be the down-to-earth, real-world, "scientific" explanation for these incredible movements of birds, insects, and other similar planetmates. Instinct implies a kind of foreknowledge, premonition, or clairvoyance wilder than anything imaginable (and all contained within that microscopically small package of DNA), but somehow the idea of telepathy — what I am calling mind-sharing — is considered unscientific and too fantastical to be believed.

The same with dolphins and fish. We see their precise synchronous movements, as they move perfectly together in swimming and jumping, and we say that is instinctive. We cannot know how they could possibly perfectly choreograph their movements far more precisely than any contestants on *Dancing with the Stars* are able to, even after much training. Actually it is more like the choreography of groups of humans that is arrived at after months of hard work to get it right.

Even then, we are not able to maintain that perfect choreography if we were to make random new changes in our movements. Yet birds have infinitely creative and seemingly random changes perfectly choreographed into their movements. Changes which are instigated by.... Well, here you see again, how magical! Instigated by no one in particular; they just occur for all participants simultaneously, not even a leader or a director in sight. Yet imagine those human dancers making endless new patterns in their routines, unplanned, spontaneous, without direction, and perfectly synchronized in the movement and steps among all the participants. Never going to happen, right?

Yet we attribute the ability of the dolphins, fish, birds, and insects to do that to *instinct*, and then we do not have to try to understand it anymore. We give something a name and consider it job done.

Then we say the idea of *shared mind* — a shared field of energy comprised of knowledge or, as I have been asserting, Experience (subjectivity, consciousness), which is the only thing that exists, being shared among multiple perceivers at the same time — which also might explain it, is fantastical. Yet this idea of consciousness shared is an idea that our consciousness research is leading us toward.[4]

In this light, it is likely that ideas like instinct will have as much importance in the future as the convoluted theories of astrologers who, prior to the heliocentric revolution in thought, attempted to make sense out of the movement of the stars. Consciousness research, with its findings in related fields such as quantum physics, transpersonal psychology, prenatal and perinatal psychology, and the new biology will, in time, demonstrate to all of science (it has been demonstrated to those of us in these fields already) that it is consciousness, Experience, subjectivity that is fundamental to Reality. Science will eventually acknowledge that insubstantial yet profound no-thing — that Experience, Consciousness, or mental-emotional stuff — is shared between beings, who we formerly thought were absolutely separate from each other but who we will then know actually are not and actually share identity, in a sense. In doing so it will bring clarity to our understanding of these fantastical behaviors of planetmates and make the idea of instinct to be like the emperor with no clothes — sad and laughable.

At any rate, what I am saying is that many planetmates have a kind of shared mind … they participate in a kind of field of mind or understanding … and that gives them the ability to know things they were not taught. In a sense, the species did the learning over the course of its evolution, and it is shared mentally by all members. If that sounds unbelievable, realize that what I just described is exactly the way one new biologist, Rupert Sheldrake, describes his theory of *morphogenetic fields*.[5] More about that later.

In any case, now we have lost that shared mind. We have lost that ability. More correctly, we believe we have lost it, for we retain some ability of shared mind, or telepathy. Still, for the most part we ignore it, dismiss it, or at least downplay it, goaded on by the emptiness inside, wrought of so much forgetting.

What instinct has to do with secondary altriciality and culture is that

a) In the womb just before birth we experience an hellacious time which splits us off from our connection with Divinity. This is known as *fetal malnutrition,* and because it is a traumatic time, which we needed to push out of our mind, we suppressed others of our abilities along with it. Among them is that mind sharing with other beings and that felt connection with Divinity. But then,

b) Since our brains are too big to be able to stay in the womb the twenty-one months it would need for us to be born at the level of development comparable to other species when they are born, we are born prematurely with our brains not fully developed enough. Perhaps not developed enough to do that "mind sharing" that other species are able to do?

c) At any rate, then we are born with even more pain, birth trauma. This causes us to lose any last traces of connection with Divinity or the participation of the individual consciousness in that of the group. So, indeed, we are born with a "blank slate." Not because we have nothing, no instinct, no sense of self, no prior understandings or proclivities, or even instructions, but rather because all that we did have, unlike all other species, was wiped off our "slate," our consciousness, during those prenatal and perinatal times of excruciating pain, which caused us to block all that out. We are born with a *tabula rasa*, a mental blank slate, because we have repressed out of our consciousness (we have created an unconscious) all that we are and could be if we had not suppressed, repressed, and forgotten who we are. So that,

d) Onto this blank slate we pour all the necessary learnings we need to survive; we do this through a process of parenting. However, unlike the mind sharing of other planetmates, we are only going to get any learnings we do as funneled through an even more narrowed consciousness, one even more split from Divinity or the mind we share in common with the Universe. And that more narrowed consciousness is that of our caregivers, one's parents, usually. Thus,

e) Culture — which is the accumulated, infinitely varied, and unavoidably flawed understandings of how to behave and survive in the world, developed over time, and different in every society — steps in where mind sharing ... what we disrespectfully call *instinct* ... should be. So here scientists are correct in saying that planetmates have instinct and we have culture to do the same thing for humans. Only, framed the way it usually is by scientists, it is used as another way of touting our superiority instead of being explained in a way that would tell what that substitution of culture for instinct actually is: Culture is an artificial substitute for what we have lost in splitting from Divinity ... or shared mind ... and it is a sufficient-for-survival construct. Yet culture is not as refined, or as close to Truth and Reality, or perfect, even, as what other planetmates have that is called *instinct*. Culture, in this way, is collective Ego. For Ego can be defined as the artificial consciousness construct that each individual develops to be able to function, after one has lost one's more expanded consciousness that one had in the womb. This development — that of Ego — also has its own chapter in which to shine, coming up next.

Enter the Ego

In any case, this story of our last four weeks before our grand entrance into the world, our societies, and our families, is one of increasing pain at our origins. Something had to happen. All of that feverish repression of pain must have had *some* consequences for us experientially.

Indeed, it did. What we next look into is the creation and construction of that psychic component unique to humans — the Ego.

5

The Fifth Descent — Ego:

Loss of Eden — Origins of Ego, Savagery, and the Apocalypse … Being Half-Born Makes Humans Reckless

"The fateful process of civilization would ... have set in with man's adoption of an erect posture." — Sigmund Freud, Civilization and Its Discontents

"Civilized man has exchanged a portion of his possibilities of happiness for a portion of security." — Sigmund Freud, Civilization and Its Discontents

We Ain't Born Typical … and Loss of Eden

Our birth separates us from Nature. It makes us distinct from all other species, and it is expressed mythically as a loss of Eden, a loss of a Golden Age. A loss of an Eden, a fall from grace of some sort, is a universal human myth. In it, we leave off a direct relationship or connection to a higher power or ultimate reality. We become instead more dependent and of lower status. We must rely on the "good will" of Nature and are no longer connected to it. We have become vulnerable.

Now, as I said, this is indeed what happens with our altricial nature. We have a *secondary altriciality*, which means we are born more helpless and premature than any other species. We are only half-ready for life at birth. We are half-borns, essentially — only half ready for life at birth ... relative to other species.

What this means is that there is a huge gulf between us and all other species, all other planetmates, in all things ... beginning with the way we view Reality. For humans, more than any other species, see Reality through a fog of trauma, stress, pain, neurosis, and tension unlike anything known to other beings. We are the suffering species; we are the ones uniquely commissioned to forget through trauma and then learn again through pain ... bringing to Reality whatever unique perspective, or Experience, implicated in that.

What this means has profound ramifications for everything about our existence, including our situation today, as we stand on the brink of an apocalyptic ecocide and humanicide, unlike anything experienced, or even imagined, on Earth in its previous four and a half billion years.

Being Half-Born Makes Humans Variable ... and Reckless

Our birth defines us humans, and it represents a separation in our understanding of life from all other — nine million and more — of species of planetmates. The additional thing is that it is related to a helplessness of our newborns, more helpless after birth than even the most helpless of newborns of other species.

So we have birth trauma with a physically and mentally undeveloped fetus having to confront a most horrendous ordeal of making a huge head fit through a narrow pelvic opening. Then we have additional trauma in that we have an excessive neediness and reliance on the environment to provide those needs afterward — those physical and neurological needs.

However the outside world and its events are infinitely more random, haphazard, and uncertain than the events of any species before birth. Biology is simply a lot more consistent than are the actions of humans or the outside world. So those analogous needs of ours that are going to be imperfectly met because of the randomness of human action and the outside world are going to be met near perfectly and consistently for other species inside the biological confines of their existence before birth.

Thus our traumatic birth, plus our imperfect satisfaction of needs after birth, makes for a wide variety of types of humans and personalities. Yet all of them are in some way more deprived and stressed than they would be without those first two elements.

So the ones who are responsible for providing the satisfaction of those postnatal needs of the infant are going to be such impaired adults. Consider then how well they are likely to perform in providing for the excessive neediness of the newborn compared to the automatic and near perfect satisfaction of needs for other species at that same relative biological stage of development being in a perfectly providing biological surround of one sort or other.

Parents Are Imperfect

Human parents are responsible for overseeing and assisting in the successful development of our newborns at levels of development that are taken care of by biology — refined to perfection over the course of billions of years — for other species. That includes our own species at its earliest beginnings, before that birth trauma and prematurity began ... which is millions of years ago.

Nature does not vary. It is as precise as the laws of physics and biology. It does for all species what it has done for billions of years. It has perfected itself in any process over the course of that immense period of time ... *anything less than near perfection has been eliminated through natural selection.* All species benefit from such perfection of Nature, as do humans over the course of most of our nine-month gestation.[1]

But then we are born.

Leave off for now how even fetal development is affected by substances that the mother ingests as well as the thoughts and feelings she experiences. Certainly, that adds additional variability to what humans end up becoming. Still, it is generally true that our fundamental needs as part of our staying alive and growing to maturation are taken care of near perfectly in the womb, as are other species.

This changes at birth. At this point forward, the needs, essential for survival and growth, have to be provided by *imperfect* human adults. These adults are as different in personality as can possibly be. For they are the consequence of themselves, as well, having gone through the unique set of birthing circumstances and widely varying satisfaction of needs in their earliest life. Indeed, humans are as different from each other as in the world of Nature entire species are different from other species! So, add loneliness, as well as alienation, to our pain as the suffering planetmate. Beginning to sound like being human on Earth is for the Universe the equivalent of that hell we have fashioned in our minds, isn't it?

Anyway, this near infinite variation of human personality results in near infinite differences in the ways newborns will be attended to and nurtured. Newborns are helpless and dependent on the good will of their caregivers to survive and thrive; and the differences in the good will, or lack thereof, and skill and intelligence of caregivers is, of course, as varied as are the differences between human personalities.

These differences in personality, affecting the differences in the ways newborns will be cared for, create the vast differences and myriad possibilities of personalities that people can have. This determines the kind of caregiver people become as adults. This, in turn, affects how those caregivers will care or not care for their newborns, and so on around again.

Ego and Its Origins

This fact alone separates us from Nature, for it means we will have near infinite constructions and relations to Reality and Nature — none of which are perfect or even consistent with other humans. It means we will construct an opposite and alien reality. And this opposite construct we prop up with all kinds of twisted, bizarre "truths" to explain ourselves to ourselves.

Furthermore, this schizoid tendency in humans sets up a fundamental insecurity regarding Reality and Nature — a feeling of inferiority and insecurity and uncertainness about oneself and one's nature. However, such feelings require a compensatory mechanism. That compensatory mechanism is *Ego* — quite different from the self of other beings in Nature. For Ego is comprised of the compensatory mechanisms of denial, inflation of self, and superiority vis–à–vis Nature, the All That Is, and Nature-God Itself.[2]

Ego Tells Us We are Superior to Nature

Part of this repression and compensation means that impairments that we have because of our unique birth and insufficient satisfaction of early needs, such as language, will be touted as proof of our superiority over Nature. We have no inkling that the superiority belief is a result of our prematurity and its consequences of uncomfortable feelings of insecurity and inferiority.

Superiority Is Our Defense Against Our Felt Inferiority

Regardless, we will increasingly build up this superiority defense and its resulting Ego for the purpose of beating back the otherwise debilitating feelings of insecurity and inferiority. We have a confused and unsteady consciousness, creating an alternate reality from Nature.

Wordism

The result is a situation akin to what Plato described in his "Allegory of the Cave." For the result is that words suffuse our minds and distract us from actual Reality with a non-stop stream of nonsensical repetitions of word symbols. We tout our wordism as a supreme accomplishment, instead of the aberration, the flaw in our reality perceptors, that it actually is. This causes us to never really hear or understand each other. For these word symbols not only imprison and isolate us in a world of swirling bookmarks of Reality, but they are tagged to but dimly reflective of Reality.

This flurry of mental symbols, this mind fog driven by non-satisfaction of early needs, keeps us blind to wondrous Reality itself, inside the present moment, in which all other beings live in clarity of purpose and life meaning and with direct intra- and interspecies, and inter-entity communication.

True to form, we then construe this insanity vis-à-vis Nature as a benefit in awareness, thus reinforcing our superiority defense. Actually, however, living in a world of symbols and not realities covers up our lack of knowledge of our meaning or reason for being, as well as it also represses the fear that would normally attend to that.

So, instead of the truth that we were unfortunate enough to be deprived of full and perfect nurturing by a near perfect, divine Nature, as other species are until they are ready to be in the world; instead of the obvious truth that this prematurity leaves a scar of hurt and rejection, also, helplessness and hopelessness; and that this occurs right at the beginning of known flesh existence, so as to create the very unusually twisted and unwholesome roots of our consciousness; our true state is further hidden from us by the fact that our unfortunate and tragic separation from goodness must itself be covered up so that our newborns do not die, out of pure despair, right at birth!

Ego as Opiate and Opposite

All in all, this many-fold obscuring of our horrid plight is accomplished through the creation of an alien consciousness construct, which serves both to separate us from the realization of our lack … acting very much like an opiate in that regard; as well as to act as an alternate but *opposite* construction of self … opposite from the truth of our true nature. This alien construct performs splendidly in taking all our flaws, like language, and turning them into supreme accomplishments, in this way acting as a euphoriant.

This alien consciousness construct, this child as well as parent of all our wrong-gettedness, is what we call *Ego*.

Our fully grown caregivers are instrumental in creating this Ego. For they are both the models and the delivery systems for this diminishment and perfect wrongness of Consciousness. Prior to this development, however, for millions of years, humans were planet-mates, like all other species. We were Earth Citizens and part of Nature.

The Result: Plato's Cave

The upshot of all this is that, viewed either psychologically or historically, it can be said that the metaphorical Fall from Grace in Eden, which is our birth with its excruciating perinatal trauma psychologically, and is our switch to an agrarian and sedentary lifeway historically, is such that ever afterwards humans are indirectly related to God and Nature. By this I mean they are indirectly related to the processes of reality of either the physical or metaphysical sort, including their own inner life, their subjectivity.

Essentially, in becoming human, it is as if God said to Herself, "How about I forget everything, absolutely everything, and then see what I might create out of pure nothingness. It will be interesting. And 'God knows' (lol) what I will do then. Beyond that, how about I create time, where everything does not happen at once, so as to make an entertaining *story* out of the whole process. To be fair, though, I cannot interfere with the process of creation of something out of nothing, for then it would be me doing it again. So, regardless of how I might feel about it, in order for the most incredible, loving, beautiful things to come into existence, I have to allow for the most atrocious, abominable, and hellacious things to be created, as well."

Regardless, in the adoption of Ego humans turned their back on the beneficence of God, or Nature, and they sought to go it on their own, to control Nature, to focus on survival. In that they were focused then on the world, they could see only a reflection of the Divine. They were confusing the map and the territory.

And in that reflection they sought to discern God's will. In those shadows we seek to understand Truth.

6

The Sixth Descent — Mistrust:

Mistrust of Nature, Mistrust of Divine Providence … Our Experience of Birth Determines Ever Afterward Our View of the World

"The cold, hard fact is that our experience of our birth — that is, the amount of pain and discomfort we experience in the process of delivery added to those first crucial moments and hours of our 'introductory' experience of the world outside the womb — determine ever afterward in our lives the degree of positivity or negativity with which we will view the world and other people."

Our Devolutionary Path to Ego and Away from Nature

The Descent of Our Earliest Humans

However, our early humanoid/hominid forebears were still much different from what we call *human* today. From our perspective, we would call them "animals," however unfairly to both, and see them as no different from the planetmates of Nature. Early humans, protohumans, were nomadic foragers who did not hunt or eat meat and were relatively peaceable, living harmoniously in Nature. This long period of tranquility changed as gradually the effects of premature birth built up anxiety and stress in successive generations to greater degrees.

Fear and Control

Humans behaved more and more in ways at odds with Natural ways, becoming more twisted and backwards. Birth pain and trauma and pain from having needs insufficiently met by caregivers in the first years of life, while primarily dependent, caused tension, anxiety, overstimulated brains and states of consciousness to be common among humans. Yet the core of that craziness was this increasing obsession about control. And the need to control arose from an overblown fear of uncertainty, which was rooted in an absolute, however unjustified, terror of the unforeseen and unknown.

Our human state of omnipresent fear caused our earliest progenitors to lose faith in the goodness of Nature/the Divine as it is. They became increasingly fearful of what would happen in any future time and so spent their time seeking to determine that future through fervid controlling activities in the present, which both consumed their consciousness and became their lived existence.

One way of looking at this process is that pain caused us to be self-reflective, self-conscious, and introverted ... inordinately so. You might say that so much of our lives at its beginnings — that is, prenatally, perinatally, and in infancy — involved being confronted with things we did not want or expect, experiencing the lack of things we did want but could not find ... and we were so often left in pain or aching because of these things ... that it caused humans to begin "overthinking" things in a problem-solving attempt.

In the pain that rose up in the gap between need and its fulfillment arose fear, thus timidity about acting, thus a tendency to pull back from immersion in the moment and its process of movement and activity ... out of fear, but also as a way to attempt to foresee events before we would go forward or take action That's right, part of what makes us human is founded on humans being more introverted than any other species. And with this pulling back, this over-thinking, we made ourselves an object, or a factor, amid the other factors in the problem to be solved.

Pain caused self-consciousness. *Self-consciousness* is a state arrived at by anxiety — by fear of being in a threatening uncertainty, which causes an incessant self-scrutiny in hopes of better managing and controlling present and future events. It took us out of the world, out of actual Reality, and put us into mind, a substitute world, a Plato's cave. And in mind, the most glorious angels of creative possession as well as the most horrific monsters of fearful obsession were born.

Uncertainty — Cons and Pros

Life is uncertain because we do not know the future consequences of our present actions. However, that lack of surety does not have to be seen in a negative way. Indeed, one could as easily see that unplanned aspect of life as part of a joyous adventure, as our pre-birth-pain ancestors and our planetmates today might see it. One could be delighted, or at least enthralled and not bored, by being continually surprised by life's exigencies.

Think of the way one experiences a game, say a video game, that one is involved in. There is no end of fascination, anticipation, in-volvement, interest, excitement, enjoyment … fun. So much so that one is pulled to become addicted to it. And, by the way, consider that addictive quality of us as perhaps the reason we spirits keep coming back to this world of Form. The point is that one might live in a state of curiosity and anticipation as to what will be presented by fate. However, that fact of uncertainty instead caused the pre-humans dread.

So our natural state is one of being, awareness, and bliss; and our lives could be ones full of surprises; they could be playful and always interesting. However, because of our pain of birth, our lives became ones of impatience, mistrust, defiance toward Nature/the Divine in all its forms, and became set toward fighting imaginary threats in a state of fervid, obsessive controlling of things inside and outside of us. Whereas early humans might have seen the basic needs of physical existence, like sustenance, food, and so on, as gifts from

God, our crazed state has caused us to seek to control this aspect of existence, to make it less certain.

Basic Trust, Basic Mistrust, and Birth

As I have said, the worldview of our hominid and even to some extent our gatherer-hunter existences, and especially that of our protohuman, was trusting of Nature. The world was felt to be good, not antagonistic, so dependence on it was not seen as a problem. That sense of being cared for made life overall easier than what we know beginning with the agrarian revolution and the rise of "civilization." Our primal forebears had a "basic trust" in regards to Nature.

But the agrarian revolution and all "advances" after that imply a "basic mistrust."

Ego occurs concurrently with the buildup of mistrust. For how we handle mistrust is to say, "You're not going to take care of me. So I have to do it all by myself. I have to split off from you and control and manage everything … if it is going to get done at all correctly." Hence the Ego is the beginning of the control of everything that has led to the crisis today.

What happened to make us more fearful, more anxious about our human condition? These differences of basic trust versus basic mistrust are fascinating considering their possible relation to birth trauma.

Our Experience of Birth Determines Ever Afterward Our View of the World

Erik Erikson (1950, 1968) proposed that the earliest relation of the infant with the mother sets the foundation of the later attitude toward the world. A caring, sensitive, and responsive environmental and caregiver response — in particular, the mother's — can be the basis for an attitude of basic trust toward the world … a fundamental faith in its goodness. Meanwhile a harsh and insensitive early experience — wherein the child begins to feel it cannot get its needs met

— becomes the basis for a feeling of unshakeable mistrust toward the world.

However, with our understanding of the influence of our first experiences of the world — that is, postnatally, usually in a delivery room and hospital nursery — on our basic attitudes toward that world, we realize that these fundamental orientations are formed much earlier. Importantly, birth is a huge influence on that primary stance of trust or mistrust. First impressions are hard to overcome, as they say. Sure enough, if the first encounter with the world outside the womb ... immediately after birth ... is painful, and characterized by harshness, insensitivity, and unresponsiveness to one's needs, then the infant comes to view the world mistrustfully and feels it to be a hostile place.[1]

What also of the pain of birth itself in setting up an attitude of trust toward the world or mistrust of it? The cold, hard fact is that our experience of our birth — that is, the amount of pain and discomfort we experience in the process of delivery added to those first crucial moments and hours of our "introductory" experience of the world outside the womb — determine ever afterward in our lives the degree of positivity or negativity with which we will view the world and other people.[2]

And this is where it gets interesting in seeing how we became humans and different from all other species.

7

The Seventh Descent — Hunting:

Killing of Planetmates and Eating Flesh Began Our Descent to Savagery and the Apocalypse Today

"...increasingly separated from Nature, from feeling, and from clear apprehension of reality, humans became insensitive. In becoming more numbed to their empathy and fellow feeling, they became inured enough to the spilling of blood, so that making life and death decisions over fellow planetmates became easier."

Descent to Savagery

In acting out our fear of uncertainty, arisen from our birth trauma, in a desperate fury to control everything, our first attempt to make everything to be as certain as can possibly be involved adding planetmate flesh to our former, predominantly vegetarian, diet. Previous to that we had been happy accepting God's varied and often surprising gifts through foraging, but eventually we began hunting, as well. This began our descent into savagery.

Insensitivity, Killing, Hunting

Prior to the prematurity trauma, it had not been in our long-ago-primate ancestors nature to kill, let alone eat, flesh that resembled their own — animals, planetmates. But with their lives of increasing tension and with their continued loss of touch with Real Existence, their days became increasingly taken up in a substitute world of monochromatic ghostly symbols, managed by that artificial consciousness construct of Ego.

Hence, increasingly separated from Nature, from feeling, and from clear apprehension of reality, humans became insensitive. In becoming more numbed to their empathy and fellow feeling, they became inured enough to the spilling of blood, so that making life and death decisions over fellow planetmates became easier. After that, it was not long before we were intruding on God's domain by making such vital decisions about each other, as well. We were able to murder.

I will address murder in the next chapter, for now I wish to focus on how we came to be hunters and meat eaters.

First, hunting and murder are some of the negative results of that pulling back from full immersion in Experience, out of fear, which I described in the chapter previous. Pulling back means retreating from the full experience of the body with all its feelings. That is the definition of insensitivity. In standing back, we were able to view everything around us as objects, including ourselves and our bodies, and we were able to manipulate them to attempt to control future events.

Pulling back from the present had us living more in the future, because of fearful anticipation, as well as the past, where we obsessively sought clues to aid us in attempting to control the future. Still, pulling back from feeling, from sensitivity, allowed us to make decisions to do things that in a fully experiencing and feeling, a fully sensitive state, our empathy — our feeling of union with other life — would have blocked us from doing.

Loss of "Safety Net"

We first began killing out of our fear that there would not be enough sustenance for all — that is to say, we began feeling we needed to compete over resources.

The "Good Mother" of Wilderness

Remember, an empathetic and spiritual attitude — which is one that, even today, characterizes some who live within Nature — is that they know without doubt they are interwoven with and therefore infinitely loved and sustained by a higher power, or Divinity, who is perfect in Her care and nurturing in every way, even the tiniest and most insignificant.[1]

We see the remnants of such trust that we shared with planetmates before we split off from them even in the modern gatherer-hunters that anthropologists have studied. For they predominantly express that Nature, the "wild," wilderness, the forest is felt to be a higher entity or aspect of reality, which is of a beneficent nature. Nature, "the wild", is often looked at as a good mother, eager and willing to provide whatever one needs, and in abundance. "The forest" is seen as the "safety net," which we inadequately try to reproduce in our social welfare programs in modern times, for having cut off, and for the most part made illegal, our ability to seek sustenance from wilderness.

However, in primal cultures, the world unmodified by the human touch is the Great Mother or backup that one knows one can resort to if catastrophe ensues and one is left without community or means to survive. This safety net of Nature allows for people a certain adventurousness and ability to take risks that civilized society no longer affords.

Conservatives Hate "the Mother"

The reason conservatives and patriarchal sorts hate welfare programs and socialism is that it smacks, to them, of the mother ... and they, being more caught up in acting out prenatal pain than their liberal brothers and sisters, hate the mother. My book, *Wounded Deer and Centaurs: The Necessary Hero and the Prenatal Matrix of Human Events*, explains this in detail, along with the ramifications that are concurrent with it.

Prenatal Conformity

For now, I wish to point out that among those factors is the fact that prenatal suffocation — where what we get of blood is affected by the position and movement of our body in the womb — promotes a kind of prenatal conformity. This is where we learn that we might "get more" ... of food and oxygen, but later it will be money, land, resources ... if we do not move around too much. We constrain our movements. That is, indeed, the definition of conservative: a fear of and unwillingness to change. Along with that is a reluctance to be "flexible," a rigidity of opinion, personality, and belief. Inhibition is the style, which bespeaks that free movement, i.e., change, or free thinking, for that matter, will be disastrous.

In addition to that, it was change, from an earlier relatively bliss-ful time in the womb, that resulted in all the suffering of the last month of gestation. So why would change *ever* be good, is at the root of conservative thinking. More than that, why would change not be the reason that everything got so bad, so messed up, they think. For certainly — and, boy, will ever they tell you — we are certainly "going to hell in a handbasket," now. Consequently, conservatives are ever seeking to return to a mythological "golden age" ... in actuality, one that was in the womb ... ostensibly, in current times and espe-cially in America, the 1950s. Not coincidentally that was a time the majority of these conservatives — evidenced by Trump and his supporters, who are primarily of the Fifties Generation — were com-ing into adulthood.

So conservatism of thought is rooted in horrible experiences in the womb where we deduced that if we moved too much we would have more likelihood of receiving nutrients and oxygen and where simultaneously we thought back to a time prior to the onset of suffering and longed for it, figuring that if things had not changed, times would still be good, so to speak.

We re-create this being conservative in our movements and conforming to our surroundings of oppression when again in later life we have a tendency to hold our breath when we are confronted with a stressful situation. For the stressful situation not only stimulates our time of prenatal suffocation, so we are pushed to hold our breath in that we are unconsciously impelled to re-create that event, but it simulates it as well in that holding our breath is the equivalent of not moving around too much in the womb in hopes of bettering or at least relieving our situation. Under stress, we become more conservative in our movements and actions, out of fear.

Prenatal Roots of Greed, Violence, Bigotry, Misogyny

There are other reasons for conservativism that are part and parcel of our fetal malnutrition. For example, greed comes of our feeling that we did not get enough at that time. A tendency to aggression and violence, characteristic of conservatives, comes from the crowdedness of that time. Prenatal irritation leads to bigotry; prenatal burning to war and explosions. Yet any of them, and all of them together, for sure, are felt to emanate from the mother.

Thus, misogyny is rooted in prenatal experience; and reactionary types act that out in all kinds of ways, including railing against anything that smacks of nurturing or of ease. For they did not get that nurturing in the womb, they unconsciously feel. They did not have that ease and were forced to suffer and work, they unconsciously know. So they are going to hate anything that indicates someone else might be nurtured or have a life that is facilitated without their having to suffer to bring that about.

Conservatives and Abortion

That reactionaries are unusually taken over by the pain of that prenatal time is also indicated by one of their primary issues. For other than greed — which comes out in their concern about taxation, as one of their major political issues — they are impelled by the issue of abortion. *A part of conservatives knows they are still that suffering fetus.* They simmer with rage at a mother — a woman seeking an abortion — who they see to not be willing to care for and nurture an unborn, for they were ignored and left wanting at that time: They were not cared for and nurtured and fed sufficiently. They will similarly be infuriated by abortion doctors who would ease that time for the mother, in providing their services. They feel they did not receive ease at that time, so why should the mother?

Conservatives and Prenatal Hatred of the "Feminine" — "Softness, Ease

Conservatives have their thoughts stiffened along tracks that lead to feelings that no good should come to anyone, except through hard work and suffering (like they experienced in the womb). That never should there be a "free lunch." That softness of any kind is not only weakness and unwanted, but is feminine as well. Therefore there is hatred at the thought of those qualities in others. They often use terms like *disgust, revulsion, irritation*, or being "*burned up*" — all of which are prenatal feelings wrought of fetal malnutrition.[2]

In any case, by contrast to the peaceable and trusting gatherer-hunters — content and upheld by the good mother of wilderness, providing a safety net, and often, ease — our descent to civilization, with its overriding m.o. of control, started with an insecurity and an incipient basic mistrust, resulting from our birth trauma, which caused us to begin to be fearful of and to doubt the beneficence of the All. This questioning of Divine Providence first manifested in our earliest forebears as a willingness to kill and eat planetmate flesh much like our own, that is, to hunt.

By the way, considering the relation of conservatism with this mistrust of ease and assistance, I do not believe it is coincidental that conservatives and patriarchal sorts in general are so taken up with their desire for meat. Not to mention the hunting and guns that are concomitant with that. If you look, you will see this tendency to put oneself out there as a killer and eater of flesh to be one of the ways conservatives have of beating their chests. Which is just another way they are trying to loudly proclaim to one and all that *they* are in no way "soft" and "feminine" ("You see!") as they wanted to be but could not in the womb.

Meat Was the Apple in the Garden of Eden.

It is interesting to see how that first fall of ours into hunting was reflected in the Eden myth. Here is how I see it. First, let me bring to mind these words from *Genesis:*

> *Because thou has hearkened unto the voice of thy wife,*
>
> *and hast eaten of the tree,*
>
> *of which I commanded thee, saying,*
>
> *Though shalt not eat of it:*
>
> *cursed is the ground for thy sake;*
>
> *in sorrow shalt thou eat of it all the days of thy life:*
>
> *thorns also and thistles shall it bring forth to thee;*
>
> *and thou shalt eat the herb of the field;*
>
> *in the sweat of thy face shalt thou eat bread....*
>
> *And the LORD God said, Behold, the man is become as one of us, to know good and evil: and now, lest he put forth his hand, and take also of the tree of life, and eat, and live for ever:*
>
> *therefore the LORD God sent him forth from the garden of Eden, to till the ground from whence he was taken.*

Prior to that Fall, *The Bible* relates how we "walked with God." We were, so to speak, on "face-to-face" terms with God. We had direct contact, direct communion with Him at all times.

In fact, one interpretation of Eve's "sin" was that she hid from God what she was doing. She listened to the serpent and kept her decision and her act from God. So what is meant by Eve keeping God "in the dark" about eating the apple? What is the apple? What is the serpent? What is God? Well, here is what occurs to me about that:

Creating of the Human Unconscious — Conscience Repressed and Higher Self Kept "in the Dark"

For those who follow my work and are familiar with the term, *the Unapproved and Hidden*, this perspective that God was put "in the dark" at the time when the apple was eaten is telling. In the dark and out of sight is exactly how we characterize that species unconscious of humans — which I am calling *the Unapproved and Hidden*. And if we consider, as I have said elsewhere (*Planetmates* and *Wounded Deer and Centaurs*) and will say again in this work, that eating the apple represents humans beginning the process of hunting/killing planetmates/eating meat, we can see that in doing so we had to repress our conscience … we had to put our higher self, our inner Divine, if you will, "in the dark." We would have had to suppress our feelings of empathy for our fellow planetmate beings and ignore our inner Divinity — our conscience — who would have advised against that … and would have haunted us unceasingly if we had.

Conscience

If you cannot shake the myth of early humans as savage and beastly, as real troglodytes, and you think such humans would not really be bothered by killing planetmates, you should look to some of the ethnographies of modern day gatherer-hunters — the San Bushmen of the Kalahari (as related in Louis G. Herman, 2013), the Forest People, the Mbuti (as related by Colin Turnbull, 1961), and Native Americans, in general, for example — and you might be surprised at the amount of remorse they express about doing so.

Joseph Campbell, in this vein and commenting on the mythological evidence left by hunting cultures of tens and hundreds of thousands of years ago, writes, "the daily task and serious concern of dealing death, spilling blood, in order to live, created a situation of anxiety that had to be resolved, on the one hand by a system of defenses against revenge, and on the other by the diminishment of the importance of death."[3] Similarly, Native Americans and other primal hunters are said to apologize to the planetmate for taking its life. In general among gatherer-hunters, it is common to take some time for some blessing of it at the time of the killing, to atone for what one has done, that is, kill it.

Sensitivity

Further, we see that there are some planetmates that our primal humans would not eat or, if they did, would feel the most remorse about. For these planetmates were thought by these primal people to be too much like humans. They clearly could not get the idea out of their head that it would be like they are killing and eating a fellow human. To understand this it might help to know, contrary to what most people have been told, that primal humans in general, far from being "savage," have more empathy for other living things than is common among modern humans. This is true for many reasons, some of which I get into in this book.

So yes, early humans and their hominid forebears had remorse and a "guilty conscience" about killing/hunting/eating meat. They felt that, because empathy is a trait characterizing many higher order planetmates, mammals, and apes. Something along the lines of it might even be part of the makeup of species even further removed from us. However, we cannot know, for those are too unlike us to have a possibility for us to recognize it. Regardless, empathy is not, as we arrogantly suppose, built up out of human consciousness. Rather, *human consciousness represses empathy*. The feeling of unity, which is the root of empathy, with others of one's kind and even beyond that is a common feeling in Nature.

Thus, in order for humans and their progenitors to kill other planetmates, humans would have had to "keep God in the dark." Which is the way of saying they would have had to repress their conscience, repress the promptings and advice of their higher self, and repress their feelings of remorse telling them they did wrong. They would have had to repress their sensitivity, which is, indeed, their inner Divinity. In the Biblical account, this conscience advising against killing and meat-eating is expressed in that God commands Adam and Eve, our prototypical humans, to not eat the fruit of one, only one, tree in the Garden. For that one tree, think mammalian planetmates. For that fruit, think planetmate flesh ... meat.

Our Depraved Craving for Flesh

When you think about it, the only change I am making in the myth — for both the Eden myth and my interpretation of it entail God saying we are not allowed to eat something — is to substitute meat for the apple. A truer rendition of *Genesis* would have it that God had said to Adam and Eve that they might eat anything they see on Earth — all fruits, vegetables, herbs, insects, fish, non-mammalian seafood, and such — but that they dare not eat flesh that is like their own. Perhaps there was a version of the myth that actually said it that way. For certainly, whether consciously or unconsciously, we would have had to hide the fact that it was flesh, not apples, that we are not to eat in order to go on doing what we wanted to do — eat meat. Hence, saying it was an apple protects us from feeling guilty about our depraved craving for flesh.

Further, for those of you right now wanting to criticize this interpretation by saying that all the things we would be allowed to eat were also alive, so would we not also be "sinning" in killing that way, let me say this:

The Myth of Rational Intent

Humans do not operate in reality along the lines of intellectual categories, which is the prevailing and most self-inflating of notions. We operate out of psychological factors, which manifest most directly in feelings. Now, our feelings are not really going around distinguishing between technically alive and non-alive things. Whereas our feelings do most certainly *feel* a difference between alive things that *are like ourselves* versus life that is quite unlike our own that we cannot relate to as well or at all.

And those feelings have a rational basis in that, indeed, mammals who are like us exhibit many of the traits of emotion, sociability, playfulness, reaction to pain, sorrow, happiness, and all the rest of those things we attribute to ourselves as human. Hence to kill another mammal *seems* to our *feelings* to be like killing a human, whereas taking the life of a plant or a fish does not have the same emotional barrier of conscience.

We tend to forget that in talking about human actions we need to consider human psychology and feeling and *not* any supposed human reasoning ability. "Rational man" presumes to use categories and reason as the basis upon which to take action. That is a myth born of inflation of self. In actuality, for the most part, "reason" comes in after the fact, after action, to rationalize what one has already done. And, as I have been saying, eating planetmate flesh led to a psychological change of feeling — a greater insensitivity, a better ability to suppress one's discomfort of conscience, a "more enhanced" ability to split from body and, consequently, Nature.

Fetal Malnutrition, Orality, and Hunting

Before leaving this chapter on human's distrust regarding getting nutritional needs met, especially as regarding food sources, and the depraved craving for meat that came of it, I wish to bring up the factor of fetal malnutrition, again. It is likely our prenatal hunger, as a trauma laid down in the human unconscious, was a goad in the direction of feeling deprived as adults so that we felt we needed to augment our food supplies … which came out first, in humans, with hunting. Remember we as a species were uniquely starved during our last four weeks of gestation, and this has had profound implications on our minds and behavior as a species … indeed, on our very human nature.

So, along with the basic mistrust, emanating from our birth and infancy traumas, which pushed us to feel we needed to augment our diet, we no doubt had that pushed as well by our unconscious trauma of being starved in the womb.

Obesity

How this manifests, for example, in relation to nutrition is that we are the only species who, circumstances allowing, will tend to eat ourselves into obesity and, hence, ill health. There is no good reason to do this. We have plenty to satisfy our nutritional needs, in such situations, and there is no real evolutionary advantage in being overweight. Take for example the ways an evolutionary advantage are usually portrayed: They have to do with increased reproductive fitness.

Yet if we look at obesity — an obesity which is common for humans in all cultures and social groups where there is an abundance of food — we see no reproductive advantage. Quite the opposite is the case, in fact. For, while there have been cultures where a curvy, hefty female profile is considered desirable by men, there are few to none where obesity is seen that way.

Obesity is not an aid to mating. It is also not an aid to child-bearing. While a healthy body for a woman is helpful during her pregnancy, an overweight, obese body is not.

Therefore, we have unconscious factors involved in creating feelings of being undernourished, regardless how nourished we are.

Orality and Greed

This also plays into orality — into the oral complex as described by Freud.

Let me explain:

Hunger is a prenatal trauma occurring in the last four weeks of gestation. We can call it *prenatal starvation*. It creates a push, rooted in our prenatal times, toward overweight as adults. It comes with its own set of ramifications for later life. Some of which you will recognize and, if you are being honest, might even notice in yourself.

Feeling starved in the womb, humans will feel underfed and undernourished throughout life, regardless the actual state of their satisfaction in regard to nutrients. Greediness is one outgrowth of that trauma; it is the major one. And it manifests in us as the drive to accumulate much more than one could ever need of any resource. Yet that could as easily be explained by prenatal suffocation; not getting enough air leads to wanting to have more of everything, too.

Love Hunger

However, there is, still, prenatal hunger (games). I think how we see prenatal hunger manifesting, for one, is in our craving for love. Remember that this reduction in the supply of nutrition, wrought of fetal malnutrition, is felt as not just an action coming from the motherly surround, contributing to misogyny. It represents, also, a very definite break with the mother and with Divinity beyond that. To a large extent, they are felt to be the same. So the deep connection with Divinity and mother that we felt earlier on in the womb is suddenly gone: The "honeymoon phase," the "golden age," is over. Eden is lost. And associated with that "breakup" is a feeling of hunger. Along with suffocation were gasping, irritation, crowdedness, burning, disgust, revulsion, poisoning, and sickening, of course. Now you know why divorces and breakups bring such suffering.

Hence, how the starvation comes out in later life has to do with our feelings around love. It is not just at the mother's breast that we associate feeding with love. It begins at this time in the womb. Regardless how well our "oral needs" are satisfied by way of nursing in infancy, we are likely to feel aching and hunger associated with love and the need for it. Think about it and how often love is associated with getting nourishment: One "hungers" for love; one "craves" love; one gets "filled up" by love; one is "left with a hole in oneself" without love.

This puts prenatal hunger in the same complex of feelings as later on, where the infant's need for food is caught up with its need for its mother and is the traditionally understood basis for human love and romance. So the roots of love hunger go deeper.

Whereas Freud's concepts of anal compulsion and anality seem to have deeper roots in prenatal irritation-burning — it being felt to be "messy" and toxic around one, while in the womb, leads us in later life to varying degrees of Obsessive-Compulsive Disorder (OCD), where we are driven to obsessively clean and organize our surroundings, and ourselves, to fend off that traumatic time of poisoning and irritation. Meanwhile Freud's ideas about orality and the oral complex have their roots in prenatal hunger. For even earlier in life than the breastfeeding phase, we are craving for feminine attention in terms of getting our needs for nutrients met.

Thus, greed is largely suffocation and is wrought of the panic at the very thought of not having enough air, which happened in the womb. However, prenatal hunger is "craving" for love ... the need for love being that hole of discontent, that well of dissatisfaction, that can never be filled. The basis for human jealousy, also, perhaps?

If nothing else it is why the lack of love, as in losing a loved one, is often felt in one's stomach. Often as an intensely painful hole — a pit which cannot be filled inside.

Loneliness

Loneliness is felt the same way, incidentally — that is, as a hole in the "pit of one's stomach" that needs to be filled and cannot be. Reflecting our prenatal state, loneliness is felt as a fading of life, a lack of richness, a disconnection from what is real and what is fulfilling … a missing out on what one is due and what is needed … all caught up with a sense that a state of death, of non-existence, is nearby, closing in, and threatening. Indeed, that is a pretty good description of how we might feel at a time in gestation where we are being deprived of nutrients and oxygen, in great contrast to what had been the case before, and are close to death.

Jealousy

Jealousy also can arise amidst such an emotional state of feeling one has lost one's source of nutrition and one feels empty, in an aching and craving kind of way. Of course, that is mixed with other elements of fetal malnutrition involving greed, which manifests as possessiveness of people, along with possessions; and which comes out as control, of people, along with things in one's environment. Nevertheless, ask any person in the throes of loneliness or jealousy, and you will hear it described in ways reminiscent of wanting to get fed, being hungry … and being empty … with death not far away … hovering, watching, threatening.

Indeed, this ties right back into obesity. For as we all know, people with eating problems will overeat because they will feel, no matter how much they have taken in, that there is still a "hole" inside needing to be filled. A "bottomless pit" are words they are wont to use, which indicates it having roots in a time where there was no way to change that situation of ongoing and seemingly eternal frustration of needs for nutrition … and oxygen.

Comfort Dining

You think it has to be that way? You think somehow that feeling lack of love has to come out so similarly to food hunger? Some are probably confused that it could even be thought of as different: It is so engrained in us that to be loved is to be "filled up" and that contentment in general is primarily centered upon the feelings of satisfaction in one's stomach when properly fed. Consider what a to-do we make about holidays and the banquets of food and how we speak of them with words indicating their connection with familial love. Consider the elaborate rituals we have around dining, especially in regards to dating; around family life; around get-togethers of friends involving both one-on-one meetings as well as parties, festivities.

However, think. Instead of contentment and love and the lack of them being associated with the stomach, why does it not manifest in feelings on one's skin, if it is touch, sex, and intimacy of that nature that is missing. People do not go around saying their skin is aching when they are lonely, heart broken, or jealous. Occasionally you will hear someone saying they "ache to be touched," but that is an entirely different thing and has its own roots in the trauma around birth where we needed the touch and bonding with our mothers and did not get it — instead being taken away to be put in bassinets and to have our skin scrubbed, and then wrapped tightly. Which punishment, by the way, will darn well teach us not to want something or someone ever again.

Yet predominantly, love and companionship are associated with eating and hunger, for we had our first major split with our mother, our first "heartbreak," in a sense, at a time in the womb when we were also starving. For all we know, the feelings we have that we actually call *heartbreak* have their roots at that time of hunger in the womb. That emptiness inside. That stress upon the system.

Indeed, if we look again at Eden, we see that immediately after being cast out of that place of contentment and connection with Divinity, equivalent to the time in the womb when we are blissful and connected to our mothers and not at odds with her, we are caught up in how we are going to feed ourselves *then*.

The "Cursed Ground" ~ The Unwilling Womb

It was all taken care of in Eden, as it was in the womb, earlier. But now, after Eden, the God of Abraham tells us: "Cursed is the ground," and "in sorrow shalt thou eat of it all the days of thy life; thorns and thistles shall it bring forth to thee; and thou shalt eat the herb of the field," and finally, and most damningly, "in the sweat of thy face, shalt thou eat bread." So the "cursed" ground … think here the placenta … shall not give up of its fruits willingly and ever afterwards getting nourishment will be associated with hard work and suffering. Sure is hard to suck from an unwilling womb.

The point is that early in the womb, we got what we needed; whereas later, getting nutrition is all caught up in pain … suffering … hence, work. We see all of that laid out in the myth of Eden in *Genesis*.[4]

Finally, for our purposes in this chapter, I emphasize that all that insecurity about getting one's gustatory needs met led — eventually and after a long time in which other pains and traumas came into the mix to further that uncertainty — to eating meat, to killing planet-mates, to hunting. And meat was the apple in the Garden of Eden.

8

The Eighth Descent — Murder:

"Kill or Be Killed" — Our Delusion of Scarcity Made for Murder

> *"...in early gatherer-hunter times, yes, we had plenty for everyone. But with fear rose anxiety over one's ability to survive, thus competition over resources — a competition which was not needed — and then the very creation of what one was trying to avoid: The possibility that one might need to kill or one would be killed."*

Hunting Planetmates → Killing Human Others

Back again now, to the basic mistrust that set up in us an obsession to add to our already plentiful supply of food; to this questioning of Divine Providence, this mistrust, which was first manifested in our earliest forebears as a willingness to kill and eat planetmate flesh much like our own, that is, to hunt. For with hunting and the insensitivity to the spilling of blood, it was only a matter of time before that same insecurity and fear for survival would cause our progenitors to be able to kill each other.

Thus, our mistrust that Nature would provide all we needed, which led to us deciding to kill planetmates, wrought of our fear of dying through lack of sustenance, was in truth only our *delusion* wrought of our crazed, increasingly ghostly existence, which was set into motion by our perinatal trauma. It pushed us to hunt, in order to add to what was already a sufficient food supply. It then allowed us to kill each other.

"Kill or Be Killed" — Our Delusion of Scarcity Makes Murder

Thus our delusion of being susceptible to death through starvation coincided with a fear that other planetmates, including human ones, would bring about that starvation by impinging on our resources.

And this led first to hunting and eventually to an ability to do homicide. It was a delusion not shared by all at first, but as more and more humans were overcome with it, humans did create the very real threat of being killed, for that reason, by their own kind. It was a self-fulfilling prophecy that once we believed we were in danger of being attacked and killed for our resources, we began being willing to attack and kill. Consequently, we created a situation where indeed we *were* in danger of being attacked and murdered for our resources by other humans.

If this is not clear enough, we need only look around us today. We see the exact same pattern in that over and again we are told that we have the ability to feed and sustain all humans on Earth at this time, if the world's resources were more equitably distributed. However, the 1%, despite knowing this, continue their hoarding of wealth and their efforts to further strip what they can of resources and money from those who have less … even to the point of targeting, cruelly, those who have little. In so doing, we end up with the killing and murders, manifest hugest and most brutally in wars, which characterize our times, along with its affiliates of criminalizing of dissent; murder of opposition leaders and those presenting knowledge or technology that might be helpful but which threatens the status quo, in developed countries; and expansion of the prison population, which is especially flagrant in the U.S.

Murder, Relative to …

Another parallel to this in modern times is the way we magnify the dangers of society in our media to the point where we feel we are threatened and need to take action. Thus, we create the very thing we feared. Let me explain: Herman (2012) presents data about murders among a particular gatherer-hunter group, which shows them to be as bad as in a city like Chicago. While that might seem high, keep in mind that it is still no more than as exists in some, what we think to be, "civilized" societies. Furthermore, as Herman points out, when you factor in war, that is, organized, institutional murder — an abundance of which we have in modern times — the danger of being killed by another human among gatherer-hunter groups is vastly less than in our times.

Beyond that, keep in mind that any gatherer-hunter group described in modern times is already going to be a *hunting* group. And, as this chapter will make clear: It is hunting, more specifically, killing planetmates and eating their flesh, that enabled us to be able to kill each other. Therefore, gatherer-hunters in our century cannot be taken as representative of what we might have been like as mere gatherers when we were protohumans. To get an idea of what humans might have been like as foragers, we need to look to our nearest primate relatives who *are* simple foragers, not meat-eaters.

Our two closest relatives, with whom we share identical DNA of over 98%, meaning we are barely removed from them, are the chimpanzee and the gorilla. And the gorilla is exclusively vegetarian. Note that gorillas do not murder their own kind, either. As for the chimpanzee, well, this cousin is more omnivorous — eating food-stuffs gathered from streams and lakes as well as occasional small animals, as can be easily gotten. But he or she does not hunt or eat meat in anywhere near the amount that humans do. Chimpanzees also do not murder — except in extremely rare situations, only recently come to light, where it might have something to do with proximity to humans and their daemon of "civilization."

Self-Fulfilling Prophecy

The additional point I am making in this example has to do with self-fulfilling prophecy, however. For in our modern media obsession with murder, assault, robbery, and guns, we, like those early foragers, newly come to hunting, create such a fearful and anxious populace that, without a doubt, we actually *create* that danger we are supposedly shining a light on. You think not? You say, how?

Well, such terror creates for many people an idea that they need to have weapons to protect themselves. In getting guns, they then actually greatly facilitate the chance that they will actually be in danger, for others around them are doing the same. We know, in modern times, how such obsession with guns as we see in the U.S., which also has a media drowning them in images of ghastly murder and brutal assault — in news reports, television cop and crime shows, and the like — actually creates the very thing that people owning guns are thinking they are preventing.

The Heights

I am reminded of something I observed in looking at a newspaper report from my hometown, which described the neighborhood in which I grew up. It turns out it had become the murder center of the region, predominantly by way of gunfire. It was not that way at all when I grew up there. Though there were the "toughs," and as a child I was wary of walking the commercial street in the area, one block away, which was appropriately named, Market Street, as was the others around my age in my immediate neighborhood. Nonetheless, while fighting was common, so much that even I had to participate on several occasions — I was confronted and it was not okay to back down — still, murder was pretty much unheard of.

Then came drugs ... and, with it, crime. As the neighborhood continued its economic decline, its property values went down, and sordid and unsavory sorts — oftentimes from the bigger cities around, of Philadelphia or New York — began filling up the neighborhoods of The Heights, which is what that part of town was called.

Anyway, in the newspaper article, they listed, oh, maybe thirty murders over the recent number of years. They described who, how, why, and by whom. I need to add the racial element, as it is relevant. For while nearly all of them involved Blacks, there was one incident involving Whites. Surrounded on all sides by a Black populace and an environment afloat in drugs, guns, crime, and murder, they too had acquired guns and … can you guess?

Yes, there was a killing there, too. Having acquired guns to protect themselves, these two White brothers, who were living together, ended up shooting each other. One died.

When I stopped laughing at the dufuses, I felt sorry for them.

I see this as a way that excessive fear leads to risky actions which then create the very thing those actions are intending to avoid, exactly as in a self-fulfilling prophecy.

This is a pretty good parallel to the twisted, fearful, obsessive thinking that brought about murder in our species at its beginnings, as well.

Competing Versus Sharing

In early gatherer-hunter times, yes, we had plenty for everyone. However with fear rose anxiety over one's ability to survive, thus competition over resources — a competition which was not needed — and then the very creation of what one was trying to avoid: The possibility that one might need to kill or one would be killed.

I want to further add that this same pattern and this same fearful obsessiveness is later what leads to the intense competitiveness that overtook our species once we began living in settled communities. For as gatherers we were characterized as sharing and cooperative. Indeed, if there is one trait found in non-civilized people more than any other, it is that quality of cooperation and sharing. Whereas, when we began living in settled communities, we began a hierarchy of haves and have-nots, wrought of the newly acquired ability to store things and thus to build up wealth.

With this inequality of means came a tension between people that was not there before, and that tension involved some folks getting less because others had more. This anxiety of inequality, hand-in-hand with the feelings of unfairness that come of it, create the drive to compete, rather than cooperate. Thus it is inequality itself, wrought of the hierarchy made possible only in settled communities, which precipitates greed in humans and the feeling they need to store up more and to take away from those who have less. This drive to compete increased, over time, with increasing population centers, increasing hierarchy, increasing complexity of density of population in cities, and more finely differentiated division of labor to the point where it is has reached the mania of competitiveness that exists in modern societies today.

I will have a lot more to say about that and similar developments in the course of human devolution/evolution later, but the point, for now, is that it is created out of the same kind of mechanism of self-fulfilling prophecy that turned hunters into murderers.

In sum, out of our delusion of scarcity of resources, we created the reality that we would need to kill in order to keep from being killed.

9

The Ninth Descent — Farming:

The Agrarian "Revolution" Was the Direst Development

"Yes, we turned life into work, when it could have been play."

"...we lost the magic of living. We focused, because of fear, on the quantity of said existence instead of the quality of it...."

Returning now to human's devolution in the course of our prehistory, in terms of the well-being of ourselves and all life on this planet, the worst development of all, however, was put into motion when we began to grow our own food.

The Neolithic Era and the Beginning of "Work"

This began the Neolithic Era and this huge change has been dubbed the "agrarian revolution." The agrarian revolution developed out of the same forces that caused us to begin hunting and to being able to murder, which have to do with our unnatural fear of scarcity of resources and lack of faith in a Divine Providence to meet our needs even better than we could alone. The controlling of vegetative food sources, *horticulture*, grew out of our impatience with the Divine harmony and plan, and our desire to control — what could also be seen as *interfering* in — Nature's perfect ways even so far as, now, the Flora Kingdom of Earth.

This development took hold of increasing numbers of humans beginning about twenty-five-thousand years ago and took on momentum approximately ten-thousand years ago, and really increased in speed and spread worldwide about five-thousand years ago. Humans began determining the life cycles of the vegetation they found in their environments. They continued their God-like determination of the life and death of other beings, as they had with fleshy planetmates, now with leafy ones, but more: For now they determined the entire who, what, where, when, and how of their existences. We record this as a revolution, yet it was a fall from Nature and into increasing ego immersion.

This was the direst development for humans in a number of ways. For one thing, it took the "magic" out of living. The richness of life, as lived in Nature, faded, as we regimented our lives along the temporal lines required for planting and harvesting. As *The Bible* points out, in *Genesis*, this was the beginning of "work."

Living in Time, not Experience, increased our separation from a felt existence.

Control and Power Addictions

It was also another form of control. Having determined the death of planetmates through hunting, and control of other humans through aggression and murder, we at this point began determining, not just the deaths, but the entire lifecycles of the Earth-rooted beings among us. Our controlling tendencies, wrought of fear and the anxiety of uncertainty, had us extending our domain of interference in Nature. We were less and less content to live in harmony with Nature; we were more and more, because of the birth trauma which put us mistrustful, at odds, and downright angry at Nature, more and more inclined to war with Nature. We wished to wrest from it that which it was everywhere and at all times previous completely willing to grant us through grace.

Thus, we began our controlling obsession with hunting. Yet we were continually goaded by an anxiety around insufficiency of resources, which had its roots in the traumas I have been describing, in particular, fetal malnutrition. So in due course, though in time relative to our existence as humans, it was an incredibly long time, we began mucking with the Flora Kingdom. We invaded said kingdom and began tampering with the natural order to wrestle it into line with our increasingly depraved fetishes for control. That obsessive-control disorder mentioned earlier, yes, had its roots way back here.

Certainly, hunting gave us the feeling of power of control over others. And power is its own kind of addiction, when one feels as helpless as humans do from a time even before birth. But like all addictions, the life come of it was reflective of but not equal to an authentic life; it was a substitute for life in Nature, with all its rich immediacy of feeling and experience. It was more a mental world of planning and strategizing; we began to have "agendas" about our presence in Nature and with other humans in our tribes. Things were not sufficient unto themselves and able to be appreciated in their wholeness. No. In controlling, in exerting our power, we needed to excise from our environment and the things and beings in it that small amount that would feed our ability to physically exist. Like all addictions, *power had us focused on increasingly important minutia at the cost of wholistic appreciation of the things of Reality.*

"This God-Like Determination"

That was true of hunting, but it was even more true of horticulture. Horticulture did not come easily, so it took a long time after hunting had been adopted. There are reasons for that which you might want to ponder ... we did not really desire such a regimented and effortful existence.

In fact, there was a variation to sedentary horticulture that involved nomadic living, which continued even into modern times. As we will see later with corralling of planetmates and the variation of it that involved nomadic herding, there was a kind of farming taken up by nomadic horticulturalists. Some tribes would travel to a certain place to grow things, then in the off-season they were nomadic. Noting this is to evidence that there was some sort of desire to be nomadic that humans did not want to give up. So they arranged compromises with their more controlling tendencies. It appears our increasing egoic desires to control vied with a more adventurous spirit regarding life.

Inevitably though, after hunting came horticulture, for through hunting we were able to imagine manipulating the flora of Nature as well as the fauna. In adopting hunting, we had been aided by our observations of Nature, for we saw that certain planetmates killed others for sustenance. Similarly, we observed that the offshoots of the beings of the Flora Empire — the nuts, seeds, and fruit — would give rise to new beings of that nature when they ended up under ground. Seeing that, and driven by our pervasive insecurity, it was inevitable we would begin taking that job over onto ourselves: We had hunted; now we planted.

We took the lifecycles of these Earth-rooted beings out of the purview of the Divine and put them under ours. By removing the determination of their coming into form and leaving it, we fed our increasing addiction to power, wrought of ever more control.

We placed ourselves in the spot formerly afforded the Good Mother of wilderness and forest and ourselves determined the fates of flora beings: We decided where they would be "born" and when, when they would end their existences, where they would live, who of them would get to be superior in numbers, how they would live, and the manner of their deaths. We took the lifecycles and ends that Nature had determined away from them and set them to our ends instead.

Hence we fought back our dread of uncertainty by "kidnapping" these offspring of Flora and putting them under soil in our immediate environs. This God-like determination of Flora we called a revolution, after a while … an *agrarian revolution*. However it was a major incursion into and overturning of any possible harmony with Nature we still had. All other beings live under the grace of Nature, or at least in partnership with it. We possessed it; we aggressively determined it. It was a major incursion of control into Nature's domain, and it could not have been more significant for our own fates as well as theirs.

The Direst Development

Indeed, for us, planting was the worst development of all. I will lay out, in upcoming chapters, how it step-by-step and over the course of history led to the attempted control of all else of our reality; how it removed from us the felicity and ease of life which is the birthright of all other planetmates; how it brought in disease and suffering not known previously and actually reduced, not increased, our life span; how it filled our lives with pain and suffering, even more than we already, as the suffering planetmate, had; how it took the interest and adventure out of life and replaced it with monotony and drudgery; how we thus swapped the fullness of life for something more routine, out of our terror of uncertainty about survival; how it led to inequality, domination, submission, loss of self and authenticity, increasing bigotry, increasing misogyny, increasing war and violence, increasing destruction of and despoliation of Nature; and how it led us inevitably to the apocalyptic brink we are standing upon today.

Most directly, this development continued the tendency toward insensitivity we had already begun as we needed to repress even more, to "toughen" ourselves, in order to tolerate such a diminished life experience. We increasingly lost our conscience, our fellow feeling, our belongingness, not just in Nature, but now also in tribe and extended family. We increasingly, for reasons I will explain, focused on family and we made those families economic units primarily and not coves of intimacy, love, joy, and companionship. We became ever more inured to the consequences of our actions and were able, given time, to pile up our atrocities against each other, as well as Nature.

We Lost the Magic of Living

So an even more reduced connection to our felt experience allowed us to further diminish that experience through the cultivation of plants; and that, because of the increased focus on survival to the detriment of all other of life's possibilities and all that was concomitant to that, acted back again upon experience to diminish our lives even more.

Remember, we need to contrast this intense involvement in the control of Nature to our former existence within Nature, which was characterized by relative ease: For with no effort on our own at all, Nature would automatically bring forth, and in abundance, everything that one would need for sustenance, for shelter, for drink, and for clothing. All one needed to do was to follow the path along Nature's cornucopia: Different seasons and different environs would throw up an incredible variation of anything we needed. Not only were our gifts from Nature more various and delightfully surprising, but our lives as well were profoundly interesting … characterized as they were by nomadic wandering, following mellifluous weather and in the company of equals who equally, as well, pulled together to acquire whatever was needed. Indeed, compared to later, our existences were more characterized by pleasure and felicity, by love and human feeling, by care and play with children and friends. These were our halcyon days, without a doubt.

With a delight comparable to children seeking out Easter eggs, we would scour and immerse ourselves in Nature in order to seek out its blessings. We simply had to discover where the Great Mother of Nature was currently "hiding" Her treasures.

But with the pain-driven and ever increasing lack of faith in Divine Providence and the increasing hardening of our sensitivities to existence, we lost the magic of living. We focused, because of fear, on the quantity of said existence instead of the quality of it. And even in the quantity of it we failed, though we did not know we were doing that at the time. As I said, we introduced new and virulent diseases into our lives with horticulture, and especially with farming and agriculture with their necessary concentrations of population as in villages and cities. So our life spans diminished. The only thing we really added to our lives with horticulture was the addictive highs of power and control, which were ever and easily dissipated and in need of continual refeeding.

Meanwhile, life in Nature had been playful. Foraging was adventurous and we were often surrounded in beauty, with delight-inducing fragrances, comforting and familiar sounds of insects and animate Nature, and refreshing dalliances with rushing water, soothing sun rays, and cool and amniotic shade.

However, with horticulture, all the adventure and pleasure of Nature was set to the side in favor of more certainty in our lives, regardless how much effort we had to expend to bring that about.

Yes, we turned life into work, when it could have been play.

Imprisoned in Time

Our hellacious beginnings wrought more than mistrust however. Impatience walked in with it, hand in hand. We were living more in time now, as I said. We had to adhere to Nature's timetables for sowing and reaping and all the rest of the requirements of farming. Our beginnings involving pain had already set us up to wish to escape from the present. This we did by conniving possible futures, which drew us forward, however ignorant it would make us of the people and pleasantness surrounding us in the present.

Yet in Nature, we would receive its gifts on little that amounted to a schedule. We simply had to show up. Fish and crab and such showed themselves as they would; vegetation, however uncertain, provided variety and alternatives, which we could take advantage of per our desires. Surprise and adventure characterized our lives, and through them we were continually reassured of the beneficence of Reality.

That by itself was a pretty good antidote to our fear of uncertainty. We were continually reminded of and reinforced in the knowledge that we were always in the hands of a kindly and invisible power that knew all, including our needs and desires, even better than we did ourselves. Being open to Nature, we would be taught, but also comforted by it. It was all at once counselor, teacher, and friend. It was most kind, though it gave us the hard lessons we needed.

And it was playful, tricky. Unexpected as any trickster, we could not help but be engrossed and engaged, and often delighted by it. It played with us and delighted us and even confounded us. Regardless, everything would work out in the end far better, we often realized, than if we had planned it ourselves. So we trusted in Nature's ways and intentions toward us.

Escape to an Imaginary Future

Not so, after we put ourselves in place as the Determiners. Ever more we found it more difficult to realize our life in the entrancing state of the Now. We were increasingly having a conceptual existence rather than an experiential one, for we were living in a planned future. The richness of life was ever more faded from our existence, as the present became only a precursor to a more desirable future ... always off ahead of us ... always out of reach. Yet ever taunting us and luring us, it was, with a promise, rarely achieved, of relief from unbearable feelings of impatience and uncertainty.

For though with sowing and reaping we could not have all we wanted when we wanted, we thought it desirable to know the timetable upon which it would arrive. The emptiness we feared would be there if we did not work hard and store up ahead of time was the realization in our lived existence of the hole in our guts from an inaccessible time when we starved. The death that we felt certain would follow that emptiness was the same death that had hidden close by during our time of prenatal aching. Living more now in time than in experience, we could give our intolerable impatience a promise of a time and an image of a future where it might be eased.

Descending from a state of full existence as this amounted to, however, when that time arrived it would be soon over, and those fearsome feelings of uncertainty and impatience would rise up ever and again. We failed to learn from that, driven as we were, and would simply concoct another future to pull us forward, full of that satisfaction we so desperately desired. Focusing on that future reward for the grueling and unfeeling existence we had adopted — wrought of the incredible expenditures of energy required by horticultural and farming "work" — we failed to open our "presents" in the here and now.

So much did we project our happiness into a future time when we would be rewarded for our suffering in the Now, that eventually we would concoct the same for our time after death. More despairing at the end of our lives, as knowledge of the futility of all of our days of struggling arose within us, we pushed our longed-for time of Aliveness beyond our period of life itself. We could rationalize our unfelicitous and unfelt existences by imagining some kind of afterlife

— the most revealing being the "heaven" of the Muslim and Christian traditions — where we could get the enjoyment of life we were depriving ourselves of while alive, to which a part of us knew we were entitled.

Descent to Domestication

Ever unsatisfied, it was only a matter of time till we came up with additional modes of control to soothe our unhappiness. Hunting and horticulture not giving us what we wanted, what we needed, but glorying in our ability to control, we focused that fetish on another food source. Having raised ourselves up as the "corn kings" of Nature in determining the lifecycles of Flora, it was only logical we would seek to be "king of the jungle" as well by dominating and controlling that of Fauna as well. We began corralling planetmates. We invented husbandry.

10

The Tenth Descent — Husbandry:

The Progression of Increasing Insensitivity, Increasing Dimming of Awareness Allowed the "Domestication of Animals"

*" ...enslavement of our family in Nature was an
abominable affront to their nobility and was a scar on
human character:... Our increasing drive to control
made us abominations in Nature."*

Out of Anxiety, Humans Cheat in the Game of Life

In due time, this time not long at all, after we humans "conquered" the Flora Empire on Earth, we began "conquering" fellow planet-mates of the Fauna Kingdom. Having taken over the determination of the lifecycles of the Flora Empire, it did not take long for our progenitors to imagine doing the same thing to those on Earth appearing to be more like them. It was not enough just to hunt and kill planetmates for food; after a while, the "brilliant" idea came to some to do the same to roaming planetmates as had been done to the Earth-bound planetmates, the flora. Humans were infused with newfound abilities of conquering — like petty emperors each of us — and we extended our purview to all other beings in sight.

Pumped up on our desperate addiction to control and swooning with power, we captured and set to our ends the lifecycles of more of the independent Earth Citizens. In this way early humans were now having even less consideration for planetmates as being independent, free beings as when they killed and hunted. In hunting, we had at least a little bit of regret at the taking of lives. Our ancestors still felt a kinship with their prey, as do the gathering-hunting societies we know of in our times.

Humans were not that far removed from the ways possible in Nature. For in hunting we were not doing anything so different from what other planetmates we saw were doing. For, clearly, there were carnivores around, and we observed them. We saw that they lived free and independent lives up until the moment when a final contest — for one of them final, anyway — would involve a showdown in which one would live and achieve a delicious aim and the other would be sent on its way, ending its game of life, allowing it to start over in another time and place.

So when our ancestors hunted, they were the same as carnivore planetmates in allowing the independent lives, noble and free, of any of their prey until the moment of a similar showdown in which, ideally, our prey, not us, would be freed to begin another round elsewhere. In this way, humans and planetmates were still kin to each other and were still children of the same mother, Nature.

However, in order to "domesticate animals" we needed to pluck our former kin from Nature's perfect blueprint and set them to our ends, driven by our brains, crazed from early trauma.

Thus, it was not only the deaths of planetmates we were determining, as we did in hunting them as prey. We ourselves fell prey to the obsession that we could feed our addiction for possessing and controlling the factors influencing our lives by determining the manner of their entire lives, as well. It was as if, being unsure of our success in the contests of Nature — having that basic mistrust described earlier — we decided to cheat.

Rather than search out and engage our planetmate relatives, as before, we took their entire freedom. Humans put planetmates in place and grew them as they had done with vegetables. And, as before, this meant much more work ... just as farming was an oppression compared to foraging. But prehistoric humans continued the downward spiral of control leading to more control in that they convinced themselves that adding to their days the efforts toward controlling animals would reduce the labor involved in controlling the rooted planetmates. That is to say, they figured the "animals" would aid in their farming. Nevertheless, along with the work of tilling the fields, husbandry or "domestication" contributed to lives of increasing labor and sweat. More importantly than that, controlling so much led to lives that were focused solely on physical needs and concerns, forgetting the ones of spirit and soul.

The "Domestication of Animals"

Thus, we began the "domestication of animals," as we called it. Which is hilarious when you think of it. For in these words we tell ourselves two things:

One, we objectify these beings with whom we share this planet. They are "animals." We are not animals. They are wild; they must be, needing "domestication." We are not; we are "homey" and unwild ... tame and civilized despite our murdering ways.

We "domesticate" them means we bring them into our domicile, our home. We would have it that we are doing them a favor in taking them out of their stressful lives in Nature, making them guests in our homes where we can kill them. Worse, where we take away any of their pleasures of being alive — of freedom of movement, of choice of provisions ... mating partners ... locale.

Indeed, that is the way we humans have thought of any that have come under our thumb and our sword — whether planetmate or indigenous peoples: That we are doing our victims a favor — even if they die — of taking them out of that nasty "wild"erness and putting them into our "organized" living. However lethal and tortuous it is for them to be with us, it must be better, we think, than their lives in "unruly" Nature. Indeed, with reasoning such as this slave owners of all times have justified, even exalted, their nefarious actions. Then wondered, clueless, why such enslaved would rise up against them, or try to run away.

For sure, most folks think that same thing today about civilization vis-à-vis living in Nature. Once, a person responded to my ideas, "Oh, you want to live in dirt." As if the earth was some kind of threat, needing to be wiped away continually, in some OCD kind of way. As if freedom of spirit meant nothing relative to orderliness and cleanliness — those purely ego desires, those desires wrought of our fears of uncertainty, wrought of our traumas of birth. And as if, outside the perimeters of the city and town, with skyscrapers, houses, paved roads, and manicured lawns, just past some border or other, it all becomes dirt. There's no rushing streams, forests, waterfalls, verdant fields and meadows, deep and cool lakes leaping with wildlife, carpets of undergrowth, aromatic foliage, air that's alive with winged things, birds, and breeze-surfing butterflies. No. Nothing. Just dirt. To not live in civilization is to live in dirt. So, thinking that way, of course any planetmates and indigenous people are better off living in houses surrounded by monotonous empty lawns than in "dirt." How could they not know that?

Secondly, we "domesticate" them, which means they are beastly and out of control, "wild" again, in a sense of being threatening as well. We murdering, hunting, enslaving, controlling humans are not wild or out of control; we are not a threat. I suppose as long as murder and enslavement are controlled they are seen as somehow harmonious and peaceable, especially compared to the random, the "wild" life-and-death struggles occurring in Nature.

Well, yes, if you look you will see that in modern times we have shown that to be exactly the way we think of things. As long as murder and enslavement are organized, they are civilized. It is the uncertainty of life we cannot abide; not the threat of death. A death determined by another in some orderly fashion, we unconsciously feel, like when one goes to war as a soldier, is preferable to one that is determined randomly and by fate ... catching one unawares, unforeseen.

For such a death — as a fighter or as "collateral damage" in war — is part of some huge organizational process we unconsciously feel to have more meaning. We at least have a sense of belonging in being part of something bigger than ourselves, even if it is a war, and our death is not put upon us … wasn't "our" fault.

Further, when one, like a soldier, dies, it is thought to be part of a higher cause. It is occurring, then, as if it is like it is a "higher power" — the vast society of which one is a part — deciding it, not oneself. It is a higher civilized power … and at least we have died within the matrix of the machine of organized life. It is not much different from the victims of Aztec sacrifices, or other barbaric human sacrifices of human "civilization," who thought they were performing a function in some natural order through their dying.

Everywhere we show ourselves that the thing we fear the most is freedom; for we fear the responsibility involved in that. We are so perversely lonely in the world, so cut off from Divinity and Nature, that we would prefer to be part of something that would kill and enslave us than have to be alone, fending for ourselves. You will notice how true that is when you see how many folks will return to the cities to die, when the bombs fall and the oceans rise, rather than have to fend for themselves in Nature. When storms larger than ever known on Earth level cities, earthquakes finish them off, virulent diseases make congregating in populated places deadly, still people will come to the cities. We humans would rather die in a crowd than "alone" in Nature, you'll see. Hey, maybe they'll make the nightly newscast! We seek the familiar and the orderly, even to our death.

And what I am saying here is we cannot imagine that anyone else, "wild" planetmate or "wild" human — that is, indigenous or primal human — would not prefer that as well.

Yet is this organization for the purpose of "civil"ization, this "domestication" really a "home" for them? For planetmates? The way they might feel it? No. This is slavery for our planetmates. Worse than that, it is prison. We take them out of their actual home, in Nature, where they are animate, alive, and soulful; and we make them mere *things* in our world.

"Domesticating" animals is another way of saying that we no longer see them as other beings, but only as things, which were apparently placed in Nature for our use, much as we imagine the trees were put there for our use as lumber to make our houses, our domiciles. They are no longer our brother-and-sister beings; they have become resources. Then in "domesticating" them, we are saying we have taken away any idea they might have any existence outside of ours: Their sole purpose in the "wild" was for us to discover how they could be used by us. Just as we assume all the plants in existence were not really doing very much in growing, living, and dying in the wild until we came along and gave them an actual role in life … a real purpose! you see … as our foodstuffs, as our crops, or as our medicines.

Herding Was Less a Fall

Now, it happens there was a parallel phase to this "domestication" of "animals" that occurred in our devolution of humans. In some cases it was a preceding one. This is the mode where we began herding. In this way — in herding planetmates, not corralling them — we maintained, often, still a semblance of a kind of nomadic lifestyle. But there was another aspect to it, besides the benefits we retained by staving off sedentary living, which had to do with the relationship we had with Nature in this mode, compared to what we would have when we became fully sedentary. For in nomadic herding, we still retained a connection to the world of Nature through the bonds we might have with the "animals" cared for.

No doubt about it, sheepherding or any herding was less a fall from grace than was farming. For in herding, there is still a felt connection with planetmates. There is still concern and care, and they are allowed a certain amount of freedom … think of Jesus as the Good Shepherd. That symbol expresses the bond of caring we have with planetmates in herding them, even as we control their lives and will use and eat them, eventually.

For by comparison, with sedentary living and corralling of planetmates we enlist them in our farming. In being sedentary and farming, we use planetmates as things: They are used to pull other things, to be milked, to serve up their children for consumption. And so on. Hence this is a further fall from herding. With farming, planetmates are used, grown, and eaten, as they were items only.

It is because of these developments — herding and farming — which often were parallel, existing side by side, that we get the myth of Cain and Abel. We see that in *The Bible*, God prefers Abel's offering, a lamb. For he was a sheepherder. His offering was more valued by God ... *he* was more valued by God ... than Cain the farmer. *The Bible* here is reflecting that our descent into farming was graver than the one involving herding.

The Progression of Increasing Insensitivity, Increasing Dimming of Awareness

So it went, hunting, murder, herding, horticulture, husbandry, in terms of the descents from grace in Nature ... in terms of the level of control involved and the corresponding thingification of the life around. Regardless of the actual historical progression of these descents of humans — and it varied, and not only that, it sometimes reversed and even swung back and forth between modes, in some places — these were the lifeway modes in order of the generating of the increasing insensitivity of humans ... the increasing descent into unconscious unaware living ... into *ignore*-ance.

In whatever progression, it included the domestication of plants — their enslavement — first; then that of animals, second. And we now were controlling not just the vegetative beings for food but the roaming and moving ones as well.

Animal "Husbandry"

We began our domination of fauna by herding them. Then like we did the plants, we began rounding these beings up and corralling them. Indeed we controlled where and when they would mate and with whom. For our intention was to determine their offspring to be along the lines of what we would wish.

Once captured, they were placed into our service in all ways possible. Indeed, we decided the who, what, where, when, and how of virtually every aspect of their lives, down to the most trivial. Thus, we created animal husbandry. I wonder, were we now the "husbands" of our planetmates? For certainly we had taken away their rights to mate on their own as they would in the wild.

We humans, at this point, were so infused with our addiction for controlling that we enslaved and set the lifecycles of these once noble beings along lines that would benefit us alone, regardless what pain and suffering it might mean for them. We ripped these Earth Citizens from the perfect place that Nature had designed for them. Our sister-and-brother planetmates — our warm-blooded kin now in addition to our flora planetmates — were plucked from their lives of adventure and awe and were instead "possessed" in the same way we humans had been possessing the land we dwelt upon and the earth-rooted beings we placed into it.

So we kidnapped them. We beat them into things to fit our desires. We fashioned them into alien, schizophrenic molds, the products of human minds made mad by the traumas of our early lives, in particular our births. These minds were fearful, obsessive about controlling, crazed, backwards thinking, and overstimulated. And we set them to focus on our planetmates and to draw them into our designs, our mad ones, and out of the perfect one of Nature.

And we called the perfect one "wild" and our mad one "domesticated" as if it was "homey" and nice, that way. The irony in that terminology was something that never dawned on us, until perhaps in these times. Though the insanity and brutality with which we treated our nearest relatives in Nature, you would think, would have been a hint to us somewhere along the way; though it was not.

Regardless their feelingness or beingness, we took our brothers and sisters and kept them. We grew them like our plants. We raised, trained them. We ate their offspring. We routinely killed and ate them as well, eventually. We determined when they would be born; we decided where they would live and the manner of that life. We decided what they would eat throughout their lives. We took the product of their teats from them, their milk, which Nature had intended for their offspring, not us. Indeed, we nurtured and killed their offspring as we wished.

We fashioned garments from their fur. We took their coats from them, sheep in particular, shaving it off even as they were alive, for use by ourselves. We forced some of them into lives of back-breaking strenuous labor, even making them pull the items, the plows, that we had fashioned to better enslave their sister earth-rooted planetmates. Yes, we enlisted them in our agricultural designs. As well, we used them for transportation, sometimes riding upon them like we do horses and camels, sometimes requiring they pull the contraptions, the carriages and buggies, upon which we rode, like kings being pulled by slaves. If they did not submit, they were beaten, tortured, met with deprivation, and often killed, cut up, and cooked for our consumption.

In order to use them, sometimes we needed to "break them," to destroy their noble spirits. Again, with our over-inflation of self we saw that as doing them a favor in giving them a life in service to us, much as later human rulers would consider how beneficent they were being in "ruling" their "subjects" and giving them places, however lowly, in the "divine order" that had them at the top.

We placed them in what essentially were jails. For some of them, those jails were roomy and included land upon which they could roam, though naturally we set the boundaries of them — corralling and fencing and determining they would never escape. For others, we assigned lives of minimal movement, restraining them all about, in place, where we could come and regularly remove secretions or the offspring of their bodies for us to use or consume, like milk, like eggs.

We forced their bodies together and moved them about, at will. We collected them and stacked them and put them in piles like they were seashells or stones. We "herded" them. We tied them in place and maneuvered them as we wished.

We had them serve up their offspring regularly to put on our dinner tables — eggs, veal, lamb. We rarely allowed their "children" to hatch and become actual fully grown descendants of theirs. Yet we poked and prodded them to produce ever more. And if we allowed their newborns to live, it would only be until we would take their lives at a later time, at our whim, and for some purpose solely our own.

No longer satisfied with merely hunting and killing planetmates — and being increasingly unthinking and unfeeling in our diminishing awareness, come of hunting and horticulture — we took away any sense of an individual existence for them, outside of what we wanted of them. This was truly a separation from Nature; we were now objectifying … that is, putting outside of ourselves and turning them into things … the beings on this planet who were most like ourselves. In objectifying them, you see, we were beginning the process that would have us objectifying ourselves, just as when we began killing them … hunting … we set into place the process that would have us being able to murder each other, too.

We captured our brother and sister beings much as one would gather up firewood. We took them from their places in Nature which had been established over the course of millions, even billions, of years … a design so perfect that it could be considered Divinely crafted. Yet that mattered no more to us at that time than it matters to us today that for the satisfaction of our desires it is of no matter that we irrevocably alter, in a matter of mere decades, the climate of this planet that has evolved over billions of years.

You see, *everything became a mere casualty of our existence. Everything was collateral damage to our desires* … and still is. We were the biggest narcissists in Nature … big babies whose desires and wants were all important; and the Mother, Nature must die and provide them. This is how we were acting out our deprivations of not getting our needs met sufficiently at our time of infancy because we were being tended to by imperfect human adults and not the perfect designs of Nature. We were the beings taking from Nature and destroying our Mother in a kind of revenge at what was done to us as prenates and infants and out of an unconsciousness caused by those traumas as well.

A Hideous Persona

Having lost our connection to Divine Providence and our sense of the God of All — It no longer being visible to us — we set our own selves up on the throne of Nature belonging to It. We deemed ourselves gods and rulers over Nature and all life. But we were ugly deities. Relative to the Divine Perfection that is the birthright of all beings and which is the way of Nature — the source of the apprehension of Reality as Beauty and Life as Bliss — we were clownish and pompous. We had no idea of the monstrous, the devilish, the hideous persona we were actually presenting to the rest of Creation.

In all these ways, we gave full sway to our desires; and we were able to justify our reckless and insensitive behavior to our conscience — what was left of it. How? Well, as in the other things previously, through use of the Ego we had created out of our early trauma, in defense of our pain, we turned our crimes, as always, into achievements.

A horrific example of how grievously we did that was given in *The Bible* in the way Abraham was going to sacrifice his own child so as to advance his own … ahem … spirituality … or his relationship to the "Divine." In the story, God, Jehovah, is said to have told Abraham to kill his son, Isaac, in a sacrificial way. Abraham is about to do just that when a few developments derail his plan. He does not follow through, yet ever afterwards — I only wish I were kidding — murderous Abraham is held up as the model of a righteous man, a man of faith. The story would have us believe that unthinking obedience — a complete surrender, actually a repression of our natural empathy, compassion, fellow-feelings, paternal love — is actually a "holy" (a wholly) thing. Hence it is better to surrender to and act out murderous and insane thoughts and voices in one's head than to be kind, be loving.

The historical accuracy of the Abraham and Isaac incident is not relevant. For it reflected our thinking at the time but, significantly, even afterward. Importantly, it shows how we manage to hide our barbarity from ourselves and rationalize it as its opposite. For notice how Abraham and all the "religious" who have looked to him and his story over all the millennia managed to rationalize a) that it made perfect sense that a person might have to kill another person, even their own child, because a "god" demanded it. And b), that somehow it is a religious transformation for Abraham to simply have the basic humanity, as any planetmate would naturally have, to not kill their own kind, let alone their own children.

The point is that using Ego we deemed our offenses to be duties; we respun our failings as additional proof of our singular superiority.

However, in this chapter we are exploring the way that happened in the "descent" into the "domestication of animals," or animal husbandry. And we need to see how it followed the "conquering" of the Flora Empire and how it arose out of the same drive to control everything-and-all-about-oneself out of fear, out of that basic mistrust.

In retrospect this enslavement of our family in Nature was an abominable affront to their nobility and was a scar on human character: It was a great shame we bore ever afterward. The point is that our increasing drive to control made us abominations in Nature. And with this latest descent it was an assault on the dignity of all planetmates.

Descent to the Sedentary

Regardless, our control of both flora and fauna in all these ways required the most drastic change in our way of life. For horticulture, and to some extent herding of planetmates, required the end of our nomadic lifestyles and the establishment of sedentary ones.

Yet when we enslaved our fellow warm-blooded Earth Citizens, it had a consequence completely unexpected. For in order to do that, one had to remain permanently in place. This augmented the necessity to do that, required by horticulture. But still, there is horticulture where tribes migrate to the "planting grounds" for those times of the year to do that, and then they can move away. Similarly, there are, as mentioned, even herders who can remain nomadic.

However, in domesticating both planetmates and plants, sedentary living — staying in one place all year round and usually for one's entire life — becomes absolutely essential. In order to raise fauna planetmates — for husbandry, farming, and the "domestication" of them — we needed to build permanent domiciles for ourselves, unlike all the temporary ones, which had been easily put up, easily left behind, during our nomadic days. And we fixed our former friends, the planetmates, in place as well, enslaving them along with ourselves.

This latest phase of our controlling — of our acting out our neonatal, prenatal, and infantile pain and deprivation, involving our changing over from nomadic to sedentary lifestyles — would be the direst phase in terms of the long-term survival of humans and for that matter all the rest of the life on Earth. Sedentary living — an unavoidable consequence of the combined domestication of plants and planetmates — is the one major root cause of the apocalypse looming on our horizon today.

"How so?" you say. Well, let us see. The next chapters explain how the "domestication" of ourselves and Nature — the living in one place or sedentary living — led inevitably to the ecocide currently in full swing and the imminent humanicide to come of it.

This "settling" or homesteading is what constituted the next descent of man. To it we now turn.

11

The Eleventh Descent —
Sedentary Life ... Homesteading:

Breaking with Divine Providence and Going It on Our Own, We Begin the Diminished Living of Civilization

"We imagined a devil in the Divine countenance, quite the contrast to our experience as primal humans when we perceived that on the opposite side of every face of fiendishness was a beatific one."

Sedentary Lifeways — More Constrained, More Controlling, Leads to Apocalypse....

More Constrained

All this controlling required the changeover of our human lifestyle from nomadic to sedentary. For humans needed to be in place to grow food, at least for the growing/harvesting season. We see evidence in our prehistoric record as well as among some non-civilized cultures in modern times of a somewhat nomadic life being matched with annual periods of horticulture. But we needed to be sedentary the full year round in order to corral and raise Fauna planetmates.

More Controlling

Keep in mind that while these descents of humans represent decreasing connection with the All That Is, they demonstrate also increasing control of what reality we have left. They are a profile of the ouster of a Benevolent Reality as the "ruler" of lives and the center of Nature, and its replacement with the oafish, plodding image of a despotic, bullying human, inured to his circumstances and insensitive to the life around him.

Two Reasons Homesteading Led to Apocalypse Today — Break with Providence and Ability to Accumulate

Specifically, our change from nomadic to sedentary lifeways had several significant effects on our species, human. Each of these is instrumental in creating the apocalypse emergency we and all life on this planet are facing at this very moment.

Break with Divine Providence

The two reasons homesteading leads to apocalypse are that, first, sedentary ways meant a near total break with the Divine Providence we relied on and experienced in Nature. Henceforth we were going it on our own, for good or ill. So this first reason relates to the idea of human's resistance to Divine Benevolence and all that comes of that. We will explore that, in particular, in this chapter and the next.

Ability to Store and Accumulate

The second reason concerns the ability to store more, with sedentary living, and the resulting tendency for humans to over-accumulate and to focus excessively on "things" as opposed to personal life experience. So this reason involves both a huge change in the focus of our lives — from life experience, wholeness of being, spiritual concerns, human and planetmate relationships, and so on, to an evaluation of one's life along the lines, merely, of what one possesses. Also and more importantly, storage led to some folks being able to store more than others. This created hierarchy in society, dominance-submission, and so much more, all of which we cover in the succeeding chapters.

The Two Effects of the Break with Divine Providence

Other effects of sedentary living are consequences themselves of that first reason — the break with Divine Providence.

First: Loss of Divine Spiritual and Personal Life Guidance

Leaving Divine Providence did not just mean we were having to go it alone in terms of providing our physical needs. No, for in breaking off from Divine Providence we lost also our connection to the guidance that comes from the Divine through the exigencies of fate. We tried to control all factors affecting us in life; we tried to remove fate from the formulation. And in doing that we lost the guidance toward the fullness of wisdom that is our right, as well as our purpose, here in Form.

Second: Loss of Divine Direction and Support for Physical and Emotional Well-Being

The second effect, also a consequence of our breaking with the great Mother Nature and the blessings come of that, was that in Nature we were guided toward a varied and healthy life, physically, as well as spiritually. The variation in nutrition; the hardiness come of interaction with variable weather; the required activity in doing things for oneself; the variety in locale; the nourishment from the wonders and beauty of Nature; the very freshness of the air, the water — all of that and more contributed to lives where humans grew strong, robust, and happy, and where they lived longer.

Whereas after the descents into flora and fauna control and their inevitable results of sedentary living, then urbanization, humans had much less variety in their diet.

Our Plans Cannot Replace Nature's Perfect Nurturing

In the same way as it is with our medicines and our nutritional supplements today, we can only take in and fortify our bodies with that which in our current state of knowledge we know we need … and that is ever changing … and growing. We continually discover more nutrients the body needs which had been left out of the prevailing ideas about proper diets and supplementation. In addition, we discover over and again new requirements of health and medicine previously unthought-of.

As examples of what I mean, consider the need for morning sunshine in regulating sleep patterns as it relates to our circadian rhythms and the avoidance of depression; the body's demands for an ever-expanding number and variety of micronutrients, hitherto un-known or not appreciated, which can only be had through an incredibly varied diet come from rich, not depleted, soils; the requirement of sunlight for making Vitamin D and for proper eyesight; the benefits of exposure to the negative ions predominating in Nature, her foliage and watercourses, for mental well being; the importance of a diet rich in protein and natural, complex carbohydrates, predominantly uncooked, as is the case in a Paleo diet but is completely lacking in virtually all modern diets, which are dependent on grains, thus gluten, and less protein, eventually more sugars of all kinds, and so on. All of these and many more are part of natural living but are left out of planned, controlled living, for they were yet to be discovered or known, or there are so many of them we cannot construct a planned life that includes all we need the way Nature provided it as we evolved in her womb over the course of billions of years. So, what we leave out, in trying to have healthy diets and lifestyles in any age, inevitably ends up being important as well, and in ways we do not know at the time.

The same way, it was, with our ancestors in going from nomadic living to sedentary life. And remember, they knew far less about the requirements for nutrition and health than we know today. Hence, in the villages, towns, and cities they sought merely to satisfy their hunger. Whereas in Nature, they were fortified and given vigor through a fantastic array of the bounty of wilderness — this was the true cornucopia of our mythical imaginings — and all without their even knowing of their needs, specifically.

We Were Better Taken Care of in Nature

You see how we were so much better taken care of in Nature and using our instincts for variety? By simply following our feelings of wanting to avoid monotony, following our desires to seek beauty and pleasure in our wanderings and in our consuming? And all the other things we do simply because we want to, when in Nature? *Simply because we want to*, which might actually be considered our instincts, by the way, if we weren't so dead set against acknowledging we have them for we prefer boasting about our difference from and superiority to Nature in any ways we can think up.

We were so much better off in Nature than when we deemed egoistically that *we* know what we needed and *we* can take care of it so much better than Nature can! Do you see how in attempting to control everything we necessarily fail? That our ideas that we can know it all and can foresee everything and provide everything for ourselves are unrealistic? And that Nature provides all one needs, easily and effortlessly, whereas when we rebel against Her and seek to go it on our own and take care of ourselves rather than allowing anyone else, Her, to nurture us, we fail? Do you see how it is machismo and egotism that keeps us from acknowledging we are dependent on a higher power, Nature, and thus prevents us from accepting the blessings and rewards come from Her and her higher wisdom?

In any case, in taking upon ourselves all these responsibilities of living and providing for ourselves, we did worse than when we were in Nature. So it was that with urbanization we began living shorter lives. Our life expectancies, at birth, on average declined from twenty-six years to nineteen years. For those of any age group, up to and including those who made it into their seventies, the life expectancies for beyond that were greater for the gatherer-hunters. So much for the "dangers" of living "in the jungle" … or "the dirt."

Heights decreased as well. Gatherer-hunters at the end of the Ice Age had an average height of five feet, five inches, for women; for men it was five feet, nine inches. After the move to concentrated population centers and the agricultural revolution, it declined precipitously to a mere five feet for women and five feet, three inches, for men.

We Re-Created Our Fetal Malnutrition in the Creation of Civilization

This constriction of nutrition with sedentary living to all appearances looks like a species' acting-out of the fetal malnutrition we humans experience before birth, as described in Chapter 4. On an evolutionary scale, compared to a gestational timeline, we, at the end of our "womb life" in Nature, restricted our nutrition with agriculture and it led to smaller people ... just as getting less oxygen and nutrition resulted in our starving and having a stunting of growth when we, as fetuses, were in our last month of womb existence. Prenatally, specifically in the last four weeks of gestation, it was the most hellacious time of our existence. And if we look back historically to the comparative time in our lives in Nature, which would be the beginnings of civilization where we declined so much in height and health, we see the same was true in our evolutionary history as well: It also was, and continues to be, the most hellish time in human existence.

Is there a connection? Does the restriction of nutrition ... the constriction of what we need down to what is barely livable ... kick up in us — from the "dawn" of civilization up till today — the pain from our time of fetal malnutrition? Certainly there is a fascinating parallel here. And the idea that this time of fetal malnutrition ... one month out of the nine, which corresponds neatly to the time after agriculture in relation to the entirety of our existence ... lends itself to wondering whether we are now, with the apocalypse approaching, in the first throes of a birth. In which case, what comes afterward? We can only wonder ... in both terror and wondrous anticipation, which is only slightly different from that time before birth, still in the womb.

Regardless, in our evolutionary history — our phylogeny and history not our ontogeny, now — those average heights subsequently began to increase again. Yet they never reached, even up to today, what they had been previous to the adoption of agriculture.

Also, with agriculture and homesteading, we began having diseases we never had before, while in Nature, which decimated human populations in virulent outbreaks. Because of a spread-out populace for gatherer-hunters, epidemics could not occur. And diseases such as tuberculosis and diarrheal illness were not heard of.

Upcoming, in Order: Loss of Spiritual Guidance, Loss of Health Direction, Storage-Accumulation

So, these consequences of sedentary living — that is, the breaking with Divine Providence with its corollaries of not getting our spiritual or our physical needs adequately fulfilled — let us take them, now, in turn. In the rest of this chapter, we will focus on how we lost Divine Guidance for our living, which altered forever our spiritual relation to the All and resulted in ongoing torment and unhappiness.

In the next chapter, we will explore how that split from Divine Providence led to a step-by-step degradation of our physical and emotional well-being. That decline reached a nadir with city life in early human history, it is true, but it continued through to the modern era. For it involves, today, the bastardization of food sources with GMO — that is, genetically-modified — crops and the reliance on cheap starchy, fatty, and sugary food items for the masses in lieu of wholesome foods. As was the case from the dawn of civilization, we are currently trading — this time on a massive scale — the benefits of quality, of existence; for quantity, of people.

Then, in the chapters following this and the next, we will deal with the other major development of sedentary living that had far-reaching consequences for humanity, ever afterward, which is the ability to store things and thus for some to have more than others. We will explore in those chapters all the effects of that — these effects being perhaps the worst of all for humans as well as the most pressing in contemporary times. For these effects include the burgeoning of a greed that is equal in size to the fear humans were growing inside themselves with all these descents from natural grace.

The Loss of Divine Guidance for Living

The first crucial reason our adoption of homesteading leads to our apocalyptic crisis today is that the ending of our nomadic life meant a near total break with Divine Providence. And that Providence has two important purposes for all planetmates, including us, which are guidance with living and direction toward optimal physical health:

First and foremost of these is the continued... continued from the womb and birth ... perfect direction and guidance of lives towards the growth and lifeways that are optimal to each Earth Citizen, as determined by the Divine. So this first of these two effects of the break from Providence involves direction — as determined by the All That Is or God — for our spiritual progress and ultimate fulfillment. The Benevolent All guides and teaches us along perfect pathways through the exigencies of what we call *fate* but which is actually the Divine Hand of Guidance. These difficulties, obstacles, struggles, deprivations, and pain are the instructional materials of the Benevolent Teacher, guiding us toward lives where we end up ever closer and more understanding of our rootedness, rather, identity with the Divine.

However, as we continued our descents from Nature, we increasingly saw difficulties, obstacles, even struggles, deprivations, and pain, as to be avoided instead of the blessings of Divinity. Hereafter, with our crazed, backwards thinking, we would determine our own ends and would resist the attempts of the All That Is, or Nature, to assist us.

We Wrestle Our Angels

Concerning resistance, with sedentary ways, humans began wrestling their "angels": Like Jacob wrestling the unrecognized divinity in the biblical account, in our switch to sedentary life we began confusing Divine Assistance with evil. We forgot the beatific face of difficulties and struggles, and we saw the deprivations and pain of life as things to be avoided at all cost instead of as the blessings, guidance, and instructions of Divinity. We set off on a course of resisting the Divine's attempts, through the struggles of life, to direct and teach and bring us back to our natural state of Unity with Divinity and its nature of Bliss, Beauty, and Awareness.

This first effect has us severing our connection with the Divine to the point of near total separation. As Michelangelo painted it, at this point we and the Divine touch at the end of a fingertip ... and that only. That is about right, and it is quite the fall from grace from what had been for our ancestors in Nature and from the way it is for *all* other Earth Citizens.

Life in Nature is about awareness, play, unity, belongingness, and nobility. Its love is quietly confident and blissful, not maudlin and ostentatiously covering up its absence in actuality. It contains the heights of enjoyment while embracing the uncertainty required for that. Its pain and discomfort are essential components of its larger, more encompassing Pleasure and Beauty.

I have been describing our increasing straying from that sort of life and the institution, in its stead, of a life reframed as a pursuit of avoidance of exigencies, obstacles, and pain.

Clearly our planetmate relatives do not seek out hardship, either. Also obviously, they do not overreact to it. Our eons of gathering-hunting existence had us feeling the same way, as we can see from their modern counterparts, today.

In Nature, the more bracing aspects of Reality are simply the darker side of a greater "light." That is, all experiences not immediately warranting appreciation are the doorways to greater awareness and bliss, later.

They are not only promises of greater rewards to come, they are the ways all beings are taught and guided by the Divine. Not only are we taught and guided, but through these exigencies of fate and these variables of experience we are reconnected with, reassured in, and remembered of that source and of its very personal and loving nature.

Indeed, whereas life is adventurous, playful, and enjoyable for humans in Nature, as well as planetmates, its inconveniences, discomforts, and hardships are seen as "audiences," if you will, with a higher and more enlightened self. You might say that, in Nature, when we perceived that life was not the exuberant flow it was normally and instead it presented blocks, bumps, and diverting events, that we were aware that it was a time of "promotion" for us … that we were "being kicked upstairs," so to speak. It was through the details of that particular difficulty that we, as it were, were called to the "head office"; that we got to commune with our best friend, the Divine; and that we were instructed for steps to come. We knew that when life slammed into a wall, it was time to "reframe" or "remap." And we had no doubt we would be shown how to do that. We hardly needed to see a psychiatrist.

We Become "Set in Our Ways" Because of "Settling"

To understand how radically different that is from what is considered normal living today, with civilization and after the adoption of sedentary living, it is helpful to do a simple comparison. Most humans in current times — virtually everyone — beginning with adulthood become more unable to change and more inflexible with each succeeding decade of living. For predominantly those days are spent immersed in the routine and the monotonous and are devoid of alive and catalyzing life experience.

This is not merely to say that we are cut off from full immersion in the major events of life — birth, death, life-altering rites-of-passage, ecstatic experiences, and the like — as we often hear from the voices of psychologists and social commentators. Of course that is true, but more importantly, more pervasively and persistently and on a daily basis we are squeezed of aliveness and of the ability to be flexible and to change and grow throughout our days, as once humans could.

In this age, and in pretty much any time after the adoption of "settling," humans are bunkered within a fortress of sedentary living, fixed in place for a lifetime. We spend our days, unadventurous as they are, plodding a well-worn daily path of employment by others for ends not our own; of career set to financial aims, not personally fulfilling or spiritually catalyzing ones; and of enslavement to goals and a model of life and it's trajectory, diluted for applicability to the masses and excised of risky elements deemed threatening to the status quo or to the structures, or the vanities, of civilization.

So it is until at the end of our days, people shake their heads in reference to us; they say we are too "set in our ways" to change; and our family and acquaintances — especially the younger, especially the more sensitive and alive of them — leave off doing anything more than "managing" their relationships with us, not bothering any more to try actual interaction or real relating with us.

We Once Had Truly Wise Elders

Contrasted with that, in our lives in Nature we had a comparatively amazing ability to actually grow and to change throughout our lives … to learn in and through life. This is why the elders of indigenous societies are so much more revered. It is not, like our contemporary curmudgeons are quick to complain, that they have more respectful "young uns" in such societies. Better young folks, such grumps avow, which is brought about through some harsh but necessary enforcement of ethic, which we currently lack.

No, it is that those older folks in native surroundings have such wisdom, such maturity, such personal growth through a lifetime of learning through varied experience that it makes them interesting to be around. That makes the time spent with them to be worth something, in interaction.

It doesn't feel like time wasted tolerating the tired old complaints, repetitive stories of trivial life experiences, and shallow wisdom and useless advice of pompous old people obviously trying to pump up their waning self-esteem as they fade further into the dark.

Yet for most of our existence as humans, as gatherer-hunters, we knew that life and the Divine taught and fulfilled us through its variability: Its changes made us flexible … and wise. And we had no desire for the monotony of a sedentary life. It is only now, in this five minutes before midnight in the twenty-four hour expanse of our "day" of existence that we even took to horticulture, to expanding over flora our controlling obsession. Previous to that, though we began separating from Divinity with the birth pain and prematurity that came with bipedalism — which indeed defines us and started our "day" as humans — we sought our assistance from our Divine surround. We searched for food in our immediate surroundings —

foraging and hunting, as it were — not doubting our success. We reveled in the plenty served up by that Benevolent All.

We Once Had an Edenal Existence

It was our Edenal existence; we lived in Bliss like all other planet-mates. And as soon as events and circumstances changed and became harder, discomforting, we knew it was time to move on.

Indeed the Garden of Eden describes an economic of foraging. Not hunting or anything else. Adam and Eve, metaphorically speaking, were simple foragers and had the same attitude toward Nature and the Other as contemporary gatherers who also see in Nature a Divine provider, one bringing forth food and resources in great abundance.

And, yes, gatherers do see Nature that way.[1] Why we do not know this about them, why we have perennially classified their lives, in the ignominious words of Hobbes, as "solitary, poor, nasty, brutish, and short" — all of which we now know, are wrong — has to do, again, with our bias as coming from civilization.

Certainly it made no sense to the early conquistadors and the Jesuits who accompanied them — our earliest chroniclers of indigenous nations, if not very good anthropologists — to correctly assess their lives. Spreading either civilization or religion, it would not benefit their cause to acknowledge, even if only to themselves, that what they were encountering were humans far more advanced than they. As Marilyn French (1985) says, felicity was no longer a value in patriarchal cultures. That means, it mattered not how much happier one was than another. What mattered was either how much more one had of things, how much more power one had or could wield through instruments, or how much better one's afterlife would be if one would darn well make sure to stay unhappy here while in Form! Consequently, we do not get very accurate, let alone unbiased, accounts of what the most primal of the peoples who were encountered by civilization were like.

We Once Were Both Innocent and Noble

Though the truth could not be completely suppressed. Everywhere they came across indigenous peoples — the New World, Tasmania, Ireland, Australia, the Caribbean — primal people are described as happy, friendly, content. They were seen as innocent, guileless, honest to a fault. Hardly baby-like, they are depicted as hardy. The native Tasmanians went about completely naked at all times, despite the fact that temperatures in that region often went down to forty degrees Fahrenheit in the winter.

This persona of the indigenous is indeed what led Rousseau, during the Renaissance, to his formulations about the "noble savage." And much of what he said was correct. Though being as how what he said did not stroke the ego of civilized folks, any more than my writings do, his ideas were relegated to being just an oddity, much as mine probably will be. Rousseau's ideas are only catalogued historically because it was good to have someone speak up for those "savages" so as to have something for "progressive" philosophers and "modern" social scientists to debunk and to have something to which one could make the opposite point ... on whatever ludicrous or shaky grounds one could find ... all riddled through with bias and self-congratulation and all debunked by the more thoroughgoing research coming out later and now.

In any case, during these Edenal gatherer days, we saw difficulties as signals to switch to a place of greater ease. We advanced to a place, sure enough, where the circumstances of our existence were easy and festive again. Times were good; we played; we loved. In this way, we were confirmed always that any choppiness in life's waters was the prelude to even swifter, smoother sailing beyond it.

Yes, we knew the light that follows the darkness as surely as we knew the dawn follows the night. We knew the beatific face of pain and the wisdom, guidance, instruction, and elevation as a person and spiritual being that it brought with it. We knew that every hardship was another clue on our way home, back to the full embrace of the Divine. It could not be more clear to our earliest humans that difficulties were a preparation, an initiation, from the All That Is, setting the stage for our grand Re-Union, and one by one taking us through the doorways that separated us from It.

We Contracted the Disease of Avoidance

Our veering off from that knowing in the last few minutes of our "day" of existence is astonishing, seen from the outside. For we are like a species that lived one day and in the last few minutes of it contracted a deadly disease. We see this and one might think that it signals our end, our extinction, our death.

But if we take a clue from the Knowledge we once knew, our view brightens. For why would this time of darkness be any different from all the others we experience in life … all of which open to a greater light? From that we can perhaps derive an assumption that our time of darkness and despair now, as our environment collapses around us, is not meant to kill us off but that in time we might even be the better for it.

You might say that life is Bliss, and that our spiritual path to greater awareness of that Bliss is through pain. Hence, it is surprising how in our modern times so many of us think the opposite of that, seeing greater spirituality and awareness to be products of being extremely good in not being aware of the seeming negatives of existence and being excellent at keeping all intense feelings and experiences away from oneself. Of course this is an extension of the thinking that led us every step downward in our descents, our devolution through history.

That philosophy of repression, masked as "positivity," being the outermost extreme of the tsunami of civilization, heaving in the direction of ever more avoidance of pain and discomfort, regardless, is currently leaning toward the point where we can look forward in the future, if there is a future, to blobby fleshy human-like things being hooked up to virtual reality devices continuously, within which they have their existence with others, though they never see them in person. I imagine they will be hooked up tube-like for nourishment. However, in the interim expect to see chip and cookie bag refuse strewn around them.

In that view of spirituality, we take the worst and most cowardly quality of us, the source of all our grief, and we elevate it to a spiritual principle! But this tendency of ours has its roots in that time eons ago when we began our descents.

However, while in Nature, in our primal understandings, we know that darkness precedes every light. That the journey to greater light, or Bliss and Awareness, follows a trail where shade and sunlight alternate; where steps to anything further along require "backward" steps to better make the leap ahead; and where going "up" and going "down" are simply aspects of the same expanding "outward."

Clearly, our early experience with darkness and pain at birth caused us to be continually forgetful of the beatific other side of distress, so we project a greater darkness ahead of us, conducive to dread. Because our beginnings are traumatic and were overwhelming and seemed unending, we are ever fearful that at any moment that can reoccur. We lack the nonchalance and simple, undoubting confidence and security we once had in the unfolding of events and of the rightness, even kindness of their manner of doing that.

But in all these ways, culminating in this sedentary life, we sought to expend greater effort toward fighting off an imagined darkness — which is impossible to exist the way we think it might — rather than to face the experience in front of us in the present, whether enjoyable or unpleasant.

Our Sedentary Life Was a Fortress

So, our sedentary life was the equivalent of building a fortress to keep out those imagined threats. It was not us building up a better life but our retreating into a cave, of sorts, in fleeing from it. It is where, inside, our hurt, angry, defiant self was determined to "make a stand" to fend off the Divine.

As I said earlier, our Ego caused us to mis-perceive everything, including our mistaking aid/assistance for attack. The Divine's attempts to come to our aid and to take us beyond where we are into something always better was seen by us as assaults from Reality Itself. We imagined a devil in the Divine countenance, quite the contrast to our experience as primal humans when we perceived that on the opposite side of every face of fiendishness was a beatific one.

A Fortress That Was Also a Prison

So, foraging fell to hunting. Hunting made murder of our own possible. These abilities to determine death along with its illusion of control of life descended to horticulture. Horticulture led to "domestication" of "animals" (enslaving of planetmates). And agriculture and animal husbandry required a sedentary mode of living. All of these are falls from the Benevolent All. They are stages of our gradual separation from Divine Providence, but more:

The thing to keep in mind about sedentary living is that we became more fixed in place. Even as our falls from grace into physical form involve constraining the free energy of spirit,[2] making it bounded so as to create the physical world, so also, afterward when in Form, we became increasingly more constrained and contained and more fixed in place when we began homesteading.

Over the course of our devolution, boastfully and mistakenly hailed as our *evolution,* we become fixed in place, controlled, increasingly so, until at the end of time, now, the only way to achieve freedom again is to have some huge explosion of release ... like a birth. So we have this drive, apparent, to kill ourselves off in a nuclear catastrophe. Our most secret of all wishes is to blow it all up — look to any modern movie to see how that desire is played upon and profited from, endlessly — so as to finally achieve release from all the ways we have trapped ourselves, imprisoned ourselves, blocked our fullness of life, stopped up our channels for the occasional ecstatic releases provided to all who are in Nature, chopped off our routes to liberation, and constrained our freedom in myriad ways ... all with civilization.

Thus, our radical separation from the All That Is caused us to mistake always the Divine lessons and blessings for evil, for wrongness. In this way we guaranteed our failure in the game of life. And as a species our cumulative failures we piled one upon another as if they were progressive achievements, not the increasing web of disaster that is reaching its culmination today.

Coming Next — Diseases and Discontents

Having done an overview of how sedentary living and civilization led to lives of spiritual and personal desolation, let us now explore ... in this next chapter on "The Eleventh Descent — Sedentary Life ... Sickness and Suffering" ... what effects homesteading had on our physical and emotional well-being and, following that, with "Drudgery and Labor," the degree of felicity and leisure allotted our days.

12

The Eleventh Descent — Sedentary Life ... Sickness and Suffering:

Eden Scorned — With Sedentary Living and Its Restricted Options for Sustenance, We Forego Perfect Assistance for Health of Body and Mind, Which Has Horrible Consequences

Human Instinct, Comfort Feeding, and the Suffering Ape: Why would we "eat the apple" ... that is, go it on our own with agriculture? Why would we defy Divine Providence in making our lots more painful or difficult?

Diet and Disease

The second purpose of Divine Benevolence relates to its quality of being perfect guidance. Divinity's direction fosters our optimal physical and mental health ... in ways we cannot approach using mere reason alone.

Defying Divine Assistance ... Human "Sickness"

Whereas, because of our birth pain and the crazed, backwards thinking resulting from it, we of all Nature insist on controlling our own diet, as well as destinies, in defiance of the Divine and refusing Divine Assistance. Regardless how much more difficult that makes life for us, we as humans do all in our power to avoid the Divine lessons brought to us through the adventures and exigencies of life — which we call hardships and suffering.

One of the purposes of Divine Assistance has to do with its quality of being beneficial in our lives; so resisting it invariably has unfortunate consequences. The other purpose of Divine Providence, which serves all planetmates, has to do with its being perfect providence, in ways that no one can see ahead of time. The Divine provides guidance in life, for physical as well as emotional-spiritual needs, far better than we could ascertain on our own.

In controlling our diet — reducing the bounty of Nature down to the meager few items that could be managed by ourselves — we not only over-rode our actual desires for varied sustenance, thus putting pleasure in this aspect of life at a lower priority to more certainty in it, here as well. Not only did we diminish the ability of our inner proclivities — Divine Assistance — to aid us in being fully alive, not just existing ... in mind and soul, not just body. But we created new physical diseases for ourselves as well.

The Wisdom of the Body

Furthermore, Divine Providence, not only directs and corrects us, so as to make better decisions, but assists us *in spite of ourselves.* This is related to the idea of *instinct,* which exists in all planetmates, though we are ... the vast majority of humans are ... woefully numb to its inner prompts at this point.

No one in Form is or can be aware of the All, so imperfection is inherent in all beings playing this game of physicality. Yet in Nature one can *feel* the directions from the Divine, the All. The wisdom of Nature, and the All That Is beyond that, comes through in the wisdom of the body.[1] Not the wisdom of the body just in healing, but in everything we feel when we are connected with it, in tune with it, *feeling* it, experiencing life in and through it.

In planetmates other than humans, we call this *instinct*. And as we discussed earlier, planetmates are so attuned with it they are able, not just to be perfect in Nature and to provide for themselves in Nature, but to be unbelievably miraculous in Nature. They are able to perform incomprehensibly difficult, "miraculous," actions, which appear to operate outside the laws of physics in ways or through means that science, as yet, has not a clue on ... and unfortunately roundly ignores so as to protect the sanctity of scientists' cherished beliefs, which they call their theories.

However, as early humans, in the very beginning, prior to and while being aquatic apes, and even for the long time afterward when we were gatherers, we were in tune with and guided by our instincts in all the practical matters of life, as well as the spiritual. And in following these Divine directions, without knowing it ahead of time, we discovered they were perfect. We found, unfailingly, that we were guided, in spite of ourselves, to our healthiest states of well-being and felicity of mind as well as our highest realizations and spiritual fulfillments.

We felt what was true in our bones and muscles, so to speak, just like planetmates, to this day, do. But our lives continually affirmed its rightness back to us. With age and in time, we found that in the prods and pulls of the exigencies of events — in these frequent "course corrections" provided through the patterns of what we today mistakenly consider to be random and undesirable events — we were navigated successfully, indeed magnificently, through the shoals and channels of life. We discovered also that in following through on the pushes and pulls of our inner selves we were similarly set in perfect attunement with our lives and purposes and health.

Eating the "Apple"

But in our ever widening separation from Divine Providence through increasing resistance to naturally provided food resources and the establishment of human-created or manipulated food sources with the intent of pleasing the palate and ignorant of nutritional needs, we not only forgo Divine Providence, as provided toward our spiritual evolution and our happiness in life, we defied The All's Assistance regarding our health and well-being.

Rebellious as can be, we laid in our plans for providing for ourselves along the lines of greatest control and least variability of routine. And within the parameters of the hugely diminished possibilities that came of that, we sought to satisfy an increasingly crazed and distorted appetite.

How and why that happened relates to this: In our crazed state of deprivational trauma, rooted in infancy, we developed cravings quite apart from what was actually good for us and which were very often self-destructive. Our ego and control addictions thus bore fruit in myriad other addictions of palate and mind, which over-shouted and thus sounded out our subtler inner directives and instincts.

Indeed, though we sought control above everything else, in doing so we became more out of control. Defying Divine Guidance, we were at the mercy of raw appetites and perverted tastes — the end products of early deprivation and pain, as well as being the ways of fleeing in the present from the tense, fearful, and impatient state that would characterize us normally. We would often choose foods that would please the palate and not necessarily nourish us.

Human Instinct

Let me explain that in more detail: Previously we had a perfect alignment between what was desirable and pleasurable and what was most beneficial to our health. We were, like planetmates, more "instinctual" in our choices. If we want to see how that could possibly be and what that was like, we need only look around us to our planetmate relatives. There is hardly a house-planted citizen who is not aware that when their pet cat is sick, you might find it chewing on grass in a wise and natural remedial way. That is a trite, yet familiar, example. However, a study of planetmates, of "animals," reveals how their diets, along with their entire lives, are guided in ways similar to that ... in ways we can only observe, not fully understand.

Still, that this guidance exists for planetmates — regardless what we call it so as to not have to notice its miraculous quality — is something we cannot doubt. From that, we need to make the connec-

tion to us, keeping in mind that we once were *exactly like that* and so
still have some of that in us. Indeed, when you look at the evolution
of this idea that humans have no instinct, *at all*, you notice it
resonates perfectly with and emanates out of the same medieval
place: That is, the rabid fundamentalism of a Judeo-Christian, pre-
scientific time awash in ideas of humans' unique distinction on Earth
superior to all other life forms and with dominion over all
planetmates. So, again, this idea that we have no instinct is just
another way we, in another pathetic attempt, congratulate ourselves
for our shortcomings and use mythical and phantom resources to
buttress our bravado.

Whereas, in fact, instinct is in us, however repressed. Studies
have been done where human infants were allowed, over a period of
time, to choose from a variety of foods and to thereby determine
their own diet, with no parental, or adult, interference whatsoever.
Contrary to what one would assume — which is that they would
invariably choose sweets or something else more pleasing to the
palate and nutritionless — they actually chose what would be considered, by dieticians, a complete and optimal diet.

We need to remember that our supposed separation from
Nature was an incredibly long and gradual process, occurring over
the course of millions and hundreds of thousands of years. Although
most abruptly since the "agrarian revolution" did we split away, still,
the process was *gradual* of losing sensitivity to those promptings,
those *feelings*, emanating from our bodies. They are still within us, in
fact. And some people, through processes that facilitate reconnection
with the body — notably involving facing and processing the traumas
of birth, womb, and infancy, which are the root causes of the
separation — are able to re-access this bodily wisdom and to feel
these promptings, just like we are all able to do in infancy, as in the
experiment described.[2]

Comfort Food, Comfort Dining to Soothe the Suffering Ape

However, with our increasing split from our own feelings and inner
promptings, our crazed brains sought foods that satisfied imaginary,
not real physical, desires. Suffering as we were, then, because of our

prenatal, perinatal, and infancy traumas more than all other planetmates, we sought to find in food the comfort and satisfaction we could not get in our early life in the fulfillment of those earliest needs and desires. We know that without a doubt even today as adults when we seek out "comfort food" over nutritional food. We know even in using those terms that we are seeking to console, caress, and solace our early deprivations with what we eat in the present.

But the root of that goes back to infancy. In particular, as a baby we needed to be fed and there was a gap between our need and our caregiver's ability or desire to fill it. So we determined we would never again feel a lack such as that. "Never again!" echoes through the collective unconscious of humans regarding that. And we sought increasing control of our food acquisition as adults. In those earliest times, in infancy, along with food, we needed comforting, soothing, care from and bonding with our caregivers as well.

With the gap between that need and our caregiver's ability or desire to fill it, we would seek later as adults to use our times of dining as substitutes for those aches of not getting what we needed in infancy, which we still carry with us, throughout our lives, never fading away. For, indeed, we see that we not only have "comfort foods." But consider all our elaborate rituals of dining and the sociability we design around it: We have "comfort dining" as well. Again, we are the only planetmates who do that; who have manifested those detailed, pervasive behaviors and activities taking up so much of our lives having to do with one and only one thing — equating dining with human connection, feeding with being consoled like one would a baby, eating with love.

The Suffering Ape

Now, why would we be so much more likely than planetmates to have this problem of needing to be comforted with our food? Let us look deeper and review what happened before and around the time of birth. Remember from earlier in the book that roughly half of our development, especially of our brain, in early life was happening outside the womb and at the discretion of our fully growns. Meanwhile all planetmates are experiencing that same relative period of

development under the near perfect guidance and precise orchestration of the Divine through the workings of their species' particular
biology. So they would experience no gap between need and fulfillment during that time.

Frustration at Our Roots, Craving Is Where We Live

However, we, with our unusual beginnings, are the only species that
does as a matter of course have that gap and hence that feeling of
frustration and craving. We would be set up to feel deprived during
the first year of our lives, especially. Then we would feel that lack in
mitigated form throughout our lives. These differences between
other planetmates and us weighed in strongly in our decisions to
break with the Divine around food and our receiving satisfactions of
our needs. And these compulsion-obsessions of ours would be
flavored with our desire for comforting and soothing — of which we
felt a similar lack at that time. Indeed, because of our carried-over
tension and anxiety from those lacks, as adults we truly could use
some comforting and soothing, additionally.

Further, in our former nomadic and foraging ways, we were led,
like our brother-and-sister planetmates, to satisfy our needs through a
wide expanse of varieties of nutritional sources. In those times, for
us, with this incredible variety of food products — the bounty of
magnificent forest and field, shore and stream — we would be drawn
to those that we would need or were better for us, health-wise,
exceedingly more often than those that would not serve us well. We
still had some of that "instinct" other planetmates had; we could still
feel in our bodies the promptings it gave us for what it truly needed.
Our appetites and palate coincided with our actual bodily needs,
indeed with our real spiritual needs as well. We, like all planetmates,
partook of Divine Providence through Nature's ways of sustenance.

We Narrowed Our Options

However, with our change to sedentary ways, we narrowed our range
of foods drastically. In fact, most often we would seek to satisfy ourselves in reliance on as little as one to four foodstuffs. They
themselves would be of the easier and cheaper to produce starchy

quality. We received cheap calories — as many folks do today as evidenced by the obesity epidemics in modern cultures — but poor nutrition. The Paleo diet, rich in variety of plant and protein sources — all kinds of meat, fish, fowl, insects, shellfish, and myriad kinds of vegetation of complex, not simple, carbohydrates — was reduced to and reliant on grain crops — predominantly wheat, rice, and corn. Each of these grains is deficient in protein as well as particular amino acids and vitamins necessary for health. Furthermore, with dependence on one or a couple crops as the mainstay of the diet, compared to gatherer-hunter days, famines and starvation became much more likely — when the weather would turn and cause crops to fail, or insect or plant-disease blights would destroy all for which one had worked so hard.

Therefore, the majority of our diet, post-agrarian, almost always would be variations on one or a handful of ingredients. This is not speculation. This is what we actually know from the early records of our lives in civilizations, living in population centers at that point — towns and cities — and not in Nature.

Which Had Dire Consequences

The producers of these items, the farmers living in the countryside, were a little better off in terms of the variety of their sustenance, but not by much. They could do some gathering in some of the wild still about them; they could have gardens with a certain amount of variety — in no way comparing with what is abundantly produced in the cornucopia everywhere around in Nature. Still, farmers were dependent, primarily, upon those few minimal mainstays of the diet that they would provide to the town and city folk around them.

Of course, we could not hope to satisfy the multitude of bodily needs for vigor and to avoid illness from such a diminished array of sources. We became unhealthy. Our paleontological and historical records, especially the study of skeletal remains, evidence that we lost height from what we were in Nature, as I said, but also that the bodies we created were weaker and more likely to fail. We are able to determine that farmers, compared to the gatherer-hunters before them, had almost a fifty-percent increase in enamel defects, which indicates malnutrition; along with a four hundred percent rise in

anemia; a three hundred percent increase in bone lesions, indicative
of infectious diseases; and far more incidence of degenerative conditions of the spine, probably having to do with an incredible increase
in hard, back-breaking labor come of agriculture.

Mothers would more often die in childbirth and our children
would quite a bit more than previously die then, at birth, or in the
first few years of life.

Most importantly, this abnormal control of our diet in defiance
of Nature's designs for us led to lives of illness unlike any other seen
in Nature. This was totally an offshoot of our ego-designed diet. Our
lives were not just less adventurous, less happy, less satisfying; they
were plagued with fatigue and sickness. Our lifestyles with sedentary
and urban living might have allowed us to fend off big predators
better, but it left the humans of early history wide open to malnutrition and the little predators of germs. Additionally, when we determined our much less diverse and unhealthy diet — because of our
insistence on our own ideas for sustenance over the sustenance
perfectly provided by Nature for our nomadic foraging — we created
diseases of which humans had not suffered previously. With these
new ailments hounding and afflicting us, our life spans diminished.

We Once Lived Longer

Yet before we wrested from Nature control of what we would eat,
and we let our Mother in Nature lead us in our diet, we indeed had
the potential for much longer lives. It is for this reason of greater
physical health that we have myths of very early ancestors living to
ages of hundreds or thousands of years, being immortal, like gods, or
semi-immortal. In these myths our forebears are depicted as vigorous
and tall, long-lived and noble ... and even god-like. Such myths of
noble and long-lived or immortal ancestors are found throughout the
world, from Western civilization with its foundation of myths from
ancient Greece and Rome to the creation stories of the most "primitive" aboriginal societies of modern-day Australia.

Why? For this long-livedness of our earliest ancestors, the ones
living in Nature, generally speaking, was true. This greater stature and
profile of nobility for them is true as well. Relative to today and prior
to our falls into sedentary ways of horticulture and husbandry, we

were healthier, more in tune with principled and invisible ways —
more "spiritual." We were more harmonious with Nature's designs,
and we had longer life spans, which could easily, life circumstances
allowing, exceed considerably over one hundred years. Although, for
reasons that I get into elsewhere, such extreme long-livedness was
not as desirable as one would think.[3]

Summary, Eden Scorned

To sum up, greater health and well-being and longer lives overall …
exceptionally long lives for some … at one time in our history is a
product of the fact that, during that period, humans' diet was still
Divinely provided through Nature. This was occurring in the time
prior to when human Ego wrested this control away and began its
own ideas of sustenance, built around the twisted desires of the
palate — itself made crazed in being swept up in the attempt to
artificially fill emotional shortcomings stemming from humans' half-
born status and resultant crazed, over-amped brain and consciousness.

All the rest of planetmates are not only taught and guided
toward their ultimate life fulfillment by Divine Providence, as was
our early ancestors, but even their physical forms are most perfectly
sustained in heeding Divine Guidance, in following bodily wisdom.
Both our existential and physical needs are most perfectly provided
by following Divine Providence and its promptings — both outside,
in terms of happenstance, but inside, in terms of instinct and feeling.
Regarding the physical: Physical needs for food, water, shelter, and so
on, are more perfectly provided by Nature in ways that are most
beneficial to the health of both our minds and bodies. Providence is
perfect for all planetmates, beyond anything anyone could come up
with themselves. When we separated from the Divine, even defied
Divine Assistance, when we decided it would be us who would control our diet, we dismissed Divinity's perfect banquet … perfect in
the sense of its effects on our primary purposes in being alive, not
just existing.

And with this insistence on our own ideas for provisions over
the sustenance perfectly provided by Nature for our nomadic, foraging forebears, we added the misery of unnecessary physical illnesses

and earlier loss of strength, and even of physical form itself, to our
unhappy lot. So, in our decisions to separate from the Divine
Benevolence and instead to seek to control our own fates we created
unparalleled unhappiness for ourselves, among all Earth beings. You
could say, essentially and metaphorically, we did not just leave Eden
or be evicted from Eden, we *scorned* "Eden."

The Suffering Ape

Added to our new diseases was, of course, the constant ill-at-ease
psychological and emotional states that characterize us because of
our unnatural beginnings, riddled with trauma. Relative to planetmates and especially to humans in Nature, we endured an underlying
and constant uncomfortable, unhappy state, poisoned with our early
birth and deprivational traumas, as they were, and now burdened
with lesser strength, fatigue, and persistent debilities of mind and
body.

Our attempt to better our fates beyond what had been set for us
by Divine Providence — which at one time had us living ebullient
lives within the flows of a Divinely-ordained Nature — was beginning to have disastrous results in terms of our overall well-being
beyond our mere physical survival, therefore. The end result of all
our separations from Nature — from premature births and fetal
malnutrition through to the decisions to separate from Divine Providence and seek to control our fates around issues of food and
location — was the creation of lives of fundamental suffering. In
acting out our fears in a mania of attempting to control everything
around us so as to better our circumstances, we brought ourselves
near unmitigated misery, instead.

The Will to Die

As it happened, then, in our descent into ill health and these new
diseases, we were seeking, however unconsciously, to bring to an end
our denied state of basic unhappiness. That is to say, yes, we wished
to die.

We are the only planetmates who kill ourselves — through suicide, war, and now environmental murder. Think about it. Though

people will jump from bridges and take guns to their heads, have you ever seen a planetmate throw itself from a cliff? How unhappy and brutish can their lots possibly be? Yet we are not uncommonly feeling our lives too unhappy and too much to bear. We "fall on our swords" in all kinds of conscious and unconscious ways.

Yes, we see that death wish exhibited today in its most extreme form with the apocalypse we are bringing upon ourselves. And throughout history we manifested it in our propensity for warring.

Violence and murder were substitute responses to our compression and misery in the womb — replacing the inconvenient and elusive, however natural, actual facing, feeling, and resolution of them in some psycho-emotional way — and these aggressions became act outs of our brutal births as well. However on a collective scale, as war, such bloody ferocity brought with it the welcome relief of a purging of miserable elements through infliction of it on others and, if nothing else, the promise of the end of the nagging unease and ongoing misery of life through death.

A romantic quality became associated with death, especially through battle for the sake of the group or through something else that could be rationalized as a "higher cause" — honor, love, religious ritual involving sacrifice, and the like. However these supposedly noble rationales were mere justifications for wanting simply to end the misery of living and were a mirror image, instead — reversed and perverted — of what is our actual and deeper destiny ... our truer purpose which arises authentically in our more fundamental and natural desire for re-union with the Divine through life experience and immersion in Nature. Thus, we began seeing our reunion with Divinity as being through death, when formerly it had been through life. We went to war, death, and killing instead of to vibrant and meaningful lives, to spirituality, and to ecstatic experiences of compassion and re-union ... of expanded and empathetic oneness with human others, with the planetmates in Nature, and the All.

Having Children Was Substituted for Aliveness

We acted out this will to die, or *Thanatos*, with our children as well. Our offspring became our immortality projects, substituting for authentic life experience. Yes, we did not want to live, and we were no longer noble and fulfilled, so we conceived children in another substitute and perverted attempt to bring that about by having someone do it for us.

Put it this way: We did not want to live, but we did not want to fail in life, either. Or at least we did not want to know we were losers in the life game. So we produced offspring — as many as possible and equal to the degree of our emptiness — to carry forward our failed life designs. We assigned them the task of carrying out and living the lives and experiencing the aliveness we knew we had failed in achieving ourselves. We "pass the buck" down to our children to live the lives we lost when we left Nature. For a part of us knows, however far we are from our lives in Nature, what our true state of life enjoyment and life fulfillment should be.

Then, in a vicious cycle, each generation would pass on these "aliveness projects" to their children at the point in the parents' lives when they were beginning to feel defeated in their own plans of fulfilling the wishes of their own parents. Which is — the application of one's life toward the parents' immortality projects and intentions — sadly, about as far as most humans would dare to dream in our post-sedentary days. We would no longer even approach the idea of the application of one's life to the deepest knowings of oneself ... to the visions and dreams uniquely and authentically one's own. Yet we had, at one time.

All these things combined, we presented ourselves a sorry figure on Nature's stage. For these so called "improvements" to our physical circumstances along with our social and cultural "evolutions" come of controlling and sedentary ways were had at great cost. We were able to greatly expand our numbers, but our flourishing was like that of a cancer upon the Earth, for it did not bring with it increased vitality. We grew, yes, but we did not thrive. All our increases of population numbers were paid for with a diminished and watered-down existence for those brought into this world.

13

The Eleventh Descent — Sedentary Life … Drudgery and Labor:

In Nature We Played and Had Ease; No One's at Fault for Our Falls But We Are Now Responsible … The Fearful Planetmate

"...cursed is the ground for thy sake; in sorrow shalt thou eat of it all the days of thy life: thorns also and thistles shall it bring forth to thee; and thou shalt eat the herb of the field; in the sweat of thy face shalt thou eat bread...." **— Genesis, The Bible**

Drudgery and Labor

For our lives were drudgery and hard work, as well. Adding to all our woes was that of strenuous lives of daily hardship. That was piled upon all the suffering come of poor prenatal and infancy nurturing, impoverished diet, and pitifully shallow life experience. Out of "Eden," now, as even *The Bible* portrays it, "by the sweat of one's brow" … from one translation … we would henceforth sustain our meager physical existence.

Play in Nature

This was in contrast to our lives in Nature, wherein the part of our lives that was spent in sustaining ourselves was contained within our play in wilderness. In Nature, we had little distinction between work and play. As Colin Turnbull (1961) relates, regarding the Mbuti of Africa, the games they play as youngsters are forms of the kinds of activities they will do as adults. They might scurry through or hide in the brush, for fun; climb and swing through trees; throw things, delighting in one's precision of aim; hunt things and dig stuff up for the pleasure and wonder of it; play at striving for accuracy with arrows, using the bow. Then, gradually, more and more of that activity has some benefit to the tribe, to the community.

There is no initiation into adulthood to provide that. No schooling, no college, not even a vision quest or some other ritual of passage — though their spiritual needs are hardly denied because of that. No. Just that fishing done for fun begins to have a use in the sustenance of family and tribe. The same with tracking and hunting. Gathering comes about naturally as aspects of activities done, in the course of play, as young ones.

Till seamlessly, without any notice made to its happening, at some point all that playful activity of the child is serving the tribe and family through the actions of a full grown adult. Though the pleasure, wonder, fun, and felicity involved in these activities does not fade away. Simply that what was done for no purpose begins to gradually have a purpose and to bring with it additional rewards, beyond play and games, of the pleasure of feeling generous and nurturing; of the hearty sense of worth in being valued by the other community members; of the warmth, heartfulness, and joy of belongingness in a tight knit and loving community; of the pride and love and feeling of self-worth of being a nurturing parent and providing for one's family.

The parallel course is taken by the girls and women of the tribe. There is no division between the fun things done, the companions one enjoys, or the things created as frivolity as children with what is done in the warm bosom of the family and tribe as adults, bringing with it, as well, all the rewards of self-worth, valuing by others, joy, felicity, and love.

Indeed, for most of our existence as humans, as primal humans, we saw every day as adventure and fun. Virtually every dawn we greeted with happy anticipation, wondering what unexpected joys it might bring. Yet we descended from those lives of pleasure into an ongoing working nightmare ... dreading the rising of the sun for what efforts it would bring, all of which were pretty much the same as the day before. "Another day, same shit," as that is expressed among working folks today. Especially so was our labor felt that way when what we did was totally at the behest of another, a higher up. I have entire chapters on that alone, coming up. For now I am focusing on the increased labor involved in our days, regardless who reaped the rewards.

In any case and all in all, in seeking to avoid death at any and all costs to present happiness, we created lives in which it was clear we actually wished for death ... where it was observably evident we were seeking it out. We not only killed each other, we not only killed planetmates of all kinds, it was supremely evident we wanted to die. So we extended our lives in all these unnatural ways, at the expense of actually wanting to live that existence.

The Fearful Planetmate

Such it is that we introduced tragedy to Nature. We became the suffering planetmate. We elevated Nature's game of life and death on high to where our numbers would increase wildly and uncontrollably, then be beaten back in mass outbreaks of disease, wars, or natural calamities — which our ever more concentrated population centers made far more severe than they had to be or would have been for us previously. We were the planetmate — the only one of over nine billion species — to introduce mass dying, warring, and killing, to Earthly existence.

Regardless, in our sedentary living; our homesteading; our creation of ever larger residences and more fortified perimeters for our properties, our towns, then our cities; we did not acknowledge this horrible descent. Why would we? For all we did and all we thought was geared to bucking up our pathetic esteem about ourselves. Whereas essentially we were huddling together like frightened children, bowing down to the products of our hands, and cowering before Nature and its ways. Furthermore, our fear had us invent phantom helpers — gods, deities — that were equal, in stature, to our pain ... to our fear ... to our ever-arising and ever-beaten-down terror.

Obviously all this reduction to the cowardly, the childish, and the infantile, had its roots in our deprivational trauma. They were all a manifestation of a denial of the way events had actually occurred to us in infancy. For they held out the promise that such satisfaction as was craved for as an infant would someday come for us as adults, somehow through all our efforts and our lives intensely focused on work. Though of course it never did. And inasmuch as we had cut off all our connection to an existence in Nature where it could, to some extent, be had, it never would or could it, either.

Our Pitiful Pleas — Religion and Capricious Gods

As for our gods and supernatural helpers? These concoctions revealed their true origins through the fact they were often cruel and contrary in their beneficence, just as our caregivers had been experienced as being. Thus our images of God are deformed. And true and real Beneficence is filtered through our fear and early pain.

Remember that all other planetmates experience a perfect nurturing in their beginnings, under the Divine orchestration of biological events, creating a perfect trust in Reality as benevolent, perfect, and generous. Whereas our experience of a variable quality of nurturing in our early infancies — always less than perfect and sometimes harsh and cruel — created for us a sense of mistrust toward existence and its designs. This inner turmoil resulted — throughout our post-agrarian history — in our projecting that struggle, that pathetic crying out for, and that desperate and pitiful plea, upon the screen of heaven and Nature.

In doing so, upon those surfaces we painted the images of our imperfect and hurtful early caregivers in the form of ambivalent gods, insensitive and wrathful deities, and perverse and contrary Nature. And the measure of our submission to these forces was equal to the measure of our suffering and pain. Feeling beaten down by the forces outside ourselves, from birth, had us begging, pitifully, from such forces throughout our lives. We sacrificed our nobility of soul upon the altars of unappreciative and vain, capricious and punishing gods … which were reflections of our caretakers in the distant past.

There Was No "Original Sin"

Our unhappy lots were not of our own choosing, it is true. We were a happenstance of Nature. We are an unexpected and singular outgrowth from a series of climatic events occurring millions of years ago, long before the apocalypse of today to which it all led. We did the best we could in surviving, by going to and into water, by standing upright to forage in it. All of our changes in morphology and anatomy were adaptations to these simple changes that were required of us by alterations in our environment about which we had no say at all. There was no ethical failing involved in any of this. The only snake persuading us was our nagging birth pain and prenatal traumas, which snakes do indeed symbolize, but which we did not have any choice in. In fact, from a moral perspective, we are the victims in this sequence of events. There was no "sin" or moral fall that preceded all this or precipitated such a harsh rejoinder as will be this response from Nature in the upcoming years.

But It Is Our Responsibility Now

Our only failing will be if we do not respond and we bring about that which we have for long desired in our deepest parts. It will be a monumental moral travesty — with horrific repercussions not just on ourselves but on all the innocents in Nature as well as our own children — if we succumb to those parts of us involving our death wish, our Thanatos, which we humans uniquely have and all the rest of the world, arising and playing under the designs of Eros, do not. We wish to die to end our laborious lives and its suffering. For the sake of the innocents, we cannot allow that.

So, while none of this was our fault, it becomes our responsibility. Looking at the entire arc of it, we might deduce that our unique and singular trajectory, bringing about all it did of bad and evil as well as good and miraculous, was a part that Nature needed to have played for some grander design of It and the Divine. Only time will tell. And books like these will be necessary for us to understand our current circumstances in order to correctly respond to them.

Human Vanity

But back then, once we separated from Nature, our crazed brains could not discern easily the Benevolent Designs the way our planetmate relatives could. We were overstressed and ever pushing the helpful prods of still remaining instinct below us. As we put up our nose at "messy" Nature, at "unseemly" wilderness, and ... most unfortunate of all ... at "inappropriate" emotion and "inconvenient" bodily feeling.

Indeed, though we acted for all the world as if we were in control and dominant, unperturbed and unaffected, we actually became increasingly enslaved to our unnatural drives and passions — the perverted, corrupted outgrowths of those unsatisfied early needs and the trauma in which they arose. Yet we took such shortcomings and the corrupted drives and passions come of them and the outgrowths of that as well and we spun them as accomplishments. We awarded ourselves, out of all Nature, with "free will," though we were about as free as addicts are in choosing their fix. We lost the sense of having the potential for unlimited variety of experiences of life, as presented through the exigencies of the Divine, which actually gives one the sense of being free. We were sick and emotionally-intellectually deficient compared to the rest of Nature.

Versus the Angels in Nature

We imagined the actual ideal satisfaction of our needs — their completion, the way they should have been satisfied — and symbolized that as the existence of angels and deities in the skies, influencing events here on Earth to aid us. We ever failed to notice that actual angels were directly before us, in the Nature we had left behind. In all the Flora and Fauna kingdom that ever helped, succored, nurtured, and pleased us in all the ways we needed to have as infants. Though we had waged continuous war on planetmates, they reacted in accordance with the Divine Benevolence of which they were manifestations. Indeed our planetmates were the unheralded angels in Nature. They came to us, against their better interests and often at the cost of their lives, and sought to assist and comfort us.

Summary — A Comparison Around Fear and Security

All in all, with so-called cultural "evolution" we have increasing control of Nature and are further split from it with each descent. So less-technological, more natural agrarian cultures would be less split from Nature, that is true. They would have concepts of relation to Nature more symbiotic, however devolved they might still be from what we were in Nature as gatherers. Thus matriarchal religions and harvest and mother goddesses of our Neolithic times were a stage between our current all-out break with Nature and the one of immersion in Nature of our gatherer-hunter days. We see that agricultural societies might revere Nature and show a strong connection to it, however they show a fear of it as well. Efforts to propitiate Nature abound, for crop health and abundant harvests depend on weather and other uncontrollable variables.

However, this fear of Nature was virtually nonexistent in humans during our earliest days as nomadic gatherers. But more, for they felt a security about their lives we cannot know today. Just considering the physical needs of survival, simple gatherer-hunters feel, for the most part, more secure than we do in the efforts of survival. This is evidenced in the way they feel and act toward material possessions, which has qualities of their being unattached to them, unpossessive of them. It takes civilization for humans to become gollums, clutching to their bosoms as their "precious" their personal items.

Quite different were we as gatherer-hunters. In comparing their need for foodstuffs with our struggle for money to survive, from their gatherer-hunter counterparts in modern times we conclude, as I have been stressing, they feel more secure and more trusting of Nature to provide their sustenance. However, anthropologists observe they feel equally unstressed about acquiring material items.

They have the same surety as they feel about acquiring food about their ability to bring to themselves requirements of living such as shelter, tools, and personal items. They feel they also will be provided freely by Nature. Regarding the physical resources required for living, they are relatively affluent and have much more ease of mind about acquiring them.

Certainly they receive no wages; they have no Social Security. But they hardly need them. Whereas we cannot go to Walmart and pick up a basketball or kitchen knife and walk out with it, they enjoy a situation analogous to that. Despite how much we tout our affluence and superiority (again!) over primal ways of life, the nomadic gatherer-hunters in our times show a disregard for and a lack of fixation on possessions we would find appalling.

The Wisdom of Ease

It is said they throw their possessions around carelessly and care little for maintaining them. Anthropologists, who almost universally come from the materialist cultures of today, consider them sloppy, perhaps foolish and reckless in their refusal to spend their time organizing, storing, and stacking their things. Which, incidentally, allows them much more time to attend to the "softer" things of life — family, spiritual relation to Nature, fun, dancing, amorous relationships, singing, ritual, trance and shamanistic work, ecstatic, entheogenic experience, and so on.

Nevertheless, what we found out is that this "sloppiness" is not actually foolish, however different it is from the way we do things. No. It was understood, eventually by Western observers, to actually make sense, in that whatever one had would easily enough be able to be replaced, down the road — with no outlay of money or resources and with minimal effort. Thus, it would be the equivalent of being able to go into a Walmart and walk away with whatever one wanted.

So it was eminently logical to not put so much time and effort into caring for one's possessions, when replacing those possessions was possible with *less* time and effort expended. Furthermore, there is the fact that whatever one owned would need to be carried from place to place, if one were nomadic, as they were. Again, it is more sensible to spend one's time doing more enjoyable things rather than obsessing about one's possessions, when if one were to lose or have something broken, it at least would not have to be carried to the next place. And, as I've said, where it could rather easily be replaced from "Nature's Walmart."

One might also speculate there is much less advantage to caring so much about the stacking and organizing of things — or for that matter, attending to the improvement of one's surroundings — when it is always only temporary. When it is going to be broken down or left behind in the foreseeable future, what is the value in spending much effort or time in nesting? Why is it not a waste of time in having and caring for things or adorning one's environment?

Which is not to say that gatherers are not artistic and creative. Indeed they are. More so are they, certainly, than humans who would outfit and fill up their homes, but let Ikea be the designer. However, what they expended their ever burgeoning creativity on — and yes it was much more of a pressing desire and impulse for them to create than it is for us — were items that could be moved, taken with one as one moves from place to place. That of course meant there was going to be much less that they would own, in that whatever one wished to hang onto would have to be carried.

Sedentary Living and Storing

That brings up the connection between sedentary living and storing. It is storage and accumulation to which we now turn. The next descent of man, reaching a peak in modern times with rapacious greed and the piling up of wealth at the expense of actual life experience, was accumulation ... over-accumulation, actually, if compared to gatherer-hunters, our early humans. Though what our early homesteaders gathered and stored would seem far less than what we consider a lot today, still it was considerably more than what could be owned by our nomadic forebears, who preceded them.

That ability to own more than what could be carried would make all the difference. For it came with a corollary that some would be able to own more than others. Storage would allow us to own things in unrestrained amounts, whereas for nomads it was severely restricted to what was moveable.

Let us take a look, now, at what happened and what it meant for us when humans ceased their wandering ways, built themselves permanent homes, and began filling their "garages" and "pantries" to bursting.

14

The Twelfth Descent — Accumulation:

The "Domestication" of Humans — The Ability to Store Things Changes Everything for Prehistoric Humans … But Not in the Way We Thought It Did — Eden Stormed … The Rich Begin Calling the Tune

"This tragic, life-diminishing spinoff of our ability to gather and accumulate excessive 'things' was a desire to control even those of our own species: Our fellow humans became the last targets of our mania for control."

The Creation of Greed

Beginning approximately ten thousand years ago — earlier in some places, later in others and in some rare and fortunate places not happening even up till modern times — the rich began calling the tune. This chapter lays out the beginnings of oppression and greed, which have taken on a heady importance in the Twenty-First Century as a small cadre of the very, very well-to-do are engaged in consolidating the entire wealth of the world under their orchestrations.

It is nothing less than astonishing to see the outlines of current events in the patterns of social and economic interaction that began in prehistory, after the adoption of farming and the end of the nomadic lifestyle. Witness, for example the worldwide Occupy events calling for economic justice, beginning in 2011, and the phenomenal outpouring of support for Bernie Sanders, a socialist, in America in 2016, calling for the same and much more. In truth, the roots of what we see in the daily newspapers — as well as what we observe in political developments in the capitals of nations, in mass movements and demonstrations of people on the streets of the major cities of the world, and in the financial reports on television — extend deep into our history of the long long ago when sedentary ways led to the ability to gather and accumulate more, since owning more did not require carrying more.

Accumulating Things

Our adoption of a non-nomadic lifestyle had — in addition to the nefarious effects from our breaking with Divine Providence — other pernicious consequences. When we became sedentary — staying in one place and growing our food, eventually corralling other planet-mates, and so on — we were able, for the first time in our long evolutionary history, to accumulate.

So, the other dire consequence of our adoption of sedentary, non-nomadic life ways was the ability to gather and store more "things" — not just food but all kinds of "things" — for we did not have to carry what we owned, like a nomad would. When we ceased wandering and set up more permanent abodes, we enabled the gathering and storage of much more than we could possibly need. However, storage of owned things created something relatively new — greed ... an "unplanetmate-like" greed.

The Invention of Possession

Let's back up. Accumulation was intertwined with a whole new kind of addictive feeling for us, which is a concomitant of our controlling mania — a sense of ownership. For the first time, we were really and truly able to *possess* ... to *own*.

Keep in mind that humans in Nature had no need, let alone desire, to *own* anything. Our environments — forest and seashore, field and streamside — were to us like vast kindly libraries from which one could borrow endlessly and return for more. Our natural surroundings were like storehouses or warehouses — repositories of all one's needs. One could attain, with little effort, all one needed and often most of what one wished, if not immediately, then eventually. And as easily as it was attained, it was discarded. All things obtained were got from the All and returned to the All; they felt not owned, but more like borrowed.

There was an unlimited supply of everything ... not in every moment, of course. But given time, or potentially, it would sooner or later be provided by Nature. All that was required was that one get it, that one accept the gift. It did not have to be "worked" for, planned for, traded for, saved up for ... or mortgaged for ... or indebted, sometimes for life, for ... or begged for from intimidating bankers and financial institutions with tendencies to impose ritual processes involving humiliation prior to complying. By contrast, in Nature, all needs were felt to be satisfied in the normal "play" of life. And they were acquired through means that left one feeling pride in one's abilities and a sense of belonging in the world; unlike today where one ends up feeling diminished, stressed, alienated and small in relation to the world, worn down, and/or humiliated.

Further, beyond just food there was no end of any other resource. Tools were fashioned, used, then discarded. They could always be made again. Indeed, why go through the work of carrying them from camp to camp if new ones could be easily made with much less effort than all the carrying would involve? The same was true of shelters. Easily wrought from the surrounding offerings of Nature, they were readily left behind when time to move on. As well, being able to do these things brought with it a sense of competence and surety in one's abilities to function in the world, providing a foundation of self-confidence on which to build the rest of one's life and from which to come in pursuing the more important or higher possibilities of living. This feeling of ease of attainment of anything desired affected our relationship to all aspects of our lives ... to all aspects of our environment ... and to each other.

By contrast, I have described in detail how our fear-and-controlling mania led us eventually to seek control of flora and fauna planetmates. Keep in mind that controlling is best attained by ownership. In order to control something, one had best have power over it. And this curious idea of ownership and possession were the elements involved in having supreme power over something — giving one the ability, which later became a "right," to use and abuse at one's whim.

Essentially, in our behaviors of ownership — power over, possession — we took an element of life that all planetmates engage in to only a small extent and blew it up and stretched it out, umbrella-like, to cover all aspects of our experience of life.

Let me explain. First, all planetmates have a semblance of ownership: Flora "possess" the nutrients and water they take in from the soil ... they "own" them. Fauna planetmates "own" the vegetation they eat, at the very moment of consuming it. The prey that the carnivore planetmates devour are "owned" at the minute they are caught. But keep in mind that, once acquired, these items spend little time in such a state of possession before they are consumed and that what remains is discarded. There is freedom therein; the time of owning is surrounded by the greater majority of time when one is completely unburdened.

Similarly, what one has taken in is returned to Nature in an altered form, after bodies have removed the part to be used for fuel. So, this engagement with the environment is more like borrowing than actually possessing or owning. The biological rhythm, the pulse of life — rooted in our very respiration, our inhaling and exhaling — is all about this taking in and then giving out. There is a balance between the individual and the Other (the outside). One is not depleted at the expense of the other. One is not dominant over or more important than the other. Receiving, giving ... birth, death ... consuming, defecating ... loving, being loved ... acting, resting ... breathing in, breathing out ... ebbing, flowing ... waxing, waning ...

day, night … they are all aspects of the eternal cycle of things that encompasses all Reality.

This lack of ownership of anything and mere borrowing within the rhythms of greater wholes is true of all planetmates, with a few rare exceptions. And in no instance does any planetmate seek the possession or ownership of anything for long. Even property. For while many planetmates will seek to have control of a specific territory, and will even mark it and defend it, that is no different from us in our early gathering lives having domains of influence for each different group of us. But these domains were not possessed or owned; no permanent attachment to them was achieved or, even, wanted.

For, to possess involves responsibility in maintaining and defending the thing possessed. It is a *burden* to own; not just in that one will have to bear or carry it, but also that one will have to bear responsibility for it. Whereas, none of our foraging forebears wanted to enslave themselves to any possessions of land. For such ownership could only happen at the cost of forgoing the enjoyment and experience of ever more new and varied lands, "down the road," so to speak.

Correspondingly, while there is occasional conflict among planetmates over territories, as there was for our foraging bands of forebears, these conflicts are and were easily resolved and easily walked away from. For with endless supplies of everything, including land, the costs of losing life or incurring injury over defense of anything are simply not worth the prize. Further, one is not "owned by" or "identified with" any particular possessions or ownership. Our early forebears essentially "owned everything" and yet "owned nothing." Owning everything meant there was always more of whatever. And owning nothing meant that one's ego or identity or status or stature was not involved in the possession or ownership of anything in particular. Hence, in either case, one could move to avoid conflict and, having unlimited choice, simply make other choices in those instances where one's desires bumped up against any other one's.

And the Worship of Things

However, by growing our food and possessing planetmates for our use in a fixed place with a permanent domicile, we were able to store food, but other kinds of "things" as well. This was because when we were nomadic we, naturally, had to carry everything we wanted to "own"; whereas when we "nested" we not only did not have to carry possessions but we were able to create and build storage areas to protect our accumulations. In this way we gathered and stored more than we could ever possibly need. The ability to possess more and store it led to the desire to possess exceedingly, for some of us. There were reasons why humans would be pushed toward greed, this way, other than just that humans are that way by nature. For we are not, by nature, greedy, as I have been describing.

Let us look more deeply into this.

With the beginnings of the concept of possession — of little importance prior to sedentary lifeways — Eden became owned, but more: With the focus on individual ownership, we began ourselves being enslaved by what we possessed. With storing — the ability to gather and place things together, that were thus "possessed," for use at a later time — we fully manifested the already burgeoning addiction we were having for things.

It is hard to see such an addiction, today, for it is the norm. However, in our devolution this obsession with possessions and this enslavement by the very things we owned was quite a contrast to the lives of full experience we once had ... and enjoyed. For with this dis-ease, we made objects the center of our existence; we lived our lives around them. Preservation of human life became secondary to the preservation of things. Things became more important, far more important, than people — their lives or their feelings.

The Requirement of Defense of Stores

But it did not end there. For once stored and built up, such "wealth" would attract others and so require defending in a manner much more determined than any previous defending of territories for foraging rights and the like, because these stores were not easily replaceable. They represented huge investments of time and resources to build them up, contain them, defend them. They could hardly be stumbled upon "down the road." Besides, *sedentary* implies one does not have access to resources potentially all and everywhere but only in one's immediate and "owned" vicinity. So there being no journey, there is no "down the road" for sedentary folks.

Think how that might have increased violence and aggression between humans. Sure enough, with sedentary living we begin having "security needs" — as it is said today. Folks having much more of their time and efforts wrapped up in things and their ownership, they would be willing to fight and die for them, unlike before. We see the roots of war and conquest here, with these simple beginnings in the ownership and defense of stores.

And with storage, then accumulation, then defense, there followed another development. These things led to another cancerous outgrowth in our increasing addiction to controlling our experiences as opposed to discovering the adventure that Divinity would have for our development and furthering on the path back to unity with The All.

Dominating Others

Remember, in Nature it was a burden to possess, both literally and figuratively. This applied to territories, to food … but, keep in mind, also to others of us. It was of no more use to seek to "own" or "possess" another person than it was to do the same for territory or anything else. For it would bring with it an unwanted responsibility and limitation of life experience at the cost of a more precious freedom and the normal expanded possibilities of living. It made no sense for early human men to dominate women, for example. Everyone having self-determination meant everyone had self-responsibility and took care of themselves, primarily. Again, to own anyone or have power over anyone is a lot of extra work, taking away from the pleasurable experience of the variety of life lived unrestrainedly. Possession, purely and simply, is hardly worth the effort in a world of limitless supply.

However, with sedentary living all that changed. We became something different from anything we had ever known.

Controlling Others

This tragic, life-diminishing spinoff of our ability to gather and accumulate excessive "things" was a desire to control even those of our own species: Our fellow humans became the ultimate targets of our mania for control. It was added to our desires to control our experiences, the timing of events, our sustenance and food sources ... which involved controlling our planetmates of the Flora and Fauna Kingdoms of Consciousness ... our lifestyles, that is to say, becoming sedentary, and so on.

So accumulating things had effects on our unplanetmate-like greed and our unplanetmate-like desire to control, now — sadly, even this — others of our own species.

The Devitalization of All Other

Our Ego was consolidating its position as the ruler of all and the only real thing in existence. We had removed the life essence from all of Reality, its soul; we saw it all as being inanimate and thus diminished, usable for any ends to satisfy the Ego. At this point, we became heady with possessing things, seeing them as defenses against feelings of deprivation ... again. And fearfully focused on relief from feelings of want, our controlling mania sought the manipulation of ever more in our environment — now, even this, our fellow humans in our communities.

We needed to see them as less animate to do this, so we did. We built up, more and more, this idea that we were the reason for Existence and that even our human planetmates were mere props for our existence ... to be used however we would wish.

The stage was set for the valuing of some lives over other lives, for the dramas of domination and submission, for the oppression of a subservient class by a dominating class, for the division of labor in a way that higher ups would decide what those lower in the ranks would do in ways both subtle and brutal, and thus for this new thing of hierarchy in human societies. Remember that foraging-hunting nomadic groups were relatively egalitarian. With civilization, that ends; autocracy and royal rule become the norm. It is to that, this next, this thirteenth descent, hierarchy, to which we now turn.

15

The Thirteenth Descent — Hierarchy:

The Beginning of Oppression, Nascent Culture War, Class War … Ten Millennia Ago … and Human's Burgeoning Sycophancy

"The stage was set for Big Accumulators, who had accepted a reduced spiritual and personal richness for a richness of 'things,' to overpower and silence the voices of those who refused such a diminished richness of experience and narrowing of their personality."

"We must not forget, however, that in the primal family only the head of it enjoyed this instinctual freedom; the rest lived in slavish oppression." — Sigmund Freud, **Civilization and Its Discontents**

The Beginning of Oppression, Hierarchy

So, our "unplanetmate-like" desire for more control we extended eventually beyond the range of the planetmates of Nature to even those of our own species. Accumulating things created a means, for the first time, by which to really do that. Hence the ability to store, in excess, led to controlling others.

Big Accumulators

Those humans who gathered more or accumulated more, by whatever means — let us call them *Big Accumulators* — could have more influence over those who gathered and piled up less; let us call them the *Small Accumulators*. Big Accumulators had more "say" and sway over Small Accumulators in that they represented the security humans lost when they left Nature.

Previously, one's ultimate dependence was upon Nature, who was bounteous and generous. With sedentary living, lives were more routine and certain, but liable to disaster and insecurity at the same time in that they leaned heavily on a few major pillars of support, as I have laid out, which, when threatened, left them helpless. Having left Mother Nature, the wealth of the Father Patriarch — that is to say, the Big Accumulator — became appealing, to look to as a potential source of support. They appeared "strong" — these "strong men" of early history — in relation to all other people and most of all when was one "weakest." Indeed, it is in this time that the ideas of strong and weak began being so important to humans. By that I mean, when we left Nature, for the first time we truly felt weak and dependent.

In due time, however, the mere influence of Big Accumulators led to much more, pushed by the daemon of fear and its companion, the fever of power. Big Accumulators sought more than influence over Small Accumulators; they went after getting control. And in this they succeeded. They were able to garner control of the actions of Small Accumulators through their ability to use their excess possessions to gift or reward those whose actions would conform to what they wanted. They used their wealth to benefit those, and only those, whose behavior fit with their ends.

So, our unplanetmate-like desire to control created an unplanetmate-like greed, sadly, for we saw that gathering more enabled us to control the actions of those of us who gathered less. Inevitably, humans discerned that by being greedy and selfish, by gathering and storing excessively — by becoming Big Accumulators — they could achieve the domination they had over the lives of the rest of Nature, through farming and corralling, now also over the lives of their fellow humans who were Small Accumulators.

Small Accumulators

Small Accumulators were not necessarily less able to gather more. Keep in mind that gathering more required an obsession and preoccupation with that; thus it required an unremitting focus on what are now called *greed, manipulation,* and *power.* So the more congenial and less crazed and obsessed of us would not wish this; especially as it required the relinquishing of the other pursuits of life not involving accumulation — for example, the relational, emotional, spiritual, and creative pursuits.

Many — who would choose to accumulate only that which was needed to sustain life and little more, so that time would be available for more fulfilling pursuits — thought the narrowing of focus to simply possessing more a sad diminishment of experience, which it was.

We see the difference between the values of the Big Accumulator and the Small Accumulator today expressed in the parable of the grasshopper and the ant. This is one of Aesop's Fables, and it, along with many versions of it, have been told as part of children's socialization for hundreds of years. And in the way that parable is told, we can see whose values won out in history and who became dominant so their version alone would be told. If you remember, in "The Ant and the Grasshopper," the ant plods slowly but steadily toward its goal of accumulation, "storing" up, as it were, for the future. This is the way of the dull but dedicated Big Accumulator, supposedly. This is how you become rich ... or at least secure, content, and happy.

The grasshopper does not store and plan for the future and is considered lazy, whiling away its time in supposedly "useless" pursuits. This is the more alive, fun, happy, and aware Small Accumulator, albeit slandered. You can imagine the grasshopper chewing a bit of grass and lounging; looking off and "daydreaming" in contemplating the clouds, sun, and pleasant weather; playing a fiddle. Remember, this is more like the way we were for the ninety-five percent of the time that we were humans, having plenty of leisure time for pleasurable and growthful pursuits. However, as every school child is frightened into learning, such non-work-like pursuits lead to disaster when the future comes.

Conforming Underlings

In any case, in our history this choice by the Small Accumulators to use some of one's time in the pursuit of a fulfilling life, as opposed to just the pursuit of piles of "things," also left them vulnerable to the Big Accumulators who could tempt and persuade the Small Accumulators to act in concert with them through promises of gifts and rewards, taken from their stores of excessive accumulation. When they succeeded, Small Accumulators became what we might call *Conforming Underlings*, ready, if not eager, to conform to the wishes of those who "buttered their bread," so to speak. The rich were calling the tune and the Conforming Underlings were the ones taking up the dance. I will say, in a little, what the other Small Accumulators did in response.

The stage was set for Big Accumulators, who had accepted a reduced spiritual and personal richness for a richness of "things," to overpower and silence the voices of those who refused such a diminished richness of experience and narrowing of their personality — a narrowing of personality that left out the grandeur of existence more for them than for any other "thing" of Consciousness … living or "nonliving" … on this planet.

The Controller-Conformer Alliance Versus Authentic Humans

Making matters worse, both conforming behavior and controlling behavior had survival advantages over more natural and authentic behaviors. For Big Accumulators and their conforming allies could combine their power to harness even more excessive resources. Driven by unreal fears of uncertainty and death from deprivation, Controllers went even further to garner power and resources through gobbling up all they could and leaving others in states of severe neglect. Then surrounded by people in severe deprivation, they could call any tune they wished, for those in states of want would be more amenable to themselves becoming Conforming Underlings and to serving the Big Accumulators ends, thus further increasing their power and excessive accumulation.

Not only did Big Accumulators and their allied Conforming Underlings have the benefit of access to more of the resources of physical survival; but Big Accumulators, out of that same uncertainty and fear rooted in early birth trauma, would be pushed to deprive others in their sphere of influence of these survival resources.

Big Accumulators *could* do this because they derived excessive strength and power combining their own power with the power of their Conforming Underlings.

Big Accumulators *would* do this because their crazed brains saw no end to their fear of deprivation, got no relief from their blown-up fear of uncertainty, hardship, pain, and struggle; and so saw no end to their desire to drive others into states of deprivation that would make them more amenable to control and to also becoming Conforming Underlings, doing their bidding and serving the ends, not of themselves, but of their high-accumulating overlords.

Hierarchy

Three groups emerged — *Controllers*, who were the Big Accumulators; *Conforming Underlings*, who were the Small Accumulators who succumbed to being wannabe Controllers; and the *Authentics*, who were the Small Accumulators by choice, the keepers of the old ways. And the Controller-Conformer Alliance everywhere put continual pressure on the authentic Small Accumulators whenever and wherever they were.

This was the beginnings of class divisions and the hierarchy in society come of that. All hierarchy in all "civilized" societies evolved from these simple societal distinctions regarding life goals and life designs arising in response to this new phenomenon of excessive storage, which today we call *wealth*.

Nascent Culture War, Class War ... Ten Millennia Ago

These class distinctions around riches divided people, but it did not benefit the Controllers for it to be seen as it was. As it was, as a simple disparity in wealth, it could lead to a Conformer-Authentic Alliance arrayed against the Controllers. So it was everywhere disguised. This potential class war was recapitulated as cultural divisions, instead. Potential class war divisions were portrayed always as actual, and fostered, elements of culture war.[1]

Culture War Is Class War Disguised

That is to say, the obvious disparities in wealth between the two sectors of society were shrouded in bogus cultural differences which the Controllers could assert was the actual reason for the division. Beyond that, they could use those disparities to get Conforming Underling support for their ends by hiding their designs behind cultural differences. Then they could use those cultural differences to legitimize the construction of moral and legal distinctions that would further add to their power in institutionally establishing and furthering their agendas. They would create morality and laws along ends to suit themselves. These latter aspects I will unveil and deal with in due course.

For now, though, let me give an at-hand example of the way this concealing of class divisions behind fostered and bogus cultural differences was done. In the story above about the ant and the grasshopper, you probably did not think twice about my description of it, even though you might have questioned my bias. But remember in the story I said the ant was a representative of the Big Accumulator? I bet you did not question that. It is what we have always been told: That is, that those who work hardest get the rewards. Ergo, those who are rich are folks who have worked hard to become that way.

Even those who have criticized the story over the centuries have not questioned that the ant represents a Big Accumulator. During the winter, with the ant all fed and comfortable in his big house, the grasshopper comes to beg a little help. The grasshopper is starving, you see. The ant refuses and "gifts" the grasshopper instead with a lecture about morality and how he should have spent his time working hard during the summer, like the ant did. The criticism of the story in the past has been around the ideas of charity and selfishness ... basically saying that the ant should have some mercy and charity in his heart, regardless.

Yet that the ant is a rich person who worked hard for his comfortable circumstances is not addressed. Oh, we see that idea of the hard-working Big Accumulator everywhere portrayed, not just in this one story. However, if it is so true why does it have to be propagandized so much? You see, it is because it is not true that it needs to be instilled in our children to pave their highway to becoming Conforming Underlings. The story is part of the shroud of deceit — one involving so much more of culture and society than merely that story — that Big Accumulators needed to erect to block out their ends. To control the minds of their underlings, Big Accumulators in every "civilized" world, through subtle use of their power, determine the form of its stories — what will be told ... what will be promoted ... what will be celebrated.

So what we would not be allowed to notice is that, in fact, the ant is not the Big Accumulator at all. Indeed, it is unlikely the ant represents much of a true version of a reality in any way. Big Accumulators usually do not get where they are through working hard and storing up. What is stored, for Big Accumulators, usually has its genesis in what one was given, most often through inheriting it or in what one has stolen. And hardworking Small Accumulators who become Conforming Underlings usually do not become Big Accumulators, however great their efforts and sweat. And they do work hard, for that is demanded of them.

Here is the crucial thing: The story of the ant and the grasshopper represents what Big Accumulators *want Small Accumulators to believe!* Why? To cover up the way things actually work. Let's look at the story again: The story is actually the model for the Conforming Underling for how to behave in life for the benefit of the Big Accumulator. It is the promise given Small Accumulators to persuade and tempt them to become Conforming Underlings. It is typical of propaganda put out by Big Accumulators everywhere to take the focus off the fact they actually did not acquire their wealth that way.

Yet it portrays the values that the Big Accumulators — the wealthy and rich everywhere — want ordinary folks to abide by and believe.

Conformer — "Tea Party" — Psychology: Why Underlings Hate Authentics, Assist the Wealthy

Those who are mesmerized into compliance with these beliefs will adhere to them religiously, too ... which is a further advantage for Controllers. For having paid so dearly in allegiance to these concoctions through sweat and lost happiness in life, Conforming Underlings are immensely invested in their being true. Beyond even that, Conforming Underlings will aid the Controllers in the promulgation of these beliefs because of that huge investment of life spent and wasted in hypnotic allegiance to them.

Why People Cuddle with Their Chains

For, as in so many areas — as shortly in this book we will see in the way we raise and treat our children — those who have been oppressed or in any way damaged demand that oppression and harm of all around them so as to hide their own misfortune from themselves. They will fight with all their hearts for untrue values that they succumbed to, so they will never be triggered into realizing how much they have lost, how much they could have had otherwise, how much they have been enslaved. So they will not just become Conforming Underlings, they will collude with the Controllers to bring the same oppression they experienced onto all errant Small Accumulators.

Conforming Underlings hate and attack Authentics wherever they are. For Authentics represent the threat that Conforming Underlings will expose to themselves and will realize, with catastrophic emotional results, the fraud that is their life.

So this is how latent class war becomes manifest as culture wars. It shows how class divisions, inherently unjust, get covered up as culture wars.

The Loss of Self, the Rise of Sycophancy

Regardless, what followed in the near term is that there was pressure on Small Accumulators in a number of ways. Remember, Small Accumulators were what we originally were and describes the state in which humans were happy. So, Small Accumulators were embodiments of the "old ways" … the natural ways. They were "more conservative" in seeking to choose richness of life experience over possession of things. But their numbers became fewer, and the old ways increasingly sank into oblivion for these reasons:

The major way Small Accumulators began to disappear is through their accommodation to the power of the Big Accumulators: They covered up their desire for a more authentic and richer life, in response to the increasing pressures put upon them from deprivation orchestrated by the Controller-Conformer Alliance. Small Accumulators by choice became fewer in number as many sought to be Big Accumulators.

Poverty and Table Scraps

But, Small Accumulators (the poor), as they say, we have always with us. And that is true. For, outside of those choosing to be Small Accumulators — in awareness of the broader life experience it makes possible — there were and will be always those who, for reasons of fate, Divine intention, inordinate fearfulness, and/or inability to be or "bad luck" in becoming Big Accumulators would be small accumulating not out of choice. These Small Accumulators — who would if they could be Big Accumulators — would be easily swayed to conform to the wishes of the Big Accumulators.

Why is that so? Why would those wishing to themselves dominate and control end up becoming submissive and allowing themselves to be dominated? It sounds contradictory. However, quite simply, in allying with the Big Accumulators, such wannabes of accumulation could maintain the hope — most often illusory — that they could become the same. Like dog planetmates who at times have gathered around the tables of humans, hoping for scraps, such Small-Accumulators-by-fate would be attracted to Large Accumulators.

The Cult of Power

Indeed, a pseudo-religious quality came to be attached to Large Accumulators, by these Small Accumulators. It was thought Big Accumulators — in particular, the "strong man" most in control among them — had a sort of power or energy, contained within his body, of a great degree ... far more than ordinary humans ... which it was possible to feel when in proximity with him. It was even thought that it could "rub off" on others. We observe this throughout history and culture, and we see it embodied in the cults of celebrity and power today.

However, this purported power and its imagining that it could accrue to oneself if one was in its vicinity was, essentially then, a symbolic rationalization of this idea of thinking that one could become a Big Accumulator — sooner or later, one way or the other — through proximity to and alliance with Big Accumulators.

The Meaning of *Conformity*

That is why such Small Accumulators would submit to the wishes of Big Accumulators. They would become the best and most loyal allies to the ones who had more. In deferring to them ... repressing their own individuality in order to do that ... they would maintain their hope of satisfying their own greed at some point. This is what is meant by their becoming *conformers*. They would alter their behavior — they would *conform* it — in a way to be pleasing to their overlords; and they held little value in having their outer behavior match their inner experience, which is the very definition of *authenticity*. They would be liars to themselves and the world, narrowing the purview of their life from the richness of experience that is possible to a focus on physical survival alone.

Again, early deprivation created excessive fear of being left wanting in life, leading to extreme measures. And these compromises with integrity included allowing a loss of self. These Conformers would become solid, albeit often sycophantic, allies with the Big Accumulators or Controllers.

Led to Domination by Controllers

So there were, and are still among humans, these three styles of being human: Big Accumulators or *Controllers*; Small Accumulators by choice, keepers of the Old Ways, who might be called *Authentic Humans;* and these would-be Big Accumulators, these loyal sycophants to the folks who had more, who might be called *Conforming Underlings.*

Notice that the desires and designs of these three groups are split along a particular line. Controllers and Conformers are allied in their aims, and those aims are directly opposed to those of Authentics. So, though Big Accumulators were far less numerous than Small Accumulators, their alliance with Conforming Underlings gave them power far beyond their small numbers. This Controller-Conformer alliance would, nearly everywhere, come to dominate in the struggle for resources over those Small Accumulators who sought to hang onto more natural and authentic behaviors and lives.

Motivations and Strategies of the Controller-Conformers

Here is a deeper look at how the Controllers accomplished that domination.

Organization — the *Modus Operandi*

Naturally this alliance of Controllers and Conformers would mean their numbers would be greater than the Authentics they opposed. However, the power that came with control of great resources allowed the Controller-Conformer alliance also higher degrees of organization. For humans could be compelled along lines not to their choosing, rather in accordance with the designs of those at the top through the power of gifts and rewards from the Big Accumulators.

Organization of people is arrived at through the complicity of those being manipulated. We would these days say that rich folks can pay others to do their bidding and work toward their ends and not the ends that people would choose if not coerced and bribed that way. So coercion through distribution of resources by the few —

bribing or paying — allowed greater organization of activities along the lines beneficial to the elite.

Incidentally, this is why Democrats in America always have had and will continue to have more difficulty in wielding power and being organized ... for individualistic motives cannot be harnessed. Whereas those who seek power have that one aim in common — power, wealth — and around it they can always and everywhere be organized ... as we see with the Republican–Tea Party Alliance today. It does not matter what Conformers think or what other values they might have; for, in allegiance to power and wealth and harboring the secret terror that they have been duped and robbed, their behavior and even their thoughts are malleable. Their minds are arbitrary; and they are amenable to adjustment to have them conform to what is needed in the greater pursuit, the greater value, of power ... and the maintenance of the lie into which they have invested their lives.

Hence, public truth is as easily manipulated for the Controller-Conformer Alliance as private truth is for the conformer. It simply does not matter what is real or actual when in the pursuit of power and wealth, only. Anything can, and will, be asserted if it furthers their ends ... regardless how obviously ridiculous, nonsensical, or obviously self-serving it is — as we saw most recently in Donald Trump's campaign for presidency. The fact that Trump was believed by such a huge percentage of the population testifies to the irrelevancy of truth for Conformers. This wealthy, royalist-exuding Trump has managed to come across as a reformer for the little man against the powers that be. Some actually took him on as being a kind of hero speaking against the 1% of the world. When clearly, of that wealthy elite, he is a chartered member, if not some kind of ersatz officer. Even his tax proposals, which would lavishly increase the purses of the filthy rich at the expense of everyone else, did not open Conformer's eyes to his being arrayed with those, not with, but against them.

So this pattern of achieved power, through organization around the untrue and inauthentic, is true of Democrats and Republicans in America today. However, it corresponds everywhere with its counterparts in history — history's so-called "patriots" and defenders of the "father land" aligning themselves with wealthy elites, the Controllers and privileged, against their rebellious and authentic opposition. This is why fascism arises so easily (I say with trepidation as Donald Trump, with the assistance of Russian hacking and an FBI Director with a political agenda, is being installed as president of the most powerful country on Earth). This is why royalists and loyalists to the crown have dominated over reformist, revolutionary movements throughout history. This is why uprisings for fairness and democracy throughout history — from the Middle Ages to Tiananmen Square, Occupy Wall Street, Syria, and Turkey today — are so readily crushed by the Controllers, wielding their sycophantic, uniformed forces. For Conformers turn their eyes, if not actively participate. Afterwards, in media and historical accounts, there is nary a backward look by such — society's "silent majority."

Fear and Omnipotence — the Motivations

Yet the Controller-Conformer alliance would be even more success-ful because they would go further than that. Not only could they organize the activities of large numbers of people to benefit the Controllers in the acquisition of greater amounts and storage of re-sources, thus increasing their power and ability to do that all the more, in vicious cycles of greed and power. Not only would this in itself allow them to rise in dominance over the more natural, indi-vidualistic Small Accumulator — the Authentics. But their raging fears of want and deprivation had no bounds; they expanded their *control* over other humans way beyond what was involved in simply winning out in the resource contest. Their crazed and fearful brains pushed them to seek god-like, total control — omnipotence, auto-cratic control, sovereignty, in essence. And they still do, by the way. They created the kings and royalty of yesteryear, the dictators and potentates of history, and the oligarchy – the rule by the wealthy of a society – of today.

Backing up, remember that the Big Accumulators (the Control-lers) shared something with the Conformers — an excessive fear, again from that early birth trauma, of lack of resources and its ultimate consequence, death. The Authentics risked more, in pursu-ing the ends of the soul; so they either had less fear, for whatever reason, or their desire for a richer experience of life was greater and caused them to take on the burden of that fear.

However, the Controllers and Conformers — fearing death, deprivation, and uncertainty to an extreme degree — would feel that nothing less than the control of all resources and the conformity of all other humans to their will and ends was required. With excessive fear, or diminished appreciation of life in itself, or both, they felt that the only way to find relief from their overpowering anxiety about existence came in attempts to control everything, to control all variables of existence, especially the ones related to accumulation, and all the humans in any way involved with any of this.

So the Controllers and Conformers would not merely seek to gather and accumulate resources, they would seek also to eliminate any competition for these resources, however slight or inconsequential, however small or disorganized that competition might be, in the form of the natural, authentic, but also individualistic Small Accumulator.

Scarcity and Poverty — The Stick

They did this in a number of ways, beginning with gathering and hoarding as much of the available resources as they could. Hoarding in this way would leave the non-conforming Small Accumulator — the Authentic — with less than enough even to survive. Living outside of Nature now, relatively speaking, folks were more dependent on each other and on the good will of the Big Accumulators. So, magnified by the power of organization, through hoarding and even through stealing in various ways from the less powerful in society, the Controller-Conformer alliance put incredible pressure on the Small Accumulators. In doing this, the Controller-Conformers would create *scarcity* — an impoverishment of things and resources that did not need to be ... and rarely was when in Nature. They created *poverty* along with it. They created also starvation and death for the Authentic.

Think back, now, scarcity does not exist in Nature. You can see that if you but look. Imagine any natural setting. The only way you can view that environment as not prodigious with possibilities for sustenance, shelter, or any of the physical needs is if one has narrowed one's understanding of what satisfies one's needs. Looking at any environment from the perspective of seeking one or a few items in particular is the only way most environments can be seen to be at all lacking. But expanding one's understanding of what can be used to satisfy one's physical needs to what is usable and possible, one cannot help but see Nature as a cornucopia. In our mythologies we display our lost understanding that Nature is really that way and that we have simply stopped seeing that.

No. What we have dreamed up instead is this idea of scarcity. Yet scarcity is not a true perception of Nature. It is one that has been perpetrated, going along with civilization, by us humans ourselves — in particular, the Controller-Conformer alliance — for their ends alone ... specifically the ends of every society's elites. How better to persuade authentic Small Accumulators to become Conformers or at least to bend to Controller's wills than to make it that they have no recourse of resorting to Nature on their own — whether true or not? Indeed, the Controller-Conformer alliance, in gathering and hoarding resources well beyond any need, sought to create that scarcity in reality. They would elicit compliance by eliminating alternatives.

This was in many ways the same as the way humans elicited compliance from other planetmates — "domesticating" them — by corralling them and eliminating their possibilities of sustaining themselves except through the humans controlling them. The obvious difference is that humans, in general, would not be corralled ... well, not in any obvious way. I will leave out for now the creation of urban centers and the enforced dependence of the population on city and village economics for the satisfaction of needs. Still, at least ostensibly, authentic, small-accumulating humans were not corralled. They, at least initially, had freedom of movement, however self-enslaving they were to their domiciles and in their sedentary lifeways.

Yet a virtual domestication of humans by the Controller-Conformer alliance could be brought about by limiting resources available to any but themselves. By creating scarcity in the environment, in general, they could make all humans in that environment dependent on and looking to them who had stored and had gathered those resources.

Status, Prestige, Ostentatious Display — The Carrot

They went even further: The Controller-Conformers would employ other stratagems to persuade the non-conforming to become "domesticated" — just like the planetmates that humans had corralled. Causing deprivation was the stick, but persuasion to become Conformers and to enjoy the benefits of "social conformity" was the carrot. The values of compliance would be paraded about for all to see — in finer clothes; more desirable, more luxurious residences; fatter remunerations and material rewards; awe-inspiring edifices and buildings for underlings to labor around and be intimidated by; lavish celebrations and repasts; and, not to be disregarded, rewards of dubious worth in terms of titles, prestige, posts, awards, honorariums, positions, and medals, or their ancient equivalents. In fact, as time went on, it became ever more important to display such differences in status through ostentatious dress and possessions.

Fancy dress would say two things: For the Conformer, it would say, "I am better than you" to the hold outs of the Small Accumulators or the less successfully sycophantic of the Conforming Underlings everywhere around. In this way it would reward the Conformer for her or his sycophancy by providing its opposite — an ego inflation — in relation to other people. And to the Authentic or the Small Accumulator of any sort it said, "You can have this if you obey." That is to say, conform and you will be rewarded. Further, it said that not only can you increase your possessions by conformity, but also you can increase your status and have other Small Accumulators be sycophantic to you, too.

Thus, ostentatious dress and elaborate displays of possession and domicile established hierarchies of importance. Each level garnered for its members the psychological satisfaction of being sucked-up to from those below, while the members of each level would be led to feel inferior to, jealous of — and so be persuaded to emulate and suck-up to — those on the level above.

Humiliation, jealousy, dominance, submission, power, obedience were all orchestrated in these games of hierarchy. Yet the bottom line was that Authentics were pressured both by being starved and beaten into submission with the stick of scarcity as well as by being persuaded into conformity using the carrot of status, possessions, and the reward of psychological tokens in the new game of one-up-manship.

Harassment, "Morality," Law — More M.O. of Autocracy

If neither worked — the stick of scarcity or the carrot of status and conspicuous consumption — then there was harassment, scapegoating, belittlement, ostracism, and ridicule. If conformity could not be persuaded, it would be demanded and coerced. Controller-Conformer elites would create and sustain sets of rules to suit their ends, to which at least Small Accumulators must be obedient, if not always themselves.

Creating law in this way, they created outlaws. Defining criminality, they created criminals. For laws and rules would not be to benefit the greater good of all but simply that of the Controllers. Hardly would such rules sit neatly upon the desires of the members of society themselves, in particular, the Authentics. Nor were they strictly adhering to any natural morality around reduction of suffering and honoring of life — quite to the contrary! As it turned out.

Thus the establishment of societal codes was a covert way by which the Controllers could mark the Nonconforming Authentics as criminals. This was helpful to them for, by rationalizing it as "law enforcement," it enabled them in the use of physical force, capture, enslavement, physical punishment and torture, and even death.

Murder — The Ultimate "Solution"

The third way small accumulating Authentics had their numbers come under pressure — outside of desertions to the ranks of Conformers because of the persuasive forces of scarcity and reward — was through outright attack and brutality. In the last analysis, the Controller-Conformer alliance could eliminate any use of resources by anyone with ends of their own and not of the alliance through torture, imprisonment, and death.

Controller-Conformers Prevailed

So Controllers and Conformers would have extreme advantages over Non-Conformers, and they would dominate in the circles of increasing densities of societies. They would reduce the numbers of any opposing them — that is to say, any with traits or qualities that were not controlling or sycophantic — by persuading them, by killing them, or through the fact that Authentics would move away. Authentics would succumb to the wishes of the Controllers or they would be enslaved and killed, thus dying out; or they would run away to live in groups farther and farther away from the reach of the Controller-Conformer populations. Controlling and conforming traits thus won out, in humanity's struggle for survival through natural selection, over natural, authentic traits.

All in all, over time and in these ways, the old ways that were harmonious with Nature — noble, self-confident, and free — were swamped in favor of new ways of dominance, power, sycophancy, repression of personhood and emotion, bullying, obsequious behavior, punishment, humiliation, and enslavement ... with much smaller groups of Authentics living either silently or away from the population centers.

Leads to the Apocalypse

In this work I have been describing an increasing separation from Nature, beginning with when we were still planetmates — that is, still one with Nature — to now when, being the most estranged from Nature, we are about to bring down all the world to feed our psychotic ego cravings.

Cultures are equal, as anthropologists proclaim. Such academics refrain from making moral comparisons between cultures or groups of them, as, for example, gatherer-hunters versus sedentary-"civilized" societies. Still, different cultures' levels of technological complexity lie along a spectrum. On one end are the nomadic with the least amount of technological complexity — no need for it since one can only carry and store so many "things" — to the other end where we are sedentary and control more things, and with increasing systems of technological control and management, depending upon our level of technological complexity and advance.

The reason that becoming sedentary — with its corollaries of accumulation and hierarchy — is the actual base root of the apocalypse we face today is that if we were still nomadic, we would never have been able to "own" enough "things" — or Flora or Fauna for that matter … or other people — to be able to create the technological complexity, or the power systems … of alliance and coercion … to manage them, which allows us to have this awesome ability to self-destruct totally and irrevocably, which we indeed now have.

That said, in human history our ever-expanding controlling obsession rose up and continued to inundate everything in line. In the next few chapters, we will look at how these elements of power, bullying, and domination extended themselves to the women of our societies, our children, and ultimately even ourselves. What follows immediately, then, is how and why women came under attack and were the next targets for control.

16

The Fourteenth Descent — Misogyny:

Domination of Women, Gender Inequality, Why Women Came Under Attack

"The pressure on women to be conforming was so great because it was the place where conforming men, if nowhere else in society, were given free rein as controllers."

"Unto the woman he said,
I will greatly multiply thy sorrow and thy conception;
in sorrow thou shalt bring forth children;
and thy desire shall be to thy husband,
and he shall rule over thee." — **Genesis, The Bible**

Inauthenticity Rising

We see that Controllers and Conformers had survival advantages over more authentic and less conniving humans. The Controller-Conformer Alliance dominated in the struggle humans created; it won out easily over the more Authentic humans. The traits that characterized the Controller-Conformer Alliance, therefore, were to increase in humans as they would pass these traits to their offspring through both example and heredity, and these offspring would be both greater in number and have survival advantages themselves over those more authentic humans.

Humans became over the millennia increasingly inauthentic.

The upshot is that the more twisted humans — those especially who were Controllers and Conformers — beat out more Authentic humans ... which for reasons of being closer to Nature included many women.

Women Came Under Attack

This increasing depravity and separation from Nature is what accounts for human's being capable of the current environmental crisis and with creating the possibility of planet death — as the result of human endeavor and "ingenuity" — at any moment.

But at its beginning....

One extremely important facet of this Controller-Conformer-Authentic dynamic concerned the women in our societies. Remember that at this point of our separation from Divinity through excessive controlling activity and ego-aggrandizement we, having focused on conquering and controlling everything about us in Nature, were beginning to dominate and control each other in the same way. We focused on Small Accumulators, especially the Authentics among them, but a huge part of that group were female. So women became targets for all aspects of this controlling mania — domination, denigration of character, diminution of personhood, coercion, attack, corralling, enslavement, abuse, murder, and so on.

Now, why human females would be singled out might not be apparent initially. We would think that they would be as likely to be Controllers as males. Some women, indeed, were Controllers, though not many. For there is something that sets women apart in this entire dynamic, making them less likely to become Controllers, more likely to be Authentic, and to be special targets for attack and controlling by the Controller-Conformers.

Nature, Birth, Misogyny, and Why Women Got Scapegoated for Everything

What sets women apart is their special connection with Nature and birth. Keep in mind that all this controlling has its roots in birth trauma and infancy deprivation. Remember also that all this is about controlling all aspects of the natural world. Quite simply, because our females figured so prominently in both the birth trauma *as well as* the infancy trauma, they would unconsciously be blamed for it all. In attacking women, both women and men would act out their early pain. They would transfer their intensive efforts to beat back the residues, inside themselves, of their painful pasts, onto the outside and would beat back the symbol of that pain — women.

Misogyny

Humans are the only misogynistic species, because humans are the only species with excessive birth and infancy trauma. Among all of Nature, the female of the species prevails — that is to say, is central, more important, and usually dominates, if there is any inequality of genders.

Relation to Birth and Infancy

However, in humans, at birth, we experience a struggle with the female body to be born, more so than any other species. We would continue that struggle with, beating back at, and attack upon the female body later in life — both men *and* women would feel this push to do so. This explains, by the way, why women have never been able — until modern times, that is — to unite and fight back against the injustices perpetrated on them.

In any case, after birth and in early infancy, we were left wanting in having our needs sufficiently satisfied. In particular, we craved nursing, feeding, and attentiveness from our mothers. Since we could not help be at least somewhat dissatisfied with what we received — even the best mothers cannot respond perfectly, like Nature and biology can — we would for the rest of our lives first think of society's females as being the source of our dissatisfaction. Women would be scapegoated for all human ills.

It was not women's fault, of course, that they would be associated with these traumas. We would call it being in the wrong place at the wrong time. Indeed, if justice and reason ruled emotions, women would have been rewarded and appreciated for their roles in taking on these difficult times and tasks in our lives. Women, after all, suffer severely during birth, just as we do as neonates. They, though not perfectly, work hard to fill our needs after birth. Essentially, they are like the doctor who might get blamed for the disease, the hospital that might be targeted as being the cause of death since so much of it occurs there, the fireman who might get blamed for the fire ... heck, there's always one when he's around, coincidence? ... or the good Samaritan responding to the crime who might get accused of it — because he was *there.*

Simply through association, and quite unfairly, women would be targeted as the source of all our problems. We would associate women with eating an apple that would end the Earthly paradise; with a jar, or box, which when opened released all evil into the world. Amazingly, but understandably, we would create images everywhere in the world of the female vagina as ringed with voracious teeth — a perfect depiction of the pain we felt when we first came through that doorway into the world.[1]

So, women, first and foremost, after Nature itself, would be attacked and corralled in our controlling mania as it began being directed now even at ourselves.

Relation to Nature

There was another reason why women would come under attack. Being associated with those times of pain was the driving force behind our targeting women for enslavement and abuse. Nevertheless, those very fundamental aspects of being female — giving birth and nurturing infants — are the very connections with Nature that we can never deny. We can and did try to separate ourselves from all aspects of Nature, to set ourselves apart and above. However, in the activities of birth, sex, and the care of infants, we are most clearly part of Nature — down here on Earth with the rest of our planetmates. We may not acknowledge it, but we cannot but know it.

Thus, women in being primary participants in birth and infancy have a connection with Nature that is harder for them to deny; and it is a connection that our males would be aware of as well. In being connected to Nature, human females would more likely be like those Authentics — that is, more interested in emotional, relational, and spiritual, rather than in power and controlling, pursuits. Burdened with giving birth and having a greater role in parenting, they would be more likely to be Small Accumulators, too. So, they would be singled out for excessive coercion and demands for conformity by Controllers for those reasons — that is, women being more akin to Authentics and more likely a Small Accumulator.

Yet in the fact that men would know that women have a special connection to Nature, our females would be lumped in with Nature as another thing to control. Indeed, since sex is the major aspect of adult life that men experience as being related to Nature and to be unable to be controlled — at least, not without a lot of difficulty, for the sex act *requires* loss of control, as does loving in any form — and men would associate sex with women, that would be another reason women would be controlled. For in controlling women, men could, again, work to deny their connection with and dependence on Nature.

Bonding and Breast-Feeding — Other Reasons Women Are More Likely Authentic

Women were less likely to be Controllers for another reason. This has its roots also in the factor of women giving birth and being the more likely caregivers —— being mothers, that is. It has to do with bonding. And the differences around bonding, from earlier in our history to now — especially as regards the controlling proclivities of women — are telling: Women give birth, then naturally have a period after birth of connection with their child that involves bonding and the establishment of a deep connection with their baby. It is a deep emotional-biological pattern, supported by all kinds of hormones and other bodily responses.

Quite simply, mothers who do not have this bonding with their children feel more estranged from their children throughout life, less empathetic toward them; and their children feel more alienated from their mothers. On the other hand, mothers who have this period of bonding — and keep in mind this was virtually always the case up till more modern times when the birth process became dominated by medical-technological devices and procedures — have supremely better feelings of empathy and connection with their children, throughout the child's life. This is further reinforced by breast-feeding, which is another natural process disrupted by the hubris of modern medicine and the vanity of modern lifestyles.

In these ways, women are biologically primed to be giving and loving caregivers. They are aligned with their feelings that — simply and quite frankly — *care* how their child feels ... what their child's experience of life is like. Hence, poor parenting — which would involve treating the child like a thing, managing it, dehumanizing it, and controlling it — are less likely. For the mother would be much aware of the fact that is hurtful to the child, causes pain to the child, and so would not do it. Mothers, with bonding and breast-feeding, are much more likely to be nurturing, caring, permissive of their child's behavior, allowing of their child's errant acts, and accepting of their children in general, as they say, more likely to be "unconditionally loving."

Not so, in the situation of mothers and children who are not allowed the bonding after birth and who do not have the experience of breast-feeding in common. These children are much more likely to receive the kind of "poisoned parenting" — characterized by controlling and thingification of the child. This is coming up in another chapter, too, by the way.

For now, the point is that up till modern times, the natural, biological processes of bonding and breast-feeding are things that kept women in the domain of being more likely to be authentic and less likely to be Controllers. For with their children, if nowhere else, if there was bonding and breast-feeding, women would be reinforced in humans' natural feelings of empathy, which discourages the devitalization of the Other required for controlling and domination. Women would be taught in ways of nurturing, caring, emotional responsiveness, relationship, and many of the other characteristics of authenticity. None of these, nor either the ability to be aware of another's suffering, is conducive to controlling other living things. Women made poor Controllers, overall; and they had less desire, much less, to want to be that way.

However notice also that these — bonding and breastfeeding — are aspects of Nature; these are bodily processes and functions. So they become also reasons women would be seen as closer to Nature, less "transcendent"-analytical-rational-detached than men; and they would become more reasons to hate women. And, oh, by the way, to be hated, especially, by men that did not receive such nurturing. As for there being a link between lack of bonding, breast-feeding in societies and the likelihood of misogyny, I will leave that for you to judge. I think there is evidence in some societies that there is such a correlation.

Women's Lot

Now, these special characteristics of women and the extra coercion that would be brought to bear upon them because of those characteristics would split women along two lines of behavior.

Women's Choices

These would be sets of behaviors but also, and for the most part, they would be ways that both women and men would come to see women.

Conformity

One set of behaviors and perceptions of women would be the conforming ones. In these behaviors and attitudes women would succumb to the coercions and become obedient. They would become as sycophantic as can be. They would adopt the perceptions of themselves as being less than human because of their association with Nature. They would go along with what was being demanded of them and would become docile, subservient, "domesticated" — just like the "animals" that humans at this time were owning. Indeed they would go along with being viewed as possessions and things and would become self-hating and obsequious to the values of power, control, and masculinity.

Authenticity

The other set of behaviors and perceptions are what might be called authentic ones and were related to being an Authentic Human. In this choice, women would *not* concede personhood. They would not want men or others controlling their freedom, bodies, sexuality, relationships. They might, for the sake of their relations with their children, ape all the mannerisms of conformity and submission when necessary, but they would *resent* it. They really *were* still closer to their natural selves and to Nature and could not or would not, to themselves if nowhere else, deny it, regardless the pressures to conform and the punishments for non-conformance. Women would know their worth and nobility, however secretively.

On the other hand, men would perceive this assertion of the natural in women as the gravest offence and affront to all their efforts at controlling and dominating. Consequently, men's view of these women had women being lumped in with all men's other distorted views of Nature: By men, women were, like Nature, seen as wild, uncontrollable, bestial, animalistic, uncontrolled. They were associated with those forces in Nature that resisted domination and murder, too, as, like Nature's planetmates who did so, they were considered vicious and unforgiving — furious and Furies.

The Result — Inner and Outer Conflict

Thus, there was a polarity evident in women's feelings and in the perception of them in society: One matches up with the Conformers and was the pull of obedience, for the women, and the perception of their docility, by others. The other was in resonance with the Authentics — and all the natural and beneficent forces of the Divine — and resulted in women's desire to be free, noble, and self-determining … like humans in general once were. This was perceived, especially by men, as rebellion, license, viciousness, and *evil* (the opposite of *live*) — which is exactly the opposite of what it was. For the Authentic urge was life-affirming and felicitous, loving as well as free.

The Burning Times

It is the fact that these disparities between women and men along the lines of Nature and Authenticity … versus fearful conformity and inauthenticity … came to the fore so much in the Middle Ages that we had the unbelievable abomination of The Burning Times. It is not that women were actually engaging in ritualistic communion with Nature, as a witch, pagan, or their equivalent … though in some cases, in absolute defiance of the true insanity of the Catholic hegemony over minds, sex, and behavior around them, that would indeed have been the most sane, and authentic, response. Rather, it is that even the most conforming, subservient, obsequious, self-effacing, mousey, retiring, self-sacrificing, and "holy" of women were still … female. And females were associated in all minds … and rightfully so … with Nature; in that women are more natural and cannot deny — because of menses and birth — the workings of Nature and the body, like men can. Unfortunately for men, by the way.

Women's Place in the Hierarchy

This is how our females became the most important and obvious expression of the Controller-Conformer-Authentic dynamic. In it we can see all the elements of persuasion, coercion, obedience, sycophancy, rebellion, jealousy, and humiliation that were at play in all our — humans' — efforts at extending our controlling insanity into the realms of people, too, beginning with the most natural of us.

All these pressures toward conformity and sycophancy in humans could not help but make for the dominance of Controller-Conformer numbers, and thus traits, in our populations. Remember, conformity and controlling behaviors were aligned not only in their ends but within the person. For every conformer is a wannabe controller. And every conformer would be rewarded for their obedience by getting to be controlling in some other area of their life.

And as Scapegoats for Sycophantic Men

In fact, the pressure on women to be conforming was so great because it was the place where conforming men, if nowhere else in society, were given free rein as controllers. Just as in the societal hierarchies that developed out of this Controller-Conformer dynamic — which would have those on one level sucking-up to those above while being rewarded with sycophantic behavior from those below them — so also conforming behavior for all men would be rewarded with sycophantic behavior from women, who would be everywhere at the bottom of all hierarchies.

Of course, women would seek reward for their conformity, too. People or planetmates lower on the totem pole could always be invented. Women could participate vicariously in their husband's rewards of obedience from those below him; they could extract it from other women, under certain circumstances; they could get it by participating in racism or classism ... which was pervasive through-out "civilized" societies ... and in the offshoot of them, slavery; they could wield it in their relations with their children, and often did, which is a whole other issue important enough to be discussed on its own ... and it will be in the following chapters; and if nothing else there were always the planetmates and Nature that would be bent into service to satisfy these unwholly, unnatural "needs" (actually, de-sires) to be deferred to and to scapegoat others for one's own circumstances.

Women's Responses and the Results

If human females chose to accept none of these outlets for their resentment and they insisted on being Authentic and living along the lines of Nature, they suffered. And many of our women did just that. In being connected to Nature through birth and nurturing, through parenting and family relationships, they would be ever reminded of those values of Nature and of their natural ways. Values of intimacy, love, full experience of life, and felicity would make those of power and domination seem pale by comparison.

They Suffered for Being Authentic

Hence, just like compassionate planetmates who took on lives of service to suffering humanity — we see this especially in those we refer to as *pets* — a great many women did, too. They suffered for being Authentic. Because of this, women are always and everywhere more likely to suffer from unhappiness, depression, anxiety. These are not related to "biological" differences between women and men; these are not attributable to "hormones" or the like. This greater propensity to feeling sadness has to do with psychological differences between women and men which have the one — women — being more likely to feel the oppressions of civilization. Women suffer for they are more authentic and closer to having actual feelings, real human feelings, than their male counterparts.

They Were Rewarded for Being Authentic

This more expanded capacity to feel real emotion — not merely the rageful outpourings come of repression of feeling, as in men — is why women are much less likely to have lost the ability to cry. Sadly, saying this in a patriarchal, predominantly repressed, culture, I need to point out that weeping is a healthy attribute, conducive to wholeness and authenticity, whereas repression of feelings is the very definition of inauthenticity. I should not have to do that — to point these things out — however I am aware of the context in which I am writing.

Indeed, women actually are more like planetmates, they are more like "animals"; but this is meant in the most salutary way: That human females are closer, in general, to Divinity, to natural life; and thus they are more likely to take on suffering rather than participate in the power and punishment games.

Rites of Passage Into Diminished Aliveness ... Women and Men

Men's choices were quite different, though they suffered and were rewarded as well. A big difference is that men suffered and were rewarded for being largely inauthentic, while women were miserable and reaped the rewards of greater authenticity.

Men, you see, became the "outer crust" of the family unit — the part that would most interact with that insane, controlling-dominating society surrounding every home unit. Men would be the buffers between the forces of domination and control and pressure to conform in the outside world and in society, and the homey world of hearth and spouse and offspring. They would be split in two in this way.

Throughout their lives, in fact, there would be more pressure on men to be conforming to the demands of society. We see this everywhere exhibited in the more brutal rites of passage into adulthood for men. We notice how all these elements combine when we see the patterns of puberty rites across societies and as related to women and men. Men are most brutalized in the more "advanced" societies — that is, post-agrarian, "civilized" ones.

They are not brutalized; they may even be non-existent, these rites of passage, in the most "primitive" societies. Or these initiation periods might take the form of more authentic ways of transformation — vision quests or its equivalents. As I mentioned earlier, the Mbuti of Africa do not have initiation rites for puberty. They only participate in the ones of their more "civilized" neighbors, who are dependent on farming and towns, out of a kind of playful solidarity but not much more. They do not take the rites seriously and have a kind of humorous disdain for them and their neighbors who seem so foolishly caught up in them.

Meanwhile, in all societies the rites of passage for women are less brutal, are more likely to be non-existent, and might even be pleasurable. Certainly they might involve a measure of humiliation, especially regarding the fact of menses — and, this, exclusively occurring in patriarchal societies, who additionally are the most misogynistic — as ways of funneling women to their "proper" subservient and retiring roles in that society. Yet rites for adolescent girls might also be pleasurable ... or include aspects of pleasure. For womanhood is meant for women to be an opening for girls into to the worlds and behaviors of child-"rearing," family, and sexuality — none of which are against Nature and all of which can be the best sources of pleasure and fulfillment in life. Whereas for men, the adulthood demanded of them is invariably about going against Nature — "Away from the mother world, Forward to the Father world" as the Jungian, Erich Neumann, summarized it.[2]

Becoming a man, in more "civilized" societies, involves having a "second birth" — one that is not in Nature, but is "out" of Nature ... that is, it is seen as "transcendent," separated from it, from Nature. Quite frankly, the male role became increasingly, and acknowledgedly, unnatural. These passages into adulthood involved preparing a man to be willing to not be happy, to not have that as one's goal ... to not care about felicity or satisfaction in life. The rites of passage began increasingly to be about transforming a boy into someone who would adopt the role of being a mere tool in the hands of an elite ... willing to spend his life carrying out ends that are not his own, are often distasteful, and in any case are one's that one's heart is not into and one must force oneself to do.

We are trying to reverse and change all this in modern times, in some societies, that is true. And for both women and men the trend is toward more natural, more authentic, roles. That is immensely laudable. However, we need to never forget that this brutal and unhappy imposition of roles for both women and men, come of civilization, is the way it has always been, beginning with the controlling of Nature, and it is unnatural and conducive to unhappiness for everyone ... even the elite for whom these behaviors of society are orchestrated.

For even in fulfilling the ends that elites have aligned themselves with, elites can never be satisfied for those attainments do not fit with actual or natural ends or needs. Those goals of the well-to-do, and all who look to them as their models — all the Conforming Underlings and societal sycophants — are simply the end products of insatiable desires arising from pain ... the pain of early unmet needs. So no amount of satisfaction is enough. This is why greed is unlimited, is insatiable. No amount of possessions or degree of control and power can put out the fires of fear and unhappiness arising from early deprivations and pain.

Cultural and Biological Constraints on Aliveness

We see this in some of the other practices come of civilization. Circumcision is one. Circumcision is the way men are told, in civilized societies, that it will be their role in life to conform. How better to do that than to take a part of a man's body and change its shape from the natural. What better metaphor for having to change for the wishes of Other from being as one was intended to be by Nature.

Even more compelling is the fact that this deforming would be targeted on the part of a man that is the symbol of man's power and pleasure — his reproductive power and his sexuality. For, ever after that circumcision a man is reminded unconsciously that his power is only to be applied to the ends of someone outside himself and that his pleasure in life must be sacrificed as well. It is not much different from the ways and meaning of the branding of cattle we do.

Women are similarly "corrected" along the lines of their pleasure by the way; but not as pervasively in cultures, albeit more brutally. There is clitorectomy in some societies for women, telling them not to take pleasure in the bottom half of their bodies and instead to focus their energies outside of themselves, on pleasing others. And where there is not clitorectomy, there is nearly universally, in "civilized" worlds, an extra injunction put upon women to not be too sexual. The demonization of sexuality is predominantly put upon women, not on men. And all in society, including other women, collaborate to repress women's natural needs for pleasure using approbations — as we see in our times with usage of words like "slut," "cunt," "whore," "bitch." Sadly, despite all our gains in the liberation of women in recent decades, that aspect seems impervious to change.

How Women Pay for Their Relatively Greater Authenticity

However you look at it, then, women pay endlessly for their status of being allowed to have a connection to Nature and protected from brutal forces of control in society and being able to cling to themselves a smidgen of authenticity. They must, if they are able to at all enjoy their authentic connection to actual life values, do it secretively and not be too overtly happy about it; lest they rain down upon themselves more approbation and violence.

Sex

Furthermore, especially in patriarchal societies, women are set up to try to diminish any such satisfaction in those authentic behaviors in innumerable ways. Examples of this include removing from girls the right to choose their mates; allowance of their use as sexual objects, for sexual slavery, and, most damningly in some societies, their availability for rape; and sexual coercion of adults and young women, as prostitutes, concubines, and the like, and as young girls to incest, rape, and sexual use … beginning sometimes at ages as young as four years old, sometimes even as infants.

This last one is telling. For we hear there is an incest avoidance among humans. It is said to be our only real instinct. It is one more of those things humans beat their chest about and look down upon the rest of Nature around. Yet the fact is that there is against incest a taboo, which is prevalent among human societies because, indeed, humans are the one species, of all primates, who are prone to incest. Hardly is there an incest avoidance inherent in human psychology. Our primate cousins do not engage in incest; humans do.

There has been a pedophilic use of young girls that pervades history and in various societies and cultures right up to and into today … and again it is more likely in "civilized" cultures. Though it is vehemently denied.

It would be truer to say that what is universal in humans is a *denial of incest*, not incest itself. It is something humans always and everywhere cover up, avoid, and deny. This is not to say either, that incest is common, though in some societies, for example, ancient Greece, it was. What I am saying is that it exists all about and much more than one thinks and among people you would never suspect. It is a practice that is passed down through the generations and equally hidden by all participants involved. This is an issue I have taken up elsewhere[3] in more detail and will say more about in an upcoming chapter. However, the best source for this pulling back of the curtains of history on our incest denial is Lloyd deMause.[4] What he reveals shows the lie to our assertions of human morality, especially as regards how we treat our children.

And, oh, by the way. The topic of control of children is indeed the next descent we will be looking at, in the next several chapters, actually.

Work

And everywhere women do the majority of the work. It is probably in the demands of labor, morning to night, that women are most punished for having an authentic streak in them. Anthropologists acknowledge that worldwide, on average, it is women who do the vast majority of the work required. In gathering, child-caring, cooking, labor around the domicile; while men are more likely, even in gatherer-hunter societies that are more egalitarian, to be the ones to do occasional hunting or to lounge, hang out, and play games of chance — which is a strangely prevalent pastime for men.

In every gather-hunter society women provide most of the food, and it mostly comes from gathering. The men are more likely to hunt; and game, meat, is considered a bit of a luxury for it is not had as commonly.

Nearly everywhere you will see women lugging things here and there; they are truly used as beasts of burden. In some societies, they are seen by men to be the ones — despite reduced stature and predominantly lesser strength — naturally designated for bearing loads. I am reminded of something I read recently illustrating this. A Western observer had acquired the services of several natives in a primitive backwater to carry his belongings, including heavy electronic and other devices for use in his profession as an anthropologist. The men were resistant to picking up the larger items, but he elicited their compliance in taking on what was to him the obvious assignment of tasks. Yet, later in the trip, after they had been separated, he found the small, frail women carrying the equipment, some of it weighing nearly as much as them. Meanwhile the men trotted along ahead of them … and lugging very little. The point is not that this is an unfortunate anomaly; it is actually a tragic commonality among human societies up till modern times.

I am talking about the change to civilization, however. And whereas these behaviors I am describing come with farming and corralling of planetmates — for gatherer-hunters are much more egalitarian in all ways, including work, sex, decisions, having a voice, and more — they do not cover the behavior in urban areas up to modern times. Women in suburbia do not lug things so much anymore. However, one can judge for oneself — and this has been an area of quite some dispute right up to the present — if women still do more work. Considering just that women are still mostly responsible for child-caring, now also are responsible for career and making their own living in the world, and yet receive on average less than a man for doing the same work, my vote is in the category that things have not changed. Women still work more and harder.

Summary — Inauthenticity Rising

Still, though slumbering in the hearts of many women and some unusual men — the Authentics — natural and authentic traits would wane as being characteristics of humans. For, of course, those humans who accumulated more and controlled others, in alliance with their conforming and sycophantic underlings, would be able to win out in the struggle over resources over those more authentic and less conniving of us. For these traits of unnaturalness do provide a temporary edge in the competition we created for ourselves. We created unreal struggles, and imaginary achievements and defeats, out of our crazed and fearful brains; and the ones who went along most with those unnatural pursuits and forged personalities to fit it could not help but dominate in those contests. Essentially, because of these ruthless traits the more twisted of us would be able to win out more often in the struggle for survival over more authentic humans.

These ways succeeding, controlling and conformity traits would ascend as traits in our population. For, not only would these dominating and subservient traits be passed along to our children through heredity, but also through nurture and example. Our children could not help but be lured from their pulls toward natural ways, which they, by Nature, experience more strongly as they are younger and more recently removed from Divinity. Our offspring with such traits would end up being great in number and our population would increasingly see and produce such inauthentic, more twisted humans.

This was the final fall in our devolution from wholesome be-ingness to the twisted and inauthentic state we find ourselves in today. Hunting, domestication of plants and "animals," and hierarchy ... equivalent to "civilization" ... are the three major falls of humans from belongingness in Nature. All else, all descents of "man," ema-nate from them. Thus, the twisted behaviors and minds that define our species began the final evolution to the most inauthentic and unwholesome beingness that characterizes us today — a state so unwholesome as to create this rare, nearly unprecedented possibility of planet death (Mars was one), as to actually be capable of bringing down all life on Earth, along with the death or our kind, our own species, in a relatively instantaneous future.

Next, the unfortunate state in which we began to place even those humans who came of our own bodies ... our offspring, our children.

17

The Fifteenth Descent — Child Use ... A Tale of Expanding Control:

Devolutionary Review, Obsessive Control, and Child-"Rearing"

"With each dubious evolutionary 'advance,' we enlarged our capacity for and appetite to control everything around us."

Obsessive Control and Child-"Rearing"

Our descent into ever more controlling of all aspects of our surround, as we have seen, included our ways of having our survival needs met; our lifeways ... nomadic to sedentary; the Fauna Empire of planetmates around us; the Flora Empire of planetmates; others of our own species; and even our own selves, our own otherwise authentic beingness, through conformity and sycophancy. All coming under control over time, and over time increasing control of all these, it is not surprising, however sad, that this obsessive control would be applied to our offspring in their dependent state as well.

With each dubious evolutionary "advance," we enlarged our capacity for and appetite to control everything around us. In this chapter, I begin showing how the obsessive control increasingly characterizing us as humans, in regard to so many of our supposed human accomplishments, is eventually applied to our children. I have explained how our descents are rooted in the imperfection of the fulfillment of our needs in childhood. However, in this chapter, I begin to lay out the unholy facts of the negative spiral of child abuse we descended into as those imperfections of our infancy, creating our damaged adults, are turned back around again onto our children. Those damaged adults create ever more damaged children ... and from them, again then, even more damaged adults. And back around again.

Keep in mind that it is the mania to control our lives excessively that separates us from Nature and makes of us a consciousness opposed to the natural. For we set yourselves apart and above Nature to control Her.

The core of that drive to dominate and what distinguishes us as humans and separates us from the other planetmates, as I have been saying, is our aberration of premature births — relative to the rest of planetmates — with its result that newborns are dependent on adult caregivers for, relatively, an exceedingly long time. Indeed, we humans can be defined by the fact of our prematurity and the consequent long period of dependence, by infants, on fully growns for survival.

Furthermore, humans are the planetmates who experience a brutal birth, coming into life far before we are ready, which sets off a crazed overcompensation of mental activity to defend against the pain of it. Additionally, humans are the planetmates who have an excessively long infancy, where our needs are only partially met, which results in extreme controlling behavior applied to every aspect of life and all other beings in our world afterwards, in adult life.

Controlling Our Young

Now, a special example of our increasing controlling-dominating be-haviors involves the way we see our children. Controlling and domi-nating our young is special because, remember, it is because of the characteristics of our infancy and birth that this devolution of ours away from Nature began. Our prematurity and dependency as infants causes the feeling of lack, of insufficiency, that in life pushes us to mistrust and control.

Remember also, our newborns — prematurely born, helpless, and thrown out of Nature's Divine blueprint for perfect nurturing — would die out of pure despair if not for the creation of the alien construct of Ego. And the delivery system of this Ego is predominantly the fully growns who are attendant upon the needs of the helpless prematures.

Our Earliest Learning

Thus, our earliest learning of this world is about the fact we did not get what we needed when we needed it … that is, as an infant … and that we were left all alone to stew in that misery. So we fear, forever after, that we will not get what we need, again, and that we will die of that. Without really deciding it, driven by fear, we focus nearly all our energy and thought upon making sure those terrorizing feelings of hunger and abandonment will never happen again, in any possible future, by controlling all we possibly can that is happening around us in the present. Our intent in dominating all aspects of our surround is to wage war against a feared scarcity or shortage of life-sustaining resources, which we once experienced and — rightfully so — felt to be the gravest inequity and deadliest injustice.

We Apply, in Turn, to Our Young

But that urge to control — having its roots in our infancies — we turn around and direct back at our own infants, in their turn. For all kinds of reasons arising from that early experience of intense craving and longing — which I will elaborate upon shortly — we further hinder our children's satisfaction of their early needs from what it would be for them otherwise.

To give one example of why we would do that, for now: Just as women who have undergone a forced clitorectomy as a girl and experienced a diminished life pleasure because of that, so they as adults cannot help but want to do it to their own girls. Sadly, we humans cannot bear the pain of knowing how much we have been diminished. Consequently, we bring down the rest of the world to our level, so we will not be reminded and thus triggered into our pain about it. Thus, when it comes to our neglect and abuse of our babies, we, like those maniacal cliterectomizing aunts and mothers, as adults having experienced severe deprivation and unbearable pain and aloneness as infants, and experienced a diminished life experience because of it, are driven to inflict the same suffering on our babies and children as well.

Regardless, in controlling our infants excessively, we increase the drive our children will have to control everything around them when they become adults … in a vicious circle.

Sure enough, in our "progress of man," our own infants became the next category of beings to come under our maddened gaze as targets for our controlling. They were convenient candidates for the next layer of domination, being, as they are, completely dependent upon our fully growns for survival for that long period in infancy; and being that, to a lesser extent, for their entire childhood, they are very little able to fend for themselves without the assistance of adults.

Devolutionary Review — A Tale of Expanding Control

Some review regarding our trajectory of control is called for. In hindsight, our "evolution" … actually our fall from Nature … amounted to an increasing controlling fetish. I have been detailing how it began — pushed by that overheated brain and feelings of inadequateness of needs met in infancy — with a drive to control our food resources as adults.

The Hunger Games

Mistrusting Nature to provide for our sustenance — as it had done for us in the past and as it is done for all other planetmates — we began expanding the area of our control over food gathering by including planetmate flesh in our diet. We began hunting fauna and killing the animate planetmates for our pleasure and to beat back those dreaded uncertainty feelings.

The next stage of our taking over the details of the ways in which we would sustain ourselves involved our dominating the Flora Empire. We invented horticulture, and through farming we were able to control the lives of plant beings and suit them to our increasingly unnatural tastes and to add to our food resources.

Our descent into ever more controlling of all aspects of our environment next involved corralling planetmates. With husbandry, we took away their freedom and saw them as little different from the plants we grew and consumed. Plucked from their habitats in Nature, fauna planetmates were, as it were, "grown" in our circumscribed habitats to be used as slave labor and/or to be parted out as food and other objects for our use.

Notice how each of these steps involves an increasing inability to view other life as sentient and deserving of respect or consideration. Under the self-centeredness of ego consciousness, we were seeing all about us as having their reason for existence as being us.

Sedentary Living and Accumulation

These developments required a sedentary mode of living, for we could not continue our natural nomadic ways while seeking to grow in place planetmates of either the vegetative or the warm-blooded variety. And this switch to a fixed domicile allowed us to act out, through excessive storage and over-accumulation, our paranoid fears of excruciating want.

Sedentary living also allowed us full sway of our defensive mania of creating substitute projects for the real adventures of life, which, now being sedentary, we could say we *owned* ... for we had a place to put them and they did not have to be carried. So, we could go wild in our frenzies to possess and to build edifices and contraptions, equal in magnitude to our fears, which could serve in staving off that feared future of insufficiency and the dreaded pain of want. We became big on creating implements to expand our powers of control and to aid us in our outer defensiveness against our inner fears. We built structures, furnishings, tools, and devices — while sedentary — in the hopes of avoiding that sense of extreme, life-or-death need while being totally helpless to do anything about it, which we experienced in infancy. We owned, built, controlled, invented, and dominated all about us out of our terror of an imagined helplessness in the face of possible death.

Again, Ego's demands were to fortify itself against any and all threats to survival — imagined or real. This time, excessive accumulation and manic struggle in the creation and possession of items that might serve as insurance against future discomfort was the manner of our waging war with uncertainty. Though this lifeway satisfied these irrational desires and lusts to have and to control, it was unnatural for us, relative to what we truly wanted and needed; and it required a further diminishment of our experience of life. Specifically, sedentary living took the joy of play and adventure out of our lives and substituted sameness and drudgery — all under the promise of avoiding a lack or insufficiency of resources that was almost entirely imaginary.

The Controlling-Conforming Games

Then, with increasing accumulation — allowed through sedentary living and control and domination of food sources — our next "advance" of control could manifest: We began to seek power over and to determine the behavior of other humans. The hunger games gave way to controlling-conforming ones. Status and hierarchy became the symbolic representations of our unease and insecurity — our nagging sense of lacking something we needed. And women were the eventual targets for domination in these games; for all men could put themselves above at least these members of society, as their reward for conformity to others.

The methods of our control over other humans extended into cruelty, torture, and killing, in order to extract obedience. Again, our conscience allowed this through our continued removal of the idea of aliveness to all in our environs but ourselves … but our egos. In seeing all life around us as unfeeling, as not conscious or not having a soul, we had no tether on our, now thoroughly, insane and twisted proclivities for manipulation, use, and abuse.

All this led, in time, to our seeing even those aspects of ourselves that were outside of our ego as being a threat. We were at odds with the natural in us — that is, that which could not come easily under control or domination. Our natural self — our real self — includes everything involving our biology … sex, for example … and the parts of our mind that naturally rebel at our sycophancy and domination in relation to others … our errant or "negative" thoughts and our doubts, for example. More on that in upcoming chapters.

We could not as easily deny consciousness or aliveness to parts of ourselves in order to make them "deserving" of control, so we did the next best thing and saw them as being not us and as alien. If we had to acknowledge their status as conscious and intentional, we would put ourselves above them by thinking of them as subhuman or bestial … and eventually we amplified that to their being evil and demonic entities … thus further increasing our imagined distance from them. So if we were to grant their existence as being real and as *in* us, we saw them to *not be part of* us, really. We labeled ourselves "possessed" and gave these parts of us a separate identity of devil.

The result is that we deemed aspects of our personhood to be targets for control and domination, too: We sought to control our sexuality, our biological functions, and our thoughts, as aspects of our controlling-conformity. Putting them outside of what we told ourselves was us — that is to say, our ego — they also could be put below us, as we had the women among us. Very similar to women also, we ascribed them — sex, biological functions, errant thoughts — a status as parts of the natural world, which we felt had ejected us, at one time, and now, as retribution, would come under our thumb.

In seeking to control ourselves this way, we were rewarded also by the fact that the feeling of dominating and bullying our own body compensated for our submissive and humiliating behaviors toward those above us in status who dominated and controlled us. Notice today the pride men take in building up their bodies excessively. If one is bullied, a laborer, a peon, or a corporate pawn, one can still be a Controller in relation to one's body and can ape all the domination of it that one feels raining down upon one in societal circles. In the domain of religion, one can engage in self-flagellation — literal or symbolic — in a desperate attempt to align with the Controller and participate in their domination of self and Nature, by punishing the Nature one cannot deny, one's body.

All told, we sought to align our minds, even, with "transcendent" — but actually unnatural, sterile, and unalive — principles beyond our body, which actually were unconscious alignments with Controllers above us. Thus, we sought to control our thoughts, our sexuality, and our bodies — along now with our external behavior — in our massive sycophancy and burgeoning inauthenticity. In all these together — introjected devils, repression of bodily needs and desires, separation and detachment from the body in alignment with the wants of authorities, and self-flagellating sycophancy — we were laying the basis for what would later become insane theologies, rooted in fear and paranoia. And, yes, much more on that coming up as well, when we will look at religion and its role in control.

The Creation of "Sin" and the Unconscious

Let me explain that last part in more detail: We had a tendency to conform to the wishes of those who had power over us, especially those who wielded that power through excessive accumulation — those who were "richer" than us. We controlled our external behavior to match what they wanted. But in doing so, we caused a split within us. Part of us did not want to be inauthentic — the part of us that was natural. So there was conflict within us; one part of us put out complaints at what we were doing. It wanted to rebel, and it sent out disturbances in our mind as its way of undermining our efforts at subservience and inauthenticity. Basically, being a suck-up was disagreeable to the real part of us.

So, to continue our conforming behavior and to have any semblance of peace with ourselves we needed to find a way to deny that part of us that was real. We needed to repress its complaints. We did this by rationalizing our sycophancy as being a value: We called it *obedience; patriotism; loyalty;* "being a man"; "growing up"; conforming to "hard reality" … not that "idealistic nonsense"; operating in "the real world" … not that "silly" or "namby-pamby" one; and such.

We categorized our rebellious feelings — and, especially for men, our "soft," our "feminine" ones, or the ones of the body — as an evil. We created what we call *sin*.

Do you see how the outer dynamic of controlling-conforming was being brought inside us and we were beginning to reflect inside us the hierarchical arrangement outside? Inside ourselves, we created our own representation of a Controller who demanded conformity and obedience of those below "it" — that is to say, the unacceptable, rebellious, and natural parts of us. Much later Freudians would call that harsh inner controller a *superego,* and our natural impulses would be labeled an *id.*

The Constriction of Self

But it did not stop there. For naturally the dictates we would give ourselves on the inside would be personal introjections of the demands of our superiors. What came under scrutiny were the parts of us that were unacceptable or simply not advantageous in our dealings with our higher ups. Importantly, however, these items of our personhood not advantageous to those we depended upon for survival began to include more than simply behaviors they did not like, but indeed, anything natural or biological.

For it was "inconvenient" to higher ups that we might have needs. In their minds we were not quite alive, after all: We were relegated to the realm of "things" to be used, as was those of us who were female and all planetmates. The wealthy would enslave us, like we were doing with planetmates, if they could. And they often did. The big-accumulating Controllers created the institution of slavery. They would provide for us and allow us to have only the bare minimum as was needed for physical survival … also as was done with kept planetmates … and all too often, kept women. Any more was too much a bother, and, after all, would reduce what they had. And the Controllers' greed was as uncontainable as the fear that fueled it.

So, our real needs were an inconvenience to those above us intent on satisfaction of *their* needs: We could not be loud, sexual, obtrusive, angry, too noticeable … we could not be too alive. We could not be emotional — becoming sad or tearful, after all, would be a way of saying we had needs, too … and they did not want to be reminded of that. To the contrary, only *they* would be allowed to feel life. We would be told to "Control yourself!" "Be a man (woman)." "Be brave, be strong," to "not be such a baby."

This continued right up to today, where any excess emotion or boisterous outburst is labeled "bi-polar," is medicated, is institutionalized, is sometimes jailed, and … as I found out recently through a few youtube videos … is sometimes sufficient and justifiable cause, in America, for murder by police. Especially if you are African-American.

The Robotization of Man

To such an extent was emotion beaten out of us that, amazingly, becoming a human adult became equal to the extent to which one could keep one's face from moving. Having a "stone face" and being unemotional were considered, by civilized humans, to be "mature." Being unaffected began to be seen as the ultimate in strength, as well as maturity; and a stone-faced, dispassionate demeanor aided also in hiding one's actual feelings, of rebellion; or one's agenda, of manipulation and control … which aided one in the increasingly important deceptive arts. These were all especially applicable to men — to sycophantic underlings and wannabe, or actual, Controllers. Again, women were and are closer to Nature and to their real nature, psychologically, than men. Witness women's greater ability and willingness to weep about events, evidencing their willingness to actually face and feel life. Notice women's overall greater emotional responsiveness and the transparency of their feelings as registered in facial expressions.

Meanwhile laughter, frivolity, expressiveness, happiness, upset, and tears — all strongly evident in facial features — were to become considered childish and infantile … again, especially for men. Indeed, these were considered bad things, which when you think of it, they need not necessarily be.

But then, we are talking here about the way we added controlling our young, our children, to our list of domination "accomplishments." So, being child-like … while that could be seen as vivacious, fresh, and creative, in our young and not-so-young, and often, even, envied ... or being creative, expressive, and/or emotion-full — while we could see that as indicating deep experience of life and passion — were instead, among us, put down severely. Being deemed childish was made as much to be mortifying for us as was being seen as feminine, for a man ... and for exactly the same reasons: Child-like and feminine traits were both reminiscent of the Nature in us ... the biological and "inconvenient."

We Introjected Our Controllers

Thus, these predilections of the higher ups to wish for others to be less alive was for the purpose of making it so we could be more manageable ... and usable ... to them. Also, they did not want to see in us reminders that we were actually alive and feeling. For they wished to control us even to the extent of wanting us to act in a way as to not remind their consciences of their atrocious behavior. This would be reflected by us in our dealings with our young, when inflicting corporal punishment, as "Don't you dare cry; I'll give you something to cry about" ... as "This hurts me more than it hurts you" ... and as simply "Don't cry." In essence, the parent as Controller insists that the child not be so inconvenient as to do anything that would trigger a conscience or awareness in the adult — a knowledge that he or she is, as we say, "being a dick."

This wanting for us to not be "inconvenient" and for us to be more usable and manageable in this very day arises in the effort to make people more machine-like or robot-like. Certainly this was wanted of us in recent times for the purpose of us being usable cogs in the industrial machinery ... and so as to take our spots on our factories' assembly lines.

Later, we would be pushed to be "organization men" and "yes men" in complex corporate structures lacking soul ... or conscience. From cradle to grave, in modern times, we are molded, processed, produced, packaged, and eventually marketed — just as any of those items made in factories — through sterile processes of technologically dense hospital births; swaddling; bottle feeding; crib "management"; preschool indoctrination through children's television shows; and elementary, secondary, and then university schooling or military indoctrination. As adults we are ever fashioned through TV commercials to be fearful and so to insure ourselves against all possible calamities; to take our medicines, for unease and disease surround us at every turn, don't you know?; to soothe the resulting and inevitable anxieties and unhappiness with pills; to consume, reproduce, produce; to fill out all the forms thoroughly and correctly so we can be stored like things, catalogued, sorted, and monitored; but above all to get to work on time, alert and charged up, however numbed and unfeeling, to apply oneself to functioning at the behest of the forces controlling us.

And We Sought to Be Less Alive, for Their Sake

However, also in current times, amazingly, we are so estranged and have become so complicit in our abject subservience that we are trying to link ourselves — our minds and our senses — to machines — computers and the like. We fantasize becoming computers, in a sense, even, calling it *transhumanism* and thinking we would have more power that way ... again, more power meaning being even more controlling of our behavior. It is trans-human, yes, but only in the critical and disapproving way I have been describing us as humans. In yearning to be machines, and thus to become the ultimate in unalive and non-feeling, to such an extent have we forgotten our natural selves and succumbed to sycophancy in the service of our overlords.

We show in this also how much a burden it became to feel anything. For what we got from our feelings at this point was mostly misery and suffering. So in robotism, transhumanism, and *Spockism* — which is the unaffected, detached, desire- and passion-repressed model of spirituality — as well as in our dependence on antidepressants, narcotics, and pain-killers today, we show how we no longer wanted to be able to feel ... and still don't. Indeed we demonstrate in all these developments how we wish to be dead, including our imagining nuclear and climatic armageddon in our yearning desperations.

And We Sought Inauthenticity; We Sought Conformity

Yet back when this repression of feeling and humanity was first developing, our kin and family relations would also be seen as inconvenient to higher ups. For what was wanted of us was that we satisfy the needs of someone else, the higher ups, and not ourselves.

Hence any distractions from that were not wanted ... were not allowed ... and to the extent they could be ... were stomped down and eliminated in us.

At any rate, transgressions of the overlord's demands for us to be undemanding and unneedy ... unalive ... were handled by them by impressing on us a degree of humiliation and, often, cruelty, equal in size to their fear of "losing control" of us.

Tragedy enough, that was. But worse, the parts of us that were unacceptable to higher ups outside of us thus became unacceptable to us inside of us, too. We sought to align our inner reality with our outer one. Keep in mind that everyone else in Nature seeks to align their outer reality with their inner one. Quite simply, beings in Nature — gatherer-hunters and all other planetmates — seek to manifest a world that is conducive to the fulfillment of their needs and the expression of their inspirations. We did the opposite: We sought to deny our needs and to stifle any expression of ourselves. Indeed, we sought to not be inspired and certainly to not appear to be inspired. For that also would be inconvenient to our higher ups.

Religion and a Transcendent Ideal, Detached from the Body

We evolved certain cultural mechanisms to help us in estrangement from ourselves. Chief among these is what we call, *religion*. Through religion we could erect an edifice outside ourselves to support our inner struggle to keep from being too real, too inconvenient.

With religion, we could create a transcendent ideal — that is, an ideal separate from our biology or our personhood ... something detached from reality, actually. We could strive to achieve a separation of oneself from oneself — in particular the natural parts of us — and rationalize it as being better and superior. On the other side of this, we would diminish, repress, control, and subjugate all the "less transcendent" aspects of ourselves. We created a sacred and a profane in both the world and us, which does not exist in Nature otherwise. We would do to ourselves on the inside what we were allowing to be done to us by higher ups on the outside, as well as what we were doing to those below us in status and, if we were a man, to the women in our life.

Was an Additional Introjection of Controllers' Demands

However, therein we see the illusion and wrong-gettedness of our thinking. For indeed this transcendent ideal — furiously upheld by our religions — was nothing other than the introjected desires and demands of the Controllers above us. We were telling ourselves that we were obedient to God and "properly" fearful of God, yet it was only our sycophancy and our conformity behavior in regards to the Large Accumulators we were justifying.

It is understandable, then, how so many of our religious dictates … "commandments," for example … were thinly veiled expressions of the desires of Big Accumulators. We were told "not to covet our neighbor's goods," and in this way the Large Accumulators would have their riches protected and have us feeling guilty about our desires to rebel at this inequality of ownership. I will talk much more about that in upcoming chapters, too.

The upshot of all this was that we sought absolute determination and control over our lives through an insular, defended Ego. We sought control over everything outside it … whether that was in our environments and whether they were things or people …as well as control over everything outside the ego but still inside us … and they were desires, inspirations, emotions, biological needs, or even just "negative" thoughts. Which is to say, thoughts that at their root were inconvenient to our higher ups and would work to our disadvantage with them if they were ever discovered. In doing all this, then, we obliterated the last of any possible authentic beingness for us.

And with each fall from grace and over time we expanded our ability to control and our desire to do so.

In upcoming chapters we will look, in turn, into how that appetite was directed onto our children, in various ways, and ultimately onto our very selves.

18

The Fifteenth Descent — Child Use ... Birth and Burden:

The Experience of Birth, Children a Burden, Children and Women Became Scapegoats for Humiliated Men

Fully Growns Hardly Fit Caregivers for Newborns: We "Raise" Children Like Plants; We "Train" Children Like Animals

"...while our newborns required more, we would prefer to give less. We peaked, at this point, as far as our desires for controlling. So the unpredictability brought by newborn others was that much more unappealing."

Now Extending to Control of Our Children

Keeping these deleterious developments in mind — with all things coming under domination over time, and over time there being increasing control of them — it was sadly inevitable that this obsession would reach into that dominion we have over our young ones in their dependent state at the beginnings of their lives. The repression, control, domination, and denigration that we brought to bear on all of Nature, on those below us in status, on women, we now brought to bear upon the most vulnerable of us ... the easiest and most easily manipulated of targets ... the weakest and most dependent of the beings so far being put "under management."

We Require More Care in Infancy

Therefore, however sad, it is not surprising that our obsessive controlling would be applied to our offspring in their dependent state. Keep in mind that our newborns — unlike any other planetmates, who have not split from Nature's perfect ways — require careful nurturing by caregivers. Our newborns cannot cling to their mother's fur after birth, as our nearest relatives' newborns can. Nor can they search for and acquire nourishment from their mothers' breasts, as can other planetmates.

Yet our newborns' requirements are even more excessive, since we are burdened, in infancy as well as throughout our life, with a residue of trauma from birth. We say some of us suffer from post-traumatic stress disorder (PTSD), because of traumatic and inordinately painful and psychologically unmanageable events that happen to some of us in adulthood. How little we realize that our entire species is exactly so traumatized at that very time of our life, birth, when we are least able to integrate a shock to our systems.

Hence we as newborns require even more of comfort and bonding with caregivers and mothers, and even more attention to our needs, and nurturing, than the rest of our sister-and-brother planetmates in Nature; yet we receive less.

The Experience of Birth

Being prematurely thrown out of the womb, our newborns are abjectly helpless. Then they have to confront a processing at birth that one of our fully growns would label *torture,* if they had to undergo it. Not only are our babies subjected, while still naked, to a much colder environment than the ninety-nine degrees they are accustomed to in the womb, they are sometimes hit or slapped. Many of our cultures have this idea of "toughening" the newborn — for example, by immersing her or him immediately after birth in freezing cold water or subjecting them to some other mind-obliteratingly painful experience. Having been toughened and traumatized ourselves, our goal is to bring them into our dark world with us, so we will not be alone in our misery; it has nothing to do with any benefit to the child.

Newborns are almost always confronted with blazing lights and thunderous and assaultive sounds. Remember this is all comparative to what they experienced in the womb. Don't our eyes smart and burn when coming into a bright sunlight from a dark place? A tiny example, that is, but try keeping that in mind and applying that in trying to understand our neonates' first experiences of life in the world, after a full nine months of total darkness and relative quiet.

Then, our neonates have fingers and instruments roughly inserted into their mouths, stretching the mouth wide as if to rip off the jaw, to remove mucus. To a neonate who had nothing in the womb even close to that experience, it is felt as an oral assault ... as oral rape.

The cord is cut early leaving them gasping for breath. They are separated ruthlessly from the entire world they had known for nine months and with no substitute connection yet in the world outside ... an experience of sterile and cutting aloneness which wounds as deeply as the knife itself. Yet when they scream in horror, our fully growns laugh and smile and applaud themselves on having a healthy baby with "good lungs." Do we have any idea, or memory, of how we feel when confronted with such insane human behavior — so insensitive, so unseeing of us — as our first experiences with humans and our future caregivers, our parents? Do we really think that we could maintain after that, if we even had it before, the trust that any of our other needs will be cared for by what seems to us, at this point, to be residents of an insane asylum?

We are taken from our mother — the whole world to us up till that very moment — and immersed into what is relatively very cold water, to "bathe" us. We are prodded with needles and have things stuck up our bum. We are rubbed with harsh cloths or something similar right away, too. Do we think we might at this point be wondering what the hell is wrong with us the way we are? Do we suppose we might be getting a feeling that we are not acceptable in the world of the living unless we are cleaned up and careful of our appearance? Or that there is something different about us ... and "inappropriate" ... that we must, for the rest of our lives, hide or cover up?

We, as newborns, are often, at some point, placed on a cold metal scale and/or other hard surfaces for additional "processing." Do we suppose that being handled like a thing, right at the beginning, might impress in us the idea that maybe we are of that little worth? And at a time when our natural self is aching, intensely, for bonding, for the feeling of warm and accepting flesh against our ravaged body, and for the comfort of suckling, so as to provide a connection to aliveness in this outside world to compensate for the one brutally taken away, we instead find ourselves predominantly in contact with things and an inanimate world. Add to this the fact that our experiences so far with the "living" world have been seeming like a violent assault, and do we suppose we might be having stamped upon our tender psyche an imprint of bonding with things ... the material world ... a feeling that that is the place, the only place, of support and comfort in life? With things? With the world of mere inanimate objects?

Eventually, we might be wrapped tightly in blankets or other cloths, which take away the one advantage we *did* manage to get in coming out of the womb — our feeling of free movement. Do we suppose we are really thinking that life and humans are at all on our side? Do we think that for the rest of our lives we had better stay withdrawn within ourselves, not move around too much, not wave our arms, avoid rapid movements, be still as a yogi, or else disaster ensues?

Very often we are then even taken away from our mother. We might be left somewhere, totally alone, tightly wrapped, with unfamiliar and loud noises and bright lights around us at all times, for a time that seems interminable. We moan and complain when we are separated from a loved one as an adult ... even more so when we lose that loved one to another. How do we suppose we felt when everything in the world we knew was taken from us — that is, our mother ... who was also our sole source of comfort and nourishment and connection to life and warmth for the entirety of our life, up to that point? Do we have any remembrance of the total abject terror we experienced? Can we at least imagine?

Usually we numb ourselves at this point, as a newborn, wanting to die. We begin, at the start of our life, to try to kill ourselves to escape from this world of horror we have fallen into ... this apparent hell. They think we are sleeping comfortably. They do not know we are trying to die.

Then, in subsequent days ... days which seem an eternity ... as they are interspersed with bright light/darkness; coldness/warmth; being tightly wrapped, then allowed to move; being fed, then starving; and moved roughly around and manipulated, then left totally alone ... we come to know the terror that death, and even worse, torture, is at hand at any corner or with any change in life. Do we have an inkling of how that felt or how it might feel? Do we think we would be open to a life of change and adventure after that? Do we think we would allow ourselves to be exuberant or lively? Do we suppose we might, as I have been saying, be determined for the rest of our lives to never, ever, ever let *any*thing be out of our control again ... not anything? Including ourselves? And that to the extent we needed to control all and everything about us to ensure that, we would?

And would we not feel sure that we would need to ensure everything, to determine the ends of all processes? For do we really suppose, after all the above, we could expect anything good to happen without actually making it happen? Would we not cling fanatically to a determination that we will always and forevermore do whatever we need to do ... collateral damage be damned ... fully focused on our desperation to never fall again into that pit of excruciating darkness, pain, and aloneness ... and not even noticing those around us that our self-obsessed mania might be hurting or stomping upon?

All in all, with despair and misery at hand on a constant basis, in those earliest moments of our time on Earth, we forge a resolve, out of fear, that we will fight back whoever and whatever we need to, forever! ... lest we are put "under the knife" once again. And this resolve is the beginnings of our ego ... this resolve to control, to have power over, to conquer, to push all and everyone else to the side ... for our survival.

We do that. Or we do die. The pain is too overwhelming or for some reason we cannot muster the resolve, and we just succumb to death, out of our utter despair and misery. And they tally us up as a crib death.

Ego

So Ego saves our life ... but at great cost. For to erect the construct of Ego we need to split off from all that is good, natural, and easy in us, and loving; and instead focus around a drive to live at whatever cost. For at our youngest we are closest to Nature, our real self, and the Divine. Except for harsh experience and the trainings and teachings of those in our societies who in later life reinforce the split, we would, like other planetmates, know it, be it: We would be the Divine, we would be one with Nature. Indeed, to the extent that we can refrain from losing that child-likeness of soul and spirit, we will be closer to Divinity throughout our life.

Yet as a newborn even we will contribute to our ejection from that Edenal realm. It is we who will place the angels of death at the gates to Paradise. Forever after, the knowledge of that blessed experience before birth and the Divine Awareness we had of the Larger Reality of Beauty, Bliss, and pure Love, will lie on the other side of the deathly terror, the mind-numbing fright, of our experiences of birth and the time immediately afterward. So we will never look in that direction again. We will block out of our memory, even, that such a thing ever existed, having had imprinted in our flesh though not allowed into our conscious mind that that time is associated with the most excruciating and hellacious events we have ever experienced — our time in birth and as a newborn.

Our newborns would, thus, out of despair even die off if not for splitting off from their misery through our construct of Ego.

And how will we construct such an ego? The only thing we know of in our world at this point are our attendants — our caregivers and parents, in particular our mother. So what we learn from them is the only thing we even have available from which to build our new and unreal self. Hence, at the beginning only just from example, they and their behavior are our guides. Indeed, since we are so dependent upon them for life, the first thing we learn is who to be in order to get our needs at least met enough to keep us alive.

This is the beginning of that controlling-conformity behavior that follows us throughout our life: Our resolve is to control; our deepest drive and motivation is to dominate and have power over all the factors that influence our life so that we will live and never experience that terrifying helplessness and fear ever again. But in order to live, to just simply live, to get the basic minimum for survival — of food, warmth, comfort, rest ... and all the rest of that — we need to conform. We need to carefully observe and monitor what it is that will result in our receiving something life-supporting and what it is that we do that results in something harsh and painful. Like a pigeon pushing a lever to get a pellet, we learn quickly and well. We build our entire *modus operandi* for life out of these early lessons.

Thus, in our early lives, dependent on adult caretakers, it is those fully growns attending us that guide us. They, with all their insanity and their inability to truly take in or really notice much in the world outside their egos, must now attend to us. And, being as they are the sole models for the ego of the child at that time, they also will be the delivery systems for that unusual human construction of Ego. Our adults, in particular the parents, will be the major instruments in creating this strange and abominable thing of consciousness, this Ego.

Children a Burden

Now, let us look at childhood from the perspective of our fully growns. For human adults are not passive actors in these developments. As I have been saying, this is the ultimate and easiest arena of control for us humans. Sure enough, adults consciously and unconsciously foster and constrain the ego creations of our young ones in the course of their care-giving.

Fully Growns Hardly Fit Caregivers for Newborns

But our fully growns are at the same time consumed by the controlling, conforming, backwards thinking, and the alien and crazed overstimulation of consciousness that I have been describing. Parents, caught up in pressures from both within and without, could not help but be unfit. Consumed with baseless terrors and drowning in relentless mental machinations meant that humans would be neglectful of their children. With twisted thoughts within us, both distracted and ourselves needy, our adults are less than ideal caregivers to newborns; we are "babies having babies," as they say.

What we are always and everywhere ignorant of is our biological, species-determined inability to give adequate care to those dependent on us. We are, for all the reasons I have been listing, "not quite here," virtually all the time. We are distracted and self-obsessed. While responsible for tending our young's needs, we are forever distracted by our controlling and conforming obsessions; we are continually derailed and led astray by our backward thinking. We are barely able to focus outside ourselves, as we are constantly consumed by the alien and crazed, overstimulated consciousness that characterizes us.

We "Raise" Children like Plants; We "Train" Children like Animals

We know how we consciously seek to control our offspring. We call it "raising" our children. In doing so, again we show how we objectivize the world and how its people look to us like things to be grown for our use and consumption, much like our crops or chickens. We would "raise" our children up as if out of the ground like a cornstalk.

More kindly, we view it as "training" them; though we would never acknowledge, however true, that our aim is to mold and force upon them a shape that makes of them just another extension of us

... a mini-me. For we beat our children into things for use, and we value them to the extent they are copies of us. Again, there is that Ego of us. And here we see how our effects on our children begin to become unconscious influences: We affect them in ways of which we are completely oblivious and always and everywhere have vehemently denied. Still, I must point these things out for those of you who, because of the pressing and intense nature of these times and your unusual sensitivity to the needs of those beyond just yourselves, *are* able to hear it.

We Are Consumed with Building Bridges over Unpleasant Nows

We cannot help but be poor caregivers, with all these other things going on inside us. For children require attentiveness and focus on their needs, and we are ever self-obsessed. Our minds are busy building walls to buffer reality, and bridges over unpleasant Nows to fantastical and ever-receding futures of ease.

Looking back at the deepest origins of our feverish controlling and fearful conforming, remember that it is rooted in and driven by our underlying — exaggerated and foundationless — fears of death — the supposed end of our beingness. This fear for our survival is made keen by our incessant paranoia of becoming deprived and of facing uncertainty, as we actually did, in most horrifying ways, as infants.

So, the very same deprivations and uncertainty our planetmate relatives and to some extent our gather-hunter progenitors embraced as providing the spice and delightful play of life for us are the forces to drive our obsessive controlling. Furthermore, as we became more "human," we became that much more, not less, fearful of death. We became ever more terrified of an imaginary future containing uncontainable levels of pain of not getting what we want. We became ever more deranged when confronting uncertainty in our present.

Burden

Furthermore, remember that fear for our survival — of deprivation and uncertainty — drives our obsessive controlling and conforming.

So there was an increasing tendency, as we became more "human," as I have defined us, to not want to add the burden of caring for dependent young ones to our already uncertain state. Consumed with baseless terrors and caught up in our relentless mental machinations around them, we cannot bear the thought of adding the burden of children to all that. Hence, alongside the increasing time of helplessness and dependence of newborns was the increasing reluctance of fully growns to jeopardize their survival for their own newborns.

We are hardly able to focus outside ourselves and are lost in a matrix of long-ago schemas of feelings — from infancy and birth — pushing and pulling us all about regardless of what we are confronted with in the present. We truly are babies ... acting out a script of infantile traumas ourselves ... who are trying to raise other babies.

We would like to make up for our inabilities by having our newborns simply grow up faster and not be such babies for so long. For after all, it is only their neediness that offends us. It drags us down and requires that we leave off some of our activities and thoughts, which are in the efforts of defense, and come out of ourselves to heed another's needs. "If only they would cry less." "If only they would sleep through the night." "If only they would poop in the right place."

Forever falling short of filling our own needs in the present, as we go about doing that along with attempting to fill the ever present list of imaginary "needs" left over from our past, we cannot be good caregivers for needy others. Put another way, burdened as we are with imaginary struggles, it does not behoove us to attend to another's real needs.

Was Exacerbated by Sedentary-Hierarchical Living

These reluctant feelings did not fully manifest, however, until around the time of ultimate control and crazed beingness that occurred with the switch to sedentary and accumulating-conforming ways. Bad enough, all this was when we were nomadic, gatherers and hunters, but all of this was made worse by the switch to sedentary living. For with fixed abodes, inequality of stores, and the resulting social hierarchy came all its requirements to conform increasingly to the demands of a social arena for the satisfaction of one's needs. Remember that in Nature we enjoyed a relative independence of action in satisfying our basic needs. In Nature, we knew the relative self-assurance that one could always fend for oneself, if need be.

However, hierarchy and increased specialization of function — which was a narrowing of the fullness of life experience down to a focus on the aspect of it which could be traded in society for survival — made us dependent on the good will of others for survival. It re-created the state of infantile dependence on our caregivers. We were thrust ever, triggered ever, into feelings of helplessness vis-à-vis the Other, which now would include the social matrix within which we were nurtured and fed.

I will leave for later how this, in itself alone, transformed our ideas of Divinity, again ... this time it took on more of the qualities of the ones we were most dependent upon — strong men or a man, patriarchal elders, and chiefs — instead of the forces of Nature and its central experience of rebirth. For now, it is more important to notice that the major effect this fundamental helplessness in relation to society had upon our feelings and thoughts was the requirement, always, that one's actions be not just sufficient (for survival) but *pleasing* (to Other). So, to a consciousness caught up in pushes and pulls left over from early deprivations and trauma in interaction with an inattentive, sometimes harsh, Other (one's caregiver/parent) was added the pushes and pulls to appeal to, and be approved by, similarly unconcerned, careless, sometimes brutal Others in the present, which were one's higher ups.

This could not help but make it even more difficult to attend to the needs of our young. In the drama of intrigue and chicanery, which erupted out of the necessary interaction for fulfillment of needs with increasingly larger numbers of similarly helpless and equally desperate others in society, we were engaging the majority of the attention and focus we *did* have. Caught up in the necessary wiles of life left us with little over. The persistent and undeniable needs of children, arising at any time of the day or night, was an unwanted addition to the increasing demands and complexities of daily life.

Pain Containers

Outlets for Misery Were Sought — Women and Children

Further, because of the suffering of adults resulting from the social conformity and its humiliation, which came with sedentary-accumulating lives, outlets for that misery were sought. I focused a few chapters ago, Chapter 16, on the ways in which women came under attack as one of those outlets. However, children were the ultimate repositories for such resentments and denigrations. Being the lowest on the hierarchical rung, the least able to defend themselves, they served as the easiest of targets for abuse.

With sedentary living, children were the first and most obvious victims and the easiest to control, bringing benefits for our new way of life in the ways I will detail, such as their being able to be used as laborers to help with all the extra work come of farming. The domination of women for the most part came later; it was associated more with hierarchical social arrangements than with sedentary living. The order of these descents — domination of women, and of children — varied among cultures and occurred concurrently in others. In truth, these falls from natural grace were so gradual and so varied, it is difficult to make an overall determination of their occurrence in historical time.

Though, with sedentary living, which came before hierarchy, all humans took on greater loads of work; and that included the children. Play in Nature was left behind as children were put to labor on farms when we began homesteading. However, women were less oppressed in simple, agrarian communities. A matriarchal ethic — with a relationship to Nature and a focus on birth and rebirth, which characterized gatherer-hunter spirituality — was still prevalent. This took the form of a Goddess worship in agrarian societies. These were the days of the harvest and fertility rituals.

Nonetheless, with patriarchy and the rise of hierarchies, the reverence for Nature and the feminine were left far behind. Men put themselves above other men, and all men put themselves above Nature ... and women. Domination of women arose everywhere in the world with hierarchy and its offspring, patriarchy.

You will notice, however, I have placed the descent of misogyny before that of child use and abuse in this text. I did that for purposes of the narrative and to illustrate the line of power that was developing from Controller at the top to child at the bottom. Although, probably, children were targeted and corralled into control, overall on average, historically prior to the domination and subjugation of women.

Children and Women Became Scapegoats for Humiliated Men

The result? From the preceding chapters it can easily be guessed what transpired: Children were the lowest in the hierarchy of importance in any society. They were often abandoned or even killed, oftentimes right at birth. For they were the least able to defend themselves, and they represented the biggest additional outlay of resources and effort of anything coming into an adult's life. However, children were under the most pressure and were the most scapegoated in the hierarchical societies which came with sedentary living.

In ways very similar to the change in the perceptions of women, with hierarchy — that is, with there being controlling and demanding persons ever above one — came incredible pressure to extract from others below oneself amounts of complicity and service equal to what was being demanded from above. It was the unconscious trade-off that men sought for the sacrifice of their energy, time, and self-esteem to those above.

By that I mean that men knew and secretly resented the fact that they needed to put time and effort into the needs and wants of those above them, rather than their own. They felt they could live with that as long as they could balance that suck of energy from them to above with acquisition of unworked for boons from those below. More simply, if they had to suck-up to those above them, they could console themselves with the fact that others below them sucked-up to them. This was all decided unconsciously, of course. So men used women and controlled them in an amount equal to that which they themselves felt controlled and dominated from above. Men knew they were humiliated and denigrated to an intolerable degree by those above, but they were able to live with that if at other times they also could dominate and bully.

And, of course, women were always targets for all this scapegoating and abuse. Still, even further down — and available to be scapegoated even by women — were the children. So, again, children were felt to be both the one excludable variable in life's burdens as well as the ultimate repository for the suffering brought about by such burdens. They were not wanted and were killed or abandoned, being felt to be additional burdens on psychologically and economically distracted adults. However, if they were allowed to live, their needs would be set aside in accordance with the pathetic needs of caregivers who desperately sought dependent underlings — of any kind, women or children, fringe group or subservient class — upon which to balance the injustices of their adult lives.

It is no coincidence, either, that women, being the easiest in society to dominate, the ultimate societal scapegoats, would have thrust upon them the burden of care-giving that men did not want. Being the child-bearers they were obvious candidates; but these societal pressures that came with sedentary living increased and reinforced that relation. And men were both more anxious as well as more able — more easily beginning with sedentary life — to cut themselves away from any such responsibilities regarding children. Nonetheless, they heaped extra pressure on women. For the fact that women, being lowest in the pecking order, were the most supervised of all sectors of adults meant that although men would not want to help in child care-giving, they certainly did not want women to be so cavalier about it.

You can see that women were in the worst situation. Being the repository of the suffering of their men, who themselves were the repository of the misery of the strong men above them, women carried the heaviest burden yet were left with no one below them to pass along the burden of care-giving except for children. We can be thankful that women, overall, did not abuse their children to the same extent they were by their men. Our survival as a species probably hinged on that fact. Though of course they did to some extent.

Concerning our offspring, this task of attentiveness to children, furthermore, was a complication that just added to our considerable discomfort around not knowing things, not being able to control things ... around uncertainty. For while we sought to control everything about us, our children would be the one major factor upsetting our carefully made plans and throwing the monkey wrench into any laboriously constructed ease we were able to carve out for ourselves.

Thus, while our newborns required more, we would prefer to give less. Our newborns required ever longer periods in the dependent and helpless state as we changed over time, while with our increasing fears we felt it risky to focus on a helpless other and away from our attention to warding off present and future imaginary threats.

This reluctance to care for our newborns only became truly apparent and blatant after our transition from nomadic ways to sedentary ones, however. For this switch allowed full rein to our mania to accumulate and control and, with this increased separation from the natural, a greater state of ordinary madness. We peaked, at this point, as far as our desires for controlling. So the unpredictability brought by newborn others was that much more unappealing.

19

The Fifteenth Descent — Child Use ... Infancy and Sycophancy:

Newborns Had Better Smile and the Earliest Beauty Contest, On Human Sycophancy

"Humans, to the extent they could, built cabins of comfortable belongingness, but they rested uneasily upon shifting sands of mistrust and fear."

"It is as babies when the outlines of control and sycophancy are drawn."

Newborns Had Better Smile

It was around the time of ultimate control occurring with agrarian and sedentary-accumulating-conforming ways that non-care and death for newborns was common. Newborns were often and routinely abandoned, deprived, even killed. Our species could not, of course, thrive during this period; and we would have died off if not for the fact that some of our humans were not as crazed as others and so carried out at least the minimal amount of care-giving for some newborns to reach maturity and themselves have offspring.

Infant Conformity and the Earliest Beauty Contest

During this period, also, there were advantages for survival of newborns who had certain characteristics. Since newborns were increasingly seen as handicaps in the survival competition we created among ourselves, those that had traits fitting with the crazed perceptions of the fully growns were selected for survival increasingly. So traits in helpless newborns that made them either seem less burdensome or more appealing were selected for and increasingly prevalent. Babies had better smile, so to speak.

Overall, in our devolution, society and culture took the place of our missing connection with Nature; people became more "socialized" and "social" to make up for the sense of real belongingness and connection with Divinity they lost in the course of that devolution. The socialization process in infancy was crucial in that process of transforming from someone attendant to Grace to someone beholden to "civilized" others. It was incumbent upon newborns to succeed in their earliest and deadliest "beauty contest."

Yes, to adults, babies must be adorable. More generally, adult conformity and sycophancy has roots in the newborn's needs to win its congeniality contest, or else.

Human Sycophancy

So it was that our extremely controlling proclivities reached a peak with our agrarian and sedentary lifestyles. All that one interacted with on a daily basis was slotted for control — whether animate or inanimate. Life's deviations from what was expected became an evil; certainty was sought; routine was relied on and reinforced whenever possible. Power *over* was become an ultimate value; *interaction with* — with its concomitants of interesting engagement and learning — was looked down upon. All of this can be subsumed under the category of the increasing rigidification of Ego … the fearful Ego.

Of course the flip side of controlling was conforming or syco-phancy. The rising rigidity of Ego was coincident with an increasing debasement of our real, or natural, self. The intuitions and desires of the natural self were tossed to the side in deference to the demands of survival — whose instrument in the world was Ego. Correspond-ingly, survival was more precarious now, tottering, as it was, increas-ingly upon the good will, or at least the non-antagonism, of higher ups, as well as that of the necessary others — those equals with whom one's interacting would bring the satisfaction of needs not able to be satisfied on one's own. We might say that humans were becoming more "social" or more "socialized."

It is true that extra dependency upon others forced the develop-ment of skills and traits that were beneficial, even laudable. Yet these came at a cost to one's natural self. Humans, to the extent they could, built cabins of comfortable belongingness, but they rested uneasily upon shifting sands of mistrust and fear. Society and culture took the place of our missing connection with Nature. Still, Nature, with all its unpredictability, is far more reliable, not to mention bountiful and generous, than ever-inattentive humans with starving, often greedy, hearts.

At any rate, this extra dependency on the social world required an attention to others and their needs, which itself could come about through increased attention to the verbal and physical expressions — the conscious and unconscious communications — of others. How-ever, this attention was skewed and diminished. Rather than provid-ing insight into the deeper feelings and experiences of others, all this information was laid alongside the measure of how it could be used to satisfy one's needs — both conscious and real, as well as unconscious and counterproductive. So, therein we have sycophancy toward higher ups. But we have also manipulation, masked by peo-ple-pleasing behavior, toward one's equals.

And Manipulation, Go Hand-in-Hand

For certain, these behaviors — sycophancy and manipulation — were rooted all the way back in our earliest interactions with Other as an infant. It is as babies when the outlines of control and sycophancy are drawn. Helpless to acquire the satisfaction of one's needs upon one's own power, we as babies need to enlist the support of caregivers to the ends of our survival. Our desire is to have power, to have increasing control of our surroundings, for we had little to none in early infancy.

We could make noises, flap our arms, smile, laugh (eventually), cry, babble, but not much more. We cannot, as infant primates can, get up and go over to our mother and begin suckling while clinging to her fur ... getting our *own* breakfast, as it were. No. Mother must come to *us!* To stay safe and to feel secure, we cannot cling to our mother's fur as our nearest planetmates can, reassuring the both of us, as she goes about in the course of a day. So when our mother puts us down, as she must, to attend to other things and in that she cannot carry us all the time, our only connection with her will be through our voice. We must cry to let her know we are near and to assure ourselves that she is near. Helpless as can be, we must use cunning rather than physical ability to get our mother to attend to our needs.

To Summon the Great Mom

But how can we make that happen? Well, we use what we have. And our early baby actions, those actions-at-a-distance to influence the Great Mom, those early attempts at the construction of biological remotes to influence the ever-changing "programs" on the "screen" of life become our accomplished repertoire. With daily practice we are able to refine those tiny movements of face and hands, of crying and smiling, of noise and laughter, and to orchestrate them precisely to bring about our desired ends.

Thus, as infants, we learn to smile, point, cry, screech, and babble with finesse. Our early attempts are unplanned, automatic, crude, and for the most part, ineffectual ... like the early attempts of any future virtuoso. Yet smiling, we find, brings forth the Great Mom's countenance. We realize eventually we have the power to summon the "gods." We reach out for an object and cannot get to it. Still we try, and sooner or later, we find it drifts into our hand. For again, there has been an intercession from the Great Mom, this time brought about through the minute extension of a finger — pointing.

Crying out in pain is what all planetmates do. But we are the only one who turns it into a communication … a bit of an art form. Early on, when hungry, we were in pain and cried; we were soiled and uncomfortable and cried; we could not extricate ourselves from a painful position, and cried. These were not contrived responses; they are natural biological ways humans have of processing and releasing discomfort. There is nary a mammal who does not emote using sound. Don't kick your dog, but imagine if you did. You know she would yelp. You know your cat will screech when he is in distress and he will meow when alarmed.

So human babies will be noisy when upset; that's all there is to it. The tears that come later for infants are also a natural biological function we have developed, having to do with our origins as aquatic apes,[1] yet through them we release stress hormones. None of this behavior is concocted, or manipulative, at least at first. But then:

Very often, though not always, this wailing brought forth the goddess, the Great Mother, and most of the time things were set right. It did not take long for us to employ crying, not just out of pain, but as a way of communicating to that goddess. This form of baby praying, this self-flagellation for the purpose of being blessed by the goddess, we put more energy into so as to make it work better. So we cried until we were heard. And we learned to cry longer and louder to achieve our ends.

Being ever more successful at summoning the Great Mom, we found ourselves often in her presence. Simply the appearance of her face, the divine visage, brought forth waves of peace and contentment. Everything would be set right. But the Great Mother was not always directable in the way one wanted. We found that to the degree that we could interact with that Great Being and communicate with that face, we could achieve success. So we watched and learned from that face what was desirable, what was pleasing, and what actions of ours brought forth pleasantness — "rained down" from on high — and what brought forth nothing … or pain.

Superstition Is Related to the Capricious Quality of Human Care-Giving

However, the actions we performed did not always have a direct one-to-one relation to the desired result. Pointing at an object and finding it coming within reach worked for some of us, at some times. Still, sometimes what worked was mysterious, "superstitious," totally having no or an opposite relation to the result. And this varied with the caregiver. Thus, for one caregiver, crying brought about a changing of diapers and a welcome visitation from the goddess. For another, crying while needing changing resulted in one being isolated in a dark place and ignored. And the longer one cried, the longer one was isolated.

In such a situation, one would have confused or wrong learnings about how to bring about desired results. One might be getting a deep learning that to receive comfort — a changing of diapers, for example — one's chances were better if one acted, for all the world, as if nothing was wanted ... or needed. One might learn, paradoxically, that indirect expressions or non-expressions — keeping silent about — what was going on inside oneself ... what was needed and wanted ... was the best strategy for having a chance at having them addressed and satisfied ... however randomly or haphazardly that might happen.

Such a person, later in life, would become the silent suffering type or the aloof personality — forever appearing to be unneedy and above it all, yet always and secretly yearning. Again, this indirectness and this "superstitious" quality of one's interacting with the world was unique for humans and related to the capriciousness of human care-giving.

Becomes Sophisticated Communication

Alone among all planetmates, thus, we developed elaborate signal systems and symbolic actions-at-a-distance — involving complex movements and sounds — which would later become ritual and language — to have an effect, an indirect one, upon one's environment.

However much this separated one from one's environment, one of the happy outcomes from all this had to do with the unusual attention given by both infant and mother to each other's faces. Elaborate and complex, finely tuned, facial movements and facial adoptions — *expressions*, we call them — evolved to achieve exactly that "action-at-a-distance" effect one desired. The same type of finesse, though not as refined and elaborate, arose around one's bodily expressions. Mother and child's communication with each other, initially, is not through words but through increasingly accomplished interpretations of each other's facial and bodily appearance. Language is added as a further refinement of that, later.

Eventually, for older children and adult humans, a growing sophistication of communication develops, making possible even deeper interpersonal/social connection and belongingness ... if and when it should ever be used that way. Our better mental health practitioners make use of this ability, for positive ends. Our Authentics are certainly more likely to use it that way. While either of these might use this ability to see deeply into another — by means of the complex and cultivated understandings that arise and accumulate beginning in infancy and throughout life — for the purpose of connection, union, or love, with another; the same ability might be used by a card shark to notice our "tells" and to take all our money. Clearly the most successful salespeople make use of it that way.

Getting back to the situation of us in infancy, there was a limit to what we could do in these regards — that is, in regards to achieving satisfaction of one's needs through one's own efforts, however artful, at communication.

Vied with Infanticide and Neglect

Remember that an offshoot of the tendencies toward the increasing levels of ordinary madness for adults was their reluctance to attend to newborns. Unlike the mothers of Nature who gain great pleasure, status in their group, and life fulfillment out of their young and their caring of them ... for child-bearing and care-giving are major life experiences for them, not extrinsic or secondary ones ... human mothers and caregivers have other concerns and diversions and are burdened, as I have been saying, with extra survival, and interpersonal, demands. That is to say, to a human's already uncertain state of mind, because of early trauma, making it already difficult enough to survive, children represent additional resources needed … physical as well as psychological. So babies were a burden, which meant that non-care, deprivation, abandonment, and death for our most dependent was common and ever increasing.

Self-absorbed and/or controlling adults — riddled with imaginary fears from early perinatal traumas — would be more likely jealous than caring of even needier newborns and toddlers. Murder of newborns — infanticide — became ever more a possibility.

Some of our earliest religions even sanctified this murder as child sacrifice. Notably these were *religions,* now — they were collective efforts at supernatural connection — not the individualistic shamanism or the personal spirituality which characterized our earliest humans. So these elements of child sacrifice, when they occurred, arose *after* hunter gatherer shamanism and as products of sedentary-agricultural cultures.

This is understandable enough, considering the extra psychological and physical stresses that came with such agrarian cultures and the added obsession to control, including now even the weather. Ideas about sacrifice — rooted in our infant attempts to influence the Great Mom, however superstitiously — abounded, including child sacrifice. These sacrifices were techniques of attempting to control even Divinity, now, as regards bringing rainfall, protection from pestilence, and such.

At this point in the text, you can probably see how these sacrifices amounted to forms of self-flagellation. And this self-flagellating sacrificing was supported, most fundamentally, by our infancy trauma — "If I show you how unneedy I am by destroying what is dear to me, maybe then you'll come (Mom)." Later psychological motives for religious and ritual sacrifice came of the attempts at assuring security by aligning with Controllers, which arose with hierarchy — "If I hurt, brutalize, and control my body like you do me, and thus align with you, maybe then you'll like me (Dad)."

I know, some of you are seeing the oedipal conflict here. Indeed, while such an oedipal complex is not part of our human nature as natural humans, it does arise with "civilization," as it has its roots in the rise of patriarchy in hierarchical societies. It is hardly rocket science that with sons being so unseen and treated so harshly in patriarchal societies they would have secret fantasies of wanting to kill their fathers. No big surprise, in the context of the theory I am setting forth in this book. Still, this is a topic so huge I will have to leave it for later. I address it in great detail in the next book in this Return to Grace Series of books, titled, *Back to the Garden*.

For now, infanticide was the more common response than child-sacrifice and was something that was more widespread globally, with sedentary-agrarian societies. And for economic reasons — that is, having to do with the labor value of male children in agricultural societies — most often the children to be killed were female.

How We Survived, Nevertheless

Naturally, these traits in humans involving reluctance to care for children were not conducive to the vitality of our species, and they would have ended our line if not for a few factors and developments.

Factors That Fostered Population Growth

These included 1) the lingering numbers of Authentics and the traces of authentic/natural beingness and traits that still existed in humans, especially among women, the primary caregivers; 2) the evolution of certain traits in babies to make them more likely to be nurtured; and 3) the fact that sedentary-agricultural societies had two characteristics that fostered increases of population. These factors were the increase in food production and the use of children as investments:

More Food

First, though food that was produced was less nutritious and led to many additional diseases, there was more of it grown. This pushed population growth. Humans were less healthy and suffered more … were shorter in height and had decreased life spans … but there were more of us around. Our populations withstood the increased ratio of child mortality come of sedentary lifeways and made up for it with abundant child-bearing.

Children as Investments

Second, as I will lay out more clearly in upcoming chapters when I discuss children as investments and the family citadel, in these agrarian cultures, which required more work to produce food, there were needs for additional "hands," additional workers. And the easiest to control and most available labor pool for this work was children. So having larger families became an economic advantage; whereas in gatherer-hunter societies, it was not.

1. "Maternal Instinct" ... A Lingering Authenticity

The first factor, however, which helped to keep our species from going extinct, had to do with the fact that not all our humans were as crazed as those who would kill or abandon babies. Our species still had access to biological impulses for affection and spiritual ones of unity with the psyche of the Other. We might call these things "maternal instinct" or "bonding." Earlier I talked about how bonding and breastfeeding were natural avenues for authenticity for women.

However, do note that such authentic behaviors were hardly extraneous to who we are. They are not add-ons to some otherwise insensitive human nature. They are manifestations of the way all in Nature — just as our nearest planetmate relatives, the apes — are at their core. It is not that some of us were lucky enough to be born with this — this caring, kindness, compassion ... this empathy with others and with newborns — or that we developed it. Or that it came to us magically through some biological events we were pulled to do. No, it is that some of us never lost what is still part of all of us at some level, however buried by trauma and fear it might be.

At any rate, it was because of this quality of us that still remained, however adulterated, that our newborns received at least the minimal amount of care-giving required to live. It is not that some of us did not give more; some did. We have some exemplary caregivers and mothers. It is simply that relative to what is possible in Nature — the perfection of need satisfaction through their species biology that is possible for them before birth but for us occurs in the context of caregivers in the first year of life — we cannot help but fall short ... or, sadly, do far, far worse. Still, it is because we could not completely lose our natural self … well, at least not some of us … that a sufficient number of our young were cared for in their early years and made it to reproductive maturity, enough to save our species from extinction. They would be able to have young of their own upon maturity, so we did not die out.

Incidentally, it is for the reason that there were severe pressures, for the sake of the survival of our species, on women to not be as inauthentic as men that they were not and to this day, relatively speaking, are not as unreal as men. Meaning that women are closer to being authentic and caring as well as being more in tune with Nature, for the reasons I have stipulated in the chapter on misogyny.

2. Thus, Newborns Had Better Smile

However, there was another thing that was quite important. This part has to do, not with the number of caring, or authentic, caregivers we have, but with the kinds of babies who would receive care. For it is not wholly out of the person that caring erupts, *sui generis*, but out of interaction with the Other. So, babies with certain traits would be more likely to *elicit* sufficient caring in their attending adults. All beings are beautiful, and babies especially so. Still, there would be pressure from natural selection acting upon the characteristics that our babies … and so eventually we as adults … would have.

Keep in mind that half-born human infants are, in all of Nature, the neediest young ones, and the most helpless. This makes their care indeed quite a chore. Through natural selection, we would have more and more newborns with appealing traits. Non-fussiness, repression of needs, extreme tolerance for discomfort and pain, and traits that adults would find attractive or desirable were all selected for in our young. So these traits also became more pervasive in our species. Notice also how they fit into the sycophancy requirements that increasingly characterized our adult years in hierarchical societies.

In sum, newborns were a burden in the unnaturally intense race for survival we created for ourselves out of pain. However, to the extent that these young had traits that fit with the unnatural needs or wants of our manic adults, they would better survive and more likely grow to have offspring themselves. Yes, newborns had better smile. And, all in all, our species would be increasingly characterized with traits that had roots in our neonates' needs to stand out in the beauty and congeniality competitions or suffer the consequences of neglect, painful deprivation … even brutality and murder. That is to say, child abuse and infanticide.

The "Love" Contract

Therefore, such traits in newborns as non-expression of needs — in other words, non-"fussiness" or non-crying — were selected over traits of expression of needs. Traits of "appeal," "cuteness," smiling more as opposed to less, or anything that held even slightly the prospect of the fulfillment of the fully growns' own early deprivations, through the newborn, were selected for.

Love?

This last meant that if fully growns could see a dim hope that they could get the nurturing — from their own newborns, now — that they did not get from their own fully growns when they themselves were newborns, they would feel more inclined to extend caring to such newborns and increase their survivability over other newborns. What we call "love" towards our children was often simply the desperate hope that these newborns would eventually grow up to become the fully growns — "parents" — that our forebears had wished they had but who in actuality did not care for them … did not "love" them sufficiently … when they were small.

If a child displayed behavior that was at all resembling what a truly nurturing parent would be like, he or she would attract more of that kind of attention in return. If fully growns could see a dim hope, from their own newborns, of getting the nurturing that they did not get from their own parents, they would feel more inclined to extend caring to such of their children and increase their survivability over their children who did not hold out such a hope.

We have children to fill our desperate needs for love. We give birth so someone, unlike our parents, will love us. In this way we continue the unreal and futile struggle from infancy into adulthood and we tussle with it for the rest of our lives.

This dynamic created the unspoken "love contract" that developed between dependent young ones and fully grown attendants: If a child would act less like it had needs and more like it could satisfy needs it was more likely to actually receive some attention to its needs, however inauthentic and agenda-oriented that attention would be.

Indeed, what we place on high, use to boost our estimation of ourselves over all other living beings, and attribute to Divine origins even is most often just a swirl of ritualistic craving and trickling satisfaction set in motion by keenly felt but supremely denied hurt. That is a mouthful, certainly. More simply, looking at love's roots in infancy, "love" towards our young is at first simply a desperate hope our children will become the parents we wanted rather than the ones we got, who came up short in loving us when we were children.

This understanding sets up the "love contract." Parental "care" is offered, predominantly, in humans, in an amount equal to the evidence parents perceive that their children will grow up to satisfy the needs unfulfilled from their own infancy and childhood ... that is to say, to the extent the children might grow up to become their longed-for ideal parents.

Adult Love

This struggle we carry forward with us into all the love interests of our adult life.

Knowing this harsh truth about the roots of what normally passes for love does have a flip side, a positive benefit. For in looking at what we call "love," we expose a real love that is possible for us by setting to the side what passes for love among the great majority of us.

Let us explore this in more depth.

20

The Fifteenth Descent — Child Use ... The Love Contract:

Repression of Needs, the "Games People Play," Our Inevitable Woundedness, and the Adult Love Struggle

"...we are babies having babies. We will attend to the needs of our young ones, at least to the minimum needed, if it seems they will fill that huge hole of feeling unloved that we carry from our infancy."

Human Needs and Their Convolutions

Now, since our adults were disinclined to put in the huge sacrifice required to care for young who were for an exceedingly long time in a dependent state, the survival of our species required the evolution, through natural selection, of certain qualities in babies. This was another crucial point at which our trajectory veered off from the paths of all the rest in Nature. It also led to many of the characteristics we humans use to distinguish ourselves from other planetmates and put ourselves above Nature — self-control, excessive smiling, forced affability, inauthentic sociability, people-pleasing behavior, delay of satisfaction, repression of needs, emotional detachment, stoic behavior, high tolerance for pain and discomfort, emotional control, self-sacrifice, self-denial, self-retiring behavior, worshipping and honoring behavior, mollifying behavior, self-negligent service behavior, self-negation, obsequious behavior, obedience to authority, loyalty to society and nation, ability to "simply shut up and just do the job," sexual control-repression and celibacy, unneediness, self-effacing behavior, disciplined behavior, obsessive neatness and self-grooming, compulsive cleanliness, mental and emotional "tough-ness," false modesty, and so on. However progressive and advanced many of these might seem on the surface — especially as viewed by us — we have never considered them in light of their origins, the hidden intentions embedded in them, or in contrast to their alternatives in Nature ... that is, in contrast to a natural or more direct mode or state of being.

Communication of Needs in Nature

For one thing, many of them contain elements — distinguishing us from all other species — having to do with the *repression of needs*. How amazingly contradictory! Our species would, under the influence of all the wayward factors affecting our development as fetuses and infants, find survival value incumbent upon the ... drumroll here ... *non*-expression of needs! The utter absurdity of such a thing might not be entirely clear.

However, think: Everything in Nature requires other things in order to survive and grow. Plants require water, sunshine, nutrients. These either are accessed immediately, are at hand or, as in the mammal and primate planetmates, all of whom require a "parenting" of sorts when young, must be produced and provided by some other. That is, indeed, what is meant by the word *parenting*: It is the satisfy-ing, by the older, of the needs of the younger and more helpless.

In order to survive and grow, needs must be satisfied. However, in the larger planetmates, there is a gap between felt need and satisfac-tion of it. In the instances where one requires the assistance of the Other to achieve that satisfaction, this gap is bridged by *communication*.

There must be a message from the needing organism to the providing organism that something is required and when it has to be provided. This communication can be in the form of a cry, a grunt, a body movement. And in Nature, there is no dissembling.

Nature is honest, if nothing else: The needing being lets the providing being know when and what should be provided; and so it is done. Everything in Nature is interconnected and is ever interacting and clearly communicating with all about it. From cells to galaxies, atoms to planets, need and satisfaction coincide perfectly: One neuron does not need to persuade the next neuron to be so good as to pass along the electrical impulse.

In Humans, Babies Needed to Change to Get Needs Met

Now, humans, on the other hand, as I have been stressing, are the most in need and the most helpless in satisfying those needs in their early lives. And, as I have been detailing, greater amounts of and more elaborate communication is required, consequently, and has become part of the human repertoire.

But now there is this. Humans have both the greatest and most time-consuming task of parenting of all other planetmates, and this coincides with the greatest amount, overall, of reluctance by caregivers to provide it. Something had to happen for our species to not die out from lack of poor parenting. What happened was a change in our babies, making them different from the rest of the young in Nature.

I have said how, "babies had better smile." That is part of it. Yes, babies had to become adorable. Also, there is a maternal instinct, certainly. Maternal instinct, however, is simply at base the caring and unity all planetmates feel with and for each other, predominantly. But humans' "instinct" is covered up and distorted by all the unique and difficult factors of our coming into the world. Thus, our maternal "instinct" has to be triggered: It needs more help bringing it out and sustaining it.

Bonding

This happens in the course of what we call *bonding*. We are beginning to understand how important it is for the mother and newborn to be with and interacting with each other right after birth and for as much time as possible in the crucial days following. It is through that interaction that maternal "instinct" is brought forth. Without that crucial time together, most of our mothers never get past the aloofness and entrapment within themselves that our unnatural early experiences put upon us. Such moms never quite feel the "unity" with the newborn which makes the newborn's needs equivalent to their own and which is the basis for truly caring about satisfying those needs.

However, bonding is facilitated by the qualities, not just of the mother, but of the child. Babies with traits making them likely to be wanted by the adult will be more cared for and will thus survive and thus pass along those traits. So, to survive, human babies and newborns, through the process of natural selection, developed qualities to accomplish that. These would be subsumed under the rubrics of "cuteness," "appeal," "adorability." Babies had to be lovable to attract response that would bring satisfaction of its needs.

Non-Expression of Needs in Humans

In light of the fact, however, that parenting is such a chore for humans and adult humans are needy themselves, an additional class of traits would develop: *Babies would develop traits involving the repression or non-expression of their needs.* Non-fussiness, high tolerance for pain and discomfort, numbness, and unfeelingness would be placed under this column. Hence, having needs but either not allowing oneself to acknowledge or react to them or not letting the Other know of them would be an advantage in getting those needs, actually, fulfilled at some point. Consider just one implication of that: In order to get real needs fulfilled, to some extent one had better not be aware of them! In such a situation — peculiarly human — happiness becomes completely random ... happening by accident, only.

Returning to the situation in infancy, in addition to traits of adorability and appeal — cuteness and smiling and laughter — traits that involved non-fussiness, crying less, non-expressiveness, numbness, and unfeelingness on the part of the infant were selected for.

And the Hidden Agendas of Adults

Of course, there had to be a combination of both expression of needs as well as non-communication of needs in order to survive. There has to be a combination of unfeelingness-numbness and effusive entertaining adorability. And every baby who survives develops this. It is the major practice of every day of its life … to an at least sufficient degree … sometimes to a masterful level. Amazingly, human babies must learn to both communicate directly as well as to dissemble, to be both responsive as well as repressed. Human babies must learn to direct, but not appear to. They must be charming, but not obtrusive; seen, but not heard. Through this charm and manipulation offensive, these little politicians must bring about the satisfaction of their deep desires and needs, yet appear to be "above" such concerns.

Again, we see the factors which pushed the twisted consciousness and behavior of humans. Humans have "hidden agendas." They might say one thing, and the other human must figure out what that person is *really* meaning … which might be the opposite of that.

Some cultures would develop this to an insanely and mind-bendingly elaborate social ritual. "No, thank you, I don't want any" might mean "Yes. I want. But ask again." Or "Please, no. Don't bother" could mean "I wish you would. But I want you to insist on doing it." The actual meaning might need to be deduced through masterful and intricate discernment of the context of the statement, its tone and manner of inflection, the body language of the speaker, and so much more.

Extra Communication, Extra "Intelligence"

Indeed, much of the *extra* communication humans have developed, compared to other planetmates, has to do with this added dimension of confusion. A planetmate might meow or grunt its desire. It is not confusing. It says, "I want." A human hearing a communication of need must often discern it through a maze of possibilities of what that expression *might* mean … other than what is meant on the surface. And much more of language is elaborate convolutions of thought built around and upon such confusion.

Furthermore, much of the extra "intelligence" we humans credit ourselves with — accounting for the extra brain growth, size of head, birth pain, and then extra information-processing involved in repression of that pain, in a vicious cycle — has to do with this extra mentation involved in dealing with our confusing communications and relationships with each other. Our extra brain growth is because of the extra maze of neural pathways required to keep ourselves buffered from remembering our painful past, required to keep us confused, and part of this ... an example of this ... is just this confusion around communication with each other and the excessive thought processing involved with handling it appropriately, which has its roots in early infantile need deprivation and the mental machinations around it.

A good way to see the extent to which humans engage in superfluous activity around miscommunication, inaccurate response to it, efforts at resolution, and so on, is to look to the plot of virtually any television sitcom. The plot goes something like this: Someone does or says something that is misunderstood. All kinds of consequences ensue, often hilarious, as well as frustrating, to the audience for they are in on the actual meanings and intentions of the participants. Developments unfold which bring the personalities back in line with their understandings of each other and a resolution and reunion is had by the end of the show, leaving everyone, and the audience, happy and satisfied. Like fairy tales, sitcoms take actual realities, deal with them, and then provide a happy solution, a "happy ending," to help us to bear the burden of our frustrations in life.

The sad part about each of them — fairy tales and sitcoms — is that life is not actually like what they portray. The problems addressed are true — often brutally so in fairy tales — but the happy endings hardly ever occur. So also, the resolutions of miscommunications we see in sitcoms are the ways we wish things would work in life. If they did, folks would not become estranged from each other and end up harboring resentments to each other. However, in fact, most often misunderstandings abound in human relationships and fabricate the structures of our confused lives, with so much unnecessary mentation and activity ensuing from so much miscommunication and inability to comprehend the confusing signals and behaviors of our significant others. All of this emanating from our confused learnings in infancy.

And the "Games People Play"

The result is that humans have these, "games people play." Planetmates sure as hell do not. We humans engage in all these rituals as if we are beings on opposite sides of a wall, unable to see each other, communicating elaborately and madly with movement and sound — all of which are severely constrained in some places and consequently overdone and dramatized in others. How hard we work. How tiring we seem to be. How complicated our lives. How haphazard and inept our connections with each other.

Meanwhile, Nature implies the idea of everything being interconnected. Needs and satisfaction are two sides of the same coin. By separating them — aching, urges, and wants, on the one hand, and satisfaction, relief, and pleasure, on the other — so far from each other, we widened our separation from all of Nature, made ourselves more isolated, and contributed to our being the most suffering of all planetmates.

Delay of Satisfaction

This separation of need and satisfaction we label an ability — calling it a capacity for delay of satisfaction, for delay of pleasure — and we tell ourselves it makes us superior to Nature. Adorning ourselves with this crown of extra control of ourselves, we make our dissatisfaction and suffering an accomplishment. This, along with all our other dubious "achievements." Still, we never notice how this *power over* is bought at the cost of *interaction with*. Which is to say, interaction with, our body … engagement with, Nature and reality … connection with, humans and other living beings in harmonious accord.

This separation of us from satisfaction means we push the world away and retreat into a fortified circle, a command center of the mind, allowing survey and oversight of the experiences of the body, but not immersion in those experiences … not really feeling them. We tell ourselves we are free from the urges and pushes of the body, this way. We say that we "are not an animal" or "beast" in having this seeming control of our needs.

And Its Dire Consequences

Yet we never see or acknowledge how this control is paid for with irrationality and uncontrollable acts afterward, often around other events and behaviors. By this I mean we might control our sexual urges only to end up beating women and children and going to war. We might play the "heroic," strong and silent type, or the suffering martyr, but, caught up in our inner suffering, we may not notice those around us needing our assistance ... we might be insensitive to *their* cries of pain ... we might run roughshod over their lives and forget that there is life force and Divinity in them, as well. We might be celibate but unable to refrain from use of the hickory stick on our charges. Our long history of war, torture, domestic brutality, religious atrocity, rape, enslavement, and genocides should be telling us something about ourselves in these regards.

Let me be clearer on how we are different from other planet-mates regarding the satisfaction of needs. To take one example: In Nature, one of the dog planetmates might get hit or bit and would yelp. Whereas a human might get hit and not cry out. We might repress that need to express pain — and it *is* a need — because we have learned, in infancy, that to cry out when hurt brings even more hurt later. This failure to respond in the present to the urges ... "instincts" ... of the body leads to manic mental activity afterward. The repressed need drives extraneous thoughts which keep one enslaved in the mind and separated from experience in Reality. It should be clear how repression of any other biological needs — sex, food, water, freedom of movement, comfort — does the same thing.

One is often blocked from the immediate satisfaction of needs, that is true; and that applies to all planetmates, including humans. Being frustrated from satisfaction is one of those exigencies of life and fate which teaches us, ideally. Being able to navigate both frustration and satisfaction of needs equally well is what is desirable and what characterizes our planetmates. What makes humans different is our self-denial when there is no need for it. Again we have taken over the determination of our spiritual path. Again we show how we defy the Divine by seeking to control It ... just as we sought to control our caregivers as babies ... and not to learn from It. Rooted in our infancy and the inadequate and capricious qualities of our care and need satisfaction at that time, we seek afterward to deny ourselves, again, in an unconscious way of seeking Divine reward. Our denial, suffering, praying, and self-flagellation — figurative and literal — are ways we seek to bring forth advantage later: They are sad and distant reflections of our baby attempts to influence the Great Mom.

Hierarchy of Needs

And they are not just pathetic; they are ineffectual. For it is not in the non-satisfaction of one's needs that one rises up in life. It is the satisfaction of needs that allows one to go beyond them to higher concerns and "needs." When one has satisfied one's needs for food and water, one's mind and body naturally orient themselves toward the satisfaction of needs and desires for connection and intimacy with others ... in community, family, and one-to-one personal and love relations. When one is contented in interaction with community, family, and intimate others, one naturally is drawn to the satisfaction of creative and spiritual urges.

Certainly one can attempt to pursue relational, creative, and spiritual ends when one is in dire need, and one can, with effort, achieve results. However the product of those endeavors is skewed and diminished by the fact that the entirety of one's being is not directed toward those ends as — whether one knows it or not, whether it is a conscious or unconscious thing — one's body and the corresponding parts of one's mind are busy deflecting bodily urges at the same time. One "rises up" not by cutting oneself off from one's body but by standing solidly upon it.

Detachment and Faux Transcendence

Clearly, one's achievements while in a state of deprivation or distraction are distorted and sometimes counterproductive. For this path of detachment from one's body and its needs does not lead to spiritual wholeness and connection. Rather, its result is an emotionless, self-obsessed, compassion-less, humorless, and empty state of consciousness and being ... cut off from one's body ... which is labeled "transcendent" ... but which is simply split from Reality, Nature,

God, and Divinity, and which is solitary and supremely defended ... and lonely.

No, one does not transcend body and Nature to become one with God. For God/Divinity is *in* Nature/Reality. One can rise above body and call it spiritual, but it is simply human Ego that one has glorified. And the God that one worships in doing that is not one that we are made in the image of, it is one that is made in the image of us ... with all our faults, narcissism, vanity, cruelties and insensitivities, false accomplishments, and vain adornments.

Non-Expression and Sycophancy

So, in humans alone, non-expression of needs would be part of the communication repertoire developed by our young to achieve ... secretly or unconsciously ... the satisfaction of those needs. And repression of needs — that is, the attempt, consciously at first, later unconsciously, to not feel them — became a survival skill in relation to humans in our social world, however much of a disadvantage it is in relation to our biological survival, per se, or in relation to our world of Nature. We might repress our needs and get cancer ... but *they would like us!* Hopefully, there'll be lots of folks at our funeral.

Individual decisions to adopt these ways are not done intentionally, of course. Being required for survival it became part of our set of species traits. Furthermore, developed in infancy, it would result in our species having the only politicians and sales people. The only martyrs and "saints." And the only crazed and babbling people wandering the streets.

It should be clear how well these traits fit in with and how much more they were reinforced in the sedentary societies with their hierarchical social structures, where non-expression of needs — denial of self, feeling, and personhood — were desired of underlings by higher ups in order to support the dominator's illusion that their controlling tendencies were of no real harm or consequence to any others: Underlings acting less human and less real helped higher ups in their illusion that they were ... less feeling and real! Being tough and unfeeling told Controllers, not just that we were manipulatable ... for we would take whatever they dished out ... but even that we were needing and desiring direction and controlling from them. The more we acted like a robot, the more they felt we were unconscious and unfeeling and needed their help. The more we acted infantile and unthinking, they more they felt we needed their direction and paternalism, lest we die or kill ourselves all off.

The result is these things in infancy contributed to the ability of some of us to enslave others and to make all of us slaves — in ways profound and different from the rest of Nature — in our minds.

Love

In sum, non-expression of needs became of survival value in a species who were reluctant to care for their young because of their own unmet needs from infancy and childhood. And cuteness and adorability — smiling more as opposed to less, fussing less, being engaging, attentive, and entertaining, connecting more with the eyes — was of survival value for the same reason but also for another. This has to do with what we call *love,* in particular, *parental love.*

Parental Love?

Remember, we have an emotionally damaged adult — one who unconsciously seeks the satisfaction of needs left over from childhood in all the activities of his or her life and whose motives and intentions are ever skewed in ways symbolic or reflective of those needs. So, how do we suppose this adult views a tiny, unformed Other (a baby), who is dependent upon them? This adult also sees its newborn through its veil of emotional thirst and deprivation.

This part, regarding parental love, is perhaps the hardest for us to see, for it is here that we lay down the gauntlet — here, if nowhere else … and both women and men alike — about our superiority to Nature. If you have been able to agree with me so far, this is the acid test of your ability to view reality and yourself outside of Ego — outside your emotional deprivations and their consequent overcompensations of self-congratulation. For this apperception of ourselves as I am advancing is easily taken as an affront to that which is at the core of — now, even our women's — ego esteem: That is, the idea of human love, especially parental love, being pure and, again, transcendent and above, and making one superior to a supposedly unfeeling and brutish Nature.

It is not that humans are not capable of love. We are, of course. Yet we would not need to defame Nature's love and to glorify our own if our love was as untainted with selfishness and as transcendent as we profess. As I have been detailing (see Chapter 5, especially), this congratulation of ourselves on this point serves to offset the basic inferiority we feel in comparison with Nature and its planet-mates. Beyond that, this vanity about the quality of our love does yeoman's duty toward helping us to forget and deny the pain and deprivations we ourselves endured under the "care" — as infants — of those who were deluded similarly to the way we now ourselves cling to being deluded; that is to say, our own mother and caregivers.

Having been seen, as infants, through the famished eyes of adult caregivers who noticed in us the traits, behaviors, and characteristics of us that were reminiscent of the satisfaction of their needs, we felt the incredible hurt of not being truly seen: We experienced that our own needs were not going to be attended to — they would not even be noticed — unless they fit in somehow with our parents' wounded-ness or could be made to be seen by them, somehow, as potential relief of our parents' suffering. We experienced that whatever needs were noticed by the Other would be reinterpreted along lines to fit their needs, not our own. Unseen at times and misunderstood at others, we felt most alone; and we carried forward that hurt as central to our construction of an adult personality.

The Care Contract

It follows that when we ourselves had a child, that child would be seen and understood primarily to the extent that, and in the ways that, our child's behavior and ways fit with our leftover desires to be seen ... in a vicious circle ... from generation to generation. Quite simply, our babies would be seen and loved to the extent they mirrored for us the parents we wished we had. Then our children, being unseen and deprived this way, would grow up to be adults who, having their babies, would see and attend to them to the extent they mirrored what they wished *we* had been like.

Again, we are babies having babies. We will attend to the needs of our young ones, at least to the minimum needed, if it seems they will fill that huge hole of feeling unloved that we carry from our infancy. That is the essence of *the care contract*. We will nurture and foster the thriving of our children to the extent that it seems they will have the qualities that we wished had been in our caregivers in infancy. And when those characteristics are lacking, we will seek to plant them into our young ones and/or develop our children along those lines … lines which are in accordance with the relief of our hurts and the satisfaction of long ago needs. We wish to turn our infants into the parents we wished we had. We love our children to the extent that they hold out the hope that they will become that — our longed-for parents. But, no, we cannot bear the thought that our love is tainted with selfishness this way.

The Adult Love Struggle

Still, can we notice how this kind of parental love becomes the template for all that we see to be love? I have described how we have created our gods in the image of our parents in infancy — making them capricious, as our parents were, and yet potentially nurturing … if only we could be a certain way … as we wished they had been. Do we see that we view all our relations, and our love, through the veil of these deprivations as well?

We choose our lovers and mates out of these same unmet needs: We are drawn to those who are imperfect and capricious in their caring — in a way matching or reminiscent of what we received in childhood and infancy — but we pick them out by seeing in them the behaviors and ways that for us are a hope that we will actually get what we needed long ago. We select partners who are imperfect in a way similar to how our parents were imperfect, so that we can continue the unreal struggle — which we failed at as an infant — to turn these less than ideal people into the kind we really need. This struggle is rooted in an understandable reluctance to accept that what we got was not only less than satisfactory, but was traumatic. Consequently, ever after we try to make those events as if they did not happen — which is an impossible and unreal struggle.

So, to the extent that our adult partners do not match up with those hopes for them to be what we needed back then — and think about it, how can they? ... being both like our parents but we're thinking they will not be like them — we seek to change them in ways that they will be the end of our lonely years of yearning and unfulfillment. Thus, we see our adult loved ones and partners the same way we see our infants and children: We seem in them what we need, and we seek to make of them that which will lead to the healing of those long ago hurts.

Is Doomed to Failure

The result is we are ever doomed to failure. We cannot change people into who we want, any more than we could our parents. In fact, a characteristic pattern of humans is for us to begin having infants at exactly that point in a relationship with a partner — in a marriage, for example — when one realizes that one is going to fail at turning that person into the longed-for parent. It is no coincidence that one's attention will go, at that point, toward seeing if those long ago hurts can be quelled through an infant instead ... or, for some people, through another lover ... and thus we have infidelity or serial monogamy.

In this situation, the spouse does not satisfy, or quell, those pangs emanating from hidden and long ago deprivations, so babies and children are wanted, or another lover. Later, when the child comes up short ... and it will because a child cannot be a parent, really (I mean, seriously now) ... people often turn to religion, with its phantom parents, to continue the unreal struggle to satisfy those needs. That is why humans often get religion later in life, seeking to find in the phantom deity what they failed to find anywhere else in life. They come to religion after exhausting all possibilities for correcting an injustice which happened long ago.

When religion also fails, that is a time when one might possibly be open to hearing the harsh realities revealed in this book and facing the truth that one cannot make of one's life whatever one wants ... that life is full of pain, disappointment, and injustice.

Yet It Is Magnificent However It Goes

And not that that is right or okay, but simply that it is not that big of a deal: Life is magnificent whichever way it goes. For whether struggling to be free, pushing against limitations, strengthening oneself and alternating between frustration and accomplishment, it is all experience, it is all marvelous adventure.

The purpose of life is not to reach the goal, for it takes many lifetimes to return to Divinity. In the meantime, the goal is not even what would be desired. For the journey is all. And it is in making mistakes that one continues the journey. The imperfections of life are the rails upon which life's journey rolls along. They are necessary; however much at some point we will want, and need, to go beyond them.[1]

Our Inevitable Woundedness

In any case, when it comes to seeking satisfaction of early deprivations by means of others — whether romantic partners, children, or the Phantom in religions — we are doomed to failure. For we cannot remake people. In addition, we cannot satisfy those needs of long ago, not fully, even if we do get in the present what we needed then. We cannot undo a wound by not getting hurt again in the present. These early deprivations are a wound upon which and around which we have built our personality and our entire life plan. It has been cauterized and set long ago. So we cannot rid ourselves of it, and the ache of it, by simply not being further wounded.

Certainly, we are better off by not drawing to ourselves, as we will, those who will continually reopen that wound, who will continually mimic the primal events and retrigger the pain. Still, like we express in our myth of Chiron, this is a wound that will never heal; it becomes us; it is the burden we get to carry and the load we will need to push forward in life in order to build up our spiritual "muscles." But also, like Chiron, it can be the thing that catalyzes profound attachment-less service (*nishkam karma*), authentic giving and self-sacrifice, and true unconditional love, when it is the basis of a burgeoning empathy and compassion and an ever-growing openness of heart to others, to planetmates, and eventually to the Divinity from which we spring.[2]

Re-Membering and Real Transcendence

Regardless, and in the meantime, we can at least progress in life beyond the unconscious and tedious re-creation of hurts and re-invigoration of old and hurtful patterns. It is better to not draw to us that which will continually trigger us, but we cannot do that by denying our woundedness. It is for that reason, too — in order to stop the cycles of hope and then hurt — that it is better we face and embrace our woundedness. For in denying and repressing it, we are forever doomed to re-creating it. By reversing that separation from body — feeling the body and its aches and pains and urges again — and reconnecting with our woundedness, re-*member*-ing ourselves, we have at least the knowing making us capable of choosing something different. In this way we can free ourselves.

And the more we re-member ourselves, the freer we can be. That is the true "transcendence": It is one rooted in a re-feeling of and re-membering of the hurts and pains in one's body which are left over from the past and not a separating away from and a denying of that stored pain ... as if one is above body and Nature ... and confusing that self-congratulation and ego-aggrandizement with en-lightenment.

The Love Contract, Reprise

To sum this up then, our differences from other planetmates — stem-ming from our relation with our mothers and caregivers as infants — have to do largely with survival value being attached to non-expres-sion of needs. For certainly if it was the excessive neediness of our young that disinclined adults to want them, then if a baby had less of those qualities or seemed to have less they would be less likely to be shunned or abandoned, thus would be more likely to survive. A dependent young one suppressing its needs would manifest in it crying as little as possible, being as "unfussy" as could be.

Nevertheless, it was not just seeming to not be a burden that was advantageous. For our adults' psyche being so much founded on not getting early needs met, we would crave anything holding out hope, however futile, of getting anything resembling that kind of satisfaction in the present. So babies who had other qualities appealing to the adult — such as "cuteness," smiling more, or anything in the category of "adorability" or being "entertaining" or otherwise attractive to an adult or reminiscent of the satisfaction of those early deprivations — would make that young one more likely to thrive. If a baby was more engaging with us … as our own caregiver had not been with us; if it was happier and more noticing of us … as our parent failed to do; and of course to the extent that it would be as little a burden on us, it would increase the overall amount of vital care it would receive from us, from our fully growns, in general. Any traits in infants that for the adult caregiver held out the prospect, however dimly, of the fulfillment, through the newborn, of their own early deprivations were to increase in humans through the process of natural selection.

Since many of those early lacks had to do with being cared for, nurtured — what is commonly called "love" — it was any qualities of the newborn that seemed to hold the prospect of easing those cravings that were desired and thus were to be selected for and become more prevalent over time.

So the origins of what we call our unusually strong parental "love" is in this never-acknowledged "love" exchange. This "care contract" explains how our children managed to survive, with everything going against them. However, on our evolution to a purer love — one of Nature and built once again upon feelings of unity with Other and truly *feeling along with* another, not just in hopes of receiving in return — we would do well to look deeply into the inauthentic nature of what passes for love for us.

Real Love

Humans are, like the rest of Nature, capable of true and unconditional loving. Indeed, we have it in us to have that feeling toward all of Nature, toward all of Reality, even. However, we cannot achieve that while caught up in and blind to the hidden agendas and self-seeking desperation which mars our love and while braying to the world about our supposed superior capacity for and the supreme purity of our love.

In the next chapter we look even more deeply into the events and processes which keep us imprisoned in unreal struggles. Pulling to the side such ceilings of confusion, we better our chances of standing in the sunlight of love's actual dawning and our true freedom and happiness.

21

The Fifteenth Descent — Child Use ... Poisoned Parenting:

"The Fairest One of All," Childhood Is Our Pandora's Jar, "The Child Is Marinated in the Parent's Unconscious"

"Pure and guileless babies, white as snow in intention and closest to Divinity, are offered the apple of nurture and need satisfaction, but it is poisoned."

"...the child is marinated in the unconscious of the parent.... The conductor of these changes are the conscious intentions and the unconscious needs and qualities of the caregiver — both good and ill.... The child does not die, but its soul is murdered. It becomes less alive."

Tainted Care-Giving

Care-giving was tainted and minimal, certainly. Plus it fostered traits reflective of the emotional deprivations of the adults. In these ways human parenting contrasts strongly with that in Nature. For Nature's parents do not view their children through a dark, crazed veil of dry and thirsty deprivation, nor a floral, milky gleam of vain and pathetic estimation.

All human care-giving was tainted with this early deprivation and self-centeredness of the caregivers. However, while it did not serve the newborns needs for perfect nurturing, it allowed for some, at least, minimal nurturing for survival. Meanwhile, it acted on the newborns so that such traits that were even dimly reflective of the satisfaction of the fully growns' own early deprivations were selected for in newborns.

This period of ambivalence over children and what to do with them characterized our species for a very long period, relatively. Humans remained a small and insignificant part of all Earth planet-mates because of this. It only began to change when we started our sedentary-accumulative-conforming ways.

Children as Investments

So, however disturbed potential parents were, eventually humans began to see — and it's to be noted that in some types of cultures it took a great deal of time to get to this understanding — that there is benefit to the investment in these dying, desperate prematures, for their own survival, for the parents' survival. For our ancestors — after the switch to sedentary-agrarian ways — saw children as resources in their struggle against their overblown fear of death.

Children Are Neither Seen *or* Heard

Naturally, our children were hurt by the early inattentiveness to their real needs. Very much like with Snow White's stepmother, in our children's story of the same name ... which is so full of Unapproved and Hidden wisdom, by the way ... our infants are hidden behind a mirror reflecting only the caregiver's countenance — her needs — to herself. Our babies are not often really seen by us; their needs are dimly ascertained, mixed and diluted thoroughly with our own.

"The Fairest One of All"

"Who is the fairest one of all?" — as the stepmother queen intones — expresses that we are threatened by our babies … and jealous of them. For how dare they come into the world, being beautiful and delightful and having needs of their own, when we, in our beauty and charm, still have not managed to get all we needed back then (or now)? The stepmother wants to hang on to being the desired one, the noticed one, the wanted one … in this fairy tale of Snow White. In the same way, in real life, mothers and fathers, caregivers and adults of all kinds, are ever and too caught up in their own struggles to be noticed, attended to, appreciated, and wanted, to really see another, let alone a struggling, needy, and crudely assertive other — a child.

Children are new to the attention and ego games of adults, unpolished in their communications to express their needs, and riddled with mixed messages about whether they should even express them. So how can they compete with adults with decades of experience and thousands of hours of practice in the confused and complicated requirements of these games?

Guaranteed, children will be, to inhabit the bottoms of all totem poles and be the last on all lists of concern. Yet gifted with hereditary traits of charm and appeal, and extra abilities of cunning and excess mentation to devise new schemas of attracting needs attention, they have a fighting chance. And struggle they must, be clever they must, for all parenting is suffused with the emotional deprivation and resulting twisted consciousness of our fully growns.

Pure and guileless babies, white as snow in intention and closest to Divinity, are offered the apple of nurture and need satisfaction, but it is *poisoned*. They are attended to by fully growns, yet that attention to their bodily needs — like the comb is for Snow White when evil stepmother attends to her hair — is *poisoned* with the tainted intentions and self-centeredness of the caregiver. And parents outfit children with a way of being — a skill and personality set like their own

— with which to interact with the world and to allow them to go out into it; however, like the bodice given Snow White, the outfit does not fit. It is too tight; it is laced in a way to be too constricting.

And how can it not be? For it is not crafted to fit the child, it is made to suit the adult: These are ego, personality, and skill sets that the caregiver would impress upon the child to mold them into something which is desired by the adult and rarely wanted or helpful to the child him- or herself.

In all these ways, as expressed in the fairy tale, is shown the hidden desire to get rid of the child, expressed, historically, by infanticide and abandonment. Additionally, in all times and currently, the stepmother's intentions are demonstrated by child abuse, child neglect, and poor parenting. If not in blatant ways, this ambivalence toward the child, containing the annoyance and irritation, as well as the even more secret jealousy and hatred, shows itself in the simple reluctance to attend to the needs of the child by having the baby "cry it out."

It is seen in the decision to not breast feed the child at all; and if it is done, by pushing the weaning process. It manifests in the insistence on toilet training — which, incidentally, is not necessary in Nature or even among many of our gatherer-hunter societies — and even early toilet training. Babies must learn to poop *properly!* And soon. It is evident in circumcision and female genital mutilation and in all the many, many ways children are beaten into shape by humans to mold them into something not conducive to their thriving or happiness but simply to make them, for adults, less burdensome, less intrusive, more appealing, and … finally, even this — more *useful.*

More about that last, in just a little.

How Dare I?

But for now consider the blasphemous quality of what I am saying here. In human circles, one simply cannot say out loud what I just conveyed. One cannot say parents are really like this … like Snow White's stepmother. This is an example of how the Unapproved and Hidden manifests all about us, for example, here, in a fairy tale. Yet nowhere and at no time is anyone allowed to notice what these stories are saying. No one ever thinks, and certainly never expresses, what this fairy tale is really saying about us: That in our treatment of our young, it is us, not "animals," not planetmates, who, being conflicted, are often cruel. No, more than that, are *routinely* cruel.

Hardly is it hearts and happiness. No. Childhood, especially infancy, is that unseen, unknown land that we, becoming older, seek to put behind us and push below us … relieved just that we managed to get through it. We cannot remember much of our childhood, and almost nothing before the age of five. Why? Because we do not want to. We do not remember it, but a part of us is aware that it was difficult. That part pushes our mind to cover up those years, placing them behind and under a thick cloak of confabulation, heart shapes and unicorns, revision, and rationalization.

Childhood Is Our Pandora's Jar

On the individual level, our childhood is a perfect Pandora's Jar — something we fear, something that a part of us knows contains all the troubles of our life, were we to open it. Yet we sabotage ourselves this way: We are ever fleeing from the past only to manifest it, over and again, as fate.

We have forgotten that Pandora's myth advises us on a more fruitful attitude toward this time: That is, that in opening the jar, or box, the troubles of the world — our world — come forth, yes. But in the myth, the last thing to come out, the thing lying at the bottom, is *hope*. The myth is telling us that it is futile to fear and repress our history, our actual one — not the fanciful, sugar-coated version we have come up with in order to push out of our mind the truth. It is telling us that real change and progress can only come about through opening the jar and freeing the darkened impulses, thus bringing them into the light of day, of consciousness, where they can be seen and let go of. And that in doing this process, eventually … not immediately or even soon for anyone … real hope and real transformation can arise.

"Good Enough," Yes. But Poisonous, Nevertheless

Getting back to the nature of our parenting, it is important to realize that however far from ideal nurturing and what is possible in Nature, such care-giving was sufficient, barely, for our species' survival. In modern times, such an attitude would be enshrined in parenting canons, conveniently, beginning with Donald W. Winnicott, as care that is "good enough."[1] Nevertheless, such a corruption of nurturing served to infuse and mold the personalities of our children in unnatural ways. And not just unnatural ways, more and more this corrupted parenting pushed toward characteristics in the child that mirrored the darker impulses of our adults.

You are probably wondering, why would a parent's attempts to mold a child to make of them something positive and good in the world — however much it might be like oneself — end up manifesting one's own *undesirable* self? This question shows how this entire process is not quite being understood. For I have been saying how the parent seeks to make the child into a) something not bothersome or burdensome, b) something engaging and appealing, and c) something that is like what one wanted from one's own parents; that is to say, someone loving, attentive, and focused on oneself.

None of these are about helping the child acquire workable tools for later in life. They are not even about making the child to be like oneself. The fact is that though we tell ourselves that we are trying to make the child into the best person he or she can be in the world — with ourselves as the only good model of that — we are actually trying to turn them into something helpful to our psychological woundedness, not themselves. So to a, b, and c, we must add a d, which is related to the ways children are shaped and twisted *unconsciously* by our adult caregivers and in ways they do not wish, but cannot help.

"Not as I Do"

Here it is good to remember the saying, "Do as I say, not as I do." This expresses the idea that we wish our children to be something better than us. However, it is meant to be an ironic expression, because it points to the actual fact that children end up being taught just as much, if not more, from example as from direction. The fact is that children end up picking up both desirable and undesirable, effective as well as counterproductive, ways from the parent.

And the undesirable and counterproductive ways that are found in the adult are exactly reflective of that adult's early unmet needs and corrupted desires. That is to say, all that self-centeredness and emotional thirst in the adult, which infects their parenting, comes out as negative and undesirable actions vis-à-vis the child or are displayed in the child's vicinity and are observed by the child. For the adult does not acknowledge his or her selfish or needy intentions regarding the child. No, they are always unconscious, hidden, and unapproved.

That is the reason I know folks are so resistant to hearing what I am unveiling in this text. For our fragile egos are dependent on this idea that we are unconditionally loving; they are built upon this notion that our giving is pure and magnanimous. We are not aware of how we display and act out our early deprivations in our actions toward our children, so these are unconscious tendencies in us; indeed, they configure our unconscious. And this unconscious is not seen by us, yet it is has a huge effect on our child: It is most definitely seen and picked up by them, both consciously and unconsciously.

Why We Fail Even in Our Attempts to Mold Them

It turns out, as in my pre- and perinatal psychology circles we say, that "the child is marinated in the unconscious of the parent." That is, the child becomes, not just what we want it to become, but exactly that which we deny in ourselves and so, naturally, do not want it to become as well.

We are needy, and this lack of need satisfaction has made us, for one thing, insensitive. While we wish to raise a child who attends to us and behaves lovingly toward us, we do it in an insensitive way; for we cannot be other than ourselves. Try as we might to be like our ideal parent, if we do not have it in us, we cannot possibly give it. So, does the child end up being what we want ... loving, attentive, and need fulfilling? Or does the child become like us ... insensitive, aloof, and numbed down? Well, you know the answer. For the parent cannot teach love when the parent does not know real love.

It Is *Poisoned* … Poisonous Pedagogy

This is another reason the skills and personality set imparted do not fit the child, as exemplified by Snow White and the bodice. For it is not just consciously constructed in the image of the parent — that is, attempting to pass on positive traits of the parent — it is unconsciously constructed of all the unwanted qualities of the parent as well: It, too, is *poisoned.* The parent says, "Don't you dare hit your sister!" while smacking the child. This is poisonous pedagogy. And this is what I mean by that.

Ambivalent Mode → Trance State

Sure enough, while it does not kill the child anymore, that is to say, this ambivalence is a step above infanticide and abandonment, which are our first and earliest responses to having a child; still, it diminishes them. It bludgeons children's vitality and life force. Not quite killing the body, it murders the soul instead. In the tale of Snow White, we notice that each time Snow White is poisoned, or constricted with the tight lacing of the bodice, she *faints*. She does not die, but she becomes less alive. Sure enough, she ends up in a deathly state because of all this. She exists in a coma-like state, which is a pretty good description of the kind of trance state that this kind of tainted parenting produces in the child.

The Prince's (Princess's) Longed-for "Kiss"

The fairy tale then expresses what I have been saying are the effects this has upon our adult personality. For the tale says Snow White remains in this half-alive state until she is kissed by the Prince. She then wakes up. This is exactly what I have been saying about how we project all our childhood deprivations onto the love projects of our adult life, seeking to garner from them what we could not get as a child. We want our adult lovers to give us what we did not get as a child and thus save us from the diminished and numbed life that came of it. We hope they will wake us from our droning days of unease and longing.

Happily Ever After? It's a Fairy Tale, What Did You Expect?

The only thing not true about the fairy tale is the ending. For waking up, because of one's relationship with a partner, a prince or princess, is what we wish. But it does not happen. Fairy tales always hold out the hope of happily ever after. They reflect what we do and how we feel in our life. They do not show correct solutions to our problems or our pain. Indeed, that is why we call them, *fairy tales,* with all that connotes of being not real and being simply wish fulfilling.

Fairy tales are the way we solace ourselves about our human predicament. They demonstrate the wrong-gettedness of our thinking. They mirror the impossible struggles of our lives, just as sitcoms do. And like these TV shows, they provide a denial at the end … a psychological defense against realizing our truth. Thus, they reflect real things, then lie about them … just like all our good defense mechanisms and techniques of denial do. As well as do our most effective propagandists and conspiracy mongers, by the way.

Summary, Child-"Rearing"

Summing up, our children became different from the children of Nature, because their care was different and was influenced most strongly by shortcomings in their human caregivers. In order to survive, infants developed more traits of adorability and of both clever communication skills to get needs met as well as non-expression of needs so as to not be a burden.

Failure in these, early in our history as humans, would lead most likely to infanticide or abandonment. It follows that these traits increased in our babies as well as in our adult population in that they became permanent elements in our personalities. Insensitivity, dissembling, sycophancy, concealing intentions for the purpose of manipulation, unfeelingness, aloofness, controllingness of self and domination of others, alienation, and separation from others and

Nature became common human characteristics over time. Hence, the parenting modes — if they can be called that — that were instrumental in bringing about these changes were those of infanticide and abandonment.

In addition to these traits, additional ones which varied more by caregiver were inculcated in the child. The caregiver told him- or herself that they were instilling in the child characteristics and behaviors that were for the child's ultimate benefit. In actuality a good deal of what was instilled sought to put into the child those qualities that might satisfy the parents' own deprivations. Furthermore, without being able to help it, they influenced their child in ways that reflected also their own woundedness. The parenting mode at play in these influences on the child was that of ambivalence.

In this ambivalent mode of child-"rearing," the fashioning wand is not the one of child murder or abandonment, influencing our generations of children through natural selection. No, the conductor of these changes are the conscious intentions and the unconscious needs and qualities of the caregiver — both good and ill. So, like Snow White, in this scenario the child does not die; but its soul is murdered. It becomes less alive. And these traits in the child are passed along, not through natural selection, but through the fact that the numbed child will become the adult who will do the same to his or her own child: It is passed on down through the generations unconsciously and through example.

In sum, there was ambivalence in the desire for children. Our species swayed back and forth about what to do with them — between the poles of infanticide and abandonment, on one side, and acceptance, engagement, and nurture, on the other — for the longest period of our human existence.

22

The Fifteenth Descent — Child Use ... Family:

Childhood in Nature and in Civilization ... The Nuclear Family ... Primal Marriage and Sexuality ... Children Become Chattel

The Family "Investment," The Family Castle, Every Home an Enterprise, Every Family a Fortification ... Protection of Storage

Domination and control of offspring, mistreatment and exploitation of children, family "armies" and work groups

"It was families against the world. Children were raised in the pressure-cooker environment of the nuclear family. Monogamy and sexual exclusivity became all important, diminishing one's life experience. Women became owned as part of the economic resources of the family. Life experience was overall dampened in deference to survival and economic pursuits, and then this: The glorious and magical world of childhood disappeared and was replaced with one of economic utility."

Childhood in Gatherer-Hunter Societies

It follows that humans did not increase in numbers during the majority of our existence, which included millions of years of primate, proto-human, hominid, and early human existence — during all of which time we lived as nomadic foragers, gatherers, and eventually nomadic gatherer-hunters. Children were not particularly wanted. In addition to all the ways their exorbitant needs made them a burden, they needed to be carried from camp to camp. We did things that staggered births. Breast feeding the most recent child for as long as four years, which biologically inhibits the ability to become pregnant; refraining from sexual activity for a long time after the mother had given birth; and abortion ... our ancestors had their crude ways — all had the effect of spreading out over a long period of time the instances of pregnancy and childbirth. If the child came into the world deformed or unusually frail, they would usually remove it from its misery and then bury it.

Children Were Better Cared for ... and Loved

Having this long between births — an average of four years — meant that the children that were born, and that lived, received more attention, nurturing, and caring than is the case when children come more frequently. Having less children meant also that there was less burden in caring for the ones one had, so they were more likely to be wanted and to be attended to. Being free from the controlling-conformity pressures that came with sedentary-hierarchical societies, children were less afflicted with being scapegoated because of either father's or mother's societal subservience and unhappiness. Again, children benefitted from the fact that the lives of their parents were less onerous.

So, during this period when we had less children and when primitive abortion and infanticide were used as means of birth control, we had less children, but those we had were exceedingly more cared for. They were much more wanted, "loved," and seen than would be their human counterparts later on, after the agrarian revolution. They were, in fact, parented nearly as well as our nearest cousins in Nature — primates, apes, and mammals — despite our babies bringing with them so much extra helplessness and extra years of dependency.

We Were No Great Harm to Nature in the Beginning

Our species survived; although barely, due to this ambivalence. The factor of excessive burdensomeness of children, which might have ended our line, was offset by a natural, an Authentic, desire for children. Our numbers were not large relative to other species. There was a balance in Nature, and we lived harmoniously within it.

During this time, our species and its strange proclivities — its unusual birth, early infant deprivations, excess mentation, and distance from natural ways, compared to the rest of planetmates — did not matter much in the grand scheme of things. Humans were no great harm on Earth and caused no widespread suffering to the many planetmates outside ourselves.

Nuclear Families in Agrarian Societies

However, as our species turned its back on its nomadic roots and, blinded by an unnatural fever, pursued a circumscribed and strenuous sedentary lifeway, this stasis in our numbers began to change. While our earliest forays into agrarian-sedentary ways occurred as long as twenty-five-thousand years ago, they were not taken up by many of our species until around ten-thousand years ago. At that time, increasingly, and especially at around six-thousand years ago, there was a switch away from being nomadic to living in permanent settlements, based on an agricultural economic.

It is at this point that, though our motives were far from laudable and were selfish, we began to see some benefit in having offspring. We perceived survival advantages in family status and larger broods of children. By "family status" I mean that we became more inclined to identify ourselves with a nuclear family unit. Prior to this, we saw ourselves, primarily, as tribe members, and those human others who were included in our day-to-day world of social interactions included virtually all the members of our group.

Takes a Village in Nomadic Ones

Indeed, the burden of children was shared by the tribe, which is another reason children were more cared for at that time. If a child felt so inclined, he or she could move over to another hut or fire ring for a while, hang out with a different group of fully growns and children … who would, effectively, represent additional brothers and sisters … and be welcomed and embraced there.

In a very important way, children were viewed as being part of the entire tribe; their care was much more a group responsibility; their personalities were much more influenced by many tribe members other than the immediate caregivers; what they brought in terms of delight, adorability, fun, and love was much more shared by the entire group; and what they added in terms of additional hands and assistance benefitted, much more than later, the entire tribe, also.

So here again, children received much more in the way of attention, nurturing, and need satisfaction. And there was considerably more happiness attendant upon the state of being a child. Childhood involved being free and open, not just to the awesomeness of the physical world and world of Nature, but to the love, pleasure, fun, and interactions of the social world, as well, with its fascinating array of human behavior and emotion, and the brilliance and marvel of its "magical" members.

Primal Marriage and Sexuality

Correspondingly, as nomadic humans, while there was marriage, we were less adherent to a strict monogamy. We had various forms and varieties of sexual interactions and marital arrangements. Monogamy was most common, but even then it was less constrained. Sexuality was not the hoarded and jealously guarded commodity it became later for us. Marriage ties were more about the children — their care and the primary responsibilities for them. Additionally, marriage had to do with societal and cultural concerns, such as expanding kinship opportunities for the relatives of the married couple and maximizing the circles of sharing and reciprocation.

It had virtually nothing to do with establishing lines of inheritance or bloodlines, as it did later with agrarian societies and beyond. For owning little ... and needing little ... we had no concerns about passing possessions or property along. In fact, the mother being the child-bearer led most often to lines of descent being calculated primarily through her. There was no need, or desire, to upset that natural configuration.

Intensity of Human Experience

At any rate, we had much freer ideas about sexuality. Not only did this contribute to the spice of life and the intensity of human experience in general — for women as well as men — but it contributed to the caring of children. Let me explain:

By "intensity of experience," I mean that with the excessive stipulations and pressures upon our personhood that came with hierarchical societies, including today's, our experience — along with our needs, emotions, and aliveness — became muted, dampened. Repressed and numb, our experience lacks the color, the extra flavors and magnificence, and intensity of our lives in Nature. We have no idea what we are missing in our lives. We have not an inkling how we cuddle with our chains and contribute to our increasing numbification over the course of our lives.

Yet for most of our existence, which preceded our controlling-conforming-sedentary times, our experience was much more intense, alive, and interesting than it is for us now. And what added to that intensity and color, that exquisiteness and pleasure of our experience, was a freer and less constrained sexuality ... among many, many, many other things, by the way.

Advantages of Sexual "Open-Mindedness"

For the Child

How a freer sexuality contributed to the care of children is that it allowed — in that there would be no deprived party — for those times of sexual abstinence after the child was born and during the pregnancy itself. This kind of sexual abstinence would be a product of the sexual disinterest the mother often had while engaged in devoted attention to a young child. The mother derives much sensual satisfaction and emotional fulfillment from nursing, which for one thing pushes other kinds of sensual desire to the side. Other aspects of motherhood and the caring and nurturing of children are also both pleasurable and desirable as well as completely engrossing. So sexual disinterest is much more likely to happen for the mother in the period after childbirth. And as I have said, this contributes to a longer interval between births and, therefore, to an exceedingly desirable and beneficial attention to the most recent newborn.

For Spiritual and Personal Transformation

Freer sexuality and looser or nonexistent constraint on sexual partners contributed to human satisfaction and social/marital stability for another reason. For sexual disinterest leading to sexual abstinence also occurs for humans for many other reasons: It often occurs during the times of and in the course of spiritual pursuits. Not as a result of intention — for as I have said, self-denial is counterproductive to spiritual progress — but because of the degree of engagement and immersion in other-than-bodily pursuits at those times. A person might feel a pull toward taking on something with the total engagement of self that occurs, for example, in a vision quest or walkabout. A looseness of constraints on sexual partners can only facilitate the ability of tribe members to take such things up, being as how it leaves no sexually deprived other. So there is no pressure from another to refrain from following one's spiritual or creative inclinations.

Similarly, sexual disinterest occurs, sometimes, during periods of personal transformation, which occur naturally and spontaneously to Authentic humans in the course of their lives. For these times might require their full engagement and attention. Other times disinterest might occur is because of ritual or cultural involvement, during periods of grieving upon the death of loved ones, advancing age, sickness, and simply the changing feelings of the partners toward each other over the course of time.

For all these reasons and in all these instances, the loose constraints on the sexuality of our earliest forebears and the relative nonexclusivity of sexual partnership meant that the individuals involved were not pulled away from total immersion and focus on these experiences because of a sexually deprived and demanding spouse.

For Emotional and Mental Health

In addition to the examples given, consider how, freed from sexual obligations, one could allow oneself to fully and thoroughly grieve, when needed, or allow complete immersion in any comparable emotional experience. This, in its own way, and being at the core of mental health and personal growth, contributed to greater overall happiness, life fulfillment, and expansive abilities to experience life.

All things considered, more free-flowing attitudes toward sex allowed for amplification of life experience, greater spiritual and personal transformation, overall greater happiness, less personal conflict and neurosis, and, importantly, benefit to children. Not only were children helped by the care and attention they wrought of mothers who were not having additional newborns requiring their attention until they, the older ones, were much less emotionally needy. They were also better off due to the fact they lived in family and tribal groups which comprised more loving, giving, happy, and affable human adults, because of their overall better fulfillment and experience of life.

The Nuclear Family — In Sedentary Societies, Children As Investments

However, then we became sedentary and lived in hierarchical societies and all this changed. With agrarian economics, suddenly, there was more focus on the immediate family.

The Nuclear Family

Living permanently on land of which one claimed ownership and which one farmed separated our tribal human group of before into nuclear family units. We did not own the land in common and farm it in a communal style. No, not usually. For part of this war against uncertainty and increasing fear of deprivation, which manifested in our having become agrarian and sedentary, was mistrust and fear, not just of Nature but of each other. We had increasing alienation from each other, greater possessiveness of all things, and burgeoning greed. What came of such inner forces was that the nuclear family established borders around the land it cultivated and built walls of emotional avoidance between itself and the rest of the community.

It was families against the world. Children were raised in the pressure-cooker environment of the nuclear family. Monogamy and sexual exclusivity became all important, diminishing one's life experience. Women became owned as part of the economic resources of the family. Life experience was overall dampened in deference to survival and economic pursuits, and then this: The glorious and magical world of childhood disappeared and was replaced with one of economic utility.

Children as Resources — Workers and Soldiers

For with sedentary-accumulating lifeways there came a radical change in our perception of our children. While this change came gradually for some societies, the excess survival demands of agrarian ways put pressure on fully growns to begin seeing their young ones not as separate beings that one had a relationship with, however tainted and neurotic it might be. Rather, greed and fear led increasing numbers of us to lose focus on emotional bonds and to begin including our young in our calculations for sufficient or greater accumulation and its defense.

Large Accumulators, as I have said, had all the resources necessary to enlist allies in their acquisitive pursuits, through bribes and payment. They could hire or coerce support for even greedier and more dominating ends, using their excessive stores. So, there was no great pressure on them to increase the size of their families with additional children. There were other pushes, later, for larger families for the wealthy, which had primarily to do with the ego and vainglory of the patriarch, but that is another thing.

The Family Enterprise ... Work Group ... Children as Employees

However, Small Accumulators, at all times beginning with farming, would see a chance here, with larger families, to balance the scales a little vis-à-vis the Large Accumulators. Not able to purchase allies and helpers, like wealthy families did, Small Accumulators saw an advantage in and appreciation of the family burden — that is, extra children. For with it brought extra hands and cheap labor, once the children reached a certain age.

The Family Battalion

It also brought with it extra security for Small Accumulators. Consider, Small Accumulators knew they lived at the behest of the rich; they knew they were vulnerable. Clearly, the large families of Small Accumulators were not armies to deter possible advances from the overlords. Yet they gave at least a semblance of security in presenting a conspicuous buffer around those zones of nuclear family activity.

All these things together, with sedentary living there began an ever growing perception and determination of children as investments.

An Intrusive Mode of Parenting

It is at this point that we added another way that we influenced our children — an e, to add to influences a through d, as described previously. In this mode of parenting, children are seen even less. Caught up in our mental calculations and the corresponding fears for our survival, we saw children as a resource in our struggle. We began molding our children in infancy and childhood towards the end of their being useful, eventually, in our efforts.

The Nuclear Family Led to Brutal Parenting

Consequently, no longer was the problem one of neglect. No, we gave attention to our offspring. But the attention we gave them involved our actively intruding upon their beingness and fashioning something of that soul for our ends alone, our economic ends alone. This training was often severe, pushed as it was by our fear of want and free-floating desperation. For another reason, too — that is, our ever diminishing ability to see, let alone respect, life outside our ego — this intrusive parenting was often brutal.

This changing view correlated predominantly with sedentary lifestyles and accumulating-conforming ways. In this intrusive mode, we do not notice the separate beingness of our children ... and hardly their needs ... for we are seeing them the same way we have begun seeing everything that has fallen under our purview to control. In the extreme, we give as little thought to our children's feelings as we would to a shovel we use ... or a duckling that we raise for table. Having retreated furthest from our reality, in order to manage and control it, we are aloof and insensitive to our children; noticing only in them what can be useful for our survival or to stave off our overwhelming fears of deprivation and death.

Abraham and Isaac

A good example of this Ego — this complete self-obsessiveness allowing not even the awareness of cognizant, feeling others — is in the myth of Abraham and Isaac. This myth also demonstrates the differences between the modes of infanticide and the one of ambivalence, so it reflects those influences in our prehistory as well. Let us bring this back for further consideration.

Initially, in this story, Abraham is told by "God" — and for that we can read the unconscious and not acknowledged intentions of himself — to kill his son ... to "sacrifice" him. Okay, for starters, we might ask ourselves — if we have not had drilled into us otherwise by our pedagogy — why, in such a situation, it would be Abraham that would be thought to be making a sacrifice by killing his child. From an unbiased and innocent perspective, what seems clear as can be is that it is Isaac, hardly Abraham, who would really be losing something, "sacrificing" something — specifically, *his life!* That is the horrifying thought our children have when they hear this story; that is, until they are told otherwise.

Instead, notice that the child, Isaac, has little part in this drama. He is a mere thing to be used for the parent's ends. Abraham has a, supposed, link with God, a communication with God, and the existence of his son is of as little relevance as would be the cell phone one might use to call a friend. The fact that Abraham hesitates shows the change to an ambivalent mode. He still is not noticing Isaac or his son's needs. It is still all about Abraham and his supposed relation to his god. Even in his ambivalence he is self-obsessed.

Here we can see how our human inability to see and attend to our children's needs, especially in infancy, results in adults who are totally unable to notice the existence of their own children when they, in their turn, become grown. Abraham is aware that his son is there, but it is Abraham's needs — showing the self-centeredness and neediness of our adults — that are the important thing, not the child's. His own concerns are all that Abraham can see, much as the wicked queen stepmother in Snow White sees only the reflection of herself when thinking of her child.

We see here the switch, the progression from child murder/ child sacrifice to soul murder. It is the son, Isaac's, soul, his existence and his feelingness, that is sacrificed on the altar of his parent's preoccupations and concerns ... which have been elevated by Abraham, mistakenly and conveniently, to a status of "needs." In the myth this is sacrifice of the son's soul as symbolized by the fact that a ram is used in Isaac's stead as the sacrificial item. A ram is an animal, a planetmate. What this says is that people were ambivalent about actually killing their children. Instead of killing the child, the child's animal nature — symbolized by the ram — is sacrificed.

What is one's "animal nature"? It is one's feelingness, one's connection with Nature, one's real self, one's sensitivity, one's emotional self. With Abraham, it is no longer about infanticide, but it is still all about him, the parent. Children are being seen as mere instruments for use in the parent's agendas, as it was for Abraham: So this is no longer child murder, but soul murder. This soul is symbolized by the ram that is killed.

In this mode, children get to live, but only at the behest of their caregivers. For as long as there have been humans, children have been poisoned through interaction with the unconscious of their parents; and they subsequently manifest the repressed undersides of fully growns, which is comprised of early unmet needs and corrupted desires. However, with this "advance," this step in human "evolution," children are actively molded — intrusively — to ends not their own, as well.

Notice that with Abraham, at this point in history, humans are agrarian: They keep flora and fauna planetmates. They raise crops, and they herd sheep. This keeping, raising, and herding is a clue to how, from here on, children will be seen, as well.

Children Become Chattel

Children will be allowed to live, but only to the extent they further the agenda and ends of the adult. Children become chattel. They can be utilized, like any resource or investment, and much as humans use animal planetmates, for economic reasons and as little slaves. They can be sold and traded — and this we did and still do. Thus, children are seen not much differently from the way humans see the rest of Nature — including planetmates, flora, fauna, and even women. That is to say, as *investments*. They are seen as tools, also. More about that later.

Children as Investments

Fundamentally, children are thought of as investments. They are commodities. We began evaluating everything in the world along cold economic lines. Why? Because of our unnatural fears of deprivation and death, we have built our entire world and our entire consciousness oriented toward that — our economic lodestar. Plus, with a sedentary-agrarian lifeway, there is more work, tedious and hard work, than when we were nomads and gatherers. Our living was harder, but it was more certain, as I have been saying.

So, on this altar of certainty and increasing control, we sacrifice our children. We see them not just in terms of their level of burdensomeness, not just along the lines of getting a smattering of our unconscious needs fulfilled, though those are influences that always exist. Rather we focus all our intentions on what kind of person we can make of our children for our use later. Barely are we training them in ways to benefit themselves when they get older. But of course, we will do that. For language and primitive interpersonal skills are necessary for any human to function ... and to be of use.

Rather we are seeking to *train* them to be better investments, more useful tools or pawns, in our survival struggles.

Thingification and Soul Murder

This is why we might call this an *intrusive* mode of parenting. In this, we wander boldly and blindly into the soul of our child and we rearrange its elements in a way that we can use it. At this point, we have gone from infanticide and abandonment, to soul murder, to children being seen as things ... as inanimate ... not as live or animate beings with intention ... but as objects in space, matter to be used. This is called *thingification,* and it represents a more separate state from Nature than even soul murder.

Thus, it behooved us to intrude upon and dominate that innocent child's consciousness, to train that "investment," in order to maximize its usefulness when it was older. This is very much as we might put money into stocks and bonds as an investment in hopes of a future return. Our minds were calculating how much of physical resources we might need to "invest" in our child and how much "return" we might get ... and when. And if there was not a profitable payoff, we were unlikely to do much more than trade, sell, or abandon our child.

You Can't Get Cheaper, More Obedient Labor Than Children

For the first time, then, sedentary-agrarian ways do provide advantages to people with children. Not one child, but children are wanted, for they can be workers. A larger brood of children becomes, with this lifeway, economically advantageous. Whereas in our gathering and hunting, nomadic days, an extra child would be seen as another one to be carried along with the group and another mouth to feed, while providing little in exchange, until much later.

However, with large families, we have our little bands of workers and slaves. They are the best "employees" for they can be coerced to work, to work hard, and payment need only be in the amount of food and basic necessities that child might need to survive. We cannot get cheaper labor than that. Furthermore, they can begin to help at very early ages, thus expanding their years of economic value for us. Thus child labor becomes prevalent along with the tendencies toward larger families.

The Nuclear Family, Summary

All in all, then, while the phenomenal dependency of our offspring was an added burden in our lives, in general, that effort — under certain kinds of conditions, these sedentary-accumulating ones — could be justified. Children could be seen as additional assistance in our tussle with our imagined threats and brought in to share all that additional suffering we created in Nature through trying to control everything.

This was especially true if that dependent state — particularly in infancy but in childhood as well — was used to mold these children into the ideal conforming underlings for our harried adult forebears. Clearly, we did to our children what we had done to the Earth, to planetmates, and to our own bodies: We brutalized them into submission.

Those who were Large Accumulators could "bribe" additional efforts from others to aid them in their dramas, of course. Today we call that hiring others to work for us. Yet even those with lesser means — virtually all of us — had the ability to gain obedient subordinates through procreation. Large families were thus selected for. The larger the family, the better, as long as each subsequent child could within a sufficiently short period come to add more resources to the collective family struggle than would be removed from the total by the (minimal) survival of that child.

The Family Citadel

In this way, large accumulation was increasingly linked with large families. A brood of offspring could act like a small gang, or crew of employees in the gathering, processing, and accumulating of extra, hoarded resources. However, they could also serve as a small army and aid in the defense and protection of such hoarded wealth against other accumulators with green eyes and needy, famished hearts. Raising humans to assist with accumulation began to be seen as a survival advantage. Also, children, after the agrarian revolution, were increasingly seen as another category of conforming underlings — the least costly and most manipulatable ones of all — who would be even greater allies in the fight against the ever expanding threats to our survival.

This was so much our view of the way of things that our Ten Commandments — a rather good abstract of our fearful imaginings and our feverish, heavy-handed control — contains not only such reinforcement for the strong men of the society as "have no god before Him"; not only such protections for our authoritarian families as "honoring father and mother" and codification of the elements of resource management to benefit the ones who already have as "shalt not steal" and "shalt not bear false witness"; but even includes two entire commandments to cover jealousy. It is called "coveting" and has to do not only with protecting the hoarded wealth — "shalt not covet neighbor's goods" — but defending the engines of that production as well ... "shalt not covet neighbor's wife."

It is understandable how all threats to the fantastical survival competition were fought in all such manners: Monogamy would be elevated to a divine status — "shalt not commit adultery" — as part of the accumulation ordeal. Women were owned and seen as resources not much differently than children were. This view of women as economic resources only contributed to the already burgeoning factors of perinatal trauma and scapegoating in hierarchical societies pushing humans toward misogyny, as described in the chapter on that.

Further, it is no coincidence that our male reproductive capacity is referred to as "family jewels." While humorous, it is starkly accurate in the way we humans think on a level of our unconscious mind we keep far from awareness — again, that Unapproved and Hidden: A human's reproductive capacity began to be seen as an avenue of potential wealth, insurance against want or insufficiency, and even a ticket to possible Controller status and inclusion in society's elite.

For children began increasingly to be thought of as mere extensions of us, of our egos. The family unit that came of such expansion of fear and self-congratulation (Ego) was no longer harmonious with Nature. It had ceased being, even, interconnected with the tribe. It was not about individuals in relation to community. No. This nuclear family represented another advance in mistrust and fear, a further retreat into an ever diminishing circle, a fortress. With the creation of the family citadel, it was us against the world.

We Erected Shrines to Family Equal to our Terror of the Uncontrolled

Altogether, with Conforming Underlings bought, bribed, terrorized, or paid to be allies in our war over resources; with children conceived and raised to be obedient soldiers in its battles; and with tenets and social codes enforced with extreme severity so as to wrangle strict conformity to social ways benefiting the Large Accumulators and the petty male tyrants heading families, we had created a full on assault against our imaginary fears of death. A more spontaneous and not-so-controlled life was not seen for the benefits of fulfillment, pleasure, aliveness, creativity, and fun it offered. It was not seen that though such a life might serve up more uncertainty and pain, those would serve as guides in living and spurs to personal and spiritual growth. Instead, sedentary humans developed a strange abhorrence to such a more adventurous life, for it was an uncontrolled life, which they felt as uncertainty and pain. We once, as gatherer-hunters, saw such daily unknowns and occasional life turbulence as guides in our living. However, we came to perceive them only as reminders of that death we feared so intensely.

All in all, this added up to a thoroughgoing wrong-gettedness in relation to life for humans. Whereas a more natural or primal life would have us ever reminded of our Divine surround through the challenges, obstacles, and discomfort of life and would bring forth direction on the way to proceed in each individual's ever-expanding, numinous path of Divine return; instead we, post-agrarian humans, began to erect walls of fear-rooted control around our fleeting havens of ease. We cut off our roots into the Divine, unshakeable peace to which we are entitled. Raising up walls of possessions, captive planetmates, and conforming underlings — including women and children — and retreating from the more magnificent and magical expanses of self, we sought to make a stand against real life. A big part of this effort we called "family." We erected a shrine to it equal to our exaggerated terror of the uncontrolled.

Conforming Underlings were allies in such huge efforts, but increasingly offspring began to be seen as cheap and easily manipulated conforming underlings who, in time, would be even greater allies than those who could be coerced, bought, or paid. They were also more easily acquired. Children made ideal Conforming Underlings, especially for Small Accumulators.

In addition, offspring were increasingly seen as foot soldiers in the fight to maintain and defend so much extra accumulation. The family, all in all, became a fortress against the exigencies of life. Having children was another way we fought off the Divine.

23

The Fifteenth Descent — Child Use ... Child-"Raising" and Abuse:

Controlling Children, Farming the Family ... Every Home a Kingdom ... Children as Tools ... Child Abuse and Incest

"...ever since our agrarian-sedentary fall from Nature ... we did just as much 'family farming' between the walls of our homes as we did in our fields."

Child-"Raising" and Training

If we honestly observe our behavior toward our own offspring, we see how it mirrors our treatment of planetmates.

Like Crops, Raised

Reflecting our manner of engagement with flora planetmates, we "raise" our children like we do vegetables. For many of us of our species, over the course of our post-agrarian existence, conceiving children was akin to planting crops. We went about it in the same methodical way — without pleasure and with our mind focused on what we could eventually reap, of our actions, and how we would use and manage that "product."

Even the idea of a family — having a "brood" of children, as it is phrased — brings to mind a field of uniform and faceless — personality-less — items … a "product" of our labors. It is no coincidence that we call what mothers go through in giving birth to a child, *labor*. The child is seen as a product of her effort, a concrete achievement that can be used, like a tool, to achieve ends beyond it, and stood upon, like an accomplishment, in our relentless struggle for power and control.

Like Animals, Trained

As for fauna planetmates, we kidnap and capture our fellow Earth Citizens, and in our ignoble and unfeeling "management" we do not see them as conscious like us, as simply looking at the world and interacting with it in ways different from us. No. We would not have them walk alongside us but be as mere clay for us to mold whatever we desire with. We control where they go; what they eat; what they do, virtually all of the time; and who they will mate with and when and how. We pluck their offspring from them, like an apple from a tree, for any use of ours at all, including consumption. We force them into excruciating labor — the likes of which we would not do — and we "train" them to do tricks for us and amuse us. We see their lives to be ours. We look into what can come of such a life as theirs, and we seek to appropriate, for our own use and pleasure, what we see. Planetmates are little different, for us, from machines, which we can beat and pound to keep running and push to the maximum of their capacity.

Reflecting this perverted relationship, which we eventually developed and have now with fauna planetmates, we "raise" our children.

They also are parents' belongings. Like horses being raised for carriage, our young ones are raised and trained to carry our "baggage" — physical but also emotional. Like oxen being trained for the plow, our children are raised and trained to pull our enterprises forward. Like dogs they are trained to guard and protect our possessions. Our children we teach to perform for us and to entertain us, as they were seals. We do not manage all the details of the actual fornication of our children, as we do planetmates. Yet we, very often, determine who will be mated with who; and through cultural and personal persuasion, we extend the size of our families through them and such sexual activities of theirs.

We "grow" our children like house plants; we pet them when they are young like kittens; we have them "fetch" the way we would dogs. They are ours to be used for anything we want, like machines.

Like Tools, Fashioned and Beaten

Indeed, children are treated just like things and are even shaped and fashioned through brutal surgeries like circumcision and clitorectomy. They are molded in so many ways just like tools, to be just the way we can use them.

As it turns out, then, far from having discernment, let alone actual concern, in regard to the living, our ways of creation — that is, manipulation, training, and control — for the animate beings of the world became simply a little different than for inanimate things. We do not take a plow to the living like we do the earth — though our genital mutilation is close. Our "sculpting knife" or "paint brush" for planetmates and our children are methods of coercion, training, enforced obedience, and the like. We use the satisfaction of physical needs like food, rest, and sleep … and in more recent times, approval … as our "carrots." We use the "stick" of physical, mental, and emotional abuse; of punishments of all kind, including deprivation, incarceration, even tying up or chaining … and in more recent times, disapproval.

We do not hit our children with a hammer like we would in fashioning a tool. Instead we scold and bellow them into the shape we want. And while we might not use a mallet, we often hit, spank, whip, and beat them so their actions, their behavior, will issue forth along the lines and in the manner that would be pleasing and useful to us.

Like Furniture, Moved and Positioned

We do not pile them like logs as we do when we are building our cabins; nor do we arrange and position them like the furniture and contents of our home. We orchestrate their placement in our houses, nonetheless — storing them where they will fit in our rooms and sometimes stacking them in beds one upon the other. Likewise, we enforce the posture and positioning of their physical frames: They will "stand up straight"; they will not "slouch"; they must not cross their legs and must keep both feet flat on the floor; they must "sit up straight at the table," "not move around too much," not "play with their food"; and they must be silent — seen but not heard.

Like Dolls, Dressed to Reflect Us

Further controlling their physical positioning in our lives, we determine their comings and goings and their activities at nearly every moment of the day. We dress, adorn, and groom our offspring to reflect us, no different from the way we furnish and decorate our environs as an expression of our preferences and personalities. We put what we want into our children's minds — calling it "education" — along with their bodies. So, in a sense we do arrange them in such a pattern as suits our mental image of the perfect house, home, and family.

Like Toys, Played With

And the "colors" of our palette — in the "creation" or "raising" of our offspring — cover the entire spectrum from caring and benign to hateful and cruel. Indeed we often stray into the dark colors of torture in our crazed obsession to determine the outcomes of everything. We have routinely used them as sexual playthings.

Incest and Sexual Abuse

For, even our vaunted incest taboo — another self-congratulation, this one a favorite of our intellectuals — is a lie. How ironic that the one — the *only* one — thing that we would claim as an instinct for us would in actuality not be, and would be another one of the many things we concoct to hide the truth of us.

Indeed, it seems clear that our cultural proscriptions against incest are in place, not as an expression of universal instinct ... for if it was truly instinctual, why would it need to be culturally prohibited ... but out of the fact that we need to be kept from doing that which too many of us would otherwise do. More than ironic, how much of a howler it is that this one claim of ours to instinct — a nod to our delusion of superior morality — would actually *be* instinctual for our nearest planetmate relatives, chimpanzees and other primates, in their relation between parent and child.

You would think we would have gotten the clue that incest is in us from the many mythological stories we have involving it. We have fathers and daughters cavorting and making offspring, mothers and sons, even siblings. There is good reason it would come out in our mythologies, for myths are where we project and express the things about ourselves we cannot think, or say aloud. Our unconscious — all those things we hide from ourselves, and incest more than qualifies — is the raw material from which we concoct our mythologies.

Therefore, unlike our cousin chimpanzees — in this light seen to be more "moral" than thou — quite to the contrary of our chest-beating, in more cultures than we want to acknowledge and in all cultures more than we will let ourselves see, children have been our sexual playthings, our sexual toys — both inside as well as outside the family. Ancient Greece, pedagogical institutions of all times and cultures, and clergy — in particular, Catholic — are examples of these. It is not uncommon for cultures to have institutionalized rape of young girls; some of humans' "initiations" involve the participants' coercion into the performance of sexual services — this time, by boys — for the pleasure of the ritual conductors and attendants.

Our "civilized" abhorrence of such pedophilic activities, with its accompanying denial, is robust and severe so as to better cover up the multitude of perverted inclinations existing in many of us.

Every Family a Fiefdom

So it is that just as we plant, tend, and raise vegetative beings for our dinner use, we view other more animate beings in the same light and wish to "raise" planetmates; but our children we treat in the same ignoble way.

"Family Farming"

Increasingly, ever since our agrarian-sedentary fall from Nature — we did just as much "family farming" between the walls of our homes as we did in our fields. They were one and the same to us. We did as much to create an artificial social reality — in particular, in the family — to suit ourselves, as we worked to remake the physical world in the image of our desires. Having left behind a real Edenal existence in Nature, we were pushed ever — feeling, but never acknowledging our loss — to build up around us, using any materials available … and that included our Conforming Underlings, our women, our children, and our captive brother-and-sister planetmates … a substitute world of distracting, however fleeting, pleasures by which to occupy our minds from knowing of the hole in our being, with that loss.

Every Home a Castle

So in them — our private kingdoms, as we say "a man's home is his castle" — we placed ourselves on high and sought to place everything below us, having it subdued and looking our way for direction or in its utility. Indeed, in our personal fiefdoms, we would have it that we replace God Himself in the creation of our own pathetic reflections of personal "Edens," in which everything in sight has its reason for existing as being us.

Who Is the "Wild" Life, Really?

All that notwithstanding, we like to think of ourselves, in our morality, as above planetmates. We refer to them as "beasts," as "animals," which has a connotation of being beneath us and despicable. They are "wild"-life. We think of them as alternately controlled by instincts and yet wild. That should tell us something. But then, ignoring the magnificent perfection of Nature, we think of Nature as "wild," too.

Is Nature wild? If we think of it, it is only in relation to us and our wants that it is seen that way. Our poets, artists, and mystics see in Nature something else entirely. They see a beauty that inspires them to think of Divinity. They are on to something.

Yet they, too, are unlikely to see that perfection, as well, in the Earth's "animal"-life ... or their own children — who they think of as "wild" and needing to be "tamed." So we see that we think of wild as being what is out of our control. It might be "controlled" — within its own process and in relation to the rest of Nature — but it does what "it" wants, not what "we" want. Nor does it abide by our laws. It is "wild."

So "beasts," "animals," "wild"-life refer to things that have not yet come under our thumb. It is no coincidence that such terms are also used by us to refer to all of our own kind that are inconvenient to our wishes. Any who have different thoughts — our revolutionaries, hippies, and gypsies — are "wild" to us. Any who are in the minority of our societies or are poor or belong to other cultures are similarly "beasts" and "animals." Of course, those existing outside of our laws, our criminals, are "animals," we think. This is why you bristled at my idea that our planetmates are our angels in Nature. For, to us, to see in them a higher or benevolent consciousness is akin to bowing down to a beast.

Consequently, anything that is not in our power is "beast," "animal," "wild." And ultimately what is not in our power is anything that is considered Nature.

We Include Our Children as "Wild"

At any rate, in addiction to our ego and blinded that way, categorizing all of Nature as "wild," including God, and denying any separate intention or will, or soul, to It — *soul* having become associated only with that which is controllable — and seeking to have It submit to us, we see our children as "wild," as things without souls until we give it to them, and so needing to be controlled and "tamed." And being as they are soulless and wild "things" only, we allowed ourselves any means to bring this about … "for their own good," we say.

We proclaim, "Spare the rod, spoil the child." Making of ourselves a king or a god in our homes and classrooms. It is we, not God, who would be responsible for breathing *soul*, and morality, into the unformed clay, which we saw our children as. Conveniently, we would not notice that what we would consider *morality* and *soul* would coincide with what would please us — not God   and, additionally, would be *of use* to us.

Like Tools, Used

Thus, seeing our children as things, and soulless, and as "wild" — after our fall into sedentary-hierarchical ways — we would seek, under the guise of child-"raising" or "rearing," but also, we see, of "morality," to make of them things of utility to serve us. We would, essentially, fashion tools of them. We pride ourselves as humans as being above Nature in our tool use. We say that fashioning tools is one of the things that makes us human. From the perspective I am presenting, however, perhaps now we can see the roots of that urge to fashion tools, for tools magnify our power in controlling things. They expand our abilities to act upon and rearrange Nature and its ways. Just like our "technologies" and our rituals and recipes for bringing Nature and the Divine to heel, human tool use is a manifestation of our controlling obsession. And children got swept up into that singular mania.

So, just as we brutalized Nature, to extract from it what we wanted, and forced it along ways to suit our ends, we did our "wild" children. Yet, in fearful focus on the end-products of our efforts and the achievements to be wrought, we do not see the violence and torture we perpetrate on our own children. Even less do we see the way we wield that kind of barbarism on planetmates and all the world outside our egos.

For we use ruthless, unnatural methods of control and "fashioning," which planetmates could never imagine until our kind came along and to this day would never employ themselves. We seek to turn everything into a product of direct consumption or into a "tool" to aid our greedy over-accumulation … now or in the future. All our activities are directed toward those ends, including our family and community lives.

With these ends of consumption or utility in mind, we provide the necessities of survival for our young and for our captive planetmates. Almost always it is the bare minimum which is given, for any more would cut into the return on investment we anticipate of them. Along with, of course, it would be an extra bother on top of our already overworked sedentary self.

Additionally, we train and mold children and planetmates to be of use in our acquisitive aims. We physically constrain planetmates and force them to fit in with our designs. Our captive planetmates also are trained, molded … oftentimes whipped and beaten … sometimes even tortured … to become the kind of things that we would see as useful. Not much differently, we invest much time teaching and beating these younger things — our children — into the kind of older things we need or can use.

Child Abuse

Only recently in history have some of us even coined a term of *child abuse*. Whereas for most all children of the entirety of post-agrarian human history, such a thing was not conceivable. Everything from physical constraint to violence and torture were seen as not just necessary, but prudent and laudable. Children were "owned" by their parents, was the thinking; and they, the parents, could do anything they wanted with them, like any other of their property.

These "parenting" practices were not simply economically justified, our cultures managed to morally exalt them. We spanked and said it hurt us more than them. Seeing in our children the demon of abomination that was in us, we told ourselves and each other it was our "duty" to beat "the devil" out of them. I have already mentioned our pronouncement that the child would grow up "spoiled" — that is, like us, be selfish and demanding — if she or he was not forcefully and regularly beaten or caned.

Compared to the methods of child abuse and torture we devised to beat our children into tools, which came with sedentary ways and its work demands, our earlier infanticide and abandonment are seen as blessings for the child. In truth, we are only now awakening from a long dark reign of child abuse, which was the norm for parenting over the last ten or so thousand years for much of our species. So, childhood, just like birth and infancy, we turned into a nightmare.

For us, everything in Nature, including each other, is something to be either used immediately or to be invested in and nurtured for future consumption and/or use. We laud ourselves as compassionate in "training" and "teaching" our young and planetmates, and thereby we hide our true agendas even from ourselves. Yet, sure enough, we raise our dependent children, our vulnerable half-borns, using ways that often involve violence, torture, and many kinds of things Earth Citizens would never imagine doing to their young … not even to each other!

Who Are the Monsters of Childhood?

It is humans who are the real barbarians, the actual "wild" life, in Nature — actual abominations of Nature. We are the *real* "animals." It is we who are actually out-of-control … and yes, bestial … in ways planetmates could never be. The wild beasts, dragons, ogres, and abominable snowman of Nature and legend are us. We are the Abominable Human.

The dragons of our mythologies are the social configurations of our insanities to which we human parents sacrifice the innocence of our children. Just as, in myths, such dragons must have to it sacrificed virgins and children to keep the town from being destroyed. Essentially then, our dragons are actually our parents. For we as parents feel our economic survival, our sedentary ways — our "civilization" (the village) — depend upon sacrificing the soul of the child; exactly as Abraham sacrificed the ram — Isaac's soul or "animal" nature — instead of the actual physical child. The monsters of our child as well as adult narratives are the inordinate fears for survival to which ends are children are bludgeoned into usability from their innate nature of Divine expanse.

In these ways in our self-congratulation of our parenting and our denial of our ruthlessness, we hide our true agendas from even ourselves. Planetmates' purpose for us is to amplify our ego in any way they can be used to. We are like crack addicts who would rob our grandmother to get our "fix." The same is true for the way we view our children.

Like Drugs, as a Palliative for Our Fear

Indeed, ultimately the purpose of children to us is as palliative for our fear of death. Our grandiosity would have us continue the existence of our ego forever. To that end, children are invested in as immortality projects. They are only useful or desired to the extent they embody us.

It is for that reason, that of our blown-up fear of uncertainty and death ... ultimately rooted in our birth trauma ... that we deprive both children and planetmates of independent life by seeking to turn them into extensions or copies of ourselves.

This desire to control and fashion everything outside ourselves — including our children — in order ultimately to flee the thought of death represents an abomination in Nature. No other planetmate has such a magnified fear of death. Other Earth citizens do not keep and control the destinies of others or use them to inspire phantasms of vanity. It is a wonder we do not see what an extra burden that is for us, an unnecessary one. For in trying to craft our future that way, we cannot take in nor enjoy the blessings of the present.

Summary, Childhood in Nature and in Civilization

To clarify, in the world of our planetmates, there is neither a disinclination for offspring nor an overinvestment in them. Bonding and affection with Nature's young arises from the correct, biologically constituted, appreciation of the offspring, and this more individually so. Nature's parents do not measure their children along lines of what they can do for one in terms of emotional satisfactions, survival assistance, or personal security when they mature. Adult and child generations alike are suspended in webs of security, care, providence, and nurture through their inclusion in Nature's ways — its niches and unworked-for knowledge arising as instinct. Offspring are joy, interaction, fulfillment, and play, not burden, asset, emotional leech fields, and desperate, futile hope.

Alongside this of our planetmates, our crazed, but still nomadic, forebears were ambivalent about children and perceived families as a burden in relation to their overblown perception of the struggle to survive. However since this burden was lessened through tribe membership and sensible birth control methods and family management, children who were born were — relative to later and to today — wanted, appreciated, and more seen and attended to.

In contrast to both of these, agrarian anchors and accumulating, conniving modes fostered appreciation of increases of population, specifically, families, as beneficial in the struggle for survival. It follows that attention and energy would be put into these extra beings, seen increasingly as resources in the struggle against the monstrously over-apprehended fear of death.

The upshot is that in our ever-increasing sedentary numbers, children were considered advantageous against that imagined encroaching darkness we carried. So the lives of our otherwise doomed, helpless newborns were valued more often than not. Our desperate, suffering half-borns would increase our numbers as a defense against our personal demise.

24

The Sixteenth Descent — Work:

Instinct and Eros, The Decline of Pleasure, and the Invention and Politics of Work

In selling our time to others, we sold our souls.

"...the amount of surplus value in any society is equal to the amount of additional suffering that has been created through hierarchy and coercion. The huge structures of civilization are monuments to, and are equal in size to, the size of the freedom lost. Surplus value equals additional suffering brought needlessly into an otherwise joyous Nature and occurring as a result of human's completely unnecessary control obsession."

Following upon how and why families took over as the focus of social life, this chapter looks at how that, and related factors of sedentary-hierarchical societies, affected the daily activities of and the quality of human lives. We left behind the community and tribe life of our nomadic forebears for economic reasons that grew out of our sedentary-hierarchical societies. Sedentary ways brought with it additional work requirements. Indeed, with the societies evolving from them, humans brought actual *work* into Nature.

The Invention of Work

The more we added to our survival burden by controlling our food sources rather than accepting Nature's bounty and providence, the more work we created for ourselves. All the things Nature does automatically, effortlessly, and joyously in the creation of its cornucopia of bounty, we increasingly took upon ourselves. We no longer simply had to focus on moving ourselves and a few belongings — in the company of dear friends and family members, our tribe — to follow the food supply. Instead, we stayed stubbornly put, and dug into, cut up, carved out, and prodded, as it were, our Mother, the Earth, to extract every item of sustenance we needed rather than allow it to simply fall into our lap, as when we were nomads.

In this way, beyond simple sustenance, our single-minded attention to filling our stores as a hedge against the incursion of the imagined darkening, all about, of Nature, with its unpredictability, added additional work to our lot in life. Difficult enough, it was, to supplant Nature Herself as the manager of all the minute details of turning dirt of the Earth into edible food, but we had to build storehouses for such acquisitions. We needed to fashion and acquire tools for such work, too.

Formerly, what we consumed was mostly fresh; it was recently acquired from Nature. We did not need refrigerators. In keeping with the way in which we thingify Nature, consider that, as hunters, the meat we would consume did not spoil beforehand, for Nature in Her kindness had provided for it these mini-fridge units, which themselves gathered their own power to keep themselves running. They are called "animals" — specifically, the ones who keep themselves alive and their "meat" fresh until we "take it out of the fridge" ... we hunt down and kill the animal ... and cook it up for ourselves.

However, we could not let it be that easy. After we took over control of all aspects of our food's production, we needed to preserve what we were able to bully out of Nature, for those times, out-of-season, when nothing would be forthcoming. Endless hours of work were involved in this processing.

We required the construction of domiciles now, not just shelters, to house ourselves, our workers — who were usually our children — and all the excess implements needed for farming, food processing, and food storage. There is considerable work involved in "protecting one's investments."

Husbandry — the corralling and enslavement of planetmates for our use — was also incredibly labor intensive. Not only did we need to build enclosing structures to bring this about, but we needed to feed our captives. Feeding was work, and it was taxing. For there was no personal leeway allowed in this chore. One could not be lax or casual about it, getting around to it when one felt the urge to. No, if our planetmates were not cared for on a daily basis, without fail, we would lose our investment. So their biological requirements were added, as extra responsibility, to our own.

To Nature, We Added Work, Equal to Our Pain

Where did this additional labor come from — this huge extra workload that humans brought to the lives of the living on planet Earth? Was it produced out of the air? Actually, the additional work manifested in Nature is exactly equal to the additional amount of control we brought to Nature. And that is control that is emanating from our pain. So the extra labor and energy invested in our daily lives is equal in measure to the extra pain we have manifested in Nature.

Care of enslaved planetmates provides a good illustration of that. The planetmates we kidnapped needed to be housed, fed and watered, their sicknesses taken care of, and cleaned up after. That is a lot of work. Now, consider if that was needed to be done if they had not been corralled. Of course it was needed. Planetmates in Nature still have to eat.

But is there *work* involved? Well, for humans, obviously not; the planetmates have to do it. Yet even for planetmates there is virtually none, for all these things that humans have taken on to do for kept planetmates are done by planetmates in Nature out of their own desire and joy.

We say that the life of those in Nature is brutish and tough, with a do-or-die quality to it. In fact, that is the opposite of the truth. However, in our human wrong-gettedness, we need to keep telling ourselves that. For, as always, we need to project our own flaws and depravities into Nature, both to not see them in ourselves and so to continue suffering in "blissful" ignorance, as well as to build up our superiority defense against the inferiority we feel in that part of us that knows the truth.

In Nature, Life Is Not Difficult

To the contrary, in Nature life is not difficult, as we need to believe so as not to despair about the onerous quality of our own. Look at it this way: For humans it would be like the difference between doing something we call *work* — meaning we do not want to do it — versus our hobby or our creative activities, which are things we do for the joy and satisfaction of them. Well, nobody is standing over planet-mates insisting they take care of themselves. It is what they do! It is what they enjoy doing! It is all either pleasurable, or satisfying, or it is at least engaging ... as one feels when involved in a game or sport. It is interesting. Interacting with Nature and the rest of life is also awe-inspiring, beautiful, and often fantastical. They hardly want to stay home, sit on virtual couches, and not go "out" ... or to stay home from "work."

Many of us have cat planetmates. Do you suppose they consider it work to go after mice and small critters? You know the answer. If not, consider how they continue to enjoy, whatever their age, engaging in play around those same activities — going after a string, for example. If it was not enjoyable for them to hunt for the purpose of feeding, why do you suppose they would want to do it when they did not have to? On the other hand, you don't see human truck drivers driving their rigs around after work just for fun.

All planetmates come into the world with unique skills. Humans, as well. What we have so forgotten, astonishingly, is how life's pleasure is involved, not just in sensory satisfactions, as in passing substances over the surface of our taste buds, but in using those skills latent in us. Athletes and artists know what I am talking about. For, look into Nature and you will see planetmates, from birth, reveling in the use of the skills and unique abilities — like the cat's skills in going after prey — they are born with, which we say is attributable to "instinct" … as if it matters where it came from.

Instinct and Eros

For what is instinct, after all? We say it is a knowing that is programmed into animals, passed down through their genes, *pushing* them to do things at certain times and guiding their actions on how to do it. Any way you look at it, we see other planetmates as little different from machines or computer programs going through their processes, or like the inanimate forces of Nature interacting according to laws of physics. This is part of the way we have removed spirit and consciousness from the rest of Nature, so we could raise our own up higher. For, amazingly, we say that *we* do not have such "instinct," we say we have "free will"!

Because it does not fit with our constant need to pump up our ego and preferring to view them as machines, we have not considered how planetmates feel or what their experience is in going about these "instinctual" "tasks." Yet we could. Despite our vanities, we are part of Nature, too. We are not much different from the rest of Nature. Consider just our DNA which corresponds exactly with as much as ninety-nine percent of a planetmate's. So we have overlap with the Reality they experience and ingress to the way they experience it, too.

Instinct Is Eros … It Is Life Lived Pleasurably

Assume that we are not so different from "animals," for a second, and see if you can understand what "instinct" really is. Okay, we eat, for example. But why? Well, we know we have certain urges within our experience, which become more noticeable and then even painful the longer we fail to respond to them. They are called *hunger,* or we might say we have a craving. We do not "choose" these events or experiences. Are they not something like instinct?

Not quite getting it, I see. Okay, consider also what then we do. We bring that urge or hunger to an end by satisfying it. We do this by eating something. And do we need to tell ourselves *how* to eat? We have mouths, teeth, throats, and stomachs. Does our free will come up with the idea of how to use them, or is that "instinctual," too? Was swallowing some invention one of us had at one point, which was then taught to generation after generation?

Still is not completely clear? Alright, then think what is our experience when we eat. When we satisfy that urge, called hunger, we experience what we call *pleasure*. Put it all together and what do we have? We have an experience — a feeling, more exactly — which directs us to do something, at particular times, and guides us in the exact ways of doing it. And that we do until we achieve pleasure, or at least satisfaction. Sounds like "instinct," does it not?

However, you say planetmates have more specific directions on things to do and when to do them. You say one of our bird planet-mates knows "instinctually" how to build a nest, whereas we have to learn how to fashion our house. But consider that our *desire* to build a shelter does not have to be learned. We would say that it comes naturally out of the experience of existing in the open, encountering inclement weather, and wanting to be comfortable (to not be in pain because of it), and possibly as being proactive against the threat of predators. Have you not considered that a planetmate's actions might also come from exactly the same kind of experiential pushes? Just because we, standing outside of our relatives in Nature, do not see their imaginings or plans does not mean it is not going on for them.

You don't think planetmates imagine? You're still caught up in that idea that they are unthinking machines, aren't you? Yet, you ever see your dog and cat sleeping and notice how they twitch and move, obviously dreaming? Can we at least acknowledge that in their dreams they must be imagining; they must be envisioning? Since they imagine, how can we not say their supposed instinctual actions emanate from imagined behaviors or ways of doing something, from forethinking, which they then just happen to *want* to do? Whereas we simply are cut off from doing what we want to do. That is the only difference.

Instinct Is Actualization of Capacities

We can understand this "instinct" that is merely doing what one naturally wants to do. We still have overlap with that. Let us say you are someone who is naturally strong. Where does the desire to use that strength come from? You may be someone with a sweet voice. Where does the urge to sing come from? You may be someone with a knack for understanding the workings of things. Where does the "instinct" to delve deeply into matters and "research" them come from? Where does that "curiosity" come from?

Do you see that many of the things we do in life — from being able to eat and breathe to individual skills like singing — arise out of the fact that we are born with the *capacity* or ability to do them? Do you see that the potential for something gives rise to its actualization? And that experientially this comes across, just like hunger and eating, as an urge ... seemingly coming out of nowhere ... containing within it exact conceptualizations or imaginings on the possible fruition or manifestation coming from that urge, leading to what we call a *pleasure* when we are following through on that forethinking or imagining and especially upon its completion? But, if you viewed things that way, why would not you, looking at someone doing this, think they are acting "instinctually"?

So we and planetmates are the same experientially. They do their lives carrying out actions that arise out of messages from their bodies ... and from where those come, neither they nor we exactly know ... which provide the satisfaction and pleasure of life in their manifestation.

How specific those messages are is not a huge dividing line between them and us, as the fact they often are much more precise in the actions they carry out is easily explained by the fact they are less split off from such sources of information. We also have many things we do out of unconscious knowledge, coming to us as feelings in our bodies, which we do not see and do not want to notice ... preferring the self-congratulation of crowning ourselves with "free will," instead. And there would be much more "instinctual" knowledge available to us — and *is* available to us — were we, for reasons of our birth and infancy and the way they have caused us to run away from the feelings in our bodies, not split off from them. Indeed, to the extent that we have not run away from such pain, or to the degree that one has turned and faced and integrated that pain and reconnected with one's body, we do feel and receive such specific "instinctual" instruction.

Instinct is the Divine Within

In fact, think of it, when I say we cannot know — neither planet-mates or ourselves — where those messages, of instinct, come from, which we experience in the body, do you see that, to be more specific, they can be said to come from the Divine? For they are "instructions," as it were, that guide all beings in the care of themselves in life and the carrying out of life's actions along lines most beneficial and pleasurable. And other than a force that is comforting, beneficial, and wiser than our limited selves, what else is the Divine?

If Nature, in toto, is Divinity, as I say it is, then instincts are communications from the Divine. The prods and maps of potential actions, arising in the mind, for planetmates and humans, are messages from the Divine ... directing us along lines most beneficial to ourselves and all else.

Keeping that in mind, do you not see that existence, as experienced, is the same for us as for planetmates? That all beings have feelings that catalyze them into action and imaginings that construe their behavior and their imminent actions along particular, sometimes specific, lines? Humans sometimes call this *inspiration* and attribute its occurrence only to rare times. Although planetmates have routine access to such.

Yet we could, too. For to the extent that one is able to lower the barriers of early pain and the mental defenses that arose from it, we also can feel such Divine instruction ... of an increasingly more specific quality ... and become more "instinctual." Or, in our words, we can become Divinely inspired or guided by God.

The Decline of Pleasure, and Divinity

Backing up, so we denigrate planetmates' experience as "instinctual," when it is no different from our own experience of life. And if there is any difference, it has to do with the greater access they have, the stronger and clearer connection they have, with a wisdom and benefi-cence beyond their limited selves, which we humans have separated from, but which is still accessible deep inside us, below the levels of our early pain. Just because planetmates have more access to Mind-at-Large, which contains all information and knowledge, does not mean they are mindless, feelingless machines. Does it not mean the opposite? Indeed, they are our angels in Nature, as I keep saying. They are manifestations of a Divinity greater than us, all around us.

Keep in mind, planetmates' "instinct" is what guides them in having the experiences of the joy, pleasure, and happiness of life … something we humans have lost so much of. Quibble if you will about its source, it is irrelevant. Certainly, the fact they are more Divinely inspired is no reason to trivialize their experience, or their knowledge … any more than we should demean the brilliance of our Shakespeare or Einstein or Jesus just because they happened to have found a way to stay or become sensitive to the wisdom of the Universe and the Divine, which is everywhere around; but which we, the majority of us and for the most part, block ourselves from feeling.

And for planetmates this pleasure and joy, this "instinctual" guidance, includes their having offspring. It is another capacity that wants to be actualized, which, in doing so, planetmates feel pleasure. It also is not a chore, or work, which for humans it has often become.

Humans also know what life is that is lived under the direction of the Divine, instead of the direction of higher ups, extracting from us the suffering equivalent to the control of us, which is termed *work*. For, you ask a child digging in the sand with a shovel if that is work. Ask the athlete if clearing the bar when pole vaulting is work. Ask the halfback if it is work to sidestep all tacklers and throw himself over the goal line. Ask the sculptor if fashioning stone and watching her or his vision of it emerge from it is work.

Lion cubs fight and wrestle with each other. We say they are just preparing themselves for an adult life of struggle and fighting off predators. Really? Do you really think they are taking it on like a class, or exercise regimen, and not just having fun?

At any rate, creative people know what I am talking about. They know about the work that is not work, that is actually play and conducive to joy. They know about that magical, "instinctual" knowledge that comes to one precisely and specifically. For they know that their "works" (their "plays"?) have to be *just so*. When it fits with their "instinct" — their unconscious knowing which only comes out in actions of following it or expressing it — they know it is done and it cannot be any different. As Amadeus Mozart, in an ironic tone, in the movie about his life, said when someone criticized his composition for having "too many notes," "Just exactly which notes would you have me take out?"

For the artist in any medium, the creative product arises as if it was done somewhere else, by someone else, and one is just the channel for it. Upon its completion, it feels as if it had come forth perfect and precise in all its details … springing, as it were, "fully formed from the forehead of Zeus." So this is instinctual knowledge, of a sort, which ultimately comes to artists from a place beyond themselves.

What it comes down to, in humans claiming to not have instinct, is an acknowledgement that humans do not live their lives out of motivations of pleasure, attraction, or love — in other words, Eros. Rather our motivations are fear and dread. Fear causes us to split off from how we would otherwise feel and instead concoct schemes for future avoidance of presently dreaded events. Humans separate their consciousness from their immediate surround and their feelings in order to manipulate them along lines coinciding with their early traumas. We have agendas hidden to ourselves and others, which we mask with rationalizations such as free will, a superior love than what is in Nature, high intelligence and ability to reason, and so on.

Furthermore, denying instinct in ourselves is merely the way we justify doing things we do not want to do for powerful, feared others. When we began lining up our actions with the wants and desires of those we both feared and wanted to please, when we became *inauthentic,* we separated ourselves from our own authentic desires, wants, and needs. So we repressed our instinctual prods as part of that sycophancy. We have instinct; we have fear and do not follow that instinct; and we are unhappy for having fought off our instinct … our "desires."

When we do not have such fear, when we are able to feel again, not merely live in the future via dread, we find we have instincts, of a sort, again. To think that somehow the billions of years of evolution that made up our DNA — and which in us, as well as multi-billions of other species, had built into it instinct — was suddenly, in evolutionary time, trumped by a few relatively minor differences of us from planetmates is absurd.

The Politics of Work

Nonetheless, with sedentary ways we forgot all that inner direction, and we created *work* — which is the non-Divine actions emanating as urges, not from the inside and the body (ultimately the Divine), but from the outside, driven and pushed by coercion. Rather than the positive reinforcement one receives in following one's "instinctual" guidance, which makes of one's life a happy one; acting in response to the promptings of the outside is largely a product of negative reinforcement. One is not, as in Nature, justly rewarded when one follows its promptings, one is punished when one does not. Overall, such a life is anything but bright.

Do you not see that in claiming free will as our motive for doing things — along with embracing "discipline" … hard work … and all those other patriarchal values — we are simply aligning with our Controllers? That we are having values that are essentially against our nature, however much it suits them, so we are doomed to be miserable in carrying them out?

Life Lived for Controllers Is the Definition of Work

Regardless, at this point with agrarian culture on the increase, raising humans to aid in the work of accumulation began also to be seen as a survival advantage. For it takes a lot of investment of time and effort to control so much and to maintain and defend so much accumulation against competitors.

Conforming Underlings were allies in such huge efforts, but increasingly offspring began to be seen as cheap and easily manipulated conforming underlings who, in time, would be even greater allies in the fight against the blown-up fears of nonsurvival — that is to say, death, uncertainty, and the obstacles, challenges, and pain we increasingly avoided in our increasing wrong-gettedness as to our reasons for existing … which were meant to serve as guides in our evolution back to Divine rootedness, Divine identity, like the rest of planetmates.

Possessions and Accumulations Equal Work

In addition to all the extra work we brought into Nature through our controlling ways as it expressed itself in food production and storage, there is additional work involved in defending those stores. Unlike the "possessions" of those in Nature, which are easily acquired and just as easily discarded for they can be easily acquired again, this new classification of possessions that are our "stores" represents a dearly acquired (through "work") collection of things. They are the physical manifestation of human suffering. Hence they are valued highly for the fact that they are not easily or quickly replaceable. Furthermore, they represent quite a concentration of labor, wrought of suffering, which, if acquired, would reduce the amount of such suffering (labor or work) for someone else. So, they are viewed with extreme attraction by equally famished ... and suffering ... others. With these concentrations of labor-suffering — these stores — then, comes the need to defend them from those others.

With defense of stores, or "investment," we have another reason children were more desired after we became sedentary. Children are not just extra hands in the additional work we created in our descent into ever more controlling, they are enlisted in keeping others from stealing it. They act like little soldiers.

Coercion of Activity = Work = Surplus Value

So, with humans we have this added labor, this added, actual, *work*. Its roots are in sedentary living with its accumulation and the creation of stores. It morphs immediately into being the labor that we are compelled by higher ups to do, but do not want to do. Work became defined as the activities, organized by those in control, that those below needed to do. As organized now, however begrudging the compliance in doing it, this activity resulted in extra production over what one would have been able to accomplish on one's own. This is an idea potent with revelation of meaning for us, currently, so let us explore it.

Our Marxists like to talk about the *surplus value* of worker's labor and how the capitalist owners take that. They say it really belongs to the workers. Still, they have never looked deeply into its nature.

Marxists say there is an additional value — a surplus value — that is created through collective endeavors over what would be created individually. What they are saying is that if one adds up the value of what people create, working individually and being self-determining, it is a certain amount — say, the total number of chairs that can be fashioned by that group in that amount of time acting on their own. However, if those workers are organized and working collectively, they produce that amount, plus more — say, the number of chairs produced by that same group acting on an assembly line.

Anyone who has ever worked in a team knows this. Imagine we are clearing land for farming. We are leveling trees and pulling out stumps. Obviously, we can accomplish a lot more having workers collectively hauling heavy logs and in tandem sawing trees than if each worker is on his own straining away. Surplus value is also evident in Amish barn-raisings, where working together, structures can be thrown up in a day that would take weeks or months working on one's own with one's own strength and energy.

This is, indeed, a benefit that accrues to humans living in groups of any kind, and it was a huge benefit of tribe life.

However, with sedentary-agrarian ways and hierarchical societies we have an additional surplus value, for humans can be organized around projects in greater numbers and working in tandem and cooperatively. Combining their strength they are able to do things that simply cannot be done, no matter how long one worked away at it, individually or in small groups.

This is how the pyramids were built. It explains why such things were not done previous to hierarchical societies ... they simply could not be.

Further, with different units applying themselves to specific tasks within the project while other units focus on others, these units become more skilled, more efficient, and more productive in those tasks. The more that people operate like automatons with robot-like efficiency — eliminating what is distractingly and "messily" human — the more product we get from a given unit of time. This is the "benefit" of division of labor and, in the public sphere, of specialization in regards to task.

These factors are realized most clearly in industrialized societies; they are the reason the assembly line and manufacturing are so much more productive than the cottage industry of previous times.

No doubt, right now, you are thinking what a great idea this is. You see it as people having it easier because they are working together to accomplish more.

For producing more is our unconscious goal in a culture centered on things. Yet we never consider the quality of life of those producing it. Felicity became sadly unimportant in post-agrarian culture whose values centered upon quantities of things.

Furthermore, in regard even to the extra quantities of things produced, not only does that surplus value not come to the workers — this is the essence of the Marxists' complaint — for it goes to the ones at the top, the ones doing the organizing, the ones doing the enslaving. But also this surplus value, this extra quantity of things produced, is the product of effort that is onerous because it is coerced. We simply do not have people agreeing to link themselves together hour after hour — perhaps day after, day, perhaps month after month — pulling together against heavy loads. We do not have anyone, of their own volition, wanting to, over and over again, hour after hour, repeat the same simple actions, perhaps actions that are part of the creation of a product which they never see completed, so never getting even the satisfaction and pleasure of manifesting something in reality that was not there before.

Thus, not only are such workers deprived of the satisfaction of seeing something manifest out of nothingness through the efforts of their own hands — thus participating in the pure pleasure that comes of aligning oneself with Divinity as Creator — they are even ripped off of the pleasure of its completion. They are coerced into giving up their time, their life, in the carrying out of activities in which they find no real pleasure or joy. They hardly appreciate the product that results from their efforts. Not only was the actual decision to make what was created not theirs ... it did not spring forth from *their* desires, *their* "instincts" ... but they were allowed to participate in only a tiny part of its creation. It is about as pleasurable as chewing food that someone else has picked out for themselves, which one does not get to swallow, having to be turned over to the "employer" when one is done. Worse, one is forced to masticate only one of the recipe ingredients of the food item. Now, *that*, is the precise analogy to the assembly lines and division of labor come of civilization.

With hired, coerced labor, therefore, we have an example of work and free will — with its requirement of "will power" come of the fact that it is coerced — versus "instinct." The upshot is that for the worker, that pure pleasure involved in creating something out of relatively nothing, that feeling of awe and magic that one has for that moment identified with the creative principle of the Universe, bringing something from no-thingness into thingness, and had a sense of Divinity that way, is denied her or him.

There is no planetmate or human in Nature who is similarly deprived.

Surplus Value Equals Suffering

All in all, the amount of surplus value in any society is equal to the amount of additional suffering that has been created through hierarchy and coercion. The huge structures of civilization are monuments to, and are equal in size to, the size of the freedom lost. Surplus value equals additional suffering brought needlessly into an otherwise joyous Nature and occurring as a result of human's completely unnecessary control obsession.

Thus, the size of public edifice is equal to the amount of enslavement. Consider that next time you look in awe at a city's skyline.

Not only are such structures representative of the degree of loss of freedom and degree of suffering but also the size of Ego. These monstrosities are monuments to the degree of separation from Nature and to the size of Ego these Large Accumulators have now and have had, since the beginning of sedentary ways.

Marxists, we see, go only so far in uncovering the injustice inherent in societies. They want access to that surplus value that is wrought of that misery of having to do, just about all the time, what one does not want to do. Marxists never question whether it is at all worth it; they never look into whether people who are chained to the products of their hands are ever happy or free, regardless how much of that product comes back to those hands.

It is for this reason that the Marxist experiments in the Soviet Union and elsewhere turned out the way they did — failed. For they are built on the same idea of humans as being cogs and slaves as is their capitalist counterparts. They were still built upon a conceptualization of a human as "economic man," and consequently a determination of life's purpose as being merely material.

For so many thousands of years had humans been enslaved and working under coercion and glee-less, by the time Marxism was being formulated, that a free life — like the one in Nature — was completely inconceivable. Hence they built their prescriptions upon the wreckage wrought of our falls from grace in Nature, seeking not for human freedom and release from bondage and suffering but rather for a fairer distribution of the products of that bondage and suffering. Efforts like this are sometimes described as "rearranging furniture on the decks of the Titanic."

Cannot Create an Economic Utopia on the Basis of Anyone's Misery

Another reason our best thinkers for economic justice and our best utopian Marxists could not even conceive of solutions that addressed the real injustices of our lives and of the human predicament, in terms of what it had at this point become, is that whatever they imagined was built firmly within the context of human wrong-gettedness. That is to say, Marxists, in looking into the misery and injustice of the world, looked only so far as the suffering and injustice of humans. Sometimes they did not even look at the injustice or suffering of women ... let alone their wives. They certainly did not see the injustice and misery of children. And most significantly, they completely abjured planetmates: They sought, just like capitalists, to eke out excess goods at the cost of Nature and of planetmate suffering ... and often even of suffering of women, wives, and children.

The bottom line is that Marxist and utopian theory, up till now, is built upon the superiority of "man" and his dominion over Nature. Marxists, claiming to be atheist and impugning religion as an opiate of the masses, still built their conceptualization of humans in Reality upon the Judea-Christian notion that humans were given, by God, "dominion" over Nature and all its life. Unable to see the blatant and egregious egotism involved in that ... making them no different from the Large Accumulators they abhor, by the way ... and instead attempting to erect an edifice fueled by such unholy and desperate self-congratulations, what they constructed was shaky, flawed, and woefully inadequate. One cannot construct an economic utopia upon the misery of anyone ... not *any*one ... is what the Marxists could not see.

As I have said, nowhere and at no time have humans been able to see through their wrong-gettedness and have an inkling of the Unapproved and Hidden. Inherent in that is that humans are also planetmates and that non-human planetmates are as alive and deserving of respect and consideration as are humans: Planetmate suffering matters, you see. And Marxists attempted utopian reformulations of the same tired old human breast-thumping, as had been going on for thousands of years.

Still, such efforts, as those of Marxists, were doomed to failure also, for they did not address the true human predicament. Their remedy of a "new boss" did not take into account the fact that the new boss would be same as the old boss. For human happiness, pleasure, spirituality, and creativity are what is used to purchase those surplus economic products of hierarchical societies. That surplus does not rise up magically into existence, produced *sui generis*. Marxists, if they had been as "scientific" as they claimed, would have known the fundamental law of physics that energy cannot be created or destroyed. It can only be transformed.

So, no. This surplus value in society is not sprung magically into existence from nothing. No, what one gains in additional good — in *surplus* — is carved out of one's soul and purchased with human misery and tragic non-fulfillment in life.

People Would Rather Have Toys Than Be Happy

And where does that surplus come from? Indeed, surplus product is bought at the cost of suffering, work-type suffering. When we added surplus work to our lives, we created surplus suffering equal to that, and then, only after that, surplus product.

Yet all this "surplus" is unnecessary ... as unnecessary as the suffering involved in its production. People would rather have toys than be happy, is what it comes down to. They would rather be overfed than satisfied. People would rather appear to be having a full and rich life more than they actually want an exquisite existence. And appear to who? Herein we have that sycophancy built upon low self-regard, again. Humans would rather have the "Joneses" be impressed with the amount and quality of their possessions — so that they might think those neighbors approve them, maybe would like them, maybe would look up to and give deference to them — than to actually be happy.

Look again at that work we created in the care and feeding of kept planetmates — husbandry: The work has to be done, they need to be fed, or we lose our investment. If we were sick, tired, or simply disinclined, it did not matter and we had to forego an ease and pleasure in our body as we bullied it into submission, just as we do the Earth. We needed to make our body move and work, regardless how we felt or how we suffered or how much ill health would be incumbent upon such stresses and strains and unhappiness in our physical selves.

Similarly, at certain times of the year, such as harvest, we worked under extreme pressure. The demands of completing the harvest and storing what was wrought before weather might come in and, again, neutralize all the results of one's efforts made for very long days of back-breaking work. In these ways, in addition to all the others I have mentioned, we split off from Nature. For our body is Nature, and we operated it in spite of and often in opposition to its cries and screams, its promptings and messages to us. Is it any wonder then that we lost our ability to feel the fainter urges of the "instinct" within our body?

At any rate, it is supremely ironic how our insistence on taking over the reins of our sustenance through horticulture and farming, which was pushed by our desire to not be dependent on Nature and to be free, made us shackled to work loads and time constraints, and found us burdened under a multitude of demands and responsibilities and pressures. Good job getting that freedom we wanted!

25

The Seventeenth Descent — Religion:

Ritual, Prayer, Worship, and Phantom Gods …
Thought and Emotion-Feeling Control …
Religion Versus Spirituality and as a Tool of the
State

Replacing primal spirituality is ritual; phantom and
transcendent gods; control of thoughts and self, and
avoidance-denial of pain; and religion as a mechanism
of control of populace.

A part of us never forgot our horrific experiences at birth and in
infancy. We strove, therefore, to control every category of thing or
being in our outer life, so we would never ever be subject to such
overwhelming pain again. To do that, we needed to go against our
deeper nature and desires, as we see especially in the case of work. In
order to achieve outer control, then, we needed to struggle to control
our inner lives, as well. That includes our desires and wants, which I
have shown are aspects of the wisdom of the body — Divine Guidance, essentially; our allotment of "instincts," in a sense. Hence this

inner control would include an attempt to control God and fate as well as to suppress intuition and felt experience.

Review of Controlling Obsession

Let us review how we got here. Remember, our so-called evolution in consciousness has been largely to do with an expanding obsession to bring everything under control of our Ego. We displayed an ever-increasing fever to dominate and determine all aspects of our reality.

Previous chapters have dwelled, one-by-one, on these different spheres of our mania for management. I have also explained how this obsession brings with it an ever-increasing amount of effort. I have shown how we brought work into the experience of life for us — *work* being actions one does out of no inclination from inside oneself and only out of coercion from the outside. Finally, I have discussed the ways these controlling obsessions have interacted with each other in terms of a push as well to bring other beings — adult and young — into the effort of the adult ego to manage and manipulate all things that can be influenced. There was no end of effort for Ego in controlling everything. So there was no end of help sought from others to assist in its delusional struggle.

Thus, everything that was not seen as Ego was targeted for control. We changed our stature to upright and this led eventually to a change in the way we would be born that was more painful as well as to a prematurity of birth that led to an extraordinarily long period of dependency in which we would be at the mercy of capricious caregivers and thus feel deprivation in infancy. Our abnormal life entry and infancy deprivation led to an apprehension of mind and a mistrust toward the All That Is. Out of such fear we chose to add planetmate flesh to our diet and so learned how to kill. This foreboding caused us to be able to murder planetmates for food — hunting — and eventually each other out of that same anxiety, however unwarranted, about our ability to survive. We had begun making life-and-death decisions, formerly a Divine purview, over other life forms.

We next sought to control our other food source, which was vegetation — the Flora Empire; and we instituted horticulture, then farming. Becoming sedentary to do that, this led to our extending our net of control over the Fauna Empire — members of which we corralled, began using as a "cultivated" food source, and deemed ourselves superior enough to, to make godlike, life-and-death, decisions regarding every aspect of their lives. We began kidnapping planetmates, which we called "raising animals" or husbandry.

Following this, we were able to bring ourselves to making godlike determinations about even other humans of us. We developed a hierarchy of humans determined by the amount of possessions, i.e., wealth, and centered around those who owned a lot — "strong men," they are called in our social sciences — with ever lower levels of rings of conforming, sycophantic underlings spreading out from that. For the men of us, our humiliation wrought of conformity to higher ups pushed us to seek over our women, especially wives, a compensating domination of the same sort as we experienced. From there, pushed both by cravings for control and accumulation as well as the burgeoning work load that came with that, we extended our reach of resource revaluation and control to include our young as well.

As we had with planetmates and our cultivated plants, we would "domesticate" — meaning force into conformity with our sedentary lives, with its fixed domiciles, controlled families, and restrictions — all of Nature, if we could.

Denial of Consciousness in Others

For us to be able to conceive of doing these things, we needed to have a rationale that justified it. We needed to be able to turn it into a correct thing to do; we needed to be able to fool ourselves. In order to control everything we had to see everything as without consciousness and therefore as uncontrolled without us. So as to deny the ability of the aware beings around us — meaning flora, fauna, children, women — to have inclinations of their own ... that is, desires, tendencies, will, self-determination ... we needed to insist they were not capable of such decisions, of such choices. It would follow that by removing, in our beliefs, the ability of intention from everything around us, we would not only be allowed to control, we would be *required* to.

So to remove will and self-determination from the Universe we needed to deny consciousness in all of it, except ourselves. It would become true that the extent to which we would be able to deny consciousness in any aspect of the Other would be the extent that we would be able, "in good conscience" (sarcasm intended), to control and dominate there.

Concerning the development of the human family, we need to keep in mind that it was based on our expanding addiction to control, which had now infected our view, even, of our own offspring. We would see them, as well, to be *things*. We would attribute as little of consciousness to them as we could possibly rationalize to ourselves. Our children would be viewed, by the vast majority of civilized humans, and over the near entirety of the time of our post-agrarian existence, as having as little consciousness as the planetmates and other Earth citizens that we kidnapped and controlled for our ends. That is to say, little or no independent intention or sentience would be bestowed on them in our estimations.

It must be kept in mind that this increasing control over everything external to Ego at each point required that correspondingly there would need be intensifying control over our inner life as well. We set our wrestling-into-submission fever upon aspects of our selves, even, that the "management" of consciousness, the Ego, deemed "inappropriate," but was actually feared.

Increasing Control — Separation, Ego, Isolation

The upshot of this entire process is a separation from all else in order to control it. In separating from all else, we, of course, separate from the Divine in that the Divine is exactly that: All That Is or all that exists including ourselves.

The result was that in total separation from All That Is, or the Divine, and certainly from Nature, and other humans, including our own families and others in our social units, we created the ultimate in isolation for ourselves. And in this isolation we created our extra-natural ability for alien and backwards conception, thinking, and perception. This embodiment of a vortex of phantasms is our singular consciousness construct — again, that Ego that we do so well.

Having achieved such a narrowing of apprehension of the true nature of the reality around our ego — inside as well as outside — we gave ourselves maximum rein in reckless determination. Like trigger-happy cowboys on crack, we filled the world with us. We saw no existence outside our windows of temporal craving ... hence no consequences of the exercise of our lusty appetites other than any pain to ourselves come of our acts. Outside those relatively insignificant perimeters of our perceivable pain, we were unhinged. Even that, our pain, we sought to deny and diminish so we could have even greater sway in our bumbling amidst Nature's otherwise exquisite china shop.

And Now, to Control God

Finally, we even attempted to control things that could not be influenced. It is natural to have a lived spirituality in which one does not feel separate from All or each other. Our nomadic forebears had such a lived spirituality. So they did not pray, not in the sense we later began doing. For what reason, if Divine Providence exists and God is truly good, would anyone wish to control, cajole, or even appeal to a higher order of knowing that has one's overall goodness and interests in mind and is, as we say, *God*, or *good* itself?

Ritual, Prayer, Worship — Religion

However, as a consequence of our separation from All, we began using ritual, instead of our felt experience, to attempt to connect with the Divine. At first it was simply to seek to discern the Divine Will, which we had made distant from us in all the ways mentioned, so that we might act in accordance with It. Later it was to seek to *control* — again that bugaboo of humans — the will of the Divine, including all of its manifestations as in the forces of Nature, the weather, fate, destiny, luck, and providence for oneself and the extension of one's ego — the family. Our prayer — the spoken or linguistic form of ritual — was employed for the same purpose: To sway the Divine to itself bend along the outlines of one's (now perverted) will ... actually, one's predilections.

And what is the form of this ritual and prayer? As damaged and sycophantic adults — no one of us having received adequate nurturing and caring as infants and children and instead having been taught that some satisfaction of those needs could be had by pleasing and appeasing one's adult caregivers — we would act out that training in seeking to gain boons from the Divine. Indeed, we would deem this Divine to be blown-up versions of the caregivers we wished we had as children and infants — mothers and fathers become Mother and Father. We would seek to garner boons and satisfaction of desires from these early figures projected onto the Unknown in the same way we learned we could elicit them from the early entities of infancy … our parents, our caregivers: That is to say, through meaningless or distantly removed … symbolic … behaviors, repeated maniacally.

Our adult caregivers trained us as children to be conforming underlings, so we might be enlisted in their overblown schemes and "phantom" struggles — meaning unnecessary and self-created ones. Now, with religion, we would demonstrate to the creations we projected onto the Universal screen that indeed we are sycophantic underlings — as sycophantic as can be. We equated groveling with holiness in an unconscious attempt at control. We would seek to receive "compensation" from the Unknown and from the misunderstood Divine in exchange for demonstrating those things that worked as children with caregivers: We would express undying devotion, love, and allegiance to this Universal Phantom Mother/Father. Just as we needed to ally with the caregivers — our actual mothers and fathers — in their schemes against all others, so also we would think we could garner good will by demonstrating our alliance with this Phantom against the Phantoms of all others.

So it is, we think that we "please" this Phantom — which we mistakenly call "God" but who is not (for it is not Good) — by taking up arms against the Phantoms of others and their allies. We have projected our early family drama as a child onto the heavens. And we seek to use Conforming Underling behavior — sycophantic, mindlessly obedient, repetitive, most often nonsensical (to us), expressive of "love," devotion … what we call "worship" … and alliance against all others … which we mistakenly link with *faith*, as in "keeping the faith" and "defending the faith" — to procure "boons" and to alleviate the anxieties we have created for ourselves about this life as well as to relieve our overblown fear of death and an afterlife.

311

We seek relief from the misery we have created for ourselves — unique among all beings on Earth, all planetmates — from this Phantom in this life as well as afterward. This is the meaning of our ritual and prayer.

If Religion Is False, How Can God Exist?

By the way, if you ask me how can I disembowel ritual and prayer — the essence of religion — this way, yet still allude to an All That Is with a Benevolent Consciousness? If you wonder how I can be referring to a Divine Providence and a Divine direction and guidance for living, if such Phantoms as I am describing now are only projections of unmet need, you are not remembering what I have been telling you about our sense of a separated self. For while the essence of what I am debunking — religion — is appeasement and appeal; the essence of what I am affirming — which is commonly referred to as *spirituality* and *mysticism* — is surrender and mergence ... is re-union.

Religion and Spirituality

Religion is a product of the separation from unity with the All That Is or the Divine, and its individual observances of ritual and prayer only reinforce that separation. Whereas, the essence of mysticism and spirituality is to dissolve that barrier to the Divine — existing in our perturbed mind — and to re-acquire our true identity, which is at-one with that ... to achieve at-one-ment (atonement).

Priests

To this end we have priests who encourage our separation and play on it — which amounts to *religion*. Then they have a role as being mediators between the two separated consciousnesses; they are mediating professionals with "magical" powers and mysterious skills shrouded in jargon and ritual, incomprehensible to the majority of folks. Mediators are only required as long as separation is maintained, so resolution of the split, re-union with the Divine, at-one-ment (atonement), or return to godhead are hardly desired. Hence, mysticism and mystical practice are at odds with priestly religions and they are fought, often suppressed, by it and its allies. As long as there is no personal spirituality, there is a place, and a purpose, in society for such as those who would take over that responsibility — priests.

Voodoo Religion

Now, we have a kind of practitioner similar to priests existing in some primitive or indigenous societies, though not commonly. In fact, these beliefs about the supernatural and this practitioner tends to be associated with post-agrarian indigenous cultures, especially post-colonial ones. Which last point exposes a whole other line of inquiry regarding people in situations of oppression and utter power-lessness seeking magical avenues of power and revenge. Regardless, nomadic gatherer-hunters — our original humans — have mostly the next kind of beliefs, which are related to shamanism, not this one.

Now, these voodoo practitioners — sometimes referred to as *priests* or *priestesses* — existing in post-agrarian indigenous cultures might still be called *shamans*, but that is an incorrect designation. The pejorative of "witch doctor," while no longer used, actually reveals more about them than the term, *shaman*, for they, much like priests and actual doctors, act as practitioners — that is, professionals with jargon and mysterious powers and skills — mediating between sepa-rated realities.

The historical counterparts of such "witch doctors," indeed, would be forerunners of what later became priests and doctors. Their practices of attempted control of the mysterious are the roots of later religion, as well as medicine, with its physicians, and even psychiatry and its psychiatrists. Their means are incantations, much like prayer; and prescriptions of meaningless behavior, like ritual. And they believe in the power of spiritual objects — amulets, dolls, potions, and the like — to effect events; much as modern religious beliefs do, which embrace "holy" items and statues, "blessed" objects, and cere-monies involving imbibing magical liquids and food items.

What these practitioners do has been called *voodoo* — indeed, *voodoo religion* is a correct term to describe their beliefs — as well as is *sorcery*, *witchcraft*, *black magic*, and the like. What they all involve are attempts to control the Great Other — which was in infancy the Great Mother — and direct it along their ends. Keep in mind that these practices, far from being relics of a distant past, are pervasive in modern times in all practices that attempt to control the Divine, which includes the evangelical religions, much of the New Age religion, faith healing, and so on. So, "voodoo" is hardly confined to just sticking pins in dolls.

Shamans

However the third category of supernatural beliefs is true *shamanism*. Actual shamans are completely different from such priests and "doctors," described above; and shamanistic practice is the antipode to religious practice. Shamans ... and mystics, who are very much the same ... seek to cross or straddle that separation between worlds and beings. They do seek mergence, re-union, atonement and resolution of inner conflicts. They are routinely helped along by guides and allies of all kinds — human, planetmate, inanimate, event and happenstance, synchronicity, spirit or No-Form — around us seemingly anywhere and anytime ... in actuality, everywhere and always ... as "provided" by that Divine. Shamans also have conscious as well as unconscious intents to immerse in or become one with a higher reality. Correspondingly, shamans have behaviors which serve to aid humans in removing that separation with the Divine. We call this *spirituality*.

It is clear that the Divine is viewed completely differently in the various approaches to the Other — with religion and voodoo on one side and true shamanism and spirituality on the other. In most ways they are opposites. And it is in this sense, of discounting the one, the one seeking to use means of sorcery and prayer to cajole the Divine like we attempted to do as infants with caregivers; while advancing the other — which is the one seeking to remove the boundary through surrender, adherence to, and atonement with Nature and the Divine — that I repudiate one and elevate the other. For they are different, and opposite.

Furthermore, if one should question the existence of the Divine Itself, thereby removing the separation between us and Nature/Divine artificially by removing, in one's beliefs, that Other from which one has become separated ... that is, if you remove the separation by simply denying the existence of half of it ... then "the proof is in the pudding," as they say. For while religion depends on believing the unbelievable — which cannot help but be constantly under assault from Reality Itself in that it is erected *against* and *in opposition to* that Reality, which we mistakenly refer to as *faith* — spirituality requires no sycophantic obedience. For the Truth is that Ultimate Reality cannot be anything but helpful in that It *is* us. And why wouldn't we help ourselves? Why would the All That Is — equivalent to our higher self in the same way as Atman is equivalent to Brahman — withhold *any*thing that would aid us in tossing off our enslavement?

Such it is that by simply trying out the idea that there is a benevolent Universe, one finds that one receives help, assistance, and experiences that reveal that Other and, although it does not need to at this point, *proves it*. The Universe serves up all the evidence one needs, coming to one serendipitously, at the point when one honestly allows It to. Beyond that, It teaches us and carries us forward and into greater awareness, always, whether we know it at the time or not, and oftentimes even in spite of us and contrary to our efforts in a different direction.

This generous and assistive quality of the Universe is what is meant by, "Seek and you shall find, knock and it shall be opened unto you...." Reality does not require of us blind obedience and sycophantic worship. Now why would a Benevolent God — one we say correctly is all-merciful, all-compassionate — want that of us? No, the Divine — our denied Self — is as accessible to us as it was to our nomadic ancestors. Because It *is* us. It is as much a part of us ... actually we, a part of It ... as It is part of all life we see ... actually, the life that we see is part of It.

And, as I have said, this perception and understanding is part of a felt knowing of our consciousness that cannot be doubted, once it is realized. That is to say, once it has been re-accessed and been remembered.

Controlling God and Thought Control

So let us continue to critically evaluate the one that is mistaken and counterproductive — that is, the religions and voodoos. They attempt to not so much align with the Divine but instead to control It

315

in line with one's egoic desires, in the exact same way that "civilized" humans in general do with the Divine's counterpart, Nature. For is not the Divine actually out of our control? Not subject to our power? We would not spend all the time we do in ritual and prayer if It was doing what we wanted, would we?

You can see that through prayer and ritual we try to control the Divine. So does it occur to you that we humans are people who think we can, and should, seek to "domesticate" the gods? We would have the Divine, like our children, kowtow to our wishes and be another cog within the "machinery" of our lives. To re-unite with the Divine, in this way, means we get the Divine to merge with us! With *our* Ego.

Consider, at least, that this says of our way of thinking about ourselves and our lives that we know everything — that we are God Itself — and do not need to learn anything. Our awareness is supreme … it must be … for otherwise we would wish to merge with a higher reality or wisdom and learn from It, or at least, if separate, want to discern Its will, Its direction, and thus adhere to It, to Its guidance. Nevertheless, in the thinking that we developed with sedentary ways, and driven by fears of deprivation, we moved over to the position that God should do what *we* want, should be one of our achievements or accomplishments. For what higher wisdom or know-ledge is there — we, in all our burgeoning narcissism, began thinking — than that we want or need something and so should have it.

When you think about it, all of our modern science and technology is the penultimate — indeed it is the end result — of such an attitude toward Nature … toward God: That one not only can control the Unknown and uncontrollable but that one has the right and duty to, for one has wants and desires which are the center of one's life and represent our highest reality. To want, to control so as to acquire, and then to have or possess become what life is all about, the bottom line. It is the very definition of what today we call *consumerism,* built upon a human modeled simply as *economic man,* as our economics textbooks term us.

All this represents quite a diminishment of our appreciation of the supernatural — the other-than-known — from what humans enjoyed previously. Which included, by the way, that there was intention in the Other which was different from one's own, but that one was part of It and participated in It. So in those former instances, one was upheld, embraced, and guided *beyond* oneself by something higher or better than oneself at any particular time.

Evangelical Religion

Another example of this god control — which can reveal for us in its severity the general patterns of religious thinking involving manipulation of the Divine — is our evangelical religion of recent times. It is thought in these circles that if one can be the best possible sycophant and not have any contrary "bad" thought … but only think positive thoughts … and have supreme confidence in the outcome … that one can get the grace of the Divine and that miracles can be forced to occur. This is all based on certain, quite few and quite distinct, scriptures from *The Bible* where it is said that if one has supreme faith one can move mountains, and such.

However, to begin with, it is taking a metaphor of the magical and blessed things that can occur because one has faith that one is always in God's care and can trust that whatever is happening is meant to be, and it turns that metaphor into a prescription or recipe for control of the outcome along the lines one wishes. Control. Again. We are compulsively driven to apply it everywhere!

Furthermore, it confuses faith with belief. After centuries of insistence that the religion one belonged to was one's *faith* — meaning what one believed, as opposed to another's belief, *their* "faith" — the true meaning of faith is hardly known anymore. Although it is not hard to retrieve. For *faith* in any other context means to trust, or to hang on in the midst of adversity. It does not mean the ends will be what one insists upon, rather that the ends will be good ones, however they go.

For, you see … seriously, now … how can *we* know that God wants that particular miracle or healing to take place or that it is Its will or is part of Its Divine plan? These folks take what are more accurately termed *blessings* emanating from the *grace of God* — meaning that there is a Divine entity who is an actor with volition of Its own, separate from one's own will — and thinks of them as achievements … occurring as non-volitionally as water flowing out when one tips a cup … or the gold medal one gets upon winning the race.

This view completely removes the soul or aliveness of God — just as we did to Nature and to everything and everyone else — and reduces Her and Him to something like a principle of physics. Unlike atheists and most of science who remove the split between ourselves and Nature by denying one side of it — the Divine — evangelicals handle the problem by simply denying the Divine side has intention or true beingness to It. Science and religion are alike in that way. Each props up the ego in its desire to follow its perverted inclinations and to control everything in order to achieve their ends. There is a reason that one of these evangelical-type religions is actually called *Christian Science.*

You see that the "god" of evangelical religion is a kind of "god" that folks can control and order around by certain strenuous efforts of "will" — which are at base merely an outgrowth and reaction to one's fear — to keep thoughts out of the mind. It is attractive to those "good" people of society controlling their thoughts in syco-phantic alignment with the Controllers and the culture they orches-trate — which you will see I describe at length in the next chapter. For this religion brings into usage the good people's parallel practice in their "positive" thinking in obedience to the elites — which is a practice that keeps learning and personal growth from happening and strives to be witless.

In the same way as for the sycophants of culture, this concoc-tion, in evangelical religion, this *enforcement* of "blessings," requires a skill in keeping out the contrary thoughts and doubts that are part of growing in wisdom in life. So these "miracles" — sought and claimed — are, therefore, in no way the result of any kind of morality, kindness, compassion, or love. These folks think they can get what they want and perform miracles by the concentration of thought — the limiting of thoughts, again, not allowing any "bad" thought or "doubt" in — so, again, God has no say in it. It is another magical prescription, another hocus pocus not much different from black or white magic, voodoo, or science. It is no coincidence that this religion of "healthy-mindedness" — as William James (1899) called it — rose in prominence and belief concurrently with science and with the industrial age.

"New Age" Religion

There is also a version of, so-called, "spirituality" that applies here as well. Adherents of it often think of the Divine as being able to be assimilated through various techniques of consciousness. They would "raise their vibration," spike or jolt their pineal gland with certain concoctions or methods, use the correct crystals applied magically, say the correct supernatural words or mantras or prayers in *exactly* the correct manner — all so as to manipulate the forces of Nature and the mysterious or bring It into one's presence, instead of learn from and be guided by It. This, then, is actually religion — using forms of ritual to determine the Divine — only without a church. In this way of thinking, whether one is kind, compassionate, loving, authentic, generous makes no difference, as long as one has the correct "recipe" for Divinity. Like in our mythology of a tower called Babel, they think they can, through their own effort and using their own will and determination, raise themselves up to God, or a "higher conscious-ness."

And, just like the people of mythical Babel — as well as the evangelicals, scientists, and black magicians — they think God should have no say in it. God will "obey" and come to one if one uses the correct "technique," stumbles across the magical password to open the gates of heaven. God is no different from the forces of Nature, like electricity. It will "obey" and do what we want as long as we find the secret "trick" that "controls" It.

One variation on this is the controlling-type of meditation that is often employed among these people. Again it is about controlling one's thoughts, keeping out any wayward or "negative" thoughts. Not all meditations, any more than all spiritualities, are like this, I want to stress. However, this kind of meditation, just like evangelical religion, equates to that practice of "healthy-mindedness" that William James wrote about. It is an attempt to use spiritual-like techniques to be better sycophants for the Controllers, just as in religions.

Yet in that one *cannot* control one's thoughts — see what I say next chapter about that, in the example using the metaphor of trying to think "flowers" every time one thinks "sewage" — it results in folks who get better at the delusion that they *have* controlled their thoughts. They convince themselves, furthermore, that their numbness and repression, which results from this practice, is a form of higher consciousness ... awakening, or enlightenment even. Which is the lie they embrace, then boast about. Thus, they become more split from the truth of themselves, better at blocking out reality, more inauthentic. It is no wonder that elements of fakeness exude from them and are noticed by those around them. This is an inauthenticity that is even greater than that which we already have because of having an ego.

In any event, like we have done to all else in the Universe outside ourselves, all these sorts of wannabe spiritual adepts have reduced the most alive thing in the Universe — the aliveness of the Universe Itself, which is God — into another thing, another accomplishment, another attainment — manageable with the correct magic strings. Like the rest of Nature, God also is given no intention, will, consciousness. How ironic that such folks, in expanding their egos above all, can operate on an assumption that God, Itself, has no soul. But that *they* do! And that they will deign to raise Divinity up to where they, in their magnificence, are.

Do they really think God might not have input into their plans? We know the answer to that. For some of the wiser of them even say, "Want to know how to make God laugh? Tell Him (Her) your plans." That is an indication that some of them, having attempted it, are now laughing at their foolishness. So we see that even this mistake — like everything else — can lead one forward ... but only if one is open to learning from it and not keeping that awareness from happening by labeling its appearance in consciousness as a "doubt" or a "bad" thought.

Material and Technological Attitudes Infecting Religion

We see that it is no coincidence such evangelical and "new age" thoughts abound in our materialistic, scientistic, and supremely controlling modern world. For as much as science deals with only a material world — and ignores the spirituality and aliveness of the Universe to do so — it does so because it only deals with the things that *can* be controlled, whether for good or ill. That is why our science is interconnected with *technology*. Technology's meaning is *techniques for controlling.* With science behind it and feeding it, our technology has expanded our egoic, fear-based, drive to control into all corners of Earth and even beyond.

However such, so-called, "spiritual" paths, as I am describing, would seek to bring the same scientistic thinking into the realm of the non-material, the spirit, the soul, the Alive. Some of these adepts speak of a "technology of consciousness." This implies human as controller, again, even in the inner realms. Do we see that technologies only reveal that which they set out to? How can Awakening be confused with coming to know more of what one already believes? With no real change or transformation of the person?

Finally, does it not seem odd that, if a God exists, She would want to deprive billions of people living over the course of all of history from contact with Her — in a sense, "waiting" all those hundreds of thousands and even millions of years — till humans had developed their technology enough and stumbled across the correct techniques required to meet Him?

Fear Drives the Vanity of Prayer; It Implies the Universe Isn't Helpful Unless Cajoled

Therefore, attempting to pray, meditate, or imagine away the darkness is another way of not seeing, of staying in ignore-ance, and is motivated by the same fear of fear. *Fear drives the vanity of prayer.* It continues the idea that, if not malevolent, the All That Is is at least not very helpful unless cajoled. It reinforces the delusion of our separation from Nature and Divine Providence.

For in straining to pressure the Divine Other into acting in accordance with one's wishes or entreaties, one has to forget that one is not separate but is part of That Which Is. In any instance, one is forgetting that the All That Is is more knowledgeable and compassionate — being Everything as well as infinite Love — than one's deluded and singular, dimly lit self. It is only the greatest of arrogance continuing, to think that we could have better ideas as to the Ultimate Good — and that thereby we can orchestrate the rest of the

Universe along lines to produce it — than is had by what is the Ultimate Good by definition … along with It being infinitely compassionate, all-knowing, all-merciful, and all-forgiving … even of our sorry behinds, don't you know.

By Contrast, in Spirituality, "Evil," When Faced, Catapults the Good

At any rate, if you are such a person — having the most righteous intentions but simply going about it the wrong way, because you are without doubt surrounded by so much fear and distortion of all kinds covering up the correct way — what I am telling you here can be of the utmost significance and help to you.

For if you are like that, you can now entertain the thought that not only is it alright to let the darkness arise in you — and by that I mean no more than allow yourself to feel those emotions you have made wrong — but that it is the good and necessary thing to do. And in checking out that possibility, your efforts for good can be magnified magnificently.

For like the climber struggling inch by inch up the cliff face, we can do so much more and receive great relief if we were to know we did not have to reach the precipice through struggling away from below. But that we could let ourselves fall, to find that there has always been, not just a safety net there, but a trampoline … or that we are attached to a bungee cord. And that in either case we find ourselves going — with great ease and relief — much further and more directly where we need to go by trying *less* hard, to turn from darkness, not *more* strenuously, to keep from seeing it.

In this case, such knowing as this can be the most essential and powerful catalyst. For in giving up the impossible task of trying to remove discomfort or darkness from your life and accepting that you should let the inevitable pain and darkness inform and teach you, your actions can be infinitely more worthwhile, for others as well as yourself. This simple change can lead to greater and greater faith, but it also leads, increasingly so, to more capacity to manifest actual good in life. "Evil," when faced, can catapult the greatest of good.

Incidentally, how to go about facing this seeming darkness inside one — this Pandora's Jar of the repressed, hidden, and made wrong — is something I lay out in the final chapter of this book, on "Unplugging from The Matrix and Becoming Natural." Damn! but the twistedness in folks is going to misconstrue what I mean by facing their pain and "evil" within and is going to get wrong how to go about it — which amounts merely to *feeling* one's feelings, *not* acting them out. Yet I persevere.

Religion and the State

Something more needs to be said about religion before leaving this topic. It has to do with its relationship, not just to spirituality and the inner realms as I have been showing, but to society and the outer world. In the same way that religion fit the needs of Controllers to keep the masses enslaved and obedient to them, its practitioners had their niche in the civilized structures of society that had been contributing to the diminishment of self that came of leaving Nature.

Priests and the Division of Labor

Remember that the hierarchy of civilization is built upon the idea of a division of labor. By coercion from those above, those below can be organized and managed, regardless their preferences, to act along lines suitable to the upper ones. Folks would do what they did not want to do and would perform onerous, mindless, and meaningless tasks for interminable times at the behest of those with power and wealth. Being organized and directed, people can be put into positions of labor interacting with others in other positions. These positions are called *roles*. In this way, that surplus wealth, product, and so on — as I discussed in the chapter previous — can be brought about. And be immediately snagged and possessed by the ones in control, let's not forget.

All this requires, then, a division of labor, a kind of specialization, and roles. Certainly in primal societies there are roles of a sort. Still, they are few and are encompassing of much more of life experience beyond them. These roles are not constrained, focused on the few and the trivial.

Specialization and the Diminution of Self

With civilization comes roles and a division of labor along narrow lines, which lines of specialization are then orchestrated for the greater good of the conductors. Religion and the roles of priests fall in with this tendency.

Whereas with primal societies and shamanism, tribe members are allowed — indeed are required — to seek and discover their personal relation to the mysterious Great Other. As in everything else, primal folks are generalists. Each makes their own tools, fashions their own shelters, does gathering and hunting, sings songs and plays music as they please, creates their own artistic products, and relates individually with Nature and the Divine. These tasks are not divided up by roles such as carpenters, factory workers, farmers, singers, musicians, artists, ranchers, and priests.

However, priests and religion arise in this same upsurge of narrowed roles and diminished personhood come of the division of labor. With civilization there is a role, a person, who takes care of mediating with the Other; and one does not have to, indeed one is not allowed to.

One is not allowed to, you see, for here is another way these tendencies are woven together to benefit the elite. That is, with priests being the only ones allowed to mediate with the beyond, clerics amount to only one small segment of the population needing to be controlled in order to manage the morality of a populace. Through those in this one ministerial role, then, higher ups can achieve control of the minds and personalities of the rest of society, which they influence.

Religion as a Function of State

Perhaps you do not see or do not believe that the elite Large Accumulators calculated to create and then use religion as a tool of control. One might say that such a usage may have come of it but that the evolution of religion was driven by human needs and drives to connect with Divinity. Consider this, then. If religion was not intentionally being brought to bear as a means of oppression, why is it then that rulers insisted their subjects, not only belong to the religion instituted by the state, but that folks not have another? Right up into premodern times, religions have coincided with states and their power. We have one religion, the Church of England, ostensibly revealing that function.

On the other hand, if religions were meant to be mechanisms of interaction with Divinity, why would not folks be allowed to choose how to do that ... or not to ... as they wished? Why would not priests be allowed to be gone to ... or ignored ... as one wished? Consider the usage of psychotherapy today, for example. There is no benefit to the state for folks to engage in such a process or to meet with its practitioners — the counselors and psychotherapists. Hence, there is no state requirement for it. Notice, however, being as how psychiatry, on the other hand, *is* a method of control, there are the beginnings of enforced "enlistment" and usage of its practitioners in Western countries. Those who step out of line or express too much emotion are given a 51/50, as it is called in California, and are involuntarily detained and medicated. In some Communist and total-itarian societies of modern times there has been overt usage of such institutions and its practitioners, in fact. Reprogramming in consonance with a state-determined profile was required.

Finally, if religion was not being used intentionally to control populations, why is it that there would not only be state-approved mediators of it — priests — but that folks would be *required* to go only through them to fulfill such needs? If you do not think there was an actual *requirement* that such priests be the only mediators of such connection, notice how often folks were punished — in the Middle Ages, folks were murdered and burned at the stake — for such insistence on doing it their own way, for such effrontery, for doing it individually.

Religion and Culture

Without doubt, then, religion and priestly roles and mystifying ritual fit in with the ongoing movements toward increasing conformity; domination control; impersonal and ritualized practice in relation to Divinity and authority; sycophantic worship instead of connection with Divinity; and phantom and transcendent gods, representing separation from Nature and the body and abjuring the feelings of them and the experience of self and authentic beingness.

Religion thus conspires with the rest of society as a whole. It is seamlessly embedded within civilized culture, fostering the ends, not of personal growth, but those of benefit to certain and powerful others than self.

Now, *culture*, in a way, has a function similar to a kind of secular religion. It does many of the same things and all for the same ends. Let us take a look at what I mean by that, next.

26

The Eighteenth Descent — Culture:

The Matrix — "Wrong-Gettedness" and the A-mazing Cultural Maze … Strutting and Fretting, Signifying Nothing

"Such a fury we unleash, so as to create the smoke and mirrors of distraction and to keep us from the otherwise insidious trickling knowing of our horrifying creations and the gnawing abyss of dissatisfaction and unknowing inside us."

The expulsion from Paradise that came with sedentary ways demanded increasingly complex, however vapid, entrancements — ritual and mores — of culture as compensation, however empty, for the loss.

In becoming increasingly dominating, sycophantic, and emotionless, we created an emptiness within. To compensate, we created outside us in our social environment a maze-like, fantastical panorama — likened most recently to a *matrix*.

In this chapter I disclose the horror we do not want to know about ourselves and our beliefs.

Wrong-Gettedness … Culture

So the advantage to the survival of the individual newborn — however rooted, as it was, in the twisted motivations of the adults tending to them — of learning to be obsequious, inauthentically pleasing, and repressive of one's needs and expression became also the backbone of what humans call *culture*. For the lack of direct inner knowledge — the lack of connection to instinct, for example — that characterizes humans and was increasingly selected for with the predominance of controlling-conforming-appealing-nonexpression traits in humans, led to the ever-expanding overcomplexity of the obvious simplicity of existence. Humankind grew ever more fanciful and unnecessary traits, needs, desires, behaviors, wants, obsessions, compulsions, beliefs, visions, and thoughts — all subsumed under *Ego* — out of this separation from natural ways, this split from Nature, this estrangement from the Divine, this "expulsion from Paradise."

On the societal level, the cumulative result, or manifestation, of all individual egos — with all their infinite, however twisted, complexity — is what we term *culture*. Culture is the human substitute for the instinct we would otherwise have, just as Ego is the substitute for Self — *Self* meaning identity with Divinity. Being a separation from Divinity and Nature, culture is a separation from Truth as well. The *Unapproved and Hidden* — the Truth of humans not contained in any culture and whose essence is revealed in this book — is Truth that we do not know … cannot and will not know. Culture is what we erect in its stead: It is the overt representation of wrong-gettedness.

Is Culture Untrue?

"Is culture all untrue?" you are thinking. Well, no. It is true in a limited way. It is true in the same way the world is known to be flat. That is, within certain limitations it has its truth and hence its usefulness. Yet it is set in a context that is *not* true … not at all. And that context skews the results of all the contents of culture, making them of dubious worth.

At this point you should have a pretty clear understanding of what I mean by that, as I have given many examples. For instance, that life is hard and a struggle is true for virtually all civilized folk of all time. Yet it is given a different light when it is known that it does not have to be, is not in Nature, and was not even for us for most — in fact, for ninety-nine percent — of our existence as a species. That life is a struggle is not true in the larger context of what is possible and natural for humans and what is true for virtually all life of all times, except for humans in the few thousand years of civilization.

Language Helps and Hinders

Similarly, language is an aid in communication, yes. But from the larger perspective of the Unapproved and Hidden, it is a flawed substitute, a symbolic and roundabout way, of conveying messages: Not only does it confuse and obscure as much as it reveals and conveys, but the psychic, direct transmission of information that is its alternate in Nature is far easier and far more accurate.

Not only the mind-sharing of Nature is superior, but human mental confusion keeps us from another of our planetmates' advantages. For planetmates do not need language for they know more clearly what is going on without it being needed to be communicated. They can pick up instantly from the body language, the scent, and the facial and muscular expressions of others, together with the positioning of every element in any scene, more than could ever be communicated, by one to another, in language about what is going on in that scene.

For one thing planetmates can deduce far more accurately what is going on, since it is not being skewed or spun through the personality or agendas of any other. Added to this, they have far more information being conveyed to their senses, other than what could come from language. We can see this in the way canines are able to discern many thousands of times — up to a million times! some researchers report — more information from scent. Still, that is only one sense of many used by planetmates. We say animals can "smell fear." That is a trite example of the fact that planetmates are sensing far more of what is going on than humans are and they cannot be dissembled to … unlike humans with their language abilities who are so easily able to be fooled. So what would need to be communicated if it is already known? And known more accurately than one would get it as once removed, communicated to one through another?

Thus, human language is an aid in communication in the smaller context of human relationships and in that of being able to be written down and "stored" for use at a later time and to be disseminated to others, sometimes many others, without direct contact. However it is perhaps not an advantage, more likely it is a hindrance, in relation to the one-on-one communication that is possible otherwise for beings on Earth.

Culture Substitutes Itself for Natural Morality

Another instance: Remember I was saying, using the example of Abraham and Isaac, how if we had not been convinced otherwise by our pedagogy we would naturally see an example in that story of a murder being espoused by a supposed "god" and a sacrifice that would not be one for Abraham, predominantly, but for Isaac, who would lose his life? A grade-schooler hearing this story for the first time does not see in this any kind of interaction with a Divine being, rather one of murdering impulses within a person in a way that later the term *psychotic* could be applied. That is, until culture comes along to "teach" the child otherwise.

Like planetmates, children have a natural morality — where suffering, pain, and death are bad, and pleasure, freedom, and happiness are good — until forced to think otherwise ... until "enculturated." For, within the domains of culture, no one questions Abraham's behavior as being holy or righteous; nor the interaction with the "supernatural" as being anything but with a "god." However, in the larger context of feeling — the natural morality built upon innate empathy, love, and caring — which any planetmate or child would apply here, it is viewed as nothing less than insanity.

Similar things could be said for our understandings of love, our conceptualization of God, our feelings about extending kindness, and what it means to be a good person: All are what we think them to be, but only within a particular context. Beyond that, they are seen to be false, twisted, and corrupted.

The "Good" Person

Let us take one of those and using it as an example make it clearer what I mean. Let us look at what, in the context of culture, we proclaim to be a *good person*: The "good" people of our cultures put a lot of effort into doing the "right" actions and thinking the "right" thoughts. They engage in endless hours of religious nodding, bowing, and mumbling — what we call ritual and prayer — to "please" these Phantom gods of ours. Very few people would not attribute qualities of "holiness," goodness, and even saintliness to such people. But are they good?

"Good" people will also work, uncomplainingly, at the tasks assigned to them by controlling others, whether that be higher ups in the society — the Large Accumulators, the Controllers — or in the family, where that role is taken by husband and father in his dealings with his "good" housewife and his "good" and obedient children. Very few people would consider such compliant people to be other than the "salt of the earth," good housewives, well-behaved boys and girls, "hard-working, god-fearing, real" Americans … Germans … (insert your nationality here).

And Sycophancy, Thought Control, Obedience, and Self-Control

However, from what I have been telling you, it should be clear that the deferential and obedient of us, in the context I am presenting, can be seen as fearful sycophants who are confusing childhood admonitions — backed by terrorizing threats — to "be good little boys and girls and behave" with adult nobility and spirituality. Yet one might ask, what is wrong with that? Are they not "good little male and female adults"?

Well, yes and no. Here is where something is true within a certain limited area, within a narrow context, but is not true when viewed against the totality of Truth. For these people will seek to wrestle with their very thoughts so they will not have "bad" ones. They will repress any urges to complain, in adherence to a cultural value system that embodies obedience and control.

We say that their control of themselves — inside and out — their discipline, their conformity make them wholesome, "holy," or "good citizens." But, for starters, how can a person have only good thoughts and not bad ones? In actuality, we have no control over our thoughts at all. We have only some control over our actions; we can act or not act upon our thoughts. Hence anyone telling us they have control over their thoughts is really saying they are liars — to themselves, as well as the rest of the world — about what goes on inside them.

One cannot unthink a thought. What happens is, some thought occurs to us, which we, according to the morals instilled in us, deem "not good." It has happened, the thought; one cannot unthink it. But these sorts of people will then have a fearfulness, however unacknowledged and blocked from their awareness, that arises in them directly after that thought. That fearfulness comes from those forces I have been describing: It is a fear about pleasing more powerful others, and it has its roots in childhood, going all the way back to infancy, and even before. It is a fear of being punished or deprived of things for what one simply is ... in this case, just having a thought that arises unintended — "naturally." And one cannot help having this fear of the Other. It might even be said such fear is "natural" for humans, considering what all we have become as a result of our hellish womb experiences, traumatic births, and deprived infancies.

On Sewage and Flowers

So we have a random but natural "bad" thought and an unfortunate but natural fear arising in us. But what does this "holy" and "good" person do? This holy person tries to force the mind to go onto another thought that is not a "bad" one. It is like the first thought, using an analogy, would be "sewage." The next thought would be "oh, no!" The next thought, the concocted or replacement thought, would then be "flowers." But here is where the lie is. For the person keeps telling themselves they are thinking "flowers," however they are lying about the fact that they are really thinking "flowers not sewage," "flowers not sewage," "flowers not sewage," over and over again, trying to push the first thought out of their mind, and along with all that having a feeling of fear and trepidation.

Clearly, this upstanding citizen, this self-sacrificing mensch, this "good" father, this "good" mother, this "holy" thinker, this "positive thinker," is really not whole or positive at all. This person is a fearful sycophant, acting fearfully out of early experiences which they will never, ever remember, spending so much time thinking, "I will *not* think sewage, I will think *flowers,*" that they will never, ever find out what the thought after "sewage" might have been, if they had not fought it so much. And, yes, on its own, it just might have actually been "flowers." And I can tell you, sooner or later it would have been … and sooner than comes of fighting it.

This person is a narcissist, therefore, caught up in a focus only on themselves and how they might be coming across to others; is a sycophant trying to please imaginary others by conforming their behavior to them; and is a liar, not telling the truth about their experience inside of themselves to either themselves or anyone else. In the next chapter on soul murder, we will look at how this can even extend into sociopathy.

Oh, you think good people and sociopaths are on the opposite ends of a continuum? You have probably also been confused as to how sociopathic killers — the Ted Bundys, Jeffrey Dahmers, John Wayne Gacys, and their ilk — can come across as such well-behaved and "nice" citizens. You probably are not either seeing how some politicians and CEOs are getting their power by seeming to be so upstanding but are at the same time working behind the scenes to take all they can at anyone's expense and regardless who or how many die of it. More in the next chapter.

For now, the saddest part of all this is that this person, in holding back "sewage," becomes full of "sewage" … all the while she or he is thinking they smell like and are full of "flowers." The people around them know they are full of sewage. But those others, being often sycophantic also, are busy telling themselves the swill they see is really flowers.

Here we have an example of how wrong-getted we are able to become and how it spreads. We can see how culture aids and reinforces our wrong-gettedness and separation from the Truth of us. By this I mean that cultural values — concurrent with civilization and not with nomadic and presedentary ones — have become construed along lines to honor and reward the sycophantic, inauthentic, lying, and manipulative; and to punish the noble, authentic, the honest, and the guileless.

"Good People" Games … "Good" Actions and Hypocrisy

However, not just thoughts are controlled by "good" people. The same is true for such a person's "holy" and "upstanding" acts. Such a person might put out their hand to another, but on some level they are thinking, "I will be nice to you, so that I do not hit you." Yes, these people are what we call *hypocrites.*

You might be thinking, they are holy and good people and are not having the thought, "I want to hit you." Still, this is what happens when the "sewage" gets backed up. A stored-up reservoir of unapproved thoughts ever pushes for release by any means, for attention from consciousness at all costs, even if they have to come out in a distorted form — an impulse/thought to hit another. On the macro scale, this is what we as a species have done in creating and then acting out the Unapproved and Hidden, which belongs to us, collectively. This end result — the Unapproved and Hidden — is the product of the billions of unallowed thoughts, lies, and denials of all the "good" people of our culture.

The example of the hateful urge to hit, rather than lovingly help, is only a crude example, of course. It does have roots deep in our unconscious, though, and extending back thousands of years. We put out our hand to shake another's, for example. What this is really saying is, "My hand is not a fist. I will not hit you." "My hand is open to you — in giving and receiving mode, sharing mode — and not in a competitive or aggressive mode." "In putting out my hand I will connect with you, and not use it to fight you." Lastly, and most recently, "My hand does not contain a weapon." Now, why, unless a part of us knows that deep inside we would as soon hit another as anything else, would we go through all this social ritual of hand-shaking and its variants? All of its variants say similar things.

On another note, why, unless a part of us knows deep inside that we are as likely to be attacked by Other as friended by it, do we feel such relief upon the offering of said gestures? This goes to the inherent defensiveness of "normal" and "good" people that other "good" people know they had better appease by offering their hand ... for reasons not much different than a primate would offer its behind to an aggressor.

By the way, that unusual defensiveness of humans arises from those early human experiences of feeling attacked by Other through the traumas prenatally and perinatally, which are then reinforced in infancy, childhood, then again in cultural rites of passage. Note that this human defensiveness is unusual in its occurrence, happening much more frequently than in planetmates. For it arises in all social situations, all, even one-on-one interactions and not just in situations of actual potential aggression, as in primates.

In any case, it is that in real life those deeper messages of wanting to hit and fearing one will be hit are inaccessible to us. What we might be aware of that goes on in us — but rarely are — is less obviously hostile. It is more subtle, is most often unconscious, and becomes increasingly more unconscious over time, in the course of one's life ... hence more likely to direct our actions in spite of us. The "negative" thought — "I want to hit you" — might arise in the form of irritation, repulsion, or dislike ... or a simmering anger. We can actually feel that, but we will rarely admit those feelings occur in us ... forcing ourselves, instead, to "think flowers," again. You know what I mean.

Meanwhile, the negative thought or feeling, "you are going to attack (are attacking) me!" is not felt either. Rather, it comes out elsewhere, too. It is channeled unconsciously into all kinds of behaviors of introversion as well as defensive communications and passive-aggressive behaviors. Essentially, folks retreat from others and society, holed up in themselves; and/or they get revenge sneakily — without their even being aware they are doing it; and/or they react to all kinds of things said to them, even communications that are quite matter-of-fact or innocuous and perhaps not even pertaining to, let alone directed at them, with responses that are variations of "Well, that doesn't apply to me! I'll tell you a thing or two. How dare you say that! Let me explain how you're wrong. And I'm smart! (You're not.)" And the like. Check out the tweets of Donald Trump, and you'll have clarity and even better examples of this.

In any case, such things in people are examples of the kinds of hidden hostility and aggression, and defensiveness, that are buried within "good" people and covered up assiduously by all kinds of cultural means. While you think this is far-fetched, perhaps, think honestly about and explain to me how our kind, at the hands of all our "good" people, have been able to participate in lynch mobs; the rounding up of Jews for genocide at the time of Nazi Germany; the piling up of Jews like firewood to be burned during medieval times with its pogroms; or during The Burning Times, the torture and immolating at the stake of women who had some "free" thoughts — in other words, *not* controlled and then lied about thoughts, as the "good" people setting fire to them have and do. This unacknowledged and hidden hostility explains all the horrific, yet otherwise unexplainable, actions of "normal" humans including bigotry and racism, child battering and sexual abuse, anti-immigration sentiments, genocides, police brutality and murder of people of color, wife-beating, and ... (insert your "favorite" human abomination here).

So now, are these "holy" and wholesome people, these "good citizens" and "patriots" and "salt of the earth" — who are properly fearful and sycophantic, on the inside *as well* as the outside — really "good" and "wholly"?

For the more they tell themselves they think and feel one thing while actually thinking and feeling something else the more split down the middle they become. Till after a while, they have no clue who they are. They are liars to themselves and to all the world.

Self-Defeating Beliefs and Defenses

They cannot even become good people over time. Their disease, at all costs, fights against its cure. Indeed, it is like cancer, in that way. For to become a good person, one would have to know where one is being or has been a bad person and then change that. Such a person, however, is ever fighting to convince themselves they are full of "flowers," so how can they possibly do anything about the "sewage" that is actually in them?

Of such "good" people, the religious of them say that such thoughts about where they are being "bad" in their seemingly "good" actions and thoughts are instances of "doubt" and "lack of faith." So, rather than inform and do service towards becoming a greater "good," these inconvenient thoughts are done battle with as being demons, devils, and even the product of a Satan. So, no, in battling ceaselessly against the "bad" within themselves, they cannot actually become good. For they truly do not understand the nature of their bad enough to change it. Battling it, they keep it ever at a distance, giving it a status of devil, demon, Satan, and never acknowledging that these are simply — mostly innocuous and often innocent — parts of oneself that have been made "bad" by culture, then later, oneself.

Purification Rituals

What has been said about the effort to control thoughts — "positive thinking" — can be applied analogously to the many ritualistic behaviors "good" people engage in — secular as well as religious. A part of them knows they have sewage within themselves, so they are led to ever "purify" themselves … and the world by extension.

Yes, they will participate in repetitive confessionals; sacrifices of themselves and others; ritual purifications; self-flagellation; self-destructive behaviors to unconsciously punish themselves; obsessive-compulsive grooming and bathing, maybe even hand-washing; obsessive neatness of person and surroundings; perfectness of dress, outfit, adornment, and perfume; obsessive cleaning of their homes and cars; the persnickety grooming of their lawns, intensive control of all the things and of the nature on their grounds, including the shaping of any foliage there; and the obsessive organizing and cataloging of their items and the recording of their actions and intentions, i.e., obsessive planning. Nothing of their lives can be out of their control lest they be reminded of their "inner sewage" or it be revealed to others. They will be mortified if a spot, a stain, or dirt appears on their clothing, unconsciously feeling they have been "found out."

"Cleaning Up the Streets"

But yes, they will also see the world through this veil of "sewage" and so direct their efforts in ways to remove the "impurities" of others. Indeed, think again about those atrocities of humans, mentioned above, and you will see that almost always the people perpetrating the acts have rationalized to themselves their actions by claiming they are "cleaning up" or helping to "purify," or "save," the world.

If you think this only happened in previous times — Nazi Germany, The Burning Times in the Middle Ages, the times of slavery in America and elsewhere — consider how all of the "good" humans throughout the world today support the efforts to "clean up the streets," to "keep out the riff raff," and to "keep out the unwashed" without ever, in any instance, considering the people affected and how their efforts might be burdening and in some cases ending the lives of those poor souls — those ones simply more unlucky than oneself. These efforts are not far removed in quality — if not in quantity — from those of former times to maintain "purity" in the ranks, to suppress "heresy," to "crack down" on some group or other of society, or to "eliminate" the "undesirables"; and even in current times, the term *ethnic cleansing* expresses it and demonstrates its ongoingness. Need I mention Donald Trump, his bigoted proposals, and the surprisingly large number of Americans subscribing to them? Probably not. Yet keep in mind from many quarters these sorts of citizens are deemed the "good people" of contemporary society.

Denial Activities — How "Good" People Keep Realization from Happening

Yet these good citizens — as deemed by our cultures — also spend a great amount of time involved with activities of denial: They might spend hours sitting quietly at meaningless church ceremonies ... telling themselves it is really "flowers" they are seeing — you catching my drift? Or they might work themselves to death in a job.

They might fill up their time with chores around the house which are for the most part unnecessary and insignificant. Or they might immerse themselves in empty but culturally approved and applaudable activities such as repeating to themselves and others truly insignificant sports statistics; keeping up with the details of current fashion or the latest minutiae of celebrity lore; filling their minds and communications with the intricacies of auto mechanics, vehicle specifics and terminology; or showing they know what is new in financial and corporate trivia. These are all ways they can *prove* to themselves that they are okay and "regular" people — not the way they thought of themselves in infancy — and that others like and approve of them, not the way they felt others thought about them in infancy.

Whether they are trying to assure themselves they are "a regular guy," "salt of the earth," a loving and self-sacrificing mom, a "hard worker," a patriot, good citizen, or "god-fearing" person, it is all the same: They are trying to beat back that nagging feeling that they are full of "sewage" and trying to keep others from knowing that about them. These cultural activities are the way we lie, essentially.

Pathos and "Civility"

"Good" people are to be pitied for the degree of fear and sycophancy within them; that is true. It is sad how much life they have wasted striving to abide by the unjust dictates of a culture geared to higher ups, only. Yet they are hardly to be thought of as examples of integrity, wholesomeness, wholeness, or saintliness. They only appear that way for being so afraid to be otherwise and for imposing an amount of control upon themselves equal to that fear.

Certainly, whatever wrong they do is not "obvious" wrong, most of the time. They distinguish themselves from out-and-out "bad" people, like criminals. Though, the line between the two is most often blurred and many actions are in fact criminal. They get away with them, however, occurring as they do within the context of an appearance of outward "civility," which they take great pains to maintain. So compared to criminals, are they "good"? Or are they just better, slicker, in hiding or covering up their "bad"?

Indeed, these good and holy adults are actually pathetic — trying to be "good little boys and girls" in obedience to invisible others. They are narcissistic, being unable, like Abraham, to see the others around them and their needs, and only seeing their own "needs" … their sycophantic, fearful ones. They are liars and hypocrites; and they are anything but wholly or having integrity, they are split and deceptive.

"Good, God-fearing, Law-Abiding, Hard-Working"

Thus, within the definitions of culture, such folks are considered good people. That "good" is often followed by "law-abiding, God-fearing, hard-working" (people). However, along the measure of real Truth, this is only true in relation to other, more obvious, "bad" people. Hence, being a good person often just means being the best possible sycophant. We would be "good little boys and girls" and behave and do whatever we are told (whether it is actually good or bad), as adults, rather than be noble and authentic, and have integrity; real, empathetic love; true giving (without thought of reward); and be truly good adults.

Such "good" people of culture and society have been the good Nazis, in the past. They are the good soldiers mowing down villagers. Which is another great example of how "culture" operates to skew reality so as to cause you to do things you would not do if you were seeing reality directly, not *through* it. As well, they are the good citizens of society, imposing the most severe penalties upon all who stray over any lines, no matter how inconsequential, simply because people with wealth, and thus power, have drawn those lines. These are our, so-called, "good" people in our societies.

So culture proclaims, and it lies.

What Is Culture?

What is culture, then? *Culture* is the external manifestation of multitudes of egos; it is the accumulation of their actions. Culture substitutes for the "instinct" — the natural in us we have lost. In inserting itself into all aspects of our lives it pushes away the possibility we will ever feel that instinct arising in us, or find our body and mind becoming whole, natural, healed. Culture provides the opiate for the dis-ease of humanness, as well as it covers up the dis-ease and precludes any cure.

An Amalgamation

Culture is also the amalgamation of all that one has been told is real and true over against what one can see, discern, or would be obvious otherwise. Here's a good way to see it. You know that in reading this book it has come up against practically everything you believed to be true. Yet if you are honest, you know this makes much more sense, and it probably even corresponds to what you sensed to be true, but could not let yourself believe, let alone assert to others … could not "say out loud."

It's simple, culture is that whole, that composite of all that has been put inside you for you to use in your understanding of all outside you, which is in complete contrast to what you are learning in this book or would see on your own without those inserted prejudices. That's a good way to see it, right at hand. And that is why you have felt so uncomfortable hearing so much of this.

A Matrix

Essentially culture, like I said earlier, is the matrix. For it is all the ways we have been taught to see and interpret things, over against what we would on our own. And remember why and how there is such a disparity. Not only have we been separated from authentic apprehension of reality, but we have been encouraged and reinforced in that by outside interests with intentions to have us see and interpret things along ends to suit themselves … i.e., the wealthy, the elite.

Here is an example of that. Culture tells us the wealthy are wealth creators. If we saw clearly we would see that they are wealth takers, actually. It would be obvious to us, sans "culture," that it is the small operator who is more motivated to maximize her or his investment and thus create jobs, and "wealth," not someone who has so much that each dollar created is not seen as another addition in one's efforts to be wealthy but simply one, along with so many others, which can sit there, for all one cares, and does not need to be reinvested. Culture, also, is what tells Trump supporters that a billionaire like him can be on the side of the "little guy," and take on "the establishment," and right the injustices set up by a society favoring the rich. Astonishing, eh? This power of culture?

It is that planetmates do not have culture, by the way, that is another reason they do not need language so much. For what is conveyed through language is filtered through the intentions and agendas of others, the composite of which is slanted, then, away from seeing reality as it is. With no culture, planetmates do not need language as much for they are not seeing reality so unclearly that they would need the communication of language to interpret it.

Furthermore why would any planetmate want the confusion of others' interpretations about what one is able to see clearly? When that is offered to us humans, we say it is "bullshit," you see. Yet if we do not see it as nonsense, it still contributes only to our endless confusion about reality and who we are. Theologies relentlessly have engaged in the actions that have caused folks such confusion about their feelings and perceptions, being as how they concoct interpretations that are only consonant within realities that are imaginary, often having psychotic roots. Similarly, endless reams of philosophy have emanated from this pattern of folks — and religions, and culture — telling other folks that what they are seeing and experiencing is other than what it obviously is.

Outside the Matrix → The Unapproved and Hidden

By contrast to culture is The Unapproved and Hidden, which is the truth of reality outside the matrix. It is the way reality is seen with culture — all that accumulated product of slanted intentions and skewed agendas of others — removed. It is what is left when looking at all those same realities without such agendas or motives of others. Or oneself, for that matter — this is where the pre- and perinatal and infancy pain contributes its part, by the way, in skewing our interpretations and distorting our realities. Planetmates, remember, do not have that, either, further adding to their clarity about the reality they perceive.

So, yes, again, this book is an opening on The Unapproved and Hidden. I understand you do not know how lacking in agenda I am, how I get nothing for doing this, how I am not influenced by anyone higher up, or any of that; though I am unusual in being in a position in which that is all true. You do not know how my deepest rooted yet most accessible motivations are caring and love for others, concern and heartache over the unnecessary and self-imposed suffering I see; and with all that an irrepressible desire to step in, where no one else is doing it and so it is direly needed, and to do and say what only I, of all who I know, can say and do ... and *only* that. You do not know that my only reward, now or expected, is the feeling of knowing I have helped, done the part that only I could do, and the hope it helps relieve someone's suffering or misery now, in the future, or after I am dead. And that's *all*.

You do not know all that about me, but at least notice this: That in contrast to this, to all I am writing, you can discern in what you have been by culture indoctrinated to believe quite a bit of agenda, self-serving beliefs, and "convenient" truths. If you want you can easily see that quality in all those commonly held assumptions — the superiority of man over other planetmates being the deepest but only one of them — that my writing in this book addresses and comes up against, conflicts with. If you cannot discern my lack of guile, at least notice the agendas of those who concocted and orchestrated your beliefs and your actions that came of them. Take at least that, for certain, from your own apprehensions and interpretations of your direct experience here.

Strutting and Fretting

In sum, the Divine is Ultimate Truth. Whereas, culture is the societal embodiment of the separation from the Divine. Hence, culture contains some pretty a-mazing untruths and empty rituals. They are amazing because they are fantastical — colorful psychotic fabrications, if you will. They are a-mazing also because they are manifestations of our confused and twisted consciousness and bring us ever back to the maze — in an endless trudge through labyrinthine passages of a journey that is ultimately futile, guaranteed for failure — which is our life.

Culture Is a Weed Without Roots, the Fury We Create to Block Out Our Emptiness

You see, our gradual changes from natural life involved two things, basically: A growing ability to survive biologically, physically at whatever cost to our happiness, along with a separation from our natural inclinations and felt Divine guidance. And our ever-widening separation from the Divine meant a constant hole in the felt meaning of our existence.

Lacking roots in Nature or the Divine, we were like a weed without roots, growing madly above ground, reaching out vainly in all directions for sustenance because of the lack of direct connection to our deeper truth. This expanding outward desperately in all directions creates our culture — which is the artificial substitute and the dim empty reflection of existence.

Culture — our "matrix" — is the "much ado about nothing" and the "strutting and fretting upon the stages of life" and "sound and fury signifying nothing" of which Shakespeare wrote. Culture is a magnification of our overcomplexity of the obvious simplicity of existence, and it is the overblown array of our defenses to keep at bay our realization, our "enlightenment." Culture brings meaning to our lives, but it is a false one. It provides us motives, and it supports and sustains our efforts; but they are vain and empty goals and futile and meaningless rituals, only.

So, after the fall into sedentary-agrarian ways which multiplied the branches of culture a-mazingly, providing the opiate for our feelings of loss and the substitute for more natural ways, more of our newborns would live. As I have said, they would be given economic value — as a commodity — within that trance life or matrix we have erected. Our children would be allowed to live, but what was distributed among them was this watered-down offering, of a life drained of meaning and "juice" but mostly lacking the "colors" or "flavors" of experience we enjoyed as humans in Nature and containing instead the apprehension of the outlines of living not the immersion in its profound and lush plenitude.

This tendency for our lives to be bleached of real appreciation yet multiplied maniacally grew steadily over time coinciding with the aforementioned rise in the predominance of the traits of controlling, conforming, sycophantic and desperate striving to please and to be appealing, and nonexpression of needs become repression of personality and cobbling of ability to participate in existence's Divine creative stream. We built increasingly a false matrix in which to dwell, substituting it for the richness of experience of our Edenal existences.

Ignorance of the Divine Makes for Some Pretty A-Mazing Untruths and Empty Rituals

All in all, driven by this inner abyss of unknowing, our outer behavior expanded in spurious and fanciful activity and productions of all kind. With time, our vapid nature would spin out unnecessary personality traits, hollow and unsatisfiable needs, fetid desires, furious but vain behaviors, insubstantial wants, blind obsessions, uncontrollable compulsions, fantastical beliefs, painfully burning visions, and tortured thoughts … of all kinds and all of it magnified, then multiplied, then repressed and fought, then struggled with … and all this in grandiose dramas that are further multiplied, exaggerated, over-dramatized, and so on round again.

Such an overcomplication of life's simple existence and be-ingness we create to keep from knowing the horror of us. Such a fury we unleash, so as to create the smoke and mirrors of distraction and to keep us from the otherwise insidious trickling knowing of our horrifying creations and the gnawing abyss of dissatisfaction and unknowing inside us.

In all of these, we journeyed ever further from our roots in Nature and the Divine and made Edenal existence the most distant memory and the most certain component of everyone's Unapproved and Hidden.

Inevitably, all these ways came back to oneself. As we faded from natural and felt existence and — driven by pain, fear, and the resulting controlling mania — succumbed to ever more entrancing substitutes, we ourselves faded from existence, in a sense. This increasingly ghostly existence amounted to *soul murder*, then. It is to it, we now turn.

27

The Nineteenth Descent — Soul Murder:

The Heights of Control, Repression of Feeling and Loss of Joy, Dissolution of Empathy and Conscience, and the Scourge of Sociopathy

> *"...soul murder... was more than the killing of conscience, it was the destroying of feeling and all the empathy, love, and profound pleasure in being alive that comes with a life felt fully, immersed in the experience of it, not simply the management of it."*

To some extent *soul murder* is something I have been pointing to and alluding to all along in all the various descents from Nature. They all involve an assault on beingness, and for the soul, then, a death by a thousand cuts. The forces of culture, religion, child control, and hierarchy were most effective, we have seen, through the means of loss of self and control of inner life. Control of thoughts and self; avoidance-denial of pain and with that loss of ability to experience pleasure and joy; and ultimate loss of empathy and conscience are the main components of what is sometimes called *soul murder*. They are related, especially the last, to sociopathy, as we will soon see.

Thought and Feeling Control

Importantly, soul murder is rooted in thought and emotion control. With civilization and its mores and rules advanced to suit the rich and with the addition of religion as a mechanism to master the masses, the inner personal life, beyond even morality, was brought into line. Beginning in infancy and childhood, then added to throughout life, folks were impressed upon them the wishes of those above — parents as well as Controllers. In order to do that, outer demands needed to be introjected. For to target inner life was more efficient in eliciting compliance of the masses than mere external control. To keep the masses from noticing their chains and rising up righteously, the oppressors deduced it was imperative that folks not realize their enslavement.

However, thought control was embraced by the masses for their ends as well. With all the pain building up inside people, it required more psychological defenses to keep it at bay so as to have any chance of well-being. The happiness of ordinary folks was constantly under assault from all the injustices — womb to society. And all of that needed to be put out of mind. All mechanisms were needed, including religion, to repress the inner pushes of discontent coming from fetal malnutrition; from the trauma of birth; from guilt about the killing of all kinds that one was doing; from the immense labor that was one's life beginning with civilization; from abusing children and being abused as children; from the subjugation by the Large Accumulators and, if women, their men; and finally even from religion itself. For religion brought with it its own kind of trauma and gave rise to its own counter pushes and rages for rebellion inside oneself. These outrages, from religion arising, had to do with the repression of pleasure, especially sexual repression.

Sexuality Control

Remember, sexuality in one's Conforming Underlings was not convenient to Controllers. Indeed, any kind of pleasure was a threat to them to take the service classes away from their attention on the narcissistic higher ups. For sexuality involves a relaxing of inhibitions. Controllers however *wanted* folks to be inhibited, that is, controlled. Lack of restraint on the part of the masses was a threat.

Hence, it was simply a matter of time before Controllers would have their wishes channeled through religious dictates having the public morality involve the suppression of sexuality and for it to become demonized. Remember, sexuality is also our link to Nature, which had become categorized as wild. Nature had been demonized in order to control it, or thought of as bestial, at least. So now sex was, too. Sexuality was a potential wellspring of defiance, of "wildness," of randomness and non-conformity, if not rebellion; it needed to be put down.

All this suffering was of no consequence to the higher ups, of course, for they viewed those below as not really alive. They had to do that in order to control and oppress them the way they wanted. The masses needed to be seen and used as pawns and props in their schemes. The masses were readily available and "eager" raw material available to be used for any concoctions, for any dramas the upper crust could dream up. They were seen as no different than the planetmates held inside corral and under plow. The Controllers would deem the very sexuality of those they controlled to be another variable needing domination just like they had done with the procreation of their kept planetmates.

Pleasure Control

However, not just sex but any pleasure for the Underlings was a threat to Controllers. Like children seen but not heard, mute and constrained folks, eagerly obedient and ready to serve, was what was wanted. Downgraded, along with sex, was pleasure in this life. Inevitably, it was deemed immoral to even feel too good, to be too expressive, to be too joyous.

Religion added that happiness and pleasure could be had in another life in return for forgoing it in this one. And the more one was unhappy in this one, the more one could have it later. Hence self-flagellation, silent suffering, self-denying and negating and sackcloth-and-ashes misery were deemed good avenues for "moral" persons.

So, you see, yes … it was not much different from what one had learned in infancy: If one would simply repress one's cries, not ask for what one wanted or needed, pretend that one didn't have needs or that others' needs were always more paramount, then it was more likely that one would have one's needs taken care of. Magically, as blessings, as grace, that is. And that is significant for religious ideas later, as well.

Pleasure would be moralized against and devalued in order to have folks attend to the desires of those above. Instead what were inculcated as values was hard work, conformity, and obedience. So to all the other suffering involved in being human, which folks had to bear so they could simply function, now was added the repression of love, sex, tender relationship, and intimate feeling for another person. And since the functioning that one sacrificed one's feelings and desires for would be that which was at the behest of the Controllers and dominators, in the family and without, all this would amount to soul murder.

Feelings, Needs Control

Furthermore, emotion was perceived as being something out of control; it was messy. Such errant variables were not convenient to the ends Controllers had in mind. All of Nature, including the biology of their underlings, the server classes, needed to be subdued. Even human happiness or satisfaction would not suit their ends. For it would make the underlings think they had lives of their own that they could direct; it would lure them away from their attention to satisfying those of the higher-ups. The Controller's needs were what mattered, not the underlings.

For the Controllers in their ever-growing hubris thought of themselves as special, and the only really alive humans, and fancied themselves gods. They demanded they be treated that way; that they be raised upon high, worshiped, and revered. How inconvenient to those ends was any choice, intention, human feeling on the part of their Underlings. Indeed, the Controllers usurped the region of the inner lives of humans to themselves, conquering as much of the inner realms of their subjects as they attempted to of the outer domains of their neighbors.

To do so, religion and other forms of mind control were brought to bear. We have the beginnings of propaganda arising alongside that of public religion. They both would involve channeling the thoughts of the masses along lines deemed positive to the ends of the elite. Propaganda was a form of positive thinking inculcated into the masses.

Certainly we see this throughout history. And such straying from the ends of the elite often incurred the penalty of death.

Pharmaceutical Controls

In modern times, as well, this control by elites is sought. Now, we have modern medicine to augment the controlling mechanisms of religion, cultural mores, and tyrannical power. Pharmaceuticals are currently brought to bear upon errant thoughts.

Not too long ago lobotomies and electroshock were egregious examples of the Controllers intentions to keep everyone in line. Eventually such visible targets of ostensible control, which could and have given rise to defiance and rebellion, were superseded by subtler, more invisible means of control. These were far better in that not only could they be administered on an ongoing basis keeping people continually medicated — notice, for example, there are no antidepressants to be administered "as needed"; whereas "as needed" alternatives anymore, tranquilizers for example, have been eliminated as part of any normal protocol. Also the power of the medical establishment convinced people to cooperate with their own control. So it is that we have, essentially, pharmaceutical lobotomies, and willing victims. Granted, folks would seek this help. As I said they would contribute to their own enslavement. Having been made depressed by civilization, they were eager consumers of its antidepressants, understandably.

These tendencies contrived to convince the masses, as always, that what was done to them and offered or impressed upon them was for their own good — just as parents told children their control was for "their own good." The masses were made unhappy but were given palliatives for it, so they could continue functioning despite their gnawing unease. Depression would be a natural reaction to the lives of humans in any times beginning with civilization. That, however, along with any other errant emotion, is inconvenient to the engines of industry, commerce, production, accumulation, and daily work. Pharmaceuticals would be a kind of medical positive thinking, one which could be controlled, applied where it was needed, and so orchestrated for greater ends. It had this "wonderful" extra advantage that folks would eagerly cooperate with their own numbification and subjugation.

Emotions Control

All these methods were simply about making the masses feel differently than they would otherwise about their servitude and the misery of their lives and the traumas of their origins. Instead of allowing a natural sadness, culture and religion urged folks to "put on a happy face," essentially. To keep from realizing the injustice of one's lives — for we would have otherwise, since we still had inside us a psychology aligned with lives in Nature, where we were happy — we needed to smile, however much we felt like weeping.

Not just depression but huge losses of self-esteem would come about if one were to realize one's predicament. Such emotions in the populace would be counterproductive, so everything was arrayed to aid one in avoidance and repression and instead to substitute the delusion that everything was fine and the way it should be. Any feelings to the contrary were to be labeled as individual aberrations and dealt with, depending upon the times, with persuasion, punishment, murder, or pharmaceuticals.

Soul Murder

All these things combined to bring about soul murder and the sociopathy we see today: religion, sexual repression, demonization of pleasure, morality, and positive thinking — being the self-imposed mind and thought control. One was told to "channel" one's impulses and drives. For whose ends? Not one's own. Certainly by now, in not following one's feelings and intuitions those impulses had become corrupted, even perverted, so one could convince oneself that it was right and true to control one's nasty id. Which was a practice of repression in full disregard of the Nature and the Divine — both of which lie, like the hope at the bottom of Pandora's Jar, beneath such distortions of desires.

Eventually new-agers would twist such inner control into ideas that one could change one's reality by changing one's thoughts, but it was never considered what one was trying to change into and why. Mostly those ends were those put inside folks by higher ups: They were wealth, status, material goods, positions where one could be sucked up to like the Controllers above one were sucked up to. So such new-age "awareness," lacking social-political awareness, was simply another variation on enslavement.

It is not just in the form of new-age positive thinking that this manifesting of an alternate reality comes up. It has risen up as well in modern totalitarian states where propaganda is used to create the minds of the masses and to restrict their feelings. Folks have been convinced that merely raising one's voice is wrong, lest they be labeled "bipolar," and sent off to be held somewhere and medicated, where modern pharmaceuticals are used to control what feelings folks will have.

Added to these methods were the bread and circuses of all times, as we see today in the mindless entertainment, the sitcoms, the distraction into endless trivia or into computer games, mind-and-feeling-obliterating work. All these are meant to keep up the wall between oneself and one's natural dismay. As well as to keep one ready for being fertilized by the wishes of those above and harvested one's service from one like one were a plant.

Altogether this amounted to soul murder. It was more than the killing of conscience, it was the destroying of feeling and all the empathy, love, and profound pleasure in being alive that comes with a life felt fully, immersed in the experience of it, not simply the management of it.

Avoidance of Pain, Loss of Joy

A significant and overlooked aspect of this is what folks in civilized societies did regarding the pain of life. No one wants pain, of course. But I was explaining at length in the chapter on Divine Guidance how it is a natural part of life, which when it is assiduously avoided keeps one from receiving the direction one needs to guide one along to a greater experience of life.

A part I have not dealt with so much has to do with how avoidance-denial of pain corrupts our ability to feel joy and pleasure, too. In a natural setting, as enjoyed our primal forebears, we knew of life as being an alternation of pleasure and pain, happiness and misery. It was no big problem for them, however. For overall this flux of darkness and light is what made life that much more enjoyable.

In a game one would not enjoy victory or making a good play if one did not also experience being scored against and losing occasionally. Life would have none of its exquisite sense of surprise and discovery if there were no twists and turns in it. One could not enjoy the blessings of wandering into delightful glades if one did not travel twisted, darkened paths at other times. Life would simply not be much of a story or worth playing if there were not drama in it.

Yet, with sedentary-accumulating ways, we made that simple fact into the biggest dilemma for us. We have magnified the pain of life to an amazing extent. Light requires a darkness for it even to be seen; one would not know pleasure except in contrast to pain. We would wish to have only light, however; only pleasure, always. This is because, for reasons having to do with the twisted consciousness we carry from our abnormal beginnings — the pain we have in birth — we go through life terrified we will once again experience such pain as we had at our beginnings. We see all life through such a darkened filter. We live in trepidation of the ending of our happiness, when we could be enjoying it; and in terror that our pain, when it comes, will never be followed by happiness ever again. So we spoil even the experience of pleasure, while we amplify the misery of pain.

Regarding Paranoia

We once experienced pain in such an assaultive way we feared it would never end. At our beginnings, we have an abnormal amount of experience of feeling trapped and suffocated; and we, in our premature state, though still coming into the world, are not aware yet of the ending of pain, of the fact that it is not possible without pleasure. We experience such overwhelming pain during our births that ever afterward we believe it is possible that we could at any time experience pain greater than is possible for us to bear. Because we also at that early time mistakenly thought it possible that pain would never end, we believe such a thing is possible in life ... even in afterlife. Hence, unlike our nomadic forebears or the planetmates of Nature, we amplify life's pain with our fear that it can even be more than we could bear and with this belief that, beyond that, it could be unending. We believe, mistakenly, in the possibility of "hells," in a sense. That is to say, of endless suffering both in this life and the next.

To add to all that and because in our beginnings we experienced these things while in close proximity to a seemingly all-powerful Other — that is, they happened while inside our own mothers or while being born from her — we have this feeling ever after that there can be an intention or an actor behind the events of our life ... including its pain ... like our mother to a small extent was around our birth events. The whole world for us being Mother, at that time, and experiencing her as the only other actor in that drama of our birth, we attribute some of the inordinate pain of that time to that fact: that it is related to this Other, who was also World to us, and who we sensed as Mother.

Experiencing these imagined magnifications of life's pains in relation to her, then, throughout our life it is possible that we can even think there might be an intent or actor behind our experiences of pain and suffering at that time also. And since we have made such pain and suffering to be wrong, as well as horrifying, we of course can think of this actor as being malevolent, calling it devil or Satan.

This is how we take the ordinary pain and misfortune of life and weave it into the tapestry of our unnecessary fears, empty dramas, and supernatural forebodings.

Natural Joy and Feeling

On the other hand, in Nature, as we can see clearly among the gatherer-hunters of our age still, along with an acceptance of life's exigencies there is a considerable increase in the ability to feel joy and to have other emotions fully and satisfactorily. The reason this is so is that it is a simple fact of our psychology that when one denies and represses pain, one ends up reducing the ability to feel pleasure and all good feelings as well. As Arthur Janov (1971) phrased it, feeling is an all or nothing thing.

So with avoidance-denial of pain in civilized societies there arose a loss of ability to experience pleasure and joy. Visitors to the more "primitive" and natural societies living on Earth, in the past and currently, invariably remark on the ability of the people there to both laugh and cry. The laughter that is observed is not like that which we see with repressed civilized folk. It is uproarious, knee-slapping, some-times literally falling to or rolling on the ground, extended laughter. It takes up one's entire body. It bespeaks such uninhibited joy and lightness of being.

By the same token, such primal folks are taken fully up into any grief, loss, or sorrow they experience. When friends are leaving — even such as those White observers I mentioned — there is hugging and crying, unashamedly, by men as well as women. When there is a death, there is loud, demonstrative weeping and wailing, which goes on for days and is entered into fully and with one's entire body engaged.

It is not just the extremes of emotion and feeling that are fully embraced. Primal folks are observed to be able to be quite animated in their talking, too. They might gesticulate — according to some more restrained observers — "wildly." More accurately their entire bodies, they might involve in expressing themselves. Far from the arms-at-one's-sides soldier or professor, or the hands-folded school child or podium speaker, they say almost as much with their fingers, hands, and arms, as well as their body movements, as with their words. They are likely to engage their entire bodies in communication and to mix it up with exclamations, emotional utterances, excited variation in tone and cadence, curses, laughs, and mimicking of others or of the sounds in the environment.

Correspondingly and again unlike the inhibited folks come of civilization, they are able to truly feel for another, whether for an-other's joy or another's loss and sorrow. It is not just a pretense for the purpose of manipulation, either, as is likely of us modern folk. How do we know? For they are more likely generous and giving, having little regard for any loss one might incur in the aid of another. Along with this, as I mentioned before, is their innocent and guileless nature.

Nor do they need encounter groups or human potential seminars to learn to trust others and to be open to feelings. Astonishingly, many of their rituals and practices actually contain elements of communicating at length, resolving differences, revealing their thoughts and perspectives, exploring and sharing emotions, sharing of feelings and beliefs and inner experiences of all kinds — including dreams, inspirations, supernatural encounters. Observers frequently remark on the amount of time "wasted," as Westerners see it, in looking into and sharing their dreams, for one thing.

We see that primal peoples are not only more belonging in tribe and community than modern folk, they are embedded in it through a complex interconnection of feelings, shared experiences, and extensively negotiated understandings about the way things are and the optimal ways to act and respond so as to be in consideration of others and their feelings and understandings.

The Scourge of Sociopathy — Loss of Empathy, Conscience, and Fellow-Feeling

Contrasted with that is the total isolation and self-centeredness characteristic of the schizoid personality of civilized cultures. Similarly, soul murder involves the ultimate loss of empathy and conscience. Soul murder and schizoid tendencies make possible the abominable things I have mentioned — the ability to go to war, to engage in hate crimes, to rape and kill, to burn Jews and witches, and to murder from afar, as in our current day. They have created what today we term the *sociopath*.

Notice that sociopath is not a term only attributable to smooth talking rapists and serial murderers, these days, but is put upon some of the most powerful men and women of contemporary times. It is sociopathic behavior to send an entire nation to war — killing tens of thousands of one's own and millions of another nation — to further oneself in one's business, to advance one's corporation. Yet this has been done. And like those honored and respected "good citizens" I talked about in the last chapter, our society somehow manages to exalt such soulless figures. Our society buries its shame and humiliation in being so used and turns its buttocks to such rape from on high, in keeping with its deep fear and overriding sycophancy and addiction to security and routine. Not to mention its immersion in the consumer goods, the carrots, that come with such ability to be blitheringly bereft of authenticity, in one's self and personality, or of any integrity … let alone nobility of soul, let alone heroic allegiance to the cause of truth, in the world and one's society.

This brings us back to the rise of sociopathy. The flip side of conformity is sociopathy, and it is something shared by Controller and Underling alike. For both modes require an unfeeling person. To oppress and to be oppressed are both against one's nature, one's deepest human nature. For at base we would prefer to love, care, and exude kindness, not controlling; and we would rather feel nobility, heroism even, and integrity, not repression of self.

So at the penultimate of civilization's arc, we arrive at sociopathy. Our evolution was characterized by ever more control. And sociopaths exhibit the end result: Someone who is so controlled and unfeeling that he or she can control without conscience everything in their environment. Sociopathy is humans' obsessive-compulsiveness about things and one's environment, one's controlling proclivities, directed at all else in the social surround — including strangers, offspring, intimate others, and the faceless masses, all alike.

Such a person has become so good at conformity. Still, such repression of self is not without its consequences of an outraged bottled-up psyche fuming with resentment and anger at that. However the rebellion that arises of that inner cauldron of stifled emotions comes out in a kind of direction of those controlling-conforming skills toward sneaky ends — ends all unconsciously trying to bring down, and hating, all around that one mistakenly generalizes has caused one to be that way. Therefore, such a person can lie, cheat, steal, murder, all without conscience.

For the unconscious feeling driving it all — although not felt, of course — is that of hating everyone, wanting to destroy everything. Just as the lonely, deprived, and suffering infant after such a while, a long while, of frustration, cares not if it lives or dies just as long as it can do so in a way to bring down all else with it. Such an infant feels that its needs are all-important, including now even to destroy and hurt, and that all else is collateral damage. *Narcissist* is the word used for this in an adult. And it is the end point of our "evolution." It follows logically from all the drives and accomplishments in controlling everything and making of them an offshoot of one's desires, and into things not having any existence outside of one's needs.

So, yes, while we see this tendency of sociopathy in our Controllers and killers most obviously, it exists in virtually all civilized people in some measure. We see it in the way folks obsessively clean their homes, fastidiously determine their lawns and bushes, consume recklessly and trash mindlessly, with their environment collapsing around them and species by the hundreds of thousands and millions dying and going extinct without their giving a thought to it. In fact, part of the tendency to see such sociopathy in others is an outgrowth of hiding the part of it in oneself. People have become narcissistic and greedy, shoring up everything they can for themselves and family and at anyone's and everyone's expense, and calling themselves normal and their behavior required. Unfortunately society, the amalgamation of all such people, calls it normal and necessary, too.

Folks in modern times are unconscious of the plight of others in the world, are insensitive to those in their communities who are worse off, are numb to the calamities and despair of the unfortunate and hurting; and they insist that any others with demands and outrages, or any sorts of ostensible feelings and emotion, either shut up, get medicated, or be put away.

All of this is how we have become as a result of all of our descents from Nature. This is who we are with us in "control" of things and no longer assisted by the Divine.

But it is not the way we have to be.

Coming up, redemption, becoming natural. How we regain our primal, our planetmate nature once again, and belong once again in the family of our mother, Gaia, the Earth.

28

Unplugging from the Matrix and Becoming Natural:

The Abyss and the Labyrinth Versus Redemption, Re-membering, Reconnection with Body, Realization of One's Felicity in Life and One's Real Self

"While our human game of total forgetfulness has become an oh-so-serious and inescapable one of 'dungeons and dragons,' that of planetmates is relatively pleasant, playful, child-like, and often comical, without the doom and gloom quality of ours."

"It is only then, turning downward our eyes in the face of the darkness and the seeming 'end of times,' that we can even notice our soul, our emotion, our connection with all and Everything, our true happiness, our actual heart expansion and love."

Human Wrong-Gettedness

Laughable

Our thinking is a form of dementia to be sure. Yet it is humorous, too. It can be a source of amusement for us if we can stand back and take a look at ourselves sometime. If we could see ourselves, puffing and preening, playing ever like we are before some kind of camera and are the only one on the stage....

Ignoble

But far worse than that is the ignoble quality of our views. For the result of all this wrong-gettedness is more than just unfortunate and laughable, it is tragic and often ghastly. Notice the way these odd, demented views have directed our behavior in disastrous ways toward all else but us.

In particular, culture skews the truth of us, making of us something different, and unreal, in all of Nature. We know we are different, but we rationalize that as more evidence that we are superior. We are wrong; however there is no need for me to belabor the different ways in which we are different and wrong-getted and the different things that we completely misconstrue. I have said already much about our conceptualizations of materialism, superiority over Nature, and our vanities of "goodness"; and it should be clear the dire consequences which at the present have sprung from them. We would bring down the entire planet in an egoic orgasm of destruction and self-annihilation while patting ourselves on the back for our good citizenship, community standing, "family values," our "morality," and/or our "patriotism."

Concerning the other reckless mistruths of us, any humans of a fair mind have already had other examples of them occur to them. In peeling back the blanket of our wrong-gettedness, a world of darkness and ignorance is revealed.

Moronic

In these ways, the results of all our different ego "projects" — our vanities and presumptions — though they can appear rather silly are also rather pathetic and, ultimately, moronic. Compared to the truth of the All That Is — which planetmates are, and our early humans were, part of, more than just "knowing" — the productions of our fevered minds are random, temporal, and rootless.

Difficult to Overcome

Each of them over-complicates the understanding of Existence. No doubt that over-complication serves best to hide their lack of true foundation, their wrongness. We stand amazed by the profound and intricate sight of our magnificent unreality. It is hard — as hard as it is to leave the "matrix" — to question the foundations of our beliefs, while our eyes sparkle in reflection of the fascinating electronic array ... and our every thought supports itself on the jetsam of stupefied minds.

For this culture and this edifice of supposed knowledge and understanding built on these wrong and dangerous assumptions serves to feed those who seek understanding with a tasteless substitute for true awareness. Standing within Ego, as always, our comprehension and mastery of the details of the absurd and empty provides mental, fabricated satisfactions, and spurious feelings of finesse and accomplishment. We can convince ourselves we are on our way to mighty understandings as we pile up endless nonsensicals. We do not see the abyss that all these untruths end in, if taken truly through to all their conclusions or if we were to honestly analyze them.

The Void, the Abyss

Granted, there are a few of us who have ventured down that path. Some of our better thinkers have, in fact, peered deeply into the underpinnings of our Reality — among them, Nietzsche, Camus, Sartre. They, like our Marxists, are to be commended for making the effort, however woefully they fell short.

For in looking beyond the glitter and the stupefaction, in seeing beneath the words and all that they convey, but also conceal; in the attempt to peer into Reality itself, they have seen the Abyss. They tottered upon a brink, not knowing their hideous vision was of the ravine we created between us and Nature ... between us and feeling ... between us and our body. And that is all. They did not see that there was something beyond that ravine.

The Absurd and Meaningless Vision

Going only that far — only as far as intellect and analysis alone could take them — these existentialist thinkers claimed that, indeed, life is truly meaningless and that all that exists is the Abyss. They have proclaimed Reality absurd and random.

This is what we end up with when we have no felt connection to Existence and only mental phantasms reflecting it. So much is this true, that most of you reading this have no idea at all what I mean by a "felt connection."

This is what comes from our attempts to stand outside It — Existence and Nature — and "capture" It ... as always to understand only for the purpose of controlling. For certainly in our seeking of power and control — here even in the realms of the mind and the philosophical — we are doomed to failure.

Versus a "Felt Connection" to Reality

I have said it is possible to have a felt connection with the Divine that is sensed, essentially, in one's muscles. That is to say, it is part of Experience and the body. You could say that it is intuition that is grounded, not just mental. I have said this is related to the instincts of planetmates and that in retrieved connection with our bodies we can regain some sense of that instinct again. However, generally speaking, this kind of knowing is one that we find impossible to remember.

We have access to such instinctual feeling, of connection to our innate Divinity, in the womb and at birth. Yet everything about us and about our culture is geared toward having us forget it. And we get better and better at that forgetting as we get older.

The Labyrinth and the Minotaur

Over time we lose ourselves in our mental labyrinth, with its resident Minotaur — symbolizing, at once, Ego, our brutal overlords, the care-givers of infancy, and the distorted figure that our soul and its connection with Nature has become.

I have said that our symbolic thought and culture are what we substitute for that knowing, that awareness, that deep seeing and understanding.

So, in looking deeply into that symbolic skeletonized reflection of life — separated as it is from Reality — and the culture that is the collective embodiment of it, how can we see anything beyond it? We are looking in the wrong direction. We should be looking not out-ward into the world of symbols and reflections, but inward into the pleasure, pains, urges, emotions, and feelings of the body. We are afraid to do that, for, being wrong-getted, we have been taught that is dangerous.

"Impulses" and Our Fear of "Losing Control"

Therein lie your "impulses," you think. You think these "impulses" will get "out of control" (starting to see a pattern, perhaps?). That you will become something other than yourself, might become dan-gerous, hurtful ... "animalistic".... Has it occurred to you yet how out of control you already are? Do you really think by expanding your understanding and Experience of Reality back into the wisdom of the body you will become *more* stupid than you already are? More deranged? How is that possible?

Oh, you don't think you have a problem with a fear of impulses or of getting out of control? You think those are the concerns only of religious fuddy-duddies who are ever striving for self-control so as to not lose their ticket to the pleasant afterlife ... and fearful of their booking passage on the opposite train? Why then do you make such a to-do about folks having a "meltdown" in public, an emotional one? Why are you so tense and fearful about doing something "inappropriate" in a social setting? And why so restrained of move-ment and emotion at those times? How come so punishing of and so judgmental of someone expressing passionate conviction, ranting, or even raging? Why the social approbation? So much so that you cooperate with efforts to medicate and put away those who stray outside socially "correct" emotional lines?

Why do you run in so quickly when someone is upset? Is it to comfort them or to keep their upset from getting "out of control" and triggering your own? Why even have you made being upset a wrong and something that should be comforted away out of existence whenever it arises? And why do you look down on and, at best, condescend to folks who are emotionally transparent?

You see, every generation has its ways of exerting subtle control of emotions and of judging and condemning to keep others within those boundaries. How much, then, it is surprising for "civilized" folks when learning that to become real again, emotional meltdowns, "out-of-control" weeping, full-bodied raging, are only part of what will be encountered. Better get used to it.

Faith from the Abyss ... In the Heart of Darkness Is Discovered the Soul

It is not that comprehension of the Abyss is of no worth. To the contrary, it is only after you know it that you are at all inclined to, or brave enough to, or desperate enough to look in the direction of the feelings in your body. One's mind must crash itself upon the rocks of meaninglessness. You must watch your mental skyline of religion, ritual, cultural niceties, substitute pursuits, and egoic achievements collapse upon itself.

It is only in the wreckage of those cherished illusions and false hopes that you can look down in despair and notice the body that has taken you there, that has always been there, with its feelings, its own patterns of thought — which we call intuition — with its own inspiration, its breathing, its inhalation of goodness and exhalation of compassion and creativity. It is only then, turning downward our eyes in the face of the darkness and the seeming "end of times," that we can even notice our soul, our emotion, our connection with all and Everything, our true happiness, our actual heart expansion and love.

The Red Pill ... Here, if You Choose

Now, that is something you did not want to hear, isn't it? Indeed, this understanding brought by awareness of the Unapproved and Hidden, which makes the Matrix transparent, reveals behind it the horror of human life. It is a peeling back upon that which we do not, under any circumstances, want to know. It is an opening of Pandora's Jar, seemingly releasing all evils into the world. Is it any wonder the Unapproved and Hidden has never — in all of our history — been known by us? By any of us? Is it any wonder the maddening explosion of culture we have created to keep it at bay?

All that we see around us in society are in some ways an outgrowth of the lies we tell ourselves. For they are all perverted, backwards, bizarro distractions from our true reality. They represent endless, meaningless activities which fill up the time, within which otherwise the truth could rise up in us. Or they are the opposite constructions — the certitudes — upon which we stand and which are erected in exact defiance of the truth and reality.

That last would include the falsehoods involved in all the ego-congratulations we do — an example being that we are the pinnacle of evolution and so have been "given" dominion over all of Nature. Another would be our belief in the materialistic nature of Reality, with its concomitant that it does not contain consciousness but that we — all-important, superior and wonderful us — do. They are certitudes that are the opposite of the truth, standing upon which and operating within which we are not able to even entertain notions of the truth.

Leaving the Matrix

So difficult for most folks to do, so near impossible, in fact, is the apprehension of our denied and resisted truth and our lost self that I would not be telling you this, revealing to you the Unapproved and Hidden of our human existence, if it were not both necessary as well as accompanied by an incredible message of real hope. There is, you probably know, hope in the truth, by definition. You may perhaps have already been feeling that in reading this text. Certainly, it is better to let go of futile and wrong endeavors. Just refraining from the hopeless is hopeful in itself. It is better to take a few small steps in the right direction than to traverse a continent that takes one where one will not want to end up. Those tiny correct efforts are far more valuable than a mountain of struggle and effort that ends in failure and abject frustration.

But beyond that....

Are you depressed? Hearing this? Did you think it would be easy looking into the Abyss? Did you think that you would not find difficult that which billions of previous humans, back through history, were unable to do, because of its difficulty? Do you see the lengths to which we take our delusion of superiority? If not before, then now?

I am revealing the emptiness below it all. For certainly, when we take all of our efforts and trace them to their roots, we find there is nothing there ... like castles built in the sky is human accomplishment and culture.

Some of us, in this most crucial of all times, have had revealed to us this mirage quality of our cultural constructions. It happens by various means — illness, tragedy, drug use, travel, and education, not the least of these — and only when we are ready. Chances are you are not reading this unless you have experienced it — this vision that ends our innocence, undermining our cherished illusions and false hopes.

Some of us call this collective mirage a "matrix." Indeed, that term does describe the way our cultures substitute for Reality, making us unable to realize Reality or Truth, as well as providing the opiate for the feeling of unreality that results. Certainly, when one is reversing that trance state ... indeed, right now, for you, this might be occurring ... and this message is the equivalent of the red pill for you ... one goes through a shock, as the crutch of culture is removed ... as you become "unplugged."

The Experience and Process of Unplugging

Leaving aside the fact that in this space, this liminal one, our early deprivations can be felt and healed, still in the beginning this is a horrifying vision of unreality, emptiness, and meaninglessness. One feels that one is seeing deeply into the nature of Reality and following it down to its foundations and they are … nothing. One might have the sensation of dissolving, of becoming de-atomized, or of melting. One certainly feels like one has lost all bearings and supports and cannot "hold oneself together," anymore. One might have that oh-so-dreaded feeling that one might be losing control of oneself, be going "out of control." One might feel one is going to soar off into space; that having completely lost gravity and one's connection to Earth one will be thrown or sucked back into an endless, random Universe. One often feels like one is falling. Perhaps one has fallen off the edge of a cliff and into nothingness.

One hits various rocks on the way down and reaches out desperately for each one. Medications and recreational drugs provide relief, yes, but only temporarily. One continues falling.

One sees the love or the loves in one's life. One tries to use them to break one's fall. Reaches out to them; thinks that adherence to Love means clinging to *that* love, to building an entire life on that. But that reveals its pathetic underpinnings in infant deprivation eventually. One continues falling.

One sees another place of clinging where Love is the answer and that one will feel better if the world would only damn well abide by it! One reports oneself as Awakened! And one spews out endless condescending declarations — self- and other-congratulating and flattering — marked with hearts, flowers, unicorns and fairies, maybe; and one begins beating everyone all around into line with such Love, frustrated they will not comply … and *believe* like you do. They *must* see you are right! But they withdraw. And one notices that and questions oneself about such Love that would push others away. Or one sees at some point that such "love" as others themselves share back is desperate and clingy, or empty and inauthentic, or boring and fatuous; and one sees a reflection of oneself in that. So one feels the insubstantial, tasteless nature of that Love, becomes cynical for a while. Fingers weaken, and one loses one's grip there. And keeps falling.

Other temporary clutching spots are adhered to. Maybe wealth. A new purchase or program of personal betterment. Maybe a new position, job, or project. One can no longer deny the emptiness. They crumble in one's hands, revealing their lack of true substance.

One keeps falling, keeps bouncing off the side of the cliff but cannot break one's fall, descends ever more, feels there is nothing below one. Just an abyss.

One feels like one is falling, falling, seemingly endlessly and into a darkness, a Void. One might actually say that one is looking into an abyss or Void, and one feels vulnerable. One's ego disintegrating, one often feels open to outside energies and conceives of these negatively as being devils and demons, ... which these most certainly are not. Or one frames them as simply negative energy, or "energy vampires," or just "toxic energy." One makes, in this way, the attempt to push their origins outside oneself, where they can then be fought and blame can be used as a weapon, though that effort is futile. For however much they might be real outside of us, we are bringing them to us for they are even more real inside of us. They are the repressed and unapproved aspects of one's own experience — past and present — refusing now to be denied. And they are arising to be integrated again with ones' self, to be re-membered, in the Universe's perpetual movement to become whole again ... and this time through you.

This experience has been described by shamans down through the millennia as being cut up into many pieces. It has been called *depersonalization*, by our modern psychiatrists. It has also been called *identity loss*, and the event has been termed an *identity crisis*, by psychologists, at times; at other times, a *breakdown* ... the old fashioned-term being, a *nervous breakdown* — which terms, by the way, misunderstand the break *through* quality of the event simply out of the fact that it is not experienced as pleasantness. Indeed, one will often fear one is "going insane," or is going to "lose one's mind." The best term for it is *spiritual emergency,* by the way, and luckily there are those now who can guide you correctly along that line. Later in life it might be contained within the experiences of the mid-life crisis.

What it is, however, is simply the vision of the emptiness behind all actions and events in one's life. It is the apprehension — however clearly or not one understands it as emanating from infancy and birth — that all that one does is a product of truly inauthentic forces within oneself. It is a perception that everyone and oneself are like windup dolls, or robots, mechanically acting out directives from another place over which one has no control, regardless how insistently one had been holding previously that one had that control and "free will."

It is, however, only the collapse of the shell in which one existed; it is its disintegration and falling away as one becomes the greater self, beyond Ego, that one is capable of being.

Becoming Natural

So what do you do? Your frantic and pathetic attempts to block the process, to keep from falling, have failed … if you're lucky. If not, you have longer to tread on roads of futility until you are ready.

And if you are?

In order to realize and reconnect again with your Self, for starters, you must surrender your frantic "trying to figure it out." You must stop believing in the demons you have used to help explain that which you cannot, because you have refused to see your horrible truths. Rather, it is more important that you stop trying to understand and to control. You must allow, at least for that moment of its arising, that you might actually learn something, that you might be taught. You must let go, at least for that moment, of your sense of all-knowingness, of your self-importance and any thoughts about how you might be appearing to anyone outside of you. At least for that moment … give yourself at least this … you must "give up."

Just give up.

You must "let go."

You need only stop looking outward and let yourself be simply aware of your body, how it feels. Look down toward it, into it, not out into the world of symbols and reflections and struggles of the mind.

If you feel you cannot do that, if you feel it is impossible to feel anything or to get to a feeling, guess what? You already are. That you cannot do it ("I can't do it!") is exactly the feeling; it is often the first one encountered. Give up *trying* to feel and *realize* what you already *are* feeling. That, my friend, is It. That is you. That is what you have been "riding" on all this time while looking for you. Give up. Stop looking. Let yourself be. Real-ize.

You must only let whatever feeling there is in your body — which initially you might say or think is your mind or coming from your mind — to arise.... Don't get caught up in where it is *coming* from; that is you analyzing again, trying to figure out, trying to control. You can worry later about where such things *come* from, if you want to (but you won't). For now, don't resist, don't run away. Surrender.

You need only let yourself feel whatever is there. Even if what is there is the feeling that nothing is there. That is you, too. *That* is the feeling. Just have it. "Nothing's there!" Have it. Have "nothing's there" be who you are at that moment. And be it all that you are able to or all that it comes.

Now, how do you feel about having that?

And that is the feeling, too ... how you feel about having the feeling.

And how do you feel about that? Keep asking yourself. Be your answers. "I'm frustrated!" Be frustrated. And how do you feel about that? "I can't do it!" Yeah, you can't do it. And how do you feel about the fact you can't do it?

Keep asking. You continue discovering you ... as you are ... not as you were told to be, think you are, or think you should be.

Oh, you don't "think" (feel) you are "good enough" for this? Lol. Guess what? Surely you have it now. Yes, that is the feeling, too. And how do you feel about that?

You "think" (feel) you are *too* good for this, that it is below you, that it is silly ... difficult ... crazy ... weak ... "feminine" ... whatever....

Surely, you have this one, right? That's right, how does that feel? Be it. And how do you feel about the fact that that is how you feel?

Oh, you will find out *why* you feel that way, eventually. That comes on its own. You, again, don't have to "figure it out." And eventually you will not *have* to feel that way, either. That also comes on its own. Rather, it simply *does not* come anymore, that feeling.

At times, you will cry.

You will weep ...

... and weep.

No doubt you will cry, for along with the things that arise initially in you is the sadness of your disconnection from all that you really cared about in life. You will see clearly how you have become lost. You will begin to remember what was important to you in childhood and your heart will ache, seeing, in your mind, each step, each permutation, across the years of your life, of your fall from that innocence. You will realize how much you have lost ... of others, of yourself, of opportunities ... that are gone forever. Never coming back.

You might cry for a long, long time, as it all becomes clear to you. As you expand your boundaries becoming the bigger you including all that you previously left out. As all those things you pushed to the side as unimportant — all your emotional attachments, your family, friends, and relationships, all your feelings about your endless treadmill in your world of struggling and sorrow, all your disappointments and missed-forever opportunities, all the tragedies and assaults upon you from any corner — are remembered by you. And you re-member them.

You might even get angry and want to rage. Let yourself, for now, do that. No, I do not mean allow yourself to act it out on someone else. Just, like the crying, let it out. In a safe setting, just like the weeping, where you will not be disturbed ... and controlled upon ... release it with all your body. You may yell out; bellow and rage fiercely, desperately; groan; even scream.

It is no big deal. It will not harm you. You must learn now how to be taught, to be receptive. Let yourself *get*, for a change, instead of *do*. Let it come to you. Trust that something will come. Trust what comes. Watch as it comes, reconnects with the rest of you, and then more rises up and dawns upon you.

You might actually feel like parts of your body and your brain are reconnecting; you might feel surges of energy; your body might jerk; you might have muscle twitches as the parts of your body and mind are snapping back into each other, making you whole. Similar, subtler feelings might occur of the upper and lower parts of your brain clicking back together. You might imagine your "inner wiring" — your electrical connections between brain and body — rearranging itself, linking together, and straightening along the length of your body.

You might feel your body wanting to go through movements of its own, as if an alien thing had taken over it. This is nothing to be afraid of. That "alien" thing is really the larger you, trying to heal itself in the ways that it knows — more than your egoic mind ever possibly could — *exactly* how to do it. Your body-mind becomes whole in as precise and perfect a manner — as *instinctual* a manner — as a physical wound heals itself. You do not need to direct it. In fact, any attempt to push or guide this healing of soul only derails the process. You need only let go, and trust.

And you will feel comforted. Usually upon every release — with its real-ization and its re-connection — you feel a soothing arise in your body, an afterglow. You will feel in your body the easing of all those years of deprivation, aching, wanting, and struggling. You will feel you have come home. You will feel like you understand your life. You will not want to leave it — this place of comfort — as you look all about you at all the efforts and empty achievements that have become your life and which take up all the activity of everyone around you.

Your process of becoming primal again, becoming natural, of reconnecting with your soul, with Nature, with truth, with the Unap-proved and Hidden, and with God and Reality will take a long time. It might even require more than this life. You did not become crazy overnight. While you cannot unthink your insanity, neither can you will sanity into existence and simply decide it. If you think you have awakened and it happened in a flash, then that is just the beginning. You are probably only becoming aware of the Abyss that exists. You have much further to go.

It will take as long as it takes. And it does not matter how long it takes. The important thing is that you have given up trying to control it. You are allowing yourself to be taught by your inner guide, in its own way, and at its own pace. The practice of giving up trying to hurry anything along or direct it is part of what allows it to happen. The more you give up trying to determine who you are, the more you *discover* who you are.

Rewards on the Way

And, while becoming your real and natural self again takes years, and perhaps a lifetime or more, the end is not important for there are all the rewards on the way. Each reconnection, each re-membering of you, brings relief, awareness, clarity, and comfort at its time of occurrence; that is true. But your life, you discover, is continually transformed as well. You find rewards along the way, powers returned to you, and pleasures, poignancy, and expanding love and compassion arising in your life and abounding. You feel fulfilled; you are often happy. You feel free; you enjoy increasingly less fear. You do not need to become "enlightened" in order to have the life that is meant for you which gives you all you ever wanted.

The "Game" of Forgetfulness

Indeed, being in Form is exactly that wandering from Unity and Bliss which allows a different game, a different and unique experience, than the one of full Awareness. Some delusion and separation is inherent in the game of life. It is, as it were, a necessary component of taking up the adventure here.

For, you see, all planetmates, including humans, are, metaphorically, "video games" for the "gods." We are Divinity having the fun of playing within arbitrary limitations — of varied and fantastic scope — which we call different *species*. It is through all beings, including human and nonhuman planetmates, that Divinity gets to interact with Itself. We are Divinity, as well as Its manifestation, its Creation, its play, its amusement, its "fun." Think about it: All that we call "fun" in life involves concocting and then acting within arbitrary limitations, and teasing out the possibilities of pleasure that doing that allows. We are gods playing a sport, writing a "script," playing out a "fantasy," "goofing" on ourselves, having fun.

So planetmates forget, somewhat, coming into Form, just like humans do. It is just that they do not forget as totally as us. They know always they are immersed in the Divine and cannot be otherwise. They are like we are when playing a board game, knowing we are simultaneously the token operating within the rules of the game and a larger persona, the player, beyond that and not limited in any way.

For Humans, Amounts to a "Dungeons and Dragons"

However, our human game of *total* forgetfulness has become an oh-so-serious and inescapable one of "dungeons and dragons." By contrast, that of planetmates is relatively pleasant, playful, child-like, and often comical, without the doom and gloom quality of ours. For with our complete Divine amnesia we have managed to create a canvas of the greatest darkness in all of Nature, on which to paint our human drama.

And while we come across as nonsensical and spurious in our pronouncements in the process, this Divine reality we forget in order to do that, we could access it as our primal ancestors did. We could "breathe" It; we could let It define us; It can be our unquestioned anchor while in physical form. It is that accessible, that close. How do we know that? We know that is possible, because some humans, past and present, actually live that reality. You could, too.

We Could Be Free

The Obvious Truth is perennial truth, eternal truth, by contrast to our fleeting and insubstantial conceptions. Rooted in and stabilized by Knowledge of an immutable nature, humans can be reckless, we can be playful … we can be free. However, having "civilization" and lacking such roots in the infinite, not knowing who we are, brings into our life a dire and ominous feeling, making us conservative in our actions and oppressively serious in our perspective on everything. For, never sure of what is, we cannot be sure what we are risking, ever. We do not know that ultimately, being immortal, there is nothing to lose; and that the Reality outside our childhood fears is beneficent and understanding, giving us license to experiment and play.

Giving the Universe a Chance

But we could. And in the way I have described, simply by letting go and giving up. When we do, these freedoms and felicities are only the faintest glimmerings of the evidence in our experience, the blessings and guidance, the teachings and knowings that come — miraculously it seems — once one gives the All That Is a chance. Once one gives the Universe a chance to reveal It as It is ... not as we want it to be, out of our fevered mania. Once we give the Universe a chance to actually *be* benevolent — not just as we are coerced into saying It is in our current unaccepting-of-actual-blessedness state — we find that It is. The All That Is, we discover, is more gracious, beneficent, personally attentive and loving than we have ever imagined It could be.

The Universe is friendly, after all.

AFTERWORD

Continue with Book Eleven, *Back to the Garden: The Psychology and Spirituality of Humanicide and the Necessary Future,* and About the Return to Grace Series

Back to the Garden

The book that follows from this one in the Return to Grace Series is titled, appropriately enough, *Back to the Garden.* It is subtitled, *The Psychology and Spirituality of Humanicide and the Necessary Future.* That should tell you a lot already about what is in it. Let me be more clear, however.

Back to the Garden addresses many of the topics of this book, *Prodigal Human,* but they are rendered within a mythological, meta-physical, and spiritual framework, bringing out additional highlights and insights. In addition, it focuses in more closely on the apocalyptic features of our times — the *humanicidal* ones, as this book points out … *humanicide* meaning this compulsion we have currently to kill ourselves all off, to die and become extinct as a species, to commit species-suicide.

The book following this one shows how our current situation fits within a framework expressed in the myths of Eden, Prometheus, Icarus, Cain and Abel, Abraham and Isaac, Pandora, Gilgamesh, and others. We see how our situation has always been revealed to us through our collective unconscious, though we were not hearing; and if we did pay attention, we got the message wrong, or backwards. It shows how, as well, our entire trajectory of descents was explained and how their resolution was foretold in these myths. In this way, our collective unconscious exposes the path home ... the way that we prodigal humans, like the myth of the Prodigal Son in *The Bible,* can return and be embraced again by a welcoming and bounteous Nature and a benevolent, forgiving, ever helpful, and loving Divinity.

Back to the Garden takes our estranged state, as we saw in this book, as a starting place from which to explore how we can get back that which we lost. It looks at the environmental collapse, revealed in clear detail; it looks at current developments working against as well as for our survival; and it describes societal and personal changes that we can, and indeed *need* to make in order for humanity to survive. Thus, "the *necessary* future."

The Return to Grace Series

This Afterword is a good place, also, to give an overview of the totality of the Return to Grace Series of books. You can see where this book and the ones that follow — *Back to the Garden* and *Primal Return* — fit into the overarching narrative of a "return to grace."

The Return to Grace Series is a sequence of twelve, maybe thirteen, books I am bringing to print in the years 2013 through 2017. *Prodigal Human* is the ninth book completed. What remains to be put to paper are three or four books — Book 2, *You Say You Want a Revolution?*; Book 11, *Back to the Garden: The Psychology and Spirituality of Humanicide and the Necessary Future*; Book 12, *Primal Return: Renaissance and Grace*; and possibly a Book 13, *Primal Renaissance.* In this series of books, I lay out in great detail where we are, how we got to where we are, why we are here, why we need to change from being here, and where to go from here ... and how to do that. The remainder of the Return to Grace Series is as follows:

Book One

Book One: *Culture War, Class War: Occupy Generations and the Rise and Fall of "Obvious Truths"* (2013) describes where we are politically as a result of recent history. We are in a dire state — politically and environmentally — because a natural evolutionary development of consciousness and generational succession, begun in the Sixties, in a movement encompassing the entire world, was derailed by moneyed interests with a profit motive. Because of this advance being monkeywrenched by selfish interests, we are in a quandary in all areas of public and environmental life.

Book Two

Book Two, tentatively titled *You Say You Want a Revolution?* or *The Monster Is the Corporation* is not yet in print but exists online as Chapters 17 through 32 of *Culture War, Class War,* at the site of the same name.[1] It elaborates on the dire quality of our times, requiring drastic measures at all levels and in all areas ... a new paradigm of economics, politics, individual life purpose, human achievement, and relation to Nature.

Book Three

Our environmental predicament, in particular, is introduced in all its severity and urgency in Book Three: *Apocalypse Emergency: Love's Wake-Up Call* (2013). This book is both an appeal to our highest beingness and a call to action, wrapped in a psychological and spiritual look at why we are *not* alarmed at the moment, though we should be.

Book Four

Book Four: *Apocalypse NO: Apocalypse or Earth Rebirth and the Emerging Perinatal Unconscious* (2013) details an alarming and yet possibly opportune development of our times, existing alongside our current environmental and sociopolitical dilemmas. It shows how, through means apparently generational and psychological as well as environmental, we are seeing a rise of perinatal material in the consciousness, motives, and personalities of ourselves and everyone around, including and significantly those in power in these times.

I show how we both manifest and act out our perinatal pain in our physical environment, but also in our social environment at all levels, from individual; to group and to national, as exemplified in our politics; and to international. I show where we can place the lever of human effort and activism in order to bring about the change we need in order to survive. It is revealed within our perinatal patterns.

Book Five

In Book Five: *Wounded Deer and Centaurs: The Necessary Hero and the Prenatal Matrix of Human Events* (2016), I carry those themes forward, focusing on two factors in particular. These are, first, the deepest roots of those perinatal-apocalyptic upsurges occurring in modern life … and I trace them to actual late-gestation prenatal events of even more significance than the birth elements. The second thrust of the book concerns the phenomenon of the self-sacrificing individual required to take us forward from these times.

This *necessary hero,* it turns out, is not only apparently coming to our aid and is manifesting in greater numbers, but is imbued with just the kind of access to their own pre- and perinatal material as to make possible their leading us beyond these ties — these prenatal traps keeping us in bigotry, violence, greed, and fear and away from our deeper nature of love and compassion — which have been holding down humanity from real progress for thousands of years.

Book Six

In Book Six: *Planetmates: The Great Reveal* (2014), I have all of these — a plea from our planetmates for us to wake up; a vision of who we are in Nature and in relation to them that shows how and why we have strayed and how it has to do with perinatal factors; a revolutionary view on civilization and evolution that puts us in a new and non-complimentary light but also reveals places for change and renewal never before seen; a new-paradigm understanding of a way of being in the world and in Nature that is more natural, primal, and in touch with our basic nature; and a prophecy that in humans taking up the challenge presented, "Something wonderful is going to happen."

These are brought forth within a literary device that, within the context of an event called "The Great Reveal," has the voice of our planetmates — that is, all the life and beings who abide with us on this planet — teaching, revealing, directing, cajoling, lecturing, scolding … ranting at times … all to the end of a redirection of the human race so as to save the life on this planet, including ourselves, before it is too late.

Book Seven

Book Seven: *Funny God: The Tao of Funny God and the Mind's True Liberation* (2015) describes the new paradigm of activism required of the necessary hero as the "Tao of Funny God," which has it that only true and radical responses not rooted in the paradigms we confront can be effective. It details old paradigm *patriarchal* perspectives and how they are wrong and why they need to be gone beyond. And it explains *matriarchal* new paradigm ones that are needed.

In its second part, it lays out, in story format, a prophecy and a vision of a potential wondrous future, coming soon, something along the lines of that "something wonderful" of *Planetmates*. This vision is consistent with the findings about Nature, reality, and psychology, which I advance in other parts of the Series.

And in its final part, "The Mind's True Liberation," *Funny God* presents an expansive, indeed, towering, overstanding of human life and its purpose in a cosmic, a Divine scheme, along with a vision — a revelation on the nature of God, human life, life purpose, and on existence itself.

Book Eight

Book Eight: *Experience Is Divinity: Matter As Metaphor* (2013) explains the nature of reality and human consciousness that is consistent with the views of quantum physics and modern consciousness research, especially that of the kind I have experienced in deep experiential psychotherapy and especially in nonordinary states of consciousness brought about spontaneously and via my primal, meditation, and breathwork experiences of many years.

Book Nine

In Book Nine: *Falls from Grace: The Devolution and Revolution of Consciousness* (2014) I bring to light the devolutional model of consciousness. It tells how we got to where we are in each of our individual lives and where we need to address our attention to return to the state of grace, which is our birthright, indeed, is our true identity.

Book Ten

In this book, Book Ten: *Prodigal Human: The Descents of Man* (2016) I bring together the ideas of *Falls from Grace* and *Planetmates* in describing the evolutionary/devolutionary arcs of humanity and the individual, founded upon growing edge views from our current sciences. In revealing the descents and their processes of occurring we have seen revealed obvious correctives we can embrace collectively, to save our world, as well as personally, to save ourselves. It is the most complete and comprehensive explication of the human condition. It is an elucidation of it never before offered, envisioned, or revealed. For these reasons it brings with it hope for change and success in our personal and planetary lives that was never imagined or allowed before now.

Book Eleven

Book Eleven is *Back to the Garden,* as I said. It reveals the same predicament as this book; in fact its first few parts lay out what has been said here, but in a condensed form and with a nod to mythological expressions of it. It provides much more of the profile of our environmental plight, of our corresponding psychological array (or matrix), and of what they both reveal in terms of a spiritual dilemma of current times. Beyond that, it outlines our possible return — that "something wonderful" again — and shows why it is necessary as well as how it is truly possible, as seemingly impossible as the notion might seem at the outset.

Book Twelve

Following *Back to the Garden* will be Book Twelve of the Return to Grace Series to be titled *Primal Return: Renaissance and Grace.*

It will detail the specific ways we might change our current trajectory; and it will paint a compelling, a comprehensive vision of a possible society, a possible humanity, a possible Earth, and a possible future congruent with and enlightened by the prenatal and perinatal understandings that have heretofore been overlooked in previous attempts to present a workable model for humanity.

For comparison on what this work will be like, see the worker's utopia proposed by Marx. My vision will be different from his, for his was merely an addendum to the unnatural plight of "civilized" man — a man still beholden to the hierarchy, but himself a dominator of women, indigenous cultures, and planetmates and utilizing, still, those as resources to fuel selfish gains and advantages, regardless how equitably distributed, or "fair," they would be. A more just slavery, coinciding with oppression and exploitation of others outside the group of male human slave worker "elites" is hardly compelling, let alone utopian.

My utopian vision, to the contrary, will be constructed on our *actual* human nature, our primal one ... which happens also to be congruent with what we have learned about ourselves from prenatal and perinatal psychology. And I will fashion a template of where we could, and should, ideally end up .... as a vision to pull us forward and aspire to. Also I will detail the steps we can take to get from where we now are to there.

Book Thirteen

At this time, it looks like there will be a Book Thirteen, which will be titled *Primal Renaissance*, using the same title of my work, which was published in 1995. This version will be much updated and expanded, however. The intention here is to detail a utopian future as a vision to be a kind of lodestar in our thinking about how to change and where to go.

This utopian vision has a particular characteristic, never before advanced. For this vision shows a future in which all that we lost in coming from Nature — our primal allotment of gifts and traits and wisdom — is married with all that we have gained, of real worth, during our estranged state of civilization.

It will describe a *renaissance*, in that it is similar to the Renaissance of pre-modern times where with the collapse of Catholic hegemony, texts hidden in the monasteries of our Greek and Roman heritages were released and distributed. And this, combining with the technology of the time, the printing press, allowed the dissemination of these ideas and their intermarriage with the other ideas characteristic of the times and pervasive throughout its culture. The cross-fertilization come of that created a flowering of culture, thus a *renaissance, or rebirth*.

In the same way, this book of mine to come predicts a cross-fertilization of our repressed and denigrated primal, primitive, indigenous, natural heritages — which is knowledge and wisdom from even prior, in history, to the Roman and Greek heritages ... wisdoms and perspectives which were even more thoroughly and brutally repressed, to our discredit and supreme disadvantage — with the vast scientific understandings and technological achievements wrought of the human journey occurring since those times of gatherer-hunter simplicity, nobility, and wisdom ... in tune with a benevolent Nature and a gracious Divinity. Thus, this possible future, I predict will be a *primal renaissance*. It is no coincidence that this renaissance will be lifted as well on the wave of a radical new technological advance in communication, like the printing press was then. This time, it is called, *the Internet*.

This book is meant to open to the quality of the livable future we are heading towards, if we survive. That is to say, it will describe the cultural paradigm manifesting a rebirth of culture and humanity, the primal renaissance, which is currently being created out of a coming together of long suppressed wisdom from primal cultures and current science and technology and all the knowledge it brings with it. Such a flowering of culture, if it is done in the way it can be as described in this Series of thirteen books, which would allow a future to actually occur, would be wonderful beyond current imagining, bringing together for the first time all that we know along with all that we need to know to both correct as well as to augment and catalyze what we currently know.

And in this book, *Primal Renaissance,* I will reveal it in as clear and detailed a vision as possible, in the hopes of awakening clarity of direction in the idealistic and the movers and changers among us to bring it about.

Return to Grace

That is the overview of Return to Grace, the series. There is also an idea to condense the entire twelve or thirteen books into an abridged version of the Return to Grace Series, as a single book. For *Return to Grace,* the book, think of it as a kind of "favorite hits" book, slanted toward the theme of the crisis and opportunity presented to us in our times, these "end times."

Stay tuned.

ACKNOWLEDGMENTS

My gratitude I extend, first, to my wife, for sharing in the evolution of all these ideas, being the screen upon which to bounce them, and providing the support and encouragement and belief in this work and in me which catalyzes everything I do.

For this particular work, I want to thank again Mary Elisabeth Dupont for the critical support and input she provided when these ideas were coming out in their first, much reduced, form as *Planetmates*.

I thank the planetmates, who are all the beings on this planet, microscopic, plant, animal, and human, for their inspiration, support, and assistance. If not so much to me, then certainly to all humans in our current planetary crisis.

I wish to acknowledge "the Family," the No-Form one, especially Graham Farrant, Martha D. Ello, Shirdi Sai Baba, Peter Lavender, and Lynn Radford for all their incredible behind-the-scenes, prescient, and perfect support, and assistance.

I want to thank here some from my "Form" family, as well, and my network of Form-ly supporters — James Adzema, Sharon Adzema, Elizabeth Adzema, Timothy Adzema, Peter Radford, and Ceila Levine, in particular. I want to give a nod especially to Peter Radford. I am grateful for his creation of the eye-popping art displayed on this book's cover.

For the input and interaction that stimulated this work, I wish to thank, also, Peter Melton, Mike Ferrigan, Gene Gibson, and all the folks involved in Extinction Radio.

Lastly I need to give a nod to my loyal followers and friends on social media — Facebook and Twitter, especially — who have supported, challenged, given input on, reacted to, and simply been a loving presence to me over the last eight years, on virtually a daily basis. I have ongoing engagement with them on every single aspect of what I write and on my work and ideas in general. An incalculable number of these many thousand, in total, with their vast array of backgrounds, cultures, geographies, fields of knowledge, professions, and lifestyles, which characterizes our humanity at this time in history, have provided a context and played a role in influencing my work and teaching me. Though I know few of them in person, many are as known to me and dear as my actual family members and are equally if not more supportive and loving, assisting me that way in all my work.

All my best to my brothers and sisters in the cause of overturning this deadly paradigm and bringing to birth a new Earth that will continue on, even better, past our current ecological abyss.

NOTES

Preface

1. *The Descent of Man* was Charles Darwin's second book and was first published in 1871. It followed his revolutionary work on evolutionary theory, *On the Origin of Species,* which was originally published in 1859.

2. For this item — that we are on the verge of bringing down all life on this planet — you can look to several of my works as well. See *Apocalypse Emergency: Love's Wake-Up Call* (2013) and *Apocalypse NO: Apocalypse or Earth Rebirth and the Emerging Perinatal Unconscious* (2013).

      However — regardless how dire and hopeless this all seems — this is no reason to abandon all action. This issue of how we should react to this immense problem and what to do about it is something I take up in the works mentioned, as well as, in particular, my work *Wounded Deer and Centaurs: The Necessary Hero and the Prenatal Matrix of Human Events* (2016).

3. Helen Caldicott, *If You Love This Planet,* 2009, p. 141.

4. For the rise of patriarchy predominating as the outstanding character of human history and prehistory and man's role in that, and women's resistance to that, I wish to refer you to the work of Marilyn French. She details our history and prehistory and the rise of the patriarchal ethic in a number of detailed works. I urge you to direct your attention to her classic, *Beyond Power: On Women, Men, and Morals* (1985).

5. An *overstanding* is a lot like a paradigm. However, unlike a paradigm, which is so ubiquitous it is mostly not seen, an overstanding is a grand perspective or model of which one is aware. It is an overarching framework or template that one uses to see and *understand* with. It is a viewing point one arrives at that allows us to see all the intricate parts of a particular reality and to perceive how they are interconnected and make sense.

On the other hand, an *understanding* is about "getting it." It means, point made, concept received, perspective on a particular thing and what it is and how it works arrived at.

You might in fact say that an overstanding is a grand overview of many, many understandings that gives additional meaning to each of them and shows how they interact and are integrated with one another ... how they fit together. It is more comprehensive and comprehendible than a *vision;* it is more detailed and visionary than a *model.*

An overstanding is an understanding that encompasses a paradigm, thus allowing one to "rise up" and envision it, in all its complexity and possibilities. Whereas an understanding refers to a mental grasp of a concept, an overstanding is akin to a vision. It is a comprehension of the whole, as a whole, and not merely the individual parts.

Chapter 2

1. On bipedalism and pelvic bone changes, from "Bipedal Adaptations in the Hominid Pelvis":

Bipedal Adaptations in the Hominid Pelvis

INTRODUCTION

Two major features are unique to humans among all the living primates: A very large brain, and moving about upright on two legs exclusively. One of these, bipedalism, appeared long before the other. Many anatomical features of Australopithecus afarensis anatomy demonstrate habitual bipedal locomotion, and the 3.6 million-year-old footprints discovered by Paul Abell at Laetoli in 1978 confirm it unequivocally (White, 1980). Not until the appearance of Homo erectus, some 1.7 million years later, could hominids be considered on their way to being large-brained (Stanford, et al., 2006).

While certain adaptations seen in the knee (e.g. the valgus angle), in the foot (such as a fully adducted hallux), and to a lesser extent in the cranium (a fully inferior foramen magnum) are all strong indicators for bipedalism (Lewin and Foley, 2004), the most interesting evolutionary changes necessary for upright posture occurred in the hominid pelvis. All of these adaptations are present not only in the pelves of modern humans, but also in all members of the Genus Homo, and in the earliest known hominids, the Australopithecines.

PELVIC ADAPTATIONS FOR BIPEDALISM

The hominid pelvis displays many unique features (when compared to that of quadrupedal primates) that support bipedalism. The major adaptations are seen in the sacrum and the ilia, as well as in the overall configuration and orientation of the pelvic bones.

Available online and downloadable at

https://courses.edx.org/asset-v1:ASUx+ASM246+3T2015+type@asset+block/ASM24_Week_3_BIPEDAL_AD APTATIONS.pdf

2. On brain size and secondary altriciality in humans at *Human Development*:

Human babies enter the birth canal from the womb in the same way a chimp does but just before the actual birth the skull rotates 90 degrees in order to exit the rounded birth canal that humans have evolved. In Homo Sapiens, *evolution reached a compromise that favored even bigger brains at a further cost to birthing and efficient walking. The* Homo Erectus *pelvis was very narrow. Humans are unique among mammals in the extent to which the brain keeps growing well after birth. The scientific terms for this is secondary altriciality. It involves accelerating the birthing process and arresting the development until after birth. Monkeys and apes are born with brains half as heavy as they will ever be. A chimpanzee brain, for example, will weigh perhaps 7 ounces at birth and about 14 ounces as an adult. Human brains are about a third of their final size in newborns; they more than double in size in the first year after birth. On average, human babies are born with a brain that weighs 14 ounces but reaches 35 ounces in one year. It will continue to grow until it reaches about 45 ounces in size (at age 6 or 7).*

Gestation in humans should be about 21 months rather than the normal 9 we think in terms of. This is the process of accelerating the birthing process to enable the enlarged brain to escape the birth canal. Development of the brain then continues external to the womb for well over the first several years. What this intense development means is that a human infant is born relatively helpless. A baby can neither stand up or in any way fend for itself for a long time. Stephen Jay Gould has written our sexual maturation comes almost absurdly late in a Darwinian world supposedly regulated by a constant struggle to secure reproductive success and pass more genes along to future generations....slower development must provide some power advantage to evolve, in the face of its obvious drawbacks. In fact, must of what makes us human in the end may stem from this unnaturally long period of helplessness in the very early part of our lives.

Available online at

http://web.mesacc.edu/dept/d10/asb/origins/development.html

3. On prolonged postnatal brain growth at *Unique to Humans*:

This is one of the most dramatic distinctions between humans and other mammals (including primates). In all precocial mammals other than humans, at around the time of birth there is distinct slowing down in brain growth relative to body growth. In altricial mammals, the switch to diminished brain growth occurs at a developmental stage comparable to birth in precocial mammals. In humans, substantial brain growth relative to body growth continues for approximately a year after birth before a marked slow-down occurs. Because of this human neonates are unusually dependent on parental care in comparison with other primates for the first year of postnatal life, and sometimes labeled as "secondary altricial."

From R. D. Martin, "The Evolution of Human Reproduction: A Primatological Perspective," in *American Journal of Physical Anthropology*, 2007, p. 62.

And on postnatal brain growth at *The Rise of Homo sapiens: The Evolution of Modern Thinking:*

Human infancy is also distinguished from that of apes by the very high rates of brain growth that continue from the fetal period into the first year of life (Dienske, 1986), leading to a condition referred to as secondary altriciality. Portmann (1941) demonstrated the difference between altricial and precocial mammals. Altricial mammals usually have short gestation periods and produce helpless, poorly developed young that require prolonged care in a protective area like a nest or den. In contrast, precocial mammals have a relatively long gestation period and their young are born in a more advanced state of development with no nest or den required. Humans are unusual in that like precocial mammals, they have a long gestation period (Martin & MacLarnon, 1990) but like other altricial animals their young are relatively helpless, hence the term secondary altriciality. The state of secondary altriciality, which is one of the unique features of modern human infancy, can be estimated based on the ratio of adult/newborn brain weight and so its evolutionary history can be assessed (Rosenberg, 1992; Smith & Tompkins, 1995)....

The second major benefit of secondary altriciality is that it releases restrictions on brain size. Prior to this shift, any developmental mutation that increased brain growth faced the problem of squeezing a large cranium through the pelvis during birth. Large-brained infants would almost certainly have had much higher mortality rates, as would their mothers. By postponing brain growth until after *birth, however, mutations that increased brain growth would have been less risky from an obstetrical perspective. Once past the restrictions of the birth canal, the brain would be free to grow as large as biologically feasible. Only skeleton-muscular mechanics and metabolism limit its theoretical size.*

Thus, secondary altriciality could have been a significant enabler both for flexible postnatal development and for increased brain capacity in the emerging hominid species. Indeed, by enabling these crucial new traits, secondary altriciality marks the start of the hominid line as clearly as any other factor. It may also help to explain obligatory bipedal locomotion....

We do not know precisely when secondary altriciality originated in the hominid line. It is clearly a biological change of considerable complexity and evolutionary significance, which suggests that it developed over a considerable period. Theorists presume that the common ancestors of hominids and chimpanzees had the characteristic apelike developmental pattern, and that secondary altriciality emerged as a unique trait on the hominid branch. Modern apes have presumably retained something closer to the ancestral pattern. The genetic foundations of secondary altriciality will be an important topic for future research on human origins.

The Hominid Trinity

The major problem with the foregoing analysis is that we cannot put infant mortality aside, even temporarily. A larger, more flexible brain is useless if the infant dies before it matures. By all logical standards, secondary altriciality should have been a death sentence for the hominid line, an evolutionary experiment quickly extinguished by withering infant mortality. Clearly, that did not happen. The solution, I believe was a set of compensating shifts in hominid anatomy, behavior, and social structure....

From *The Rise of Homo sapiens: The Evolution of Modern Thinking*, by Coolidge and Wynn, 2009, pp. 104ff.

Chapter 4

1. Since this factor of prenatal malnutrition is so impactful on human devolution and fetal development, consequently playing in heavily to what I advance in my theory of human devolution or descents from Nature, I will here quote significantly from Briend's article. Others, especially those more familiar with the biological and medical

viewpoints, may find even more of import than I do in what he advances here.

> [O]f the recently developed features that single us out from other species, the adoption of upright posture caused the greatest anatomical and physiological changes. Their magnitude has been compared to that of the acquisition of flight in birds. This characteristic may be sufficiently advantageous to outweigh several coincidentally arising drawbacks. One of these, unquestionably, is a relatively difficult birth; the pelvis transmitting the weight of the trunk to the legs is the part of the skeleton most affected by this change in posture, and the path traversed by the fetal head during birth is peculiarly complicated....

> [T]he repercussions of upright posture are manifest not only at the time of birth, as generally admitted, but also in the preceding weeks by impaired fetal growth.... Certain changes have occurred also in maternal cardiovascular physiology, which tend to reduce uterine blood flow and hence fetal nutrition, principally in the last weeks of pregnancy.

> Upright posture and maternal haemodynamics

> The raising of the trunk to the upright position provoked a forward projection of .thé sacrum and of the lower lumbar vertebrae. This skeletal modification, specific to man, decreased the available space for the pregnant uterus, as a result of which it interferes near term with normal maternal haemodynamics. The aorta and the inferior vena cava that run along the lumbar spine are vulnerable to compression at the level of L4 and L5, particularly when the subject is supine. Only when lying in the lateral position is this effect relieved.

> Compression of the inferior vena cava provokes diminution of the blood volume and a drop in cardiac output, whereas these are normally considerably increased during pregnancy. When standing, a similar compounding effect is provoked by changes in hydrostatic pressure in the venous system due to gravity. The combined results of these two mechanisms on the cardiovascular system are most pronounced during the last weeks of pregnancy and are relieved only when the pregnant woman is lying in the lateral position. Any effect on uterine blood flow must be to reduce it. This is supported by the isotope studies of Suonio et al on pregnant women near term, which showed statistically significant changes in uterine blood flow associated with the move from the left lateral to the vertical position.

> These haemodynamic findings imply that the cardiovascular system of pregnant women is not perfectly adapted to the upright position, and during evolution its suboptimal efficiency may have become a limiting factor for fetal growth.

2. Some of Stanislav Grof's work and findings can be found in Grof, 1970, 1975, 1980, 1984, 1985, 1988a, 1988b; Grof and Grof 1980,

1989, 1990; and Grof and Halifax 1977. He has more recent works as well, extending over a period up to the present.

3. For a comprehensive examination of how our anthropocentrism skews all our knowledge, often reversing it from what it should be, and how removing that reveals a new world of understanding — one in which we belong, not as dominators, but as noble participants — see my recent publication, *The Secret Life of Stones: Matter, Divinity, and the Path of Ecstasy* (2016).

4. For my ideas on mind being a shared thing and on the basis of all Reality being Experience, as arrived at by the findings of modern consciousness research and quantum physics, see my works, *Experience Is Divinity: Matter As Metaphor* (2013) and especially, and more recently, *The Secret Life of Stones: Matter, Divinity, and the Path of Ecstasy* (2016).

5. For Rupert Sheldrake's ideas see, among others, Sheldrake, 1981, 1991a, 1991b, and 1995; the *New Sense Bulletin*, 1991; and Institute for Noetic Sciences, 1991.

Chapter 5

1. For a comprehensive explanation of the difference we have from the planetmates of Nature, having to do with what happens in the last stage of gestation just before birth, which is also a product of our bipedalism and the pelvic bone changes, see my *Wounded Deer and Centaurs: The Necessary Hero and the Prenatal Matrix of Human Events* (2016).

2. About my use of *Ego*, especially related to concepts of ego strength: Mainstream psychology posits ego strength as that quality of selfhood which allows integrative power of one's experience and the ability to deal with and flow with events and stimuli. Someone with less ego strength is more likely to be fearful in the course of the experiences of life and more likely to block out or run from reality, rather than to deal with it in a positive, growthful, or productive way. Yet Ego is also the system of defenses, denials, and avoidances that is used to block out reality in order to function. So that in this sense Ego would equal poor ego strength. This is confusing, and to avoid

that confusion I follow Jung in separating the two by calling the one that is defensive and avoidant of truth and reality, the Ego. Whereas the integrative function I call the Self, as Jung does.

This is related as well to a topic I get into in others of my works. Which is the difference between positive self-esteem and positive self-regard. For *self-esteem,* as commonly understood, equates to ego-esteem or defensiveness; while *positive self-regard* relates to a positive evaluation of oneself while yet cognizant of one's shortcomings and faults and is characterized by a lack of defensiveness. This latter is the Self, not Ego.

Chapter 6

1. For more along this line, see Frederick Leboyer, *Birth Without Violence*, 1975, 2009.

2. See, also, Arthur Janov, *Imprints: The Lifelong Effects of the Birth Experience*, 1983.

Chapter 7

1. I use the feminine gender here in referring to that higher power or God seen in wilderness and Nature, because in truth Nature is and was seen as feminine, for the most part, if there was any gender to be attributed to that vast screen upon which early humans and modern gatherer-hunter peoples played their life. Compare Great Mother, Divine Feminine — terms we use today.

2. See my *Wounded Deer and Centaurs: The Necessary Hero and the Prenatal Matrix of Human Events* (2016) for more on the qualities and dynamics of fetal malnutrition.

3. Joseph Campbell, *The Masks of God: Primitive Mythology,* 1969, p. 349.

4. If you wish to know more on how our universal womb experience creates our universal human mythologies — as in this example of

Edenal dynamics arising out of our prenatal ones — look to my work, *Womb with a View,* which is scheduled for release in 2017.

Chapter 11

1. See Colin M. Turnbull (1961) on the Mbuti, Robert Lawlor (1991) on the aborigine, Louis G. Herman (2013) on the San Bushmen of the Kalahari, and similar ethnographic reports for the way primal humans see in Nature a benevolent and loving beingness.

2. See my *Falls from Grace: The Devolution and Revolution of Consciousness* (2014) and *The Secret Life of Stones: Matter, Divinity, and the Path of Ecstasy* (2016), on the constraining of free energy when coming into Form, i.e., into life, as well as the falls from grace involved in incarnating.

Chapter 12

1. See Alan Watts, "The Wisdom of the Body," Chapter 4 in *The Wisdom of Insecurity,* 1951.

2. These processes I speak of would be primal therapy, of which I am most familiar, but to some extent through holotropic breathwork and psychotechnologies of re-accessing bodily feelings of other sorts.

3. I deal with death and our life-negating, experience-diminishing focus on it in two other of my works, to date, *Planetmates* and *The Secret Life of Stones.* Look especially, in *Planetmates,* to the "30th Prasad — Death. 'Kill and Be Killed': Planetmates Do Not Fear Death the Way Humans Do." In *The Secret Life of Stones,* see Chapter 29, "The Other Is Our Hidden Face."

Chapter 13

1. See Colin M. Turnbull, *The Forest People,* 1961.

Chapter 15

1. For more on how class war is disguised as culture war, see my work, *Culture War, Class War: Occupy Generations and the Rise and Fall of "Obvious Truths"* (2013).

Chapter 16

1. The ubiquitous symbol of a vagina ringed with teeth is known as the *vagina dentate*.

2. Erich Neumann, *The Origins and History of Consciousness*, 1973.

3. Regarding the prevalence of incest denial, not incest avoidance, see my works, *Planetmates: The Great Reveal* (2014) and *Wounded Deer and Centaurs* (2016).

4. For deMause on incest and its prevalence throughout history, see especially Lloyd deMause, *The Foundations of Psychohistory*, 1982, and "The History of Child Abuse," 1994.

Chapter 19

1. On tears, see Elaine Morgan, *The Descent of Woman: The Classic Study of Evolution*, 1985; and *The Scars of Evolution*, 1994. Other relevant works of hers are *The Aquatic Ape*, 1982, and *The Descent of the Child*, 1995.

Chapter 20

1. On this point, see especially in my work, *Funny God* (2015), "Part Three, Experience Is Divinity," and in my *The Secret Life of Stones* (2016), "Part Five, Matter Is Message."

2. On this, Chiron and spiritual woundedness, see my *Wounded Deer and Centaurs* (2016).

Chapter 21

1. On "good enough" and Donald W. Winnicott (1958), note Winnicott's assertion that child-caring can be "good enough," and the prevalence of that view, quoting Winnicott — in child psychology, child development, parenting circles, and their publications — as an excuse for what is done throughout child-caring, including and especially our views on child development. It provides a convenient out for parents, which becomes then a paradigm that disallows truly seeing what we do, in allegiance to protecting parent's from guilt. Yet it precludes any insight or awareness for better methods and for change in parenting behavior. Also, it dispels any criticism that might otherwise be. I expand on this in my section on Donald W. Winnicott in my work, *Wounded Deer and Centaurs* (2016).

Afterword

1. For a look at the current version of what will be Book Two, *You Say You Want a Revolution?* do a search for my blog, *Culture War, Class War,* and check out chapters 17 through 32. I authored it using my pseudonym, SillyMickel Adzema. You can also use this url:

  https://culturewarclasswar.wordpress.com/

REFERENCES

Adzema, Michael. 1995. *Primal Renaissance: The Emerging Millennial Return*. Eugene, OR: SSILLY God Ventures. sillymickel@gmail.com.

Adzema, Michael. 2013a. *Apocalypse Emergency: Love's Wake-Up Call*. Return to Grace, Volume 3. Eugene, OR: Gonzo Sage Media. Available on Amazon, Kindle, and at book stores.

Adzema, Michael. 2013b. *Apocalypse NO: Apocalypse or Earth Rebirth and the Emerging Perinatal Unconscious*. Return to Grace, Volume 4. Eugene, OR: Gonzo Sage Media. Available on Amazon, Kindle, and at book stores.

Adzema, Michael. 2013c. *Culture War, Class War: Occupy Generations and the Rise and Fall of "Obvious Truths."* Return to Grace, Volume 1. Eugene, OR: Gonzo Sage Media. Available on Amazon, Kindle, and at book stores

Adzema, Michael. 2013d. *Experience Is Divinity: Matter As Metaphor*. Return to Grace, Volume 8. Eugene, OR: Gonzo Sage Media. Available on Amazon, Kindle, and at book stores.

Adzema, Michael. 2014a. *Falls from Grace: The Devolution and Revolution of Consciousness*. Return to Grace, Volume 9. Eugene, OR: Gonzo Sage Media. Available on Amazon, Kindle, and at book stores.

Adzema, Michael. 2014b. *Planetmates: The Great Reveal.* Return to Grace, Volume 6. Eugene, OR: Gonzo Sage Media. Available on Amazon, Kindle, and at book stores.

Adzema, Michael. 2015. *Funny God: The Tao of Funny God and the Mind's True Liberation.* Return to Grace, Volume 7. Eugene, OR: Gonzo Sage Media. Available on Amazon, Kindle, and at book stores.

Adzema, Michael. 2016a. *The Secret Life of Stones: Matter, Divinity, and the Path of Ecstasy.* The Path of Ecstasy Series, Volume 1. Eugene, OR: Gonzo Sage Media. Available on Amazon, Kindle, and at book stores.

Adzema, Michael. 2016b. *Wounded Deer and Centaurs: The Necessary Hero and the Prenatal Matrix of Human Events.* Return to Grace, Volume 5. Eugene, OR: Gonzo Sage Media. Available on Amazon, Kindle, and at book stores.

Adzema, Michael. work-in-progress. *Back to the Garden: The Psychology and Spirituality of Humanicide and the Necessary Future.* Return to Grace, Volume 11. Scheduled for release in 2017. sillymickel@gmail.com.

Adzema, Michael. work-in-progress. *Primal Return: Renaissance and Grace.* Return to Grace, Volume 12. Scheduled for release in 2017. Some of it was originally published in *Primal Renaissance: The Emerging Millennial Return,* 1995. sillymickel@gmail.com.

Adzema, Michael. work-in-progress. *Primal Renaissance.* Return to Grace, Volume 13. Scheduled for release in 2018. Some of it was originally published in *Primal Renaissance: The Emerging Millennial Return,* 1995. sillymickel@gmail.com.

Adzema, Michael. work-in-progress. *Return to Grace: The Crisis and Opportunity of End Times.* Return to Grace, Volume 14. Scheduled for release in 2019. Some of it was originally broadcast on Extinction Radio, beginning in 2015. sillymickel@gmail.com.

Briend, Andre. 1979. "Fetal Malnutrition: The Price of Upright Posture?" *British Medical* Journal *2,* pp. 317-319. Available and downloadable online at

http://www.ncbi.nlm.nih.gov/pmc/articles/PMC1595686/

Caldicott, Helen. 1992, 2009. *If You Love This Planet.* New York: W.W. Norton.

Campbell, Joseph. 1959, 1969. *The Masks of God: Primitive Mythology.* New York: Putnam.

Coolidge, Frederick L., and Wynn, Thomas. 2009. *The Rise of Homo sapiens: The Evolution of Modern Thinking.* Chichester, UK: John Wiley & Sons.

Darwin, Charles. 1859. *On the Origin of Species.* London, UK: John Murray.

Darwin, Charles. 1871, 1879. *The Descent of Man.* London: John Murray.

deMause, Lloyd. 1982. *The Foundations of Psychohistory.* New York: Creative Roots.

deMause, Lloyd. 1987. "The Fetal Origins of History." In Verny, T. (ed.) *Pre- and Perinatal Psychology: An Introduction.* New York: Human Sciences Press, 243-259.

deMause, Lloyd. 1994. "The History of Child Abuse." *Aesthema: The Journal of the International Primal Association, 11,* 48-62.

deMause, Lloyd. 1995. "Restaging Early Traumas in War and Social Violence. *The Journal of Psychohistory 23,* 344-391.

deMause, Lloyd. 2002. *The Emotional Life of Nations.* New York & London: Karnac.

Erikson, Erik. 1950, 1963. *Childhood and Society.* New York: W.W. Norton & Company.

Erikson, Erik. 1968. *Identity: Youth and Crisis*. New York: W.W. Norton & Company.

French, Marilyn. 1985. *Beyond Power: On Women, Men, and Morals*. New York: Ballantine Books.

Grof, Stanislav. 1970. Beyond psychoanalysis I. Implications of LSD research for understanding dimensions of human personality. *Darshana International 10*(55).

Grof, Stanislav. 1975. *Realms of the Human Unconscious: Observations from LSD Research*. New York: Viking Press.

Grof, Stanislav. 1980. *LSD Psychotherapy*. Pomona, CA: Hunter House.

Grof, Stanislav. (ed.) 1984. *Ancient Wisdom and Modern Science*. Albany, NY: State University of New York Press.

Grof, Stanislav. 1985. *Beyond the Brain: Birth, Death, and Transcendence in Psychotherapy*. Albany, NY: State University of New York Press.

Grof, Stanislav. 1988a. *The Adventure of Self-Discovery: Dimensions of Consciousness and New Perspectives in Psychotherapy and Inner Exploration*. Albany, NY: State University of New York Press.

Grof, Stanislav. (ed.) 1988b. *Human Survival and Consciousness Evolution*. Albany, NY: State University of New York Press.

Grof, Stanislav. 1998. *The Cosmic Game*. Albany, NY: SUNY Press.

Grof, Stanislav, and Grof, Christina. 1980. *Beyond Death: The Gates of Consciousness*. London: Thames & Hudson.

Grof, Stanislav, and Grof, Christina. (eds.) 1989. *Spiritual Emergency: When Personal Transformation Becomes a Crisis*. Los Angeles: Jeremy P. Tarcher.

Grof, Stanislav, and Grof, Christina. 1990. *The Stormy Search for the Self: A Guide to Personal Growth Through Transformational Crisis*. Los Angeles: Jeremy P. Tarcher.

Grof, Stanislav, and Halifax, Joan. 1977. *The Human Encounter with Death*. New York: E.P. Dutton.

Herman, Louis G. 2013. *Future Primal: How Our Wilderness Origins Show Us the Way Forward*. Novato, CA: New World Library.

Institute for Noetic Sciences. 1991. *Noetic Sciences Bulletin*.

James, William. 1899. *The Varieties of Religious Experience*. New York: Philosophical Library.

Janov, Arthur. 1971. *The Anatomy of Mental Illness*. Berkeley, CA: Medallion.

Janov, Arthur. 1983. *Imprints: The Lifelong Effects of the Birth Experience*. New York: Coward-McCann.

Janov, Arthur, and Holden, E. Michael. 1975. *Primal Man: The New Consciousness*. New York: Thomas Crowell.

Lawlor, Robert. 1991. *Voices of the First Day: Awakening in the Aboriginal Dreamtime*. Rochester, VT: Inner Traditions International.

Leboyer, Frederick. 1975, 2009. *Birth Without Violence*. Rochester, VT: Healing Arts Press.

Martin, R. D. 2007. "The Evolution of Human Reproduction: A Primatological Perspective." *American Journal of Physical Anthropology, Suppl 45*, 59-84.

Moore, James. 1987. Colloquium presentation, 16 November 1987. La Jolla, CA: Department of Anthropology, University of California, San Diego.

Morgan, Elaine. 1972, 1985. *The Descent of Woman*. New York: Stein and Day.

Morgan, Elaine. 1982. *The Aquatic Ape*. New York: Stein and Day.

Morgan, Elaine. 1994. *The Scars of Evolution*. London: Oxford University Press.

Morgan, Elaine. 1995. *The Descent of the Child.* London: Oxford University Press.

Muktananda, Swami. 1974. *The Play of Consciousness.* Oakland, CA: SYDA Foundation.

Neumann, Erich; Jung, Carl G.; and Hull, F. C. 1954, 1973. *The Origins and History of Consciousness.* Bollingen Series XLII. Princeton, N.J: Princeton University Press.

New Sense Bulletin. 1991. "Contest-Winning Studies Support Sheldrake Theory." *New Sense Bulletin, 17*(1) [October 1991], 8.

Sheldrake, Rupert. 1981. *A New Science of Life: The Hypothesis of Formative Causation.* Los Angeles: J.P. Tarcher.

Sheldrake, Rupert. 1991a. "Is Nature Alive?" *Human Potential,* 16-21, 33-39.

Sheldrake, Rupert. 1991b. *The Rebirth of Nature: The Greening of Science and God.* New York: Bantam.

Sheldrake, Rupert. 1995. "Nature as Alive: Morphic Resonance and Collective Memory." *Primal Renaissance: The Journal of Primal Psychology, 1*(1), 65-78. Available through sillymickel@gmail.com.

Turnbull, Colin M. 1961. *The Forest People: A Study of the Pygmies of the Congo.* New York: Simon & Schuster.

Verny, Thomas, and Kelly, John. 1981. *The Secret Life of the Unborn Child.* New York: Dell.

Watts, Alan. 1951. *The Wisdom of Insecurity.* New York: Random House.

Winnicott, Donald. W. 1958. *Collected Papers: Through Paediatrics to Psycho-analysis.* New York: Basic Books.

ABOUT THE AUTHOR

Michael Adzema is an author, activist, prenatal and perinatal psychologist, philosopher, and ecopsychologist. He has been a university instructor, a journal editor, and a psychotherapist, specializing in primal therapy, breathwork, and rebirthing.

Michael was the editor of *Primal Renaissance* — a professional journal of primal psychology — and was the first person in the United States to teach prenatal and perinatal psychology at the university level, which he did at Sonoma State University in the early Nineties. In the early Eighties, working as an anti-nuke activist with Oregon Fair Share, he was one of a small group of people whose actions led to the lawsuit that ended nuclear plant construction in the United States.

He is a regular contributor to Extinction Radio, broadcast by Activate Media, formerly Occupy Boston Radio. His voice can be heard on other broadcasts, as well, speaking on topics of activism, spirituality, ecopsychology, the environment, pre- and perinatal psychology, metaphysics, and philosophy.

Over the last twenty years, Michael Adzema has managed and authored a number of popular websites and blogs, including *Primal Spirit; Becoming Authentic; Culture War, Class War;* and *Michael Adzema, Author.* Currently he publishes prolifically and often on his primary blog, *Michael Adzema, Author,* at sillymickel.blogspot.com. One can find a number of his videos on youtube, as well, under the pseudonym, sillymickel. He teaches and publishes frequently on Facebook as Michael Adzema, and on Twitter under the name, Mickel Adzema, @sillymickel.

In addition to *Prodigal Human,* he has authored, most recently, *The Secret Life of Stones: Matter, Divinity, and the Path of Ecstasy.* Also this year, 2016, he published *Wounded Deer and Centaurs: The Necessary Hero and the Prenatal Matrix of Human Events.* Going back in time he authored and produced the books, in order from most recent to least, *Funny God* (2015); *Falls from Grace* (2014); *Planetmates, The Great Reveal* (2014); *Experience Is Divinity* (2013);

Apocalypse NO (2013); *Culture War, Class War* (2013); and the companion volume to *Apocalypse NO,* titled *Apocalypse Emergency — Love's Wake-Up Call. Primal Renaissance: The Emerging Millennial Return* is a book he authored and produced in 1995. The book next up in the Return to Grace Series of Michael Adzema's works is *Back to the Garden* and is scheduled for release in early 2017.

Along with the books mentioned above, except *Primal Renaissance,* two more books are to be published in his Return to Grace Series, for a total of thirteen volumes, being released in 2013 through 2017. Their titles, tentatively, are *You Say You Want a Revolution?;* and *Primal Return: Renaissance and Grace;* with a possibility after that for one titled, *Primal Renaissance.* His books can be found at Amazon, are available on Kindle as well, and can be ordered through any major book outlet.

Introduction & anti-humanist manifesto for pantothanatics

The human race is grossly overpopulated. The climate is considerably affected by various emissions &, almost worse, the quality of individual humans is steadily declining. Research, easily found by an Internet search, reveals that cacagenics, or dysgenic fertility, as it is usually known, has brought about a reversal of the vaunted Flynn effect, the effect that still leads newspapers and other vulgarians to claim that "we" are growing smarter. Sadly, this is no longer the case & IQ has declined by roughly 7 normalized points since the end of the 70s.

The admirable Koko, the famous gorilla, has an IQ of around 90, according to a test conducted by signing. Soon she can look at people & think "stupid wankers", if she doesn't do so already. Human intelligence comes more from Neanderthal DNA than from *homo sapiens* DNA.

Humanism is very old, & it once had a point. The proper study of mankind was man, & theology was the greatest enemy. Now the earth that underlies the human world is threatened, & we need to think of her first, the earth that shelters & protects. Heidegger saw humanism as part of an essentialist metaphysics, & his later philosophy can be utilized to ground a deep ecological view of the problem we now face, where nature is being destroyed by the legions of brats that humanity insists on dropping, like mentally defective rabbits.

Antinatalism is a development of the old pessimistic philosophy of Schopenhauer & others. It tells us to stop breeding, or at least stop breeding indiscriminately. This is unlikely, since dysgenic fertility points out that the best &

most intelligent elements breed the least, the worst breed most. Just look at the noble Japanese.

The world is reaching a point where abortion should be actively encouraged; suicide & abortion are good & positive phenomena, and pestilence is a long term friend.

Some antinatalists want the human race to die out. Whatever replaces us cannot be worse. This will not happen fast enough. It is also very unlikely that the worst elements will ever fully understand their superfluity. Maybe it is time that we started killing ourselves off?

There is too much human.

human everywhere

there is human everywhere a worthless cancer his fat retarded
mouth, & in case of anarchism i would kill like fucking
Caligula with a happy ax

there is human everywhere so much less than a fang in the
night & the glorious empty eye

your safe word is "i freely consent to this murder" & there is
not pain enough in the grubby flesh to alleviate hatred; there is
human everywhere & no such thing as sex

nowhere enough

nowhere enough is memory eternity not the genuine retention; we have confabulated days & slow torture, world is what we put there a greasy smudge over the innocence earth is, tiny animals & everything living

nowhere enough is the flesh absent, or adequately present. it is a great gray wall, world is, written over it is lies & gibberish, ideologies where the dead pretend to live

the dogs invented

it was a security the dogs invented out of fighting regularly,
knives a lifetime like children might if people were better than
they are, if gorillas were not so obviously better than them &
death & vague promise but unsubtle enough

it was a security temporary the dogs invented where
tomorrow does not really matter much & yesterday is fucked

words weak

memory is just words & weak its ineffectual not even forever.
here was recollection ineffective they confabulated their baby
it was sexless their heaven was, blood & dust & things
forbidden or permissible, a duty not to be

& memory lives their last idiot religion in case it mattered
much – the last believer will crawl an idiot face-fucked fish
into his oblivion, their everyday sexless heaven does not
matter much; they are cripples with nothing left to touch or
love

love & leprosy

under the god lived love & leprosy they assumed, hundreds of kittens & smoke over some battlefield once pretending to be relevant – terror & sandwiches

there is slow water & stagnant ideology dressed for success, under night is an eternity of copses walking & fishes emerging from the primeval ocean on trembling legs, under the imaginary god lived love & leprosy & death

Myra

Myra is dressed in objection to her death the unsteady
obnoxious like the hagioscope oracle was not talking to her
but a legion of subtle nuns done dancing their obstinate
eternity like cornflakes & decay

people would become her in case of danger & her pious
insolence was more than obviously answers & nothing is more
sexless than faces. we have worn our skin like an implausible
excuse like a resurrection in restless flesh

if you harm yourself enough you do not even need death

consume

we consume need & cruelty like puppies do, the dogs are
several a resurrection, words is a moron, invented heaven.
here nothing is us the loveless & world a memory temporary.
the earth is for walking on & holding the forgotten, a reservoir
of everything that mattered when we were good enough to be
animals

they have invented since the obnoxious not & moral oughts
that perhaps never happened yet. everything is memory & to
forget

the stench of compassion

it stinks like decay & compassion, dead flesh & weakness, the illiterate genetically defective being meat to burn, thus they have invented compassion their deprecatory necessity, shit to chew for all the morons walking, & the schizophrenics are silenced like nighttime for the sin of being alive, for being spatiality extending & colonizing time

& there is nothing left to feel sorry for, corpses & whores

grinding god

& here is their god grinding its fucking mandibles in panic as
if resistance mattered, decay or the flesh is empty throughout
every several sexuality

whatever i might predicate of their god might just as well be
as correct as anything else, sex & gormless & death. these
things have all happened on many separate occasions & there
is nothing to say about them

(but not their goat-fucker god a charade his whole retarded
absence, not the empty, not all the madmen laughing,
everything else whatsoever that was the elder gods, that ever
never happened)

inadvertent

night is upon me an inadvertent suicide & the entire world is a futile temporary floating in a gross cold forever where there is always only the transfinite, nothing big enough to hide a god in anywhere

& the skin we are wrapped in is garbage & a debt, falling forward into night the curmudgeonly nothing like a scumbag wrapped in plastic, dressed in bibles & absences where words have worn their impotence cozy like a cloak

The world is reaching a point where abortion should be actively encouraged; suicide & abortion   are good & positive phenomena; and pestilence is a long term friend

Some antinatalists want the human race to die out. Whatever replaces us cannot be worse. This will not happen fast enough. It is also very unlikely that the worst elements will ever fully understand their superfluity. Maybe it is time that we started killing ourselves off?

There is too much human

dead their inevitable

dead was their inevitable like typewriter torment, there were battlefields no soldier ever walked on & torn paper wrinkled like skin, there are not memories enough to live in here a sensual weapon

anxious it is written their insensible dread where night is open eyes & the point of blood is it does not refrain from not hearing words it neither recognizes nor expects answers to weight its shoulders like guilt or innocence or anything else inessential & irrelevant

history is a priest snoozing in an intolerable hole & over the trees is air empty as prayers might once have been when they retained some meaning

perfectly ordinary orgasm

electric is in the walls a perfectly ordinary orgasm & the stolid
corpse has never yet sniggered, though he is sorely tempted as
night falls like a dead man laughing

& night was tied together from broken days & the skin that
insisted that you live in it as if it were a unity & a confirmation
of something that you strongly disapproved of in secret, since
everybody runs around with confused & stupid opinions & is
not man or woman enough to concede that he or she is an
incorrigible cunt not worth the paper they are printed on &
wasting air like being a fucking moron was going out of style

it was a corpse's conventional orgasm & made of tiny holes in
time

golden mountains

they expected gods & golden mountains, prayer or a murderer
where coffee turns into words & the ice runs over us like love
does if love ever existed. under the god is time & a razor;
under the sun is more nothing

the corpses lie their eternity & do not touch, they have ceased
being & there is nothing left in them to think or feel since this
is the past now & become meaningless like freedom is, golden
mountains & living things

the dog wants

the dog wants a fly very badly & furniture is nothing to him. he cares nothing for heaven & all the dead, there is not night enough for him & nothing to cover up all the nothing with decorous memory

time is a fang like night is, life is a razor relentless & comes with its insolent blood over the prey screaming. there is lawless in night, i hope, & room to kill

reckless genetics

here is the electric silence & static the answer, we are made of
feckless & reckless genetics there is nobody there

there are bones everywhere that have been cows & pigs once.
with every year one assumes that children grow less & less
intelligent & it is gratifying that kindly science confirms this/
we are not becoming gods here, just shit

there is not long to wait now before the great irrevocable stop;
brats have already forgotten how to think & live

telephone & the road

telephone is not identical with the road there are differences inscrutable & blatantly obvious, walking & a suicide. where we have is an absence here the hole// & summer grows like destiny forever, the foulest canker

night is a small child listening to War singing Summer on the radio in a car alone a hot day once/ & everything was dust & loveless

the 80s were made of forgotten & we have not slept in them enough our innocence. our vile flesh

death sweat

if death were sweating a short answer. here is the cocaine
insect has grown him wings a living thing

here they have flesh & fish fingers or skeleton fingers to chew
on, zombie brains & cold water

time is a worried plunge, gold in a corpse hole, if death were
forever or something we might endure like the dying there
would be memory here, a heaven already

contraceptive memory

children are contraceptive memory, their conscious a pitiful prosthesis to mumble their ugly before nightfall - they have swallowed retarded ideology as appetizing as the elderly cum of a priest might be, as worthless as any broken dream

children are contraceptive memory, insignificant & too much being in them, they have less to do with pleasure than all the dead men

time & incompetent

memory is time & incompetent killers they are wearing
tomorrow like a hat like a garbage can. before us is a water
retreating & pointless children who should never have been
born drinking dust

tomorrow earth will stand better without them when world is
gone – there is less empty memory coming & night is long

corpses at the window

the corpses stand at the window they are like children
monochrome under a forgotten summer sun; they are an
inaudible laugh in a changing room instead of a memory
falling between centuries like an innocent murderer a faint
scent of death & sulfur - a dead daughter

the corpses at the window want no more than to become
inevitable & boring, predictable & inevitable as an average
everyday suffering, less than nothing, & we shall remember to
become them

the earth extends

the earth extends its inevitable, the sweaty sex that matter is, the factual unacceptable we have always already accepted, the inevitably extended, the sexual tensor. here was a history once & now they are not noticing, the prophet is choking on the cum of a wild pig running from his dead lips like illiterate threats & insane promises

no body wants a fucking zombie prophet, & nobody wants promises. the earth extends & we are obliged to live it

on the balcony

on the balcony is no big Louise & no angels. there are no more
ashtrays, no faces, sweat & a memory

here expands land around us it is a green wait the expectant
grass the absent dead that grow the soil like a tiny orgasm

under us could be anything as long as it is possible, logically
or metaphysically, but nothing where we are looking for
meanings

on the balcony extension & a minuscule dose of being

because weight

because weight & extension, the gross mensurable, we endure these numbers & the terrible sense of locality, where is the random voluntary spurt of aesthesis, the sensational aleatory that does not demand recording in case there are answers at some specific locus, as if it could ever matter, or be material more than a random goose sounding off for some reason irrelevant

because of wait we measure death and everything impending, counting these futile dead children, as is there might be some point in listening

& they swam in

& they expected insanity a cold water to swim in their
oblivious once a radiator an expectation a god to invent
already a slow dive, a knife. thus is the subtle loveless we are
obligatory & innocuous, their extravagant incessant

here the walls emphasize themselves unsubtle, like
waterboarding or any other torture even better & sexier. it is
often good to kill, a slow sensuous, a nothing to touch. the
blood is like less boring water, it is innocence to swim in a
glorious lack. there are animals & possible, a vacuum cleaner a
can opener, sexual is incessant

breeding is the intolerant sememe the extortionate murderer
dressed in midwifery & time. blind is life tonight

here is the dead

here is the dead apparently, the coffin obnoxious the light.
there are sufficient an impotency already. memory is
intolerable there are whole countrysides in it & they are a red
defecaory inevitable. the flesh aches for the knife the absence.
we are made of everything inessential & have time & futile
passion in us to unwind

to nightfall

to nightfall a huge excess & yet the sun barely vanishes some
time where it leaves a twilight in the sky like a curse or a
fictitious fetus screaming an xian abortion like a homeless
ghost. in us are words & some superfluous blood we do not
need like memories

here iconograhics are a dead idiot. the gross is not god always
is not necessarily insane

& as the sun swells its obnoxious the crows are unsubtle dead
paper, torn from a lifeless & an entire arrogance - they are like
a gambler sitting in an antique boat made of eyes & time

almost everything receives its inappropriate significance, as if
answers mattered, as if the whorish word were made of
solemn & an extravagant blessing. all there is is the intolerant
blood dressed in its temporary flesh under the loveless sun.
salvation is to forget, is empty as a drug

what has been

what has been is the innocent potential forced to become
unsubtle rapist facticity like a worthless ancestor dressed in
his corpse like a moron standing on the balcony ugly like bird
shit, like words

what has been never even asked for existence & is not worth
proud except where it is life prevailing & obstinate its
pointless, better than any god